D1025389

Foreign Policy
by Congress

FOREIGN
POLICY
BY CONGRESS

THOMAS M. FRANCK
EDWARD WEISBAND

New York   Oxford
OXFORD UNIVERSITY PRESS
1979

Copyright © 1979 by Oxford University Press, Inc.

Library of Congress Cataloging in Publication Data
Franck, Thomas M
Foreign policy by Congress.

Includes index.
1. United States—Foreign relations. 2. United
States. Congress—Powers and duties. 3. Executive
power—United States. I. Weisband, Edward, 1939-
joint author. II. Title.
JK573.1979.F7   328.73'07'46   79-14857
ISBN 0-19-502635-7

Printed in the United States of America

UNIVERSITY LIBRARY
Lethbridge, Alberta
143722

For Phyllis Bockser Goldberg

CONTENTS

Introduction 3

I CONGRESS BECOMES A WORLD POWER

1 The Legislated Peace: Congress Ends U.S.
   Involvement in Indochina 13
   THE AERIAL WAR ENDS 13
   MILITARY ASSISTANCE DRIES UP 23
   THE FINAL DAYS 27

2 The Cutoff Complex: Congress Reverses Presidential
   Policies Toward Turkey and Angola 34
   TEACHING THE PRESIDENT A LESSON: TURKEY 35
   TEACHING THE PRESIDENT A LESSON: ANGOLA 46

II CODETERMINATION: CONGRESS ALTERS
THE GROUND RULES

3 Codetermination: Congress Recaptures the War Power 61
   THE SEARCH FOR SYSTEMIC CHANGE 61
   THE DECLINE OF THE WAR POWER 63
   REVIVING THE CONGRESSIONAL WAR POWER 68
   THE WAR POWERS LAW IN PRACTICE 71
   THE WAR POWERS LAW AND THE CONSTITUTIONALITY
      OF THE CONGRESSIONAL VETO 76

4 The New Oversight: Codetermining Human Rights,
    Military Aid, and Nuclear Export Policy   83

   THE NEW OVERSIGHT   83
   HUMAN RIGHTS   84
   APPLICATION OF THE NEW OVERSIGHT TO HUMAN RIGHTS   89
   THE EXECUTIVE BRANCH AND THE NEW RULES   93
   EFFECTIVENESS OF THE HUMAN RIGHTS POLICY   96
   MILITARY AID   98
   THE NELSON-BINGHAM BILL   98
   THE HAWK MISSILE SALE: THE FIRST TEST   100
   IMPROVING ARMS EXPORT CODETERMINATION IN PRACTICE   103
   EVALUATION OF THE CONGRESSIONAL ROLE   105
   NUCLEAR EXPORT CONTROLS   111

5 Congress Tames the Intelligence Community   115

   THE BACKGROUND OF CONGRESSIONAL ABDICATION   115
   REFORMING INTELLIGENCE OVERSIGHT   117
   THE NEW OVERSIGHT IN PRACTICE   125
   SECURITY AND COOPTION   129

6 Treaties, Agreements, and Commitments:
    Putting "Advice" Back into Advice and Consent   135

   THE DECLINE OF ADVICE   135
   COOPTION   138
   CIRCUMVENTION   141
   CODETERMINATION OF INTERNATIONAL COMMITMENTS   146
   RECIDIVIST TENDENCIES   152

7 A Foreign Policy of Laws, Not Men?   155

   CONSTITUTIONAL THEOLOGY OR POLICY PRAGMATISM   155
   WHEN BY LEGISLATION?   159

III WILL THE CONGRESS COME TO ORDER?

8 The National Interest and the Special Interests:
    Congress and the Foreign Relations Lobbies   165

   THE KOREAGATE SCANDAL   166
   LEGAL CONTROL ON LOBBYING ABUSES   172
   FOREIGN GOVERNMENTS AS LOBBIES   180

THE ETHNIC LOBBIES 186

OTHER FOREIGN POLICY LOBBIES 194

THE INTEREST CONFRONTATIONAL MODEL:
ANTI-BOYCOTT LEGISLATION 200

9 Up the Hill, Sideways: Congress in Search
of a Delivery System 210

THE UNWIELDY FLOOR 210

LEADERSHIP FROM THE LEADERSHIP 214

LEADERSHIP FROM CAUCUS 216

LEADERSHIP FROM COMMITTEES 217

RECONSTRUCTION 221

10 Expertise: Powering the Congressional Delivery System 227

THE STAFF EXPLOSION 227

STAFF EXPERTISE 232

STAFF INFLUENCE 234

THE INFORMATIONAL SUPPORT SERVICES 242

YOUR PLACE OR MINE?: TURF WARS UNDERMINE
COMMITTEE CREDIBILITY 245

THE INAPPROPRIATE APPROPRIATIONS POWER 249

THE IMPACT OF THE NEW BUDGET PROCEDURES ON THE
FOREIGN RELATIONS POWER IN CONGRESS 253

IV IN SEARCH OF THE LOST CONSENSUS

11 Strengthening Relations with an Incongruous Congress 261

"REMEMBER THE LMO" 261

THE "H" FUNCTION: LIAISONS DANGEREUSES 263

THE WHITE HOUSE 270

PANAMA CANAL TREATY RATIFICATION: THE NEAR-DISASTER 275

THE SECOND ROUND 281

LESSONS OF THE PANAMA CAMPAIGN 284

THE LIMITS OF LIAISON 286

SALT II: TEST OF THE POST-REVOLUTIONARY SYSTEM 288

Notes 295
Index 347

Foreign Policy
by Congress

Why should I mourn
The vanished power of the usual reign?

T. S. ELIOT
Ash Wednesday

INTRODUCTION

SINCE the ending of the Vietnam War, more than a President has been deposed—an entire system of power has been overturned. The Presidency itself, not just Richard Nixon, has been the subject of a revolution that radically redistributed the power of government. In this revolution, the principal losers were the President, his cabinet, the White House corps of managers, and those senior officers of the Congress—party, committee, and subcommittee leaders—who had become too closely identified with the advancement of Presidential designs. Chief among the power gainers was the Congressional rank and file.

Among the booty redistributed by the revolution was control over U.S. foreign policy, long a Presidential perquisite. With the revolution came those questions characteristic of radical breaks with an established order. Can the revolutionaries get organized or will they be themselves devoured, victims of disordered revolutionary energy? Having seized power, can they couple it with purpose? Can they protect the national interest from enemies seeking to take advantage of the upheaval?

National security in the dangerous post-1941 world of hot and cold wars had been achieved by a zealous patriotic rallying behind the Presidential colors. "Politics stops at the water's edge," Congress dutifully intoned, which really meant that democracy's writ may not be operative in the places where foreign policy is made. Off shore, the open partisan debate that characterizes public and Congressional scrutiny of domestic policy must give way to uncritical concurrence.

But once the icon of Presidential omniscience had been smashed, what could the revolutionaries offer to fill its niche? How would the

3

Congressional rank and file safeguard the national interest? Would 535 members of Congress, all seeking a meaningful role, paralyze the national will? Would "open" decision-making give advantage to our adversaries and offense to our friends?

There is some irony in the timing of these questions. For thirty years— from 1944 to 1974—the United States was, beyond question, the leading world power: undefeated in war, unrivaled in weaponry and technology, locomotive of an emerging world economy. During that period the United States might consciously have opted, as a matter of rational value allocation, to pay some costs in foreign policy efficiency and effectiveness to achieve the benefits of democratic control over our international relations. But we did not. Instead, the democratization of U.S. foreign policy has occurred precisely as our secure position of leadership began to erode, with U.S. armies defeated in Asia, weaponry matched or outstripped by the Soviets, and the dollar in disarray.

The skeptic may well ask: If we could not afford the luxury of democratic foreign policy-making in our halcyon days, how can we afford it now? And skeptics might also ask: Is this not something we have seen before? Are we not witnessing another swing of the perpetual pendulum rather than a genuine revolution?

Senator Fulbright said, in 1961:

> I wonder whether the time has not arrived, or indeed already has passed, when we must give the Executive a measure of power in the conduct of world affairs that we have hitherto jealously withheld. . . . It is my contention that for the existing requirements of American foreign policy we have hobbled the President by too niggardly a grant of power.

Pointing out that Congressional power over foreign relations puts undue strain on the Secretary of State and other high officials "who are obliged to expend prodigious amounts of time and energy in shepherding their programs through the glacial legislative process," Fulbright complained that his fellow members of Congress, "with their excessive parochial orientation . . . are acutely sensitive to the influence of private pressure and to the excesses and inadequacies of a public opinion that is all too often ignorant of the needs, the dangers, and the opportunities in our foreign relations."[1]

But in 1974, Senator Fulbright had a different message.

> Only if one subscribes to the cult of the "strong" Presidency which mesmerized American political science in the '50s and early '60s can one look with complacency on the growth of Presidential dictatorship in foreign affairs. In those days, when the magic glow of Roosevelt still flickered in our memories, when Eisenhower reigned with paternal benignancy and the Kennedys appeared on white chargers with promises of

Camelot, it was possible to forget the wisdom of the Founding Fathers, who had taught us to mistrust power, to check it and balance it, and never to yield up the means of thwarting it. Now, after bitter experience, we are having to learn all over again what those pre-Freudian students of human nature who framed the American constitution understood well: that no single man or institution can ever be counted upon as a reliable or predictable repository of wisdom or benevolence; that the possession of great power can impair a man's judgment and cloud his perception of realities; and that our only protection against the misuse of power is the institutionalized interaction of a diversity of politically independent opinion. . . . I believe that the Presidency has become a dangerously powerful office, more urgently in need for reform than any other institution in American government. . . . Whatever may be said against Congress—that it is slow, obstreperous, inefficient or behind the times—there is one thing to be said for it: It poses no threat to the liberties of the American people.[2]

If there were two Senator Fulbrights over a period of thirteen years, there seem also to be two President Carters, and they both emerged within a period of less than two years.

After his election, President Carter and Secretary of State Cyrus Vance several times—whether answering the telephone question of a little girl from Alabama or solemnly testifying before Congressional committees—reiterated their approval of the post-Vietnam restraints on Presidential initiatives imposed by Congress through such vehicles as the War Powers Act and Section 36B of the Foreign Assistance and Arms Export legislation.

More recently, however, President Carter has complained publicly of the restraints on his foreign relations discretion imposed by Congressional restrictions. In June 1978 he complained that "excessive use of legislative vetoes and other devices to restrict foreign policy actions can impede our ability to respond to rapidly changing world conditions. Reasonable flexibility is essential to effective government."

The remarks by Fulbright I and Fulbright II, as also by Carter I and Carter II, do illustrate the applicability of this metaphor of the pendulum of political fashion: from a let-the-President-do-everything to a let-him-do-nothing concept of the Presidency, and back again.

The current trend toward Congressional assertiveness in foreign policy may be the fourth such swing in American history. There are those—not the least of them in the White House—who believe there has been no revolution, and that the pendulum will soon fall back one more time, toward the President's side.

The first period of Congressional predominance came immediately after the aggressive Administration of Andrew Jackson. Beginning with Martin Van Buren's Presidency in 1837 and encompassing the terms of

Harrison, Tyler, Taylor, Fillmore, Pierce, and Buchanan, through 1861, this swing lasted roughly twenty-eight years.

A second swing to Congress began after the end of the wartime Lincoln Administration, extending from Grant through the Whig period to the end of the Cleveland Presidency in 1897. Including the Administrations of Hayes, Garfield, Arthur, and Harrison, it, too, lasted approximately twenty-eight years.

The third swing to Congress began with Wilson's second term and lasted through the Administrations of Presidents Harding, Coolidge, and Hoover. This time, the swing circumscribed a mere eighteen years.[3]

A fourth swing, if that it is, began in 1973.

Three generalizations can be made about these recurrent swings:

(1) War tends to end the swing to Congress, and the ending of a war tends to trigger a swing back.

(2) Each swing contains within itself the excesses that generate the counter-force for the next swing.

(3) The duration of the swing, historically, may be getting shorter.

The pendulum theory has been criticized as simplistic by scholars[4] who, at the very least, see countervailing movement within each tendency. On closer observation, what seem to be linear swings reveal themselves to be made up of jagged little zigzags, trends on trends, more closely resembling a cardiogram than a series of smooth bell-curves. Whatever its merits as a guide through history, however, the pendulum theory may prove to be an unreliable interpreter of the present and future. There is persuasive evidence that the present period of Congressional ascendance is not just a swing of a pendulum; that what we are experiencing is a revolution that will not be unmade. That evidence may be briefly summarized:

First, Congress has increasingly legislated its role via procedures that are on-going, rather than in one-shot policy confrontations. Most of these new mandated procedures are designed not to reverse particular policies made by the President but to require by law a Congressional input into, or review of, the Executive decision-making process itself. This "new oversight" has transformed the game in Washington by increasing Congress's access to information and power.

Second, Congress has acquired its own policy capability. It has hired itself a staff of foreign relations specialists that is almost a counter-State Department; has given itself a Congressional Budget Office to balance the President's Office of Management and Budget, a Congressional Reference Service, and General Accounting Office to match the President's National Security Council and State Department Policy Planning staff. The GAO even maintains embryo counter-embassies. These are infrastructural changes that are far more stable than the one-damn-thing-after-another transactional relations that have hitherto been the hallmark of shifts in the balance of power.

Third, Congress has vastly democratized itself in the past five years, by institutional changes. It is now far harder for the Executive, or anyone else, to domesticate. Congress has transformed the selection of committee and subcommittee chairmen, opened up committee assignments, relaxed the power of committees over the legislature's business. Members are harder to discipline or restrain. Closed rules are harder to get, discharges easier, "germaneness" less rigidly enforced. A turnover in membership has created an influx of younger, better-educated members less amenable to centralized leadership. The Executive can no longer keep Congress on a short leash by coopting a few Arthur Vandenbergs. On the contrary, the President is now dealing with 535 members, most of them reasonably autonomous, mostly emancipated from idiosyncratic, feudal committee satraps, many willing to listen to reason, but not to commands.

Fourth, related to the above, foreign policy has become a hot political item. The new members of Congress, whether on or off the relevant committees, want to be in on the action. Foreign policy gets press coverage. It interests the voters. It is the subject of a welter of lobbies. It is inextricably related to domestic pocketbook issues. Traditionally this has not been the case; heretofore most members simply could not be bothered. Now they bother.

Fifth, the Executive has made its own structural accommodations based on the reluctant assumption of a stable, continuing Congressional partnership. Liaison has been beefed up in the Departments and the White House. The "H" base in the State Department, which conducts liaison, has been broadened by encouraging substantive bureaus to open their own ancillary lines to Congress. Congress-watching and Congress-consulting have become systematized. Even where not required by law, as in the Strategic Arms Limitation Treaty (SALT) negotiations, members of Congress are being added as advisers to negotiating delegations. The sharing of intelligence has been routinized. The foreign relations bureaucracy has been politicized in the sense that it now has almost as many specialists for dealing with Congress as for dealing with any foreign country. Temporary service on the Hill is being recognized as a respectable and profitable step up the career ladder of State Department Foreign Service officers. An Old Boy FSO-staffers' network is being strung between the Hill and Foggy Bottom.

There is a *sixth* and most important reason for believing that we are witnessing more than just another swing of a pendulum. Since Congress became actively involved in foreign policy–making, a reassessment of the costs and benefits of Congressional activism has occurred, which indicates costs are lower than had been feared and that there are some unanticipated benefits as well. Open Congressional participation and public ventilation of the issues brought human rights concerns to the fore, imposed restraints on arms sales and nuclear exports, and, it may be argued, on balance improved the text of the Panama Canal treaties by— in the "leadership amendment"—clarifying several unresolved issues which might have caused friction in the future.

Even in the White House and State Department, Congressional reassertion of its Constitutional role has increasingly been understood in terms of foreign policy benefits. Much of this has to do with legitimation. When Congress challenges the President, it focuses his attention on the task of convincing the public, of "bringing the country along." With disastrous consequences, American foreign policy has long been considered too complex an issue to take to the people. The mere fact that Congress could not be taken for granted—in connection with the Panama agreements, SALT talks, Middle East policy, trade with the Soviet Union, human rights—has forced the White House repeatedly to make its case in public. In most instances, Congress and the public eventually came to agree with the Administration. In some cases, the Administration compromised. Either way, the result was a policy legitimized by manifest endorsement of Congress, which is a far more sensitive seismometer of public feeling than the Presidency. As such, it was more likely to succeed than a Presidential fiat.

Democratic legitimization achieved in this fashion has begun to build a replacement for the national foreign policy consensus shattered by the Vietnam War. The new consensus, however, is characterized by wide participation, painstaking consultation, and hard-fought compromise, whereas the old, too often, was played out as a game of follow the leader.

There are costs, of course, and they are made apparent by the circus-like aspects of the Congressional debates on Panama as well as by idiosyncratic subcommittee chairmen, self-aggrandizing staffers, incomprehensible requirements for Executive reporting to Congress, and dense jungles of legislation with impenetrable tangles of standards, roamed by monstrous subordinate clauses. There are also high-handed denials of transfer authority for appropriated funds and counterproductive denials of foreign aid to countries that offend a few legislators. These are the serious, rough edges of a political process that is by no means perfect— except, to paraphrase Winston Churchill, when compared with all the alternatives.

Neither, however, are the new post-revolutionary rules of the game immutable. Initially, the White House and State Department in the Nixon-Ford Administration opposed all the rules by which Congress had insinuated itself into the process. By the time Jimmy Carter became President, a tentative tactical decision had been made to learn to play by them, and to try to win. In the process of the game, the Administration began to work some subtle modifications in the rules themselves.

But such victories should not obscure the revolutionary new realities of Congressional power that have democratized and legitimized U.S. foreign policy. The Administration would not be acting prudently, or in the national interest, if it sought to restore the old order of Presidential omnipotence. Neither should it count on an historically determined destiny to swing the pendulum back in its favor.

What might conceivably generate another swing of the pendulum is Congressional inability to use power. Failure to create its own effective decision-making system can destroy any Congressional partnership with the Presidency. So could the unwillingness of individual members to devote the necessary time and attention to their new foreign policy responsibilities.

The legislative branch has yet to build a convincing delivery system or to win its battle of the attention span. If the public perceives Congress as unable or unwilling to act effectively in partnership with the Executive to safeguard the national interest, power will run off Capitol Hill.

It was as recently as 1975 that the prestigious Murphy Commission on the Organization of the Government for the Conduct of Foreign Policy published a study which found that

> Congress does not have the information, and some congressmen do not have the understanding, sophistication, and interest to support independent judgment. Inevitably, then, Congress is compelled to accept the grand design, the general direction, the mood of presidential foreign policy. . . . Congress could strike out on its own only with an acute awareness of its uncertainties and inadequacies, and the risks to the national interest and its own institutional standing.[5]

Yet strike out on its own it has, defying its legions of detractors; and, despite a few wild swings, Congress has not struck out. This revolution began, this study will show, as have all others: with a series of sharp, destructive attacks on the old order. But then Congress turned to reconstruction, devising an elaborate new system of rules for designing foreign policy by codetermination, rather than by dominion of one branch over the other.

I

CONGRESS BECOMES

A WORLD POWER

1

THE LEGISLATED PEACE:

Congress Ends U.S. Involvement
in Indochina

THE AERIAL WAR ENDS

JUNE 29, 1973—the Bastille Day of the Congressional revolution—the President of the United States acknowledged the right of Congress to end U.S. military involvement in Indochina and promised to stop bombing Cambodia. With that sullen concession, power over foreign policy shifted: from the imperial President and his discreet and decorous professional foreign relations managers to the undisciplined, rambunctious rabble of the House and Senate.

It was, like the British sacking of New Orleans, a victory won after the war was supposedly over. By the end of 1972, U.S. troop commitment to Vietnam had already been whittled down to 24,100. On January 23, 1973, President Nixon had made his historic announcement of the signing of the Paris peace accord ending the involvement of U.S. ground forces in the Indochina war. Under Article 20 of that agreement, the Vietcong and North and South Vietnamese governments agreed that "Foreign countries shall put an end to all military activities in Cambodia and Laos, totally withdraw from and refrain from re-introducing . . . troops, military advisers and military personnel, armaments, munitions and war material."

Soon after, on February 21, 1973, a Laotian cease-fire fell into place. But the civil war in Cambodia proved more intractable. The Khmer Rouge, unlike the Pathet Lao and Vietcong, were relatively uncontrollable from Hanoi. They set their sights on outright victory through relentless struggle, a strategy running counter to Hanoi's plans for a period of calm during which the U.S. could become disengaged before the final blow.

13

Nothing of these arcane tactical and doctrinal struggles within the variegated Indochinese Communist camp attracted notice in the United States. Amid the general rejoicing over the termination of the eight-year-long ordeal, scant heed was paid to the failure of the Paris accord to solve the Cambodian problem. No U.S. ground forces had been involved there since 1970, although U.S. airpower continued to provide support for the non-Communist regime. Now that support seemed a small but annoying dissonance amid the pealing of the peace carillon.

Indeed, so anxious were some to begin a new chapter, that they could not wait for the previous one to end. On the day before the Vietnam cease-fire was to come into effect, Republican Senator Clifford P. Case of New Jersey and Democrat Frank Church of Idaho introduced a bill to terminate U.S. air support for the Cambodians, cease-fire or no cease-fire.[1] Although Case-Church failed to become law, it sent a warning message to the White House.

An effort was made by the Lon Nol government in Cambodia's capital of Phnom Penh to interest its Communist foes in an armistice reflecting the spirit of the Paris accord. At the end of January, under intense pressure from the White House, Phnom Penh declared a unilateral halt to all offensive ground operations. Concurrently, Washington announced its own temporary ban on bombing. The Khmer Rouge's inevitable reply was to step up their attack, being convinced that the war had shifted decisively in their favor and that they had nothing to gain by negotiations. After this brief and disappointing respite, the United States announced it was resuming saturation bombing with B-52 bombers and F-111 fighter jets, as Communist forces edged closer to the capital.

This renewal of bombing came as a rude shock to popular if naïve U.S. expectations of peace and set the stage for the crucial confrontation between Congress and the Executive. It was a confrontation won outright by the Congress, clearing the way for a long string of further legislative initiatives that fundamentally altered the process by which U.S. foreign policy is made. As with the revolt of the American colonies—or any other revolution—it may be argued, quite persuasively, that the actual issue triggering the revolt was trivial and misperceived by the revolutionaries, that the uprising prompted excesses and caused undue damage. It is far more difficult, however, to show that these revolutions lacked long-term, underlying causes or that justice and renewal were not advanced by their triumph.

Whatever history's verdict will be, Congress acted for the American people. The Congressional majority, having at long last repealed the Tonkin Gulf Resolution authorizing U.S. involvement in Indochina and having seen the last U.S. combat forces evacuated from South Vietnam, understandably feared the continued involvement of U.S. pilots and bombers over Cambodia. Senate Democratic Majority Leader Mike Mansfield of Montana worried that the continued bombing was a "most dangerous" policy which "could have the possible effect of once again involving this country in a quagmire."[2] And, further to the right, once-hawkish Republican Senator Norris Cotton of New Hampshire proclaimed "a new ballgame. As far as I am concerned, I want to get the hell out of there just as quick as possible, and I don't want to fool around to the point that they might take more prisoners."[3]

The Administration could not assuage these fears, nor did it try. Instead, it contended that continued bombing was necessary to create the psychological conditions for serious bargaining. As long as the Khmer Rouge believed in an early field victory, they would have no incentive to talk.[4]

Late in April, Henry Kissinger, then the President's National Security Adviser, charged that the Paris agreement had been "totally violated" by Hanoi's massive illegal movement of equipment, supplies, and troops through Cambodia into South Vietnam.[5]

Congress, however, showed relatively little interest in defending the Paris accord, now that the politically key provision—repatriation of U.S. prisoners—had been carried out. This was what the Communists had expected. Legislators fretted about the continuing waste of funds: fully $160 million had been spent on bombing Cambodia in the period between January 27 and April 30.[6] And members were not reassured by Secretary of State William Rogers's promise: "We will not slide into another Vietnam. We will not introduce ground troops into Cambodia."[7] Skepticism had become a conditioned response after eight years of Presidential escalation, miscalculation, and lying. Nine days after Rogers's testimony, the Senate Select Committee on Presidential Campaign Activities (the Ervin Committee) began its investigation of the Watergate break-ins; skepticism turned to disbelief.

While Congress worried about wasted funds and about military re-escalation by an Administration it did not trust, it also became aroused by what it perceived as a continued Presidential assault on its most basic Constitutional prerogatives—the power to declare war and the power to determine how funds are spent. Once the Paris accord had been signed, it could be argued that further U.S. military involvement in Indochina required a Congressional declaration of war or specific statutory authorization. The White House and State Department, to the contrary, asserted that continued bombing of Cambodia was well within the powers of the President as Commander in Chief to defend the integrity of the Paris accord.

The argument is weak, the more so as Congress had not been asked to authorize that accord, much less the use of force to uphold it. Neverthe-

less, the Administration proceeded to give effect to its generous reading
of the President's Constitutional powers. In so doing, the White House
and Defense Department did not even seek specific spending authority
from Congress for the bombing. Instead, they excluded Congress from
that decision by the simple expedient of transferring money from other
categories of military funding. In this choice of tactic, the White House
could point to precedents going back to the eighteenth century, when
Congress had first allowed the Secretaries of Treasury and War to shift
funds specifically appropriated for one purpose to quite another.[8] But
opponents could also point to a long Congressional history of struggle
against the practice, particularly when crucial issues of national policy
were at stake, going back to 1797, when Representative Albert Gallatin
had successfully amended a naval funding bill by requiring that the sums
being supplied "shall be solely applied to the objects for which they are
respectively appropriated."[9]

Whatever the historic precedents, the tactic never won any President
a lot of friends in Congress. In this instance, the damage was aggravated
by clumsy handling of the key House and Senate Appropriations Committees, an error that drove these hawkishly inclined guardians of the
purse to give the Administration its *coup de grâce*.

Why did the President choose this fatal tactic?

The Administration had been finding it increasingly difficult, even
before the Paris peace accord, to get Congress to grant specific authority
and funds for the Cambodian aerial war, and so hit on the idea of
backdoor financing. During fiscal 1973 the Defense Department shifted
$750 million from other allocations to the war. However, it neglected a
key factor in successful backdoor manipulation. While the powerful
House and Senate Appropriations Committees had been willing enough
to help the Executive circumvent the rest of Congress, they were not at
all ready to deal themselves out. In connection with the money granted
to the Defense Department for fiscal 1971, for example, it had been
agreed between Appropriations and Defense that all transfers "shall be
considered to be matters of special interest to the Committees on Appropriations"[10]—the idea being that both committees would be consulted
before each re-programming.

The Defense Department, unwisely, failed to keep its part of this
thieves' contract. In November and December 1972, Cambodia was
bombed on credit, but not until February and March of the following
year were the Appropriations Committees asked to approve the bulk of
transfer requests necessary to make good the deficiency.[11] Technically,
therefore, the transfers were made with committee approval; but in fact
the crucial decisions had been made and executed months before approval was sought.[12]

The policy of credit bombing not only alienated the key committee members but also, eventually, compelled the Administration to go back to Congress for a second helping from the public purse. This it did on March 21, 1973, only to be devastated by what, in the field, would have been called "friendly fire." Both members of the Senate and members of the House Appropriations Committees lashed out against Presidential overreach. Debate stressed Executive arrogance and violation of committee prerogatives more than it focused on the strategic or political wisdom of further spending on Cambodian aerial operations.

In the House, particularly tough cross-examination of Administration witnesses was led by Democratic Representative Robert L. Sikes of Florida—later himself to be reprimanded by the House for financial sleight-of-hand.[13] Faced with questions about the funds that had been spent by the Administration without the prior approval of the committee,[14] Acting Assistant Secretary of Defense Don R. Brazier, the comptroller at the Defense Department, answered lamely: "Mr. Chairman, while those monies and those expenses have indeed been incurred, we have not literally transferred the money into those appropriations. We are now operating in those accounts at a deficiency rate. We have not in fact transferred the dollars into the appropriations and would not until this committee acted."[15] In other words, the committee was now being asked to exercise its control, but only retroactively, after the money had been spent. This sort of weaselly lawyering hurt the Administration's cause. It underscored the arguments of those who claimed that the real issue was the President's war on Congress, not the war in Cambodia.

The most controversial item in the second supplemental appropriations bill for 1973 was one giving Defense power to transfer an additional $750 million from one appropriated category to another. Roy Ash, director of the Office of Management and Budget, rushing to the defense of Defense, warned that the failure to permit the transfers could mean the termination of bombing support missions for Cambodian forces.[16]

The House Appropriations Committee, ultimately, by the narrowest of margins, approved part of the Administration's request, granting $430 million in additional general transfer authority, of which $149 million was to be available for combat activities in Southeast Asia. Opponents of even this grudging concession, led by Representative Joseph Addabbo of New York, then took the fight straight to an unorthodox forum: the influential House Democratic Steering Committee. This time they won, thereby aligning the party leadership against the majority of the committee. When the bill came before the full House, an amendment by Representative Addabbo, barring all transfers, carried easily.

Also adopted from the floor was an even more sweeping amendment by another disaffected Appropriations Committee member, Democratic

Representative Clarence D. Long of Maryland. This barred the use of any funds voted for Defense to support combat activity in or over Cambodia.[17] Long, who had been a leading hawk, was the only member of the House to have had a son seriously injured in Cambodian combat. A few days before the U.S. incursion into that country, he heard the Secretary of State testify at a closed committee hearing that the U.S. had no intention of extending the Vietnam war to Cambodia. Long claims this experience led to his becoming a dove.

The Senate, meanwhile, was proceeding somewhat more slowly. On May 2 its Democratic Caucus had adopted a resolution similar to that of the House Democratic Steering Committee, calling for a cutoff of all funds for U.S. military operations in Cambodia.

Sensing the direction of the wind, the Administration now changed tactics. This, as it turned out, was a second error of judgment. On May 7, Secretary Elliot Richardson told a closed session of the Senate Appropriations Committee that a mere $25 million of the requested transfer funds were actually needed to finance continued bombing through the remainder of the fiscal year to June 30: a direct contradiction of the urgent case made by Roy Ash a few weeks earlier. Then Richardson said that even if transfer authority were denied, the government could still find the funds necessary to continue bombing in other categories of appropriated monies.[18]

With that the Administration not only undermined its credibility—by now seeming not really to need what it had so recently requested urgently—but appeared to be telling Congress that it would go on bombing no matter what.

The Senate Committee responded: by cutting the total of new transfer authority to $170 million and prohibiting all transfer for military activities in Cambodia.[19] An amendment sponsored by Senator Thomas Eagleton of Missouri and adopted by the Senate Appropriations Committee closely paralleled the Case-Church Amendment that had been narrowly defeated in February. Eagleton's bill provided that "None of the funds herein appropriated under this act *or heretofore appropriated under any other act* may be expended to support directly or indirectly combat activities in, over or from off the shores of Cambodia or in or over Laos by United States forces" (italics added).

This went beyond even the Long Amendment passed by the House, which only applied to funds contained in the second supplemental appropriation. (Long had been restrained by a procedural point—the famous "germaneness rule"—that applies in the House but not in the Senate. The rule bars amendments being attached to a bill that have the effect of amending another piece of legislation.) Eagleton's bill, by cutting off money "heretofore" appropriated, would also have taken away whatever leftover bombing money the Administration belatedly claimed to have found in other appropriations.

On May 31, the Senate completed action on the supplemental appropriation, passing it by an overwhelming 73 to 5 with the Eagleton Amendment attached.[20] Senator Jacob Javits, Republican of New York, said: ". . . the courts have held that if we pass an appropriation, if we refrain from cutting off money, it may be an indication that we approve or authorize what is being done."[21]

Not only liberals but also influential conservative Senators who had consistently supported the Vietnam war effort, were prominent among those now voting for the cutoff. Among these were Republican Senator Milton R. Young of North Dakota, the ranking minority member of the Appropriations Committee, who observed, "we have got our prisoners of war out with honor, and what's the point of going on supporting a government that seems to have no will to fight and is corrupt?"[22] The venerable Appropriations chairman, Senator John L. McClellan of Arkansas, publicly weighed the danger of new prisoners of war being taken against the duty to enforce the peace treaty, concluding, "I have chosen to risk the consequences of stopping the bombing."[23]

Each house had now passed a bill restraining the Administration's bombing plans. The Senate's version, because of that chamber's more lenient rules, not only denied new funds but cut off any money left over from prior appropriations. The House bill simply refused new funds or transfer authority. When House and Senate versions of a bill differ, each appoints a team of negotiators to an *ad hoc* conference committee to work out a compromise. These appointments are ordinarily in the discretion of the chairmen of the sponsoring committees. After the conference produces an agreed compromise, it must be endorsed by each chamber. If no compromise is reached, the two teams report to their respective houses and await new instructions.

House and Senate conferees began to meet on June 5. The Senate side sent its doves (with the exception of hawkish Senator Roman Hruska of Nebraska). The House conferees were chosen by Appropriations Committee chairman George Mahon of Texas and reflected his antagonism to the two leading committee dissidents—Addabbo and Long, who had succeeded in amending the committee's compromise funding package on the floor; neither was named to the team of House conferees. When it became apparent that House and Senate conferees were deadlocked, Mahon did his best to prevent the House from capitulating to the Senate. He attempted to summon his chamber's *amour propre*, pointing out that the issue was one of fiscal policy, traditionally an area where

Representatives lead and Senators follow. Representative Long, however, once more outmaneuvered his chairman. "This is a principle," he told the House, "that rises above pride of authorship, and the idea of appropriations originating in the House, and therefore I feel that the Eagleton amendment gives us the strongest possible language. . . ."[24] By a vote of 235 to 172, the House accepted a motion by Representative Robert N. Giaimo of Connecticut to disavow its own conferees and to have the House recede from its disagreement with the Senate.[25]

This was all highly unusual, even historic—not only in the substance of what Congress was now doing but also the procedure by which it was accomplished. The impetus shaping a money bill had come not from the House Appropriations Committee but from individual rebellious members taking their case to the party Steering Committee and ultimately to the floor for a vote by the whole House. The full membership had repudiated the House Appropriations Committee leadership, kicked over the traces, and voted to end the bombing. The leadership had struck back by appointing conferees not in sympathy with the rebellious membership, and the Representatives had then voted to instruct their own negotiators to give way to the Senate in a matter historically of primary concern to the House. As a result of all this, not only the relations of President to Congress but of Congressional leaders and committee chairmen to rank-and-file members were profoundly transformed.

Desperately, Representative Mahon then offered a motion to delay by sixty days the effective date of the Eagleton cutoff. This motion failed by a cliff-hanging division of 204 to 204.[26]

Nevertheless, the Eagleton Amendment did not become law at this point. President Nixon vetoed the bill on June 27, stating that it would "cripple or destroy the chances for an effective negotiated settlement in Cambodia" and that it would be "nothing short of tragic if this great accomplishment [the Paris agreement] bought with the blood of so many Asians and Americans, were to be undone now by congressional action."[27] On June 27, the House failed to override the veto by a shortfall of thirty-five votes.[28]

This proved a short-lived triumph for the Administration. Congress had made sure to have in reserve several even bigger guns that would give it final victory. The Senate Foreign Relations Committee had already attached a similarly sweeping funding cutoff to the bill authorizing the expenditures of the Department of State.[29] House and Senate next attached the "Eagleton" Amendment to a funding bill that the President could veto only if he were willing to take responsibility for stopping the pay of the entire federal bureaucracy.[30] For good measure, the Senate added the same amendment to a bill extending the debt-ceiling limit, another vehicle the President could scarcely halt.[31] On June 28, House-

Senate conferees agreed to keep the Eagleton Amendment in the debt ceiling.

Seeing a steady procession of essential legislation heading its way bearing identical cutoff provisions, the White House caved in. On television, all that week, John Dean had been indicting the President before the Ervin Committee; the White House clearly was wounded. Still on June 28, the House Appropriations Committee reported a new version of the second supplemental appropriations bill that offered a face-saving way out. While again including the Eagleton Amendment, it delayed implementation until August 15 and thereby offered the President forty-five additional days to bomb Cambodia.

In a packed House chamber, the next day, the Minority Leader Gerald R. Ford of Michigan reported that the President could live with the August 15 deadline.[32] Ford cited the President's willingness to accept a ban on all U.S. military activity in Cambodia, Vietnam, and Laos, a statement that took the White House by surprise. Nixon, according to advisers, had only agreed to the now-inescapable restriction on bombing Cambodia. He was deeply distressed by Ford's enlargement of the injunction to include Laos and Vietnam.

Thus endorsed, the bill breezed through the House and Senate and was signed by the embattled President.[33] Nixon had "capitulated," Senator George McGovern of South Dakota exulted, adding that it was "the happiest day of my life."[34] Eagleton, however, was less enthusiastic. He voted against the compromise that had overtaken his amendment, asserting that if the air war was in fact unconstitutional, Congress, by sanctioning it for a short while longer, was giving its imprimatur to an illegal extension of Presidential power.[35]

Immediately before the August 15 deadline, the President and the Department of State made it perfectly clear that they would hold the Congress accountable for the consequences. In a passionate letter to House Speaker Carl Albert of Oklahoma and Senate Democratic Leader Mike Mansfield, Nixon said that the cutoff was tantamount to "abandonment of a friend" and predicted "a profound impact in other countries such as Thailand."[36] Through Deputy Press Secretary Gerald L. Warren, he warned that this action "undermines the prospects of world peace by raising doubts in the minds of both friends and adversaries concerning the resolve and capacity of the United States to stand by international agreements when they are invoked by other parties."[37]

In his memoirs the former President does, indeed, hold Congress accountable. The bombing cutoff "set off a string of events that led to the Communist takeover in Cambodia and, on April 30, 1975, the North Vietnamese conquest of South Vietnam." He adds, the "war and the peace in Indochina that America had won at such cost over 12 years of sacrifice and fighting were lost within a matter of months once Congress refused to fulfill our obligations. And it is Congress that must bear the responsibility for the tragic results."[38]

While these accusations will long be debated by historians, a critique of the systemic effects of the cutoff can already be ventured. First, the compromise between Nixon and Congress, by permitting an additional forty-five days of bombing, illustrates a problem inherent in a foreign policy made by compromise between mutually hostile forces at opposite ends of Pennsylvania Avenue. In the Cambodian War there were good arguments for stopping as well as for continuing the bombing; but none, surely, for continuing bombing up to a statutory deadline.

If the object was to spare further Cambodian suffering and prevent possible loss of U.S. pilots, then the instrumentally correct answer should have been to stop at once rather than to go on bombing pointlessly for more than another month. If the intention was to inflict costs on the Khmer Rouge in order to induce them to negotiate, only a policy of bombing for the indefinite future could hope to advance that purpose. As soon as the Communists knew that bombing would end at a legislative deadline, the aerial war lost whatever psychological capacity it once might have had to induce restraint.

Above all, the compromise failed to make sense to those whose understanding of the national purpose is the essential prerequisite for its success—the U.S. public. One cannot but feel the deep anger of a U.S. family whose son was shot down on the forty-fourth day. There is a lesson. The "let's split the difference down the middle" type of legislative compromise, so much a part of the way Congress and the President traditionally interact on domestic issues, can produce the worst of all possible worlds when applied to foreign policy-making.

And there is the germ of another lesson, concerning the limits and dangers of making foreign policy by passing laws that prohibit the President from reacting to future contingencies. The provisions enacted by Congress to terminate the Cambodian air war also prohibited the President from using any funds to employ any U.S. military forces—at any time or under any circumstances—in, over, or off the shores of any part of Indochina, including South Vietnam. This absolute prohibition reflected the public and Congressional suspicion that this President might at any time, on any pretext, resubmerge the nation in the Far Eastern quagmire. Indeed, it later turned out that Nixon had promised Vietnamese President Thieu, in private correspondence, that U.S. forces would come to Saigon's aid should the North launch another invasion.[39] Inadvertently, however, Congress probably did Thieu's cause more harm than it intended. By using the public legislative process to prohibit the

President from using force, the legislators signaled Hanoi that the South could now be plucked with impunity. The message was all too clear. The U.S. was out of that part of the world and would not return, whether the Paris agreement was honored or not.

Could that have been avoided? Since Congress is primarily a legislative body, foreign policy-making by Congress usually means the making of policy by laws. Characteristic of laws is predictability, a removal of uncertainty. Yet, in foreign relations, a degree of flexibility may be a valuable asset. Unfortunately, the deterrence of Hanoi depended upon creating in the Communist leaders' minds some uncertainty as to what the U.S. would do if, in violation of the Paris agreement, they again marched on Saigon. After August 15, however, General Giap needed only to read the U.S. statutes to know what to expect: mandatory inaction. To the extent that U.S. national interests depend on deterrence strategy, it must be accepted that tactical flexibility is incompatible with a legislated foreign policy.

MILITARY ASSISTANCE DRIES UP

As if to nail down its victory, Congress now included similar, sweeping prohibitions on Indochina theater military activity in half a dozen laws, including a continuing appropriations resolution,[40] State Department authorization,[41] military procurement authorization[42] and foreign aid bill.[43] In underscoring the obvious, Congress was proclaiming, "we have taken on the President, in a crucial issue of war or peace, and we have won." It had, indeed, become an independent, militant force in formulating foreign policy.

After ending all direct U.S. military action, members began to focus on the huge volume of economic and military aid still being provided to Indochina. Representative Bella Abzug of New York and other radicals favored a total ban on military assistance, while fiscal conservatives questioned the utility of pouring more money down what the members inelegantly referred to as a "rat-hole."

For 1974 the Administration requested $632 million in economic aid for Cambodia, Laos, and South Vietnam. Congress grudgingly granted $450 million.[44] Of $200 million in military aid asked for Cambodia, $150 million was voted, although the Senate tried to cut the request in half.[45] For Vietnam and Laos, the Executive asked $1.6 billion, of which Congress approved $907 million,[46] with the Senate at first holding out for a reduction to $650 million.[47] These figures represent Congress's fatigue with continuing Vietnam expenditures, but also the nadir of the Nixon

Administration. The resignation of Attorney General Richardson had taken place in October and the House Judiciary Committee, in December, completed its staffing for a Presidential impeachment inquiry.

Faced with these cuts, the Administration—learning nothing and forgetting nothing—again reacted with fiscal sleight-of-hand: overspending, requesting supplementary funds, then discovering unspent revenue. It thus ignored the lesson of the Cambodian aerial war showdown, that, in the prevailing atmosphere of suspicion, money found was likely to be money lost. And as in that earlier encounter, so now too, the White House was defeated primarily by the rank and file acting in defiance of the Congressional leadership. In the House, the Armed Services Committee was led by Louisiana Congressman F. Edward Hébert, a conservative Democrat and loyal friend of the Defense Department. Hébert persuaded his committee to give the President almost half a billion dollars in additional spending authority.[48] But then, in another revolutionary act, the House not only defeated Hébert's bill but also rejected his subsequent efforts to get approval for a smaller compromise package.[49]

The Senate's equally hawkish Armed Services Committee, fearful of a similar public rebuke, joined the Administration's game of fiscal hide-and-seek. It reported finding an additional $266 million in unused Presidential spending authority. Reacting swiftly, the full chamber, led in the attack by Massachusetts Senator Edward Kennedy, voted to prohibit any of the money being used for military aid to South Vietnam.[50] Speaking on the Senate floor, Senator Kennedy questioned "whether the shipment of more arms to South Vietnam will help strengthen the cease-fire agreement, or will fan the flames of violence" and charged that the President's priority "remains with the means of war, rather than with the tools for building peace."[51] Three days later, the nation was watching impeachment hearings on live television.

Under pressure of competing domestic demands, sharpened by inflation and recession, and sensing the impending fall of Nixon, Congress became increasingly reluctant to continue shouldering the Indochina burden. Testifying before the House Foreign Affairs Committee, Defense Secretary James Schlesinger argued in vain: "When we withdrew American forces from Indochina, it was understood that we would provide the military tools to enable the people there to defend themselves."[52] Secretary Kissinger added: "We do not have an enforceable legal obligation, but we have a moral and political obligation."[53]

In mid-1974 the Administration asked for $358 million in military grant assistance to see Cambodia through 1975. Of this, 80 percent was earmarked for ammunition.[54] If this were cut, Schlesinger warned, "the ability of the government to survive would be severely compromised."[55] Unimpressed, Congress authorized only about half. Of $933.8 million in economic aid requested for Cambodia, Laos, and South Vietnam, approval was given for less than half—$449 million.[56] Written into that authorization was trenchant advice to the Secretary of State on steps to phase out economic and military support altogether.[57]

The main bout, however, came when the Administration requested another $1.6 billion for military aid to South Vietnam in 1975.[58] The House Appropriations Committee proposed cutting that to $1 billion, but cautioned the revolutionaries in the ranks that "further reduction at this time would seriously endanger the ability of the South Vietnamese to continue its level of military strength required to resist communist aggression."[59] Secretary Kissinger added a warning that earlier cuts "have brought the South Vietnamese armed forces to a level of austerity which, if reduced further, might affect their ability to defend their country against continuing communist military pressure. Further cuts could weaken them to the point that Hanoi might be tempted to launch another 1972-type offensive."[60]

None of this convinced the rank and file. Judge John Sirica had just ordered President Nixon to turn over sixty-four tapes to Special Prosecutor Leon Jaworski, and the House committee had voted three articles of impeachment. During floor debate, veteran Georgia Democrat John J. Flynt, a member of the Appropriations Committee, proposed a further reduction in the appropriation, to $700 million. His motion passed easily on August 6, with sixty-eight Republicans joining the Democratic majority.[61] The House also adopted a floor amendment requiring the Defense Department to make a 10 percent reduction in its Vietnam-based military assistance and training personnel.[62] Not since the Administration of Rutherford B. Hayes had the power of the purse been so used by the legislators to control military deployment.[63]

Three days later, Nixon resigned and was replaced by Ford. This did not lead to a truce in the revolutionary war between the branches. The Senate followed the House in cutting Vietnam funding to $700 million.[64] Senator Kennedy succeeded, on the floor, in barring transfer to Vietnam of any of the $529 million allotted generally to Asian military assistance.[65]

Asserting that the North Vietnamese were now engaged in a major infiltration into the South, President Ford, on January 21, 1975, requested a supplemental $300 million for military aid for Saigon[66] and a further $222 million for Cambodia.[67] He also refused to rule out American military intervention although promising to "use the complete constitutional process that is required of a president" before committing the armed forces.[68] Not surprisingly, his aid request immediately met an exceedingly hostile reception in Congress.

In the Senate, even the leaders had now turned their backs on further calls for help. Senator Hubert Humphrey of Minnesota, chairman of the key Subcommittee on Foreign Assistance, early declared his opposition.[69] Senate Majority Leader Mike Mansfield said that more aid "means more killing, more fighting, and that's got to stop sometime. It is up to those people to settle their differences themselves in their own way."[70] Democratic Senator Joseph Biden of Delaware argued that even food and medical assistance should be refused because it would only sustain the Cambodians' will to prolong the struggle.[71]

Philip Habib, Assistant Secretary of State for East Asian and Pacific Affairs, testified that lack of money had now made it impossible to replace South Vietnamese ammunition, fuel, spare parts, and medical supplies as they were used up. "We are unable to provide *any* replacement of major equipment losses—tanks, trucks, planes or artillery pieces,"[72] he added. Apparently, however, freshman Representative Henry A. Waxman of California spoke for many of his colleagues when he replied: "We cannot promote the peace by providing the means of war. We can only induce a peace by bringing all sides to the conference table. Providing more military aid to Saigon only increases its resistance to substantive negotiations."[73]

It was clearly a dialogue of the deaf. The Administration spoke of the nearly 200,000 additional troops the North had launched into the South and urged that the United States not simply "walk away."[74] Yet that was exactly what most members of Congress, reflecting what seemed a broadly shared sentiment in the press and the country, wanted to do.

As the battles of Phnom Penh and Saigon reached their strident climax, so did the revolution in Washington. In a letter to House Speaker Carl Albert, President Ford warned that if Congress delayed additional military assistance to Cambodia, "the Government forces will be forced, within weeks, to surrender to the insurgents"—simply for lack of ammunition. "This is a moral question that must be faced squarely," he said. "Are we deliberately abandoning this small country in the midst of its life and death struggle?" The President added that the "integrity of our alliances" throughout the world "depend upon our reputation as a reliable partner."[75]

But even as hard-core a hawk as Chairman George Mahon, while saddened to see Cambodia collapse, admitted: "It is almost impossible to convince rank-and-file American citizens that there is any end to this. If ultimately Cambodia cannot survive, why expend additional hundreds of millions?"[76]

The Administration's verbal strategy, in these final days, became ever more inept. On the one hand, the President and Secretary Kissinger were cajoling Congress and the public to provide aid needed by the Cambodians and Vietnamese to hold the line. At the same time, the Administration argued that even if the situation were hopeless, the United

States should not be seen to be the agent of political euthanasia. In Congress, a broad coalition of liberals and conservatives replied that further assistance to Indochina would merely prolong the human agony and squander the taxpayers' wealth, without significantly affecting the outcome.

THE FINAL DAYS

Most nations that lose wars suffer revolution at home. When the United States lost the war in Indochina, a revolution did occur, but in the halls of Congress rather than in the streets of America's cities. Power was seized, but, as in most revolutions, it was not immediately apparent from whom or by whom. Certainly, a part of the power to conduct foreign relations slipped from the once-magisterial hand of the Presidency. And it was to Congress that this power passed. But it did not pass to the Congressional leadership, for too many had too long been the faithful courtiers of the White House. Indeed, the revolution was as much against them as against the Chief Executive. (There were exceptions, like Chairman William Fulbright of the Senate Foreign Relations Committee. Even so, the revolution did not bring him to power either, but to defeat in an Arkansas primary.) It was not easy in those early days of the revolution to discern who had inherited the power lost by the President and the committee chairmen. To some extent, it is still the great unanswered question of the post-revolutionary era. Congress has power, but in Congress, *who?*

When a revolution has overturned established power, *ad hoc* groups arise in an effort to fill the void. On February 25, a group of six Representatives and one Senator left for Vietnam and Cambodia at the request of President Ford to make an on-the-spot investigation of the final agony. Among them were critics of the war: Democrats John J. Flynt, Bella S. Abzug, Donald M. Fraser of Minnesota, and liberal Republican Representative Paul N. McCloskey of California. It was the wan hope of the Administration that if these doves saw conditions for themselves they could be persuaded to support one more dollop of aid and might then win over others.

The delegation returned on March 3 and 4. Speaking on behalf of all but Representative Abzug, Paul (Pete) McCloskey told reporters that he had, indeed, been persuaded to propose an emergency appropriation for humanitarian assistance and military aid through June 30.[77] The group appears to have been genuinely surprised and influenced by what they saw of the fighting spirit of the Cambodian and South Vietnamese forces as well as by surprisingly persuasive evidence of Khmer Rouge brutality: evidence largely ignored or skeptically discounted by the media. Representative Flynt, who had recently been instrumental in reducing funding, now testified: "If the United States continues to provide economic and/or military assistance between now and the beginning of the rainy season, . . . I think . . . we might say that there is about a 50-50 chance of effecting . . . negotiations."[78]

Nevertheless, the House Foreign Affairs Committee on March 13 voted 15 to 18 to reject this advice, even though emergency assistance for Cambodia had been endorsed by its own subcommittee.[79] The Senate Foreign Assistance Subcommittee, by a margin of 4 to 3, over the strenuous opposition of Chairman Humphrey, approved the transfer of $125 million in ammunition and military supplies to Cambodia out of Defense Department stockpiles,[80] and on March 21 the full Senate Committee on Foreign Relations proposed three monthly supplemental allotments for Cambodia, each of slightly more than $50 million.[81] The effect was not to authorize new funds but, rather, to loosen the spending ceiling imposed by the 1974 authorization and to permit some additional transfer power and other flexibility previously taken away.[82] Nevertheless, the final decision was put off until after the Easter recess in view of Congressional preoccupation with other, higher-priority matters such as tax reduction and farm support legislation.

During that week—at the end of March and beginning of April—Vietnamese defense lines fell apart. Saigon's forces abandoned more than two-thirds of the country to the North Vietnamese who then advanced to within striking distance of the capital. In Cambodia, Premier Lon Nol and his family fled on April 1, as the U.S. Embassy began evacuating its personnel. By April 2, Vice President Nelson Rockefeller conceded that it was really "too late to do anything about it."[83] "I must say I am frustrated by the action of the Congress in not responding," President Ford added, the next day. "And I am frustrated by the limitations that were placed on the chief executive over the last two years. . . . I believe that in any case where the United States does not live up to its moral or treaty obligations, it can't help but have an adverse impact on other allies we have around the world."[84]

By April 10, Congress had finally returned from its adjournment. Even though it was now amply clear that the supplemental emergency military aid bills for South Vietnam and Cambodia had died in committee, Ford used his first State of the World message to initiate a new request for $722 million in military and $250 million in economic and humanitarian aid for South Vietnam. He called for action within nine days,[85] and also urged Congress to lift the 1973 prohibition on Presidential use of military forces in Indochina so as to facilitate evacuation of Americans and South Vietnamese "whose lives may be endangered, should the worst come to pass."[86] Ford did not bother to renew his request for Cambodian assistance: "I regret to say that as of this evening it may soon be too late."[87]

Congress, caught up in revolutionary passions, again refused to heed the President. In a key vote involving only a tiny minority of members, the proposals for emergency military assistance to Saigon died on April 17 in the Senate Armed Services Committee. By the narrowest majority of 8 to 7, its membership defeated successive proposals to authorize additional sums: $215 million, $149 million, $101 million, and $70 million. A final proposal, made by the doves on the committee, would have authorized an additional $50 million but it was rejected by a vote of 10 to 5, the hawks joining to secure its defeat because they considered the amount so small as to be useless.[88]

With that, remaining Congressional attention focused on two issues: purely humanitarian assistance and legislation authorizing the President to use force to evacuate Americans and pro-U.S. Indochinese. Even this the rank and file was unprepared to grant. Representative Les Aspin of Wisconsin spoke for them when he said that Congress simply did not know what actions the President might take if there were any loosening of the statutory prohibitions. "The unhappy prospect is that a large contingent of U.S. forces would move into South Vietnam followed by fighting, casualties, and maybe, worst of all, American POW's. We would be back in the quagmire."[89]

Although Congress did not sanction it, the President nevertheless proceeded to airlift Americans, Cambodians, and Vietnamese out of Danang, Phnom Penh, and Saigon. Ford defended the legality of his actions as Nixon had the Cambodian aerial war—by citing the "inherent" Constitutional powers of the Commander in Chief, even though it was not lack of power, but lack of appropriated funds to employ the power, that was at issue.

In 1973—when these tragic events could not have been foreseen—the Eagleton Amendment to the Foreign Assistance Act had prohibited any use of U.S. forces in Cambodia and Vietnam. Now the President found himself facing a painful but inescapable choice between law and duty.

The Eagleton Amendment certainly had not had this dilemma in mind. Its purpose, rather, had been to prevent Richard Nixon's ever taking the country back into the Indochina conflict. But in barring all use of funds for any military activities in, over, or off Vietnam, Laos, and Cambodia, the letter of the law also prohibited use of the Marines to evacuate the embassy at Saigon. That Eagleton probably intended no such consequence merely illustrates a hazard of controlling foreign relations with inflexible—and case-specific—legislation. It had been the expectation of those legislators who thought about it at all, that any un-

foreseen future contingency could be dealt with by Congress quickly enacting an even more case-specific dispensation. As it turned out, this was
a false expectation. The revolution had brought egalitarianism to Congress, and an assembly of 535 equals does not rush to decision.

By late April the scene had turned surreal. Even as U.S. helicopters
shuttled back and forth "off or over" Cambodia and South Vietnam,
the Senate continued its solemn consideration of whether to permit the
evacuation. Senator Barry Goldwater of Arizona, speaking to the bill,
reminded his colleagues "that by the time this bill is passed, all Americans will probably have been evacuated from Saigon and many, many
thousands of South Vietnamese." And he added that

> when the North Vietnamese get within rocket range of Tonsonhut Air
> Base, there is not going to be any more evacuation unless we want to go
> to war. I think we are spinning our wheels. The President, and I am
> proud of him for having done this, has taken unto his own hands the
> protection of Americans and American property and American freedoms,
> wherever they might be, around this world, regardless of the legislation
> that we, in my opinion, foolishly passed last year. . . . I suggest that
> we're being a little foolish, a little redundant. We're not accomplishing
> anything. We may not pass this bill until the day after tomorrow, at
> which time, I think the whole action will be over and we will have again
> engaged ourselves in ridiculous debate. . . .[90]

Ridiculous or not, the debate continued. On April 23, Democratic
Senator Dick Clark of Iowa offered an amendment to the Vietnam Contingency Act of 1975, to require the President "not more than forty-eight
hours after the date of enactment of this Act" to "transmit to the
Speaker of the House of Representatives and the Committees on Foreign
Relations and Judiciary and Armed Services of the Senate a report setting forth a plan for the withdrawal from Vietnam. . . ."[91] Another
amendment proposed by Senators Alan Cranston of California, Clark,
and Biden would have required the withdrawal to be "accomplished in a
single operation" if feasible.[92] Senator Javits replied that he was "one of
the most ardent advocates of Congressional power over war and over the
use of armed forces" but that he nevertheless found this too much to
stomach. "I think it would be a disservice to the whole idea if we allowed the pendulum to swing so far that we are going to take over the
management of tactical operations. It just cannot be done."[93]

Both these amendments were defeated and, at the end of the day, the
Senate passed the bill by a vote of 75 to 17.[94] In the House, the comparable legislation was passed on April 24, at 2:40 A.M., after a fourteen-
hour session marked by incredible parliamentary snarls and acrimonious
debate, by a vote of 230 to 187. That, oddly, was not the end of the

matter, for the differing House and Senate versions now had to go to conference committee to be reconciled. Then both chambers had another opportunity to debate the issue. Hard-liners among the revolutionaries like Representative Benjamin S. Rosenthal of New York again argued that the bill "surrenders to the administration broad areas of discretion over the evacuation of Americans and South Vietnamese. It reflects the outworn view that the administration alone can make responsible decisions in foreign affairs." He complained that the bill "leaves the administration the determination of how many persons should be evacuated, where they should be resettled, over what period of time the evacuation should take place, and how much should be spent in the process" without providing for "formal congressional input. . . ."[95] Representative Fraser sadly but correctly summed up the prevailing mood:

> The distrust of the executive branch runs so deep in this Chamber that Members are afraid that any discretion, any grant of authority, to the executive branch will open the door to allow the executive branch to again try to make one more effort to do what ten years failed to do. . . . Mr. Chairman, let us not carry this deep distrust to the point where we will not give any authority to the only person who is capable of handling it.[96]

On April 25, the Senate passed the conference version of the House and Senate bills by a vote of 46 to 17 with fully 36 Senators not voting. Senator James Abourezk, a rogue elephant of a Democrat from South Dakota, had the last implacable word: "This bill . . . has been labeled a humanitarian bill," he said. "Actually, more than one administration has been selling snake oil to Congress, and this is just another bottle of snake oil with a different kind of label on it."[97]

On April 30, the President informed House Speaker Albert that the Indochina evacuation had been completed but that funds were urgently needed to pay for humanitarian assistance and transportation of refugees. "I request that the House of Representatives act quickly to approve the Conference Report. . . ."[98] In peevish response, the House rejected the request the next day by a vote of 162 to 246. Ninety Republicans voted with the Democrats against their own President.

With the final refusal of Congress to accommodate President Ford, and the disintegration of the remaining anti-Communist positions in Saigon, the tragedy ended. A few legal sticklers and persons burdened with a sense of history fretted that the failure of Congress to pass the bill could later be misconstrued. "It is like saying, 'when the President went into Cambodia without congressional authority, it proved he did not need it,' " Representative Fraser argued. "That is not a very satisfactory way to leave the effort that we are trying to make in Congress to share with the President the decisions on the use of combat forces abroad."[99]

Speaking afterwards of the overall result, Fraser provided a veteran revolutionary's verdict on that phase of the revolution when it temporarily got out of hand:

> Of course it was healthy, our ending the President's foreign relations monopoly. But we should not have had to cut off the Vietnamese to make our point. They just might have made it, with more help from us. We didn't just cut off their supplies, we cut off their hope. Congress demoralized them. I was all for pulling out our troops, but I never equated that with cutting off our money and supplies. Not while Vietnamese and Cambodians were still willing to fight for their country.[100]

Revolutions occur when people lose patience and, acting in anger, seize the controls. It is not the preferred method of operating a ship, although it may be the only way to deal with madness or incompetence on the bridge. It is in such a context that these events in Congress must be understood. Had there been a modicum of mutual respect and good faith, the Congress would probably not have acted as it did. It undoubtedly assumed functions that it cannot, and therefore should not even try to, perform. Members do not have the time to oversee, much less redesign, the day-to-day decisions made by the Executive in administering the laws and ministering to the national interest. Congress does, however, have both the time and inclination to play an important—and in many instances decisive—role in setting goals and outlining methods for their attainment. If this legitimate Congressional function is repeatedly frustrated by the President, if compliance is habitually replaced by circumvention, then, in the revolutionary reaction, Congress will seize not only the powers it should have but also those it should not have.

When that happens, neither the legislators nor the administrators are performing effectively, since neither is discharging its appropriate function. What is appropriate to each branch is usually discernible by looking at the instruments available to it. Congress acts by making law. Law is a vehicle of predictive certainty, the antithesis of flexibility and creative uncertainty. The foreign policy of a nation needs a mixture of certainty, which can be provided by Congress through legislation, and of flexibility, which—as the tragic-comic efforts to modify the Eagleton Amendment illustrated—cannot readily be provided by Congressional lawmaking.

When foreign policy becomes too heavily law-determined, the system loses its ability to retain creative ambiguity and flexibility of initiative and response. Sometimes, in the conduct of foreign relations, laws—conducive to displays of immutable commitment—are useful instruments of national policy. At other times, flexibility, even the elements of surprise and unpredictability, are needed. At all times, however, the choice of normative or non-normative strategies in the conduct of foreign relations is itself an important function of foreign relations statecraft that must be exercised deliberately and prudently.

Unfortunately, when Congress and Presidency are in revolutionary turmoil and all trust is dissipated, that basic choice may be made more in anger than in prudence. The decision to terminate the aerial war against the Khmer Rouge, after a forty-five-day grace period, is a painful example of a policy which should never have been encased in law. That it was is due solely to the refusal of the President to consult Congress on a matter the Constitution did not assign solely to him. But in choosing to make this point through the instrument of law, high costs were paid. The law, at least indirectly, recognized the President's inherent right, without express Congressional approval, to bomb a country with which the U.S. was at peace. It publicly signaled the Khmer Rouge that, if they remained intransigent for seven more weeks, their forces would be home free. And, ultimately, it tied the President's hands in unanticipated contingencies: during the Saigon and Phnom Penh evacuations and the Cambodian seizure of the U.S. freighter *Mayaguez*. The latter incident forced Gerald Ford once again to face the unpalatable choice between protecting the national interests and obeying the law. There should have been no law and no dilemma. Nor would there have been, had the White House realized, by consulting with a broad spectrum of Congress, that sentiment had turned decisively against the aerial war, and the President had then phased it out before there was need for recourse to the Government Printer.

But these were revolutionary times; and the changes in Congressional-Executive relations had launched both parties onto uncharted seas, where the old rules and traditional ways provided little guidance, and where wisdom could at first amount to little more than learning from mistakes.

2

THE CUTOFF COMPLEX:

Congress Reverses Presidential Policies Toward Turkey and Angola

The rank and file of Congress, rather to their own surprise, had defied what had but recently been all but deified: the National Security Adviser, the Secretaries of State and Defense as well as key Congressional committee leaders. After ending U.S. involvement in Cambodia and Vietnam, legislators were suddenly forced to face the consequences of that self-discovery.

With the recognition that they were able to impose their will upon the executive branch in key areas of foreign policy came all kinds of pressures—from within and without Congress—to interfere in a wide range of other Presidential policies. On a revolutionary's map, the road from "could" to "should" is broad and short.

Once Congress had ended the bombing of Cambodia, the withdrawal of economic and military aid for the Saigon and Phnom Penh forces was merely an afterthought, another reflection of the public's desire to shed a lost but lingering war. This rationale, however, does not account for two other contemporaneous Congressional initiatives that radically reversed Presidential policies: toward the Cypriot and Angolan civil wars. Both were unrelated to the Indochina war. Yet in each of these further engagements in the "war between the branches," there were also important echoes of the same revolutionary themes. And the outcome was the same. Again, Congress won; it succeeded in reversing Presidential policy; it acted against the advice not only of the White House but also of much of its own leadership. As before, the initiatives came not from the once-powerful committees but from the floor, from maverick members outside the Congressional foreign relations elite. (These similarities overshadow some differences among the cases. For example, the Indochinese and Angolan episodes cast the President as intervener and Congress as extricater. But in the Cyprus case, roles were reversed: Congress wanted the U.S. to intervene with sanctions against Turkey while the President urged even-handed neutrality.)

By what lights did Congress steer its course in the Cypriot and Angolan crises? Certainly not by purely ideological, or ethical, concepts of world order. By those standards, the legislators were maddeningly inconsistent. On the one hand, they voted to punish Turkey—our most powerful Mediterranean NATO ally—for having intervened in the Cyprus civil war, a conflagration raging less than 200 miles off its shores and involving the fate of several hundred thousand ethnic Turks. On the other hand, Congress stopped the Administration's efforts to counter Russian and Cuban intervention in the Angolan civil war, a conflict being waged thousands of miles from those countries and involving no interest of Moscow's or Havana's except that of satisfying their taste for expansion. A more cynical observer might conclude that opportunism is the one consistent strand of Congressional behavior. This view is accorded some weight by the sensitivity of members to the lobbying of Greek-Americans in the effort to punish Turkey. (There was no sizable Afro-American lobby to press for action against Russia and Cuba.) But this explanation does not really satisfy. It was neither lobbies—although they were a factor—nor concepts of world order which determined Congressional policy, but the state of Executive-Congressional relations. In both Angolan and Cypriot cases, the President, with maximum secrecy, had determined to make major policy without consulting Congress, and the legislators were equally determined that he should not. Deep distrust of the Presidency and a determination to "get a handle" on foreign policy decisions intimately affecting American interests, rather than any profound commitment to one side or the other in the Angolan or Cypriot civil wars, informed and motivated the majority of members.

TEACHING THE PRESIDENT A LESSON: TURKEY

On July 15, 1974, the Greek Junta had engineered a coup on Cyprus which overthrew President Makarios and replaced him with Nikos Sampson, a politician who notoriously favored union with Greece. These events made it inevitable that the Turkish government would perceive a serious threat to its own interests in Cyprus. Moreover, under the 1960 London-Zurich accord establishing the independent Republic of Cyprus, Turkey—with or without the two other treaty "guarantors," Britain and Greece—was entitled to use force if Cypriot independence were undermined.

Despite somewhat feeble diplomatic efforts of the United States Government—and, according to some reports, with its tacit acquiescence[1]—a Turkish expeditionary force invaded Cyprus by sea and air on July 20. Turkish leaders described the action as a limited police action designed to promote negotiations between the island's warring Greek and Turkish communities.

For a brief time, it appeared as if this might be an attainable objective. On July 22, Greece and Turkey agreed to a cease-fire and the next day Sampson was replaced by a Greek Cypriot moderate, Glafkos Clerides, the speaker of the overthrown Cyprus Parliament.

The fall of Sampson was paralleled by the overthrow of the Colonels' dictatorship in Athens. They were replaced by a democratic government headed by Konstantin Caramanlis, which restored recognition to Makarios. On July 30, Greece, Turkey, and Britain signed the Declaration of Geneva establishing the legal basis for the cease-fire. The U.N. peace-keeping force (UNFICYP) was given new responsibilities for patrolling a buffer zone separating the Turkish army from the Cypriot National Guard as well as for the policing of villages with mixed Greek and Turkish communities.

This diplomatic effort had been initiated primarily by British Foreign Secretary James Callaghan and U.S. Undersecretary of State Joseph Sisco. They went on to devise a patchwork plan for separate Turkish and Greek Cypriot regions linked in a federal solution. On August 12, however, this compromise was rejected by the Greek Cypriots. Two days later, the Turkish army reopened its offensive.

This time the government of Turkey said it was conducting a "new peace operation" designed to restore "the lawful rights of the Turkish Cypriot community and to stop the horrors committed against them by the Greeks and the Greek Cypriot community. . . ."[2] By August 14, as the Turkish army fanned out across large tracts of the island, the Greek government announced its withdrawal from all military aspects of NATO. By the time Turkey declared a cease-fire, on August 16, its forces had overrun the entire northern third of the country.

In human terms the dislocations were staggering. Over 180,000 Greek Cypriot refugees were driven from their lands and homes.[3] Medical, food, and housing problems matched the scale of these dislocations.

Throughout, the State Department maintained a low profile, allowing the British to lead in the mediation effort. When comment did come, it was from an unexpected quarter. On August 18, Secretary of Defense James Schlesinger noted that his department was reviewing U.S. military aid to Turkey in view of the Cyprus events. He added that Turkish moves had now gone beyond what any of its "friends or sympathizers would have anticipated and are prepared . . . to accept."[4]

In Ankara, however, there was jubilation. Prime Minister Bulent Ecevit's chief foreign policy adviser, Haluk Ulman, announced that Turkey would hereafter insist on retaining at least 28 percent of Cyprus as a permanent zone governed by Turkish Cypriots.[5] In Athens, Prime Minister Caramanlis vowed that Greece would never accept a Turkish solution and would continue the struggle, whatever the time or sacrifices required.[6]

These rumblings from the eastern Mediterranean had begun to reverberate in the halls of Congress. On August 8, New York Democratic Representative Mario Biaggi—who had not previously taken a lead in foreign policy matters and was on none of the committees dealing with aspects of international relations—publicly called on the State Department to suspend all economic and military assistance to Turkey. He characterized that country as "one of our most unreliable allies" and charged it with "continuation of blatant acts of aggression against the people of Cyprus."[7] Biaggi was sure that Turkey could be brought to heel by cutting off its military supplies. On August 14, Representative John Brademas of Indiana, with forty other co-sponsors, introduced a bill to do just that. He argued that "the time is long overdue for the U.S. government to exercise stiff pressure on . . . Turkey. . . ."[8] On the Senate side, Democratic Senator John Tunney of California—who also had not hitherto been notably active in foreign policy-making—on August 19 introduced a similar resolution to suspend all arms sales and assistance.[9]

The Executive was not unaware of this pro-Greek sentiment in Congress, but fatally underestimated its force. Senator Eagleton's legislative assistant, Brian Atwood, had warned Undersecretary Carlyle Maw of the anti-Turkish consensus emerging on the Hill and had pointed out that under existing law, the Administration was obliged to terminate military aid whenever U.S. arms were used by a recipient for other than defensive purposes. On behalf of Eagleton, he urged State to suspend weapons deliveries with a public show of reluctance and then to appeal directly to Congress for a waiver. In that way, he argued, the law could be upheld, a signal could be sent to Ankara, but the intransigents in the Greek camp would also be on notice that arms shipments would resume if they did not demonstrate flexibility. He believed that Congress would vote a waiver whenever the President made an urgent case based on progress in negotiations, or on tactical necessity, or even on the need to protect U.S. bases in Turkey.

Henry Kissinger, to whom this offer was relayed by Maw, called Senator Mansfield for a second opinion. The Majority Leader told him not to worry, there was no substantial feeling in the Senate for a Turkish arms embargo. It was on the basis of this bad advice that Kissinger proceeded. Later he was to complain that the Congressional leadership no longer could be counted on to lead, or even predict, the course of a runaway legislative rabble.

Not that State wholly ignored Congress. There were periodic consultations during July and August. Assistant Secretary Arthur A. Hartman briefed ten members on July 31. On August 2, Undersecretary Sisco talked about Cyprus with Representatives Brademas, Paul Sarbanes of Maryland, Gus Yatron of Pennsylvania, and L. A. Bafalis of Florida: the "Greek mafia," as they were called with affection on the Hill, and with rather less warmth at the other end of Pennsylvania Avenue. At this session, Brademas, too, warned Sisco that the movement for a mandatory halt in U.S. arms shipments and sales to Turkey was rapidly gaining strength. He asked whether a Congressionally mandated cutoff might not be helpful to State in stimulating a resumption of negotiations between Greeks and Turks. Sisco replied that, while a nonbinding "sense of Congress" resolution merely urging the withdrawal of Turkish troops "would not hurt," actual threats or mandatory punitive steps against the Turks would almost certainly be counter-productive.[10]

Nevertheless, Brademas pushed ahead with his bill. He had in his favor the telling argument that, regardless of individuals' policy preferences, the law required a suspension of sales. It was time for Congress to teach the Executive that it is not above the law, not even in the conduct of foreign relations. What was at stake was the integrity of *procedure*; and, as every old hand on Capitol Hill knows, even legislators who agree on nothing else usually close ranks to protect *The Process*.

Sisco continued to meet with the Greek-American congressmen. On August 15, the day after the introduction of Brademas's resolution, Kissinger received the same five members to urge once more the futility of a policy of threats and punishment. The next day Undersecretary Sisco testified to the same effect before the Senate Foreign Relations Committee. It was all to no avail. The law is the law, members muttered. It was time the President and Mr. Kissinger learned that lesson. But, while defense of procedure and distrust of the Presidency account for much of Congressional activism, some thoughtful members believed that the Administration had been wrong in its support of the Greek Colonels' dictatorship and, now that Greece had restored democracy, were wrong again in failing to side with it against Turkish aggression. These views were primarily, but not solely, expressed by Greek-American members or those with many constituents of Greek origin.

Now alarmed, the State Department scrambled to bring its critics into the picture and make them feel part of the consultative process. Kissinger and Sisco soon learned, however, that the revolutionaries' demand for "consultation" was far more than merely a demand to be informed.

It amounted to little less than an insistence that they be allowed a significant role in setting policy. When Congress demands to be "consulted" it is really asking for the right to participate in the decision. Co-determination was the goal. The executive branch regarded such a prospect with horror.

Even as the State Department and members of Congress were "consulting," during these three months after the invasion, the Administration actually doubled the rate of arms deliveries to Turkey. Most of the increase consisted of F-4E jet fighters, bombs, missiles, ammunition, and trucks: all very useful to Turkey in its occupation of Cyprus.[11]

By September 24, after it had become apparent that Ankara was not about to make any new concessions, Representative Rosenthal proposed an amendment to a funding bill then before the House to prohibit the use of any monies "for military assistance, or for sales of defense articles and services (whether for cash or by credit, guaranty, or any other means) to the Government of Turkey until the President certifies to the Congress that substantial progress towards agreement has been made regarding military forces in Cyprus."[12] Rosenthal argued that 80 to 90 percent of the equipment Turkey had used in its invasion "was made, paid for, and delivered by the United States."[13]

Despite urgent appeals, not only from Kissinger but also from Democratic and Republican House leaders, the amendment sailed through.

Kissinger and Ford now hurriedly convened a breakfast meeting with senior leaders of both parties in an effort to contain the damage. Senate Majority Leader Mike Mansfield and House Republican Leader John Rhodes of Arizona, both unsympathetic to the cutoff, agreed to introduce an amendment to the Rosenthal Amendment, thoughtfully written for them by the State Department, that would permit further military aid and credits so long as the President found that Turkey "is making good faith efforts" to reach a settlement.[14] This was quickly adopted by an obliging Senate Appropriations Committee.[15]

Once the bill reached the Senate floor, however, it was a different ball-game. The leadership proved completely incapable of delivering votes. The revolution was beyond their control. By a staggering 57 to 20, the Senate adopted Senator Eagleton's floor amendment. Without naming Turkey, it simply prohibited any funds for military aid to a country employing United States weapons in violation of the law limiting their use to self-defense.

Not only the State Department but the frustrated Senate leadership recoiled in pain at the effrontery of the junior Senator from Missouri, who was not even on the Senate Foreign Relations Committee. Majority Leader Mansfield inveighed against emotional responses and "quick fix" solutions. He summoned his colleagues to "statesmanship," but Eagleton responded that it was "time for the rule of law and that is the best form of statesmanship."[16]

Minority Leader Hugh Scott of Pennsylvania tried sarcasm.

> If this continuing resolution remains in this form, I personally see no reason why Secretary Kissinger should continue the negotiations since Congress, in making its own foreign policy, will have deprived the Secretary of the only tools with which he can negotiate, and unless the whole Congress wishes to move to New York to negotiate with Greece, Turkey, and Cyprus, I fail to see how we are going to be able effectively to serve as mediators.[17]

Eagleton replied in kind.

> The main thrust of the remarks of the Senator is that we feeble-minded 100 U.S. Senators should not have anything to say about the foreign policy of the United States . . . by asserting ourselves in foreign policy, we are not intervening in the private life or the private preserve of Henry Kissinger.[18]

The House (Rosenthal) and Senate (Eagleton) Amendments were somewhat different in form, although identical in intent and effect, so they had to be reconciled by a House-Senate conference committee. Under the rules, such a committee may produce a compromise that differs from both House and Senate versions. In this instance a conference committee, handpicked by the leadership, succeeded in writing a version remarkably like that produced at a White House breakfast and embodied in the defeated leadership version of the Senate bill. Aid to Turkey could continue if the President would stipulate that "good-faith efforts" were being made to reach a solution.

It was a clever maneuver, but not clever enough. The rank and file of both houses, having tasted power, were not to be put off in this fashion. Just as in the battle for Congressional control over Vietnam policy, so now the victory of Congress over the Executive was also a triumph of the Congressional populists over the two chambers' own foreign policy elites. Representative Rosenthal, shaking with anger, characterized the conference committee compromise "as amounting to virtually a runaway conference. The conferees did not abide by the vote of a substantial majority of the members of this body, nor as a matter of fact, substantial vote of a majority of the members of the other body."[19] Nor could the rank and file be moved by the warning of Appropriations Chairman Mahon that a mandatory cutoff would "jeopardize the interests of the United States" or by Foreign Operations Subcommittee Chairman Otto Passman's exasperated question: "Mr. Speaker, if we cannot trust the President of the United States, who can we trust?"[20]

On October 7, the House, by a lop-sided 69 to 291, rejected its own conferees and insisted on the mandatory cutoff.[21] To avoid creating another discrepancy between House and Senate versions that a conference committee could exploit, Representatives Rosenthal, Brademas, and Sarbanes met with Senator Eagleton to "conform" their versions. It was a rare moment. So passionate was the revolutionary camaraderie, that the immemorable tribal rivalries between the chambers, the immutable rules against such an execrable practice as coordination, were temporarily suspended.

The new Eagleton Amendment breezed through the Senate on October 9. However, the leadership continued urgent negotiations with the White House and State Department. A few days later, the results of this surfaced in the form of a compromise amendment agreeing to the cutoff but suspending its operation until December 15, exactly the same formula used to end Cambodian bombing. This carried narrowly in the Senate, but lost in the House, where the leadership was even less effective.[22] On October 14 President Ford vetoed the funding bill. By the narrowest of margins, a sparsely attended House failed to override the veto.[23]

So the conflict continued. Two days later, the House attached an identical cutoff to a new funding bill and the next day it, too, was vetoed by President Ford. It now became possible that the entire U.S. Foreign Assistance Program would run down for lack of funds. A third Continuing Resolution for the program was therefore rushed through both Houses the very same day. Attached to it was the White House-Congressional leadership compromise mandating a cutoff while suspending it until December 10. It was slightly modified by making the grace period conditional on the Turks sending no American-supplied "implements of war" to reinforce their garrison on Cyprus.[24] This time Ford signed the bill.

The last chance to reverse the cutoff came with the introduction of the foreign aid bill in the Senate at the beginning of December. Its prestigious floor manager, Hubert Humphrey, had become convinced that the Turks were not amenable to the kind of pressure tactics Congress had mandated. By 55 to 36, at the urgent pleading of Humphrey, the Senate agreed to a delay in the cutoff to mid-February. The House, however, refused to budge. On December 10, as required by Congressional fiat, the State Department notified its Turkish allies that the embargo was in effect.[25]

Because the Senate and House versions of the foreign aid bill took opposite positions on delaying the cutoff, the bill went to conference. A compromise was worked out that allowed resumption of aid until February 5. In part to promote this small victory for the Administration and the Congressional leadership, Secretary Kissinger had organized a well-publicized meeting with the Greek and Turkish foreign ministers in Brussels on December 11. He reported afterwards that the Turks had indicated a readiness to make some concessions providing they were not seen to be doing it under threat. Kissinger also asserted that Turkey had been on the verge of making some unilateral moves as early as October but had pulled back because of the embargo.[26]

Whatever these self-serving revelations told about Ankara, they spoke eloquently of new Administration perceptions and tactics. Gone entirely was the faith that Congress would follow the leader. It was all too apparent that life for the Administration had suddenly become vastly more complicated. Learning quickly, the Secretary had already understood that diplomacy could constitute the pursuit of Congressional relations by other means.

Although there was a widespread suspicion that Kissinger's diplomatic maneuvers were stage-managed to impress the Hill, impress they did. On December 17 the Senate passed the conference committee compromise and, the next day, the House narrowly followed suit. A round had gone to the establishment. Still, it is doubtful whether that brief resumption of Turkish military aid, any more than a short stay in the termination of the aerial war over Cambodia, was really enough of a gain to justify the struggle.

Throughout the angry debate on Cyprus, legislative legalists led by Senators Eagleton and Adlai Stevenson of Illinois and Representatives Sarbanes, Yatron, Brademas, and Rosenthal had argued that laws, not the flexible discretion and political instinct of the Secretary of State, must govern U.S. relations with Turkey. Secretary Kissinger, on the other hand, had passionately pleaded the case for flexibility rather than law. He argued that the Turks would never negotiate under the gun of what, in Ankara, would be perceived as an anti-Turkish law. Two Presidential vetoes and three Congressional bills later, a compromise of exhaustion was reached which appeared to give both President and Congress some of what they wanted. A cutoff was legislated, but its implementation was suspended for almost two months, the theory being that this would give Kissinger time to see what diplomatic flexibility and political sensitivity could accomplish.

However, as in the case of Cambodia, the compromise produced a product that was the worst of both worlds. The Greeks, knowing that intense pressure would begin to be applied against Turkey in a few weeks, saw no reason to hurry into concessions before the cutoff took effect. On the other hand, the Turks reacted to what they perceived as public humiliation without being in the least mollified by the hard-won grace period.

The compromise was further unsatisfactory in that it produced a policy lacking either principle or pragmatism. Congress had tirelessly argued that violence and aggression were being perpetrated on Cyprus by forces using American guns and bombs—a clear question of principle for the U.S. as arms merchant—while the Administration countered that the withholding of guns and bombs would merely diminish U.S. ability to influence the aggressors while leaving them free to obtain weapons from other sources. In this conflict between principle and pragmatism it is not enough to observe that foreign policy must inevitably contain a mix of both. What Congress and President wrought was, in fact, a go-stop-go policy toward arms exports that succeeded only in alienating both Greeks and Turks while producing a policy ranking low in both the scales of principle and pragmatism.

By late January, progress had still not been made on negotiations as the Congressional-Executive fight appeared about to go another round. Speaking in Los Angeles, Kissinger deprecated "the growing tendency of the Congress to legislate in detail the day-to-day or week-to-week conduct of our foreign affairs. . . ."[27] He added that "the effort to strengthen executive-legislative bonds" is complicated by the new character of the Congress." An aide, interpreting this Delphic remark, said that the Secretary had learned from bitter experience that while he could persuade the Congressional leadership, that leadership was regularly outvoted by coalitions of members in both Houses who were not in senior positions and who consequently had not been involved in the consultations.[28]

One week before the February cutoff deadline, Turkish Defense Minister Ilhami Sancar announced the unilateral withdrawal of a 1000-man Turkish brigade from Cyprus, and by the end of January, negotiations between Turkish Cypriot leader Rauf Denktash and his Greek Cypriot counterpart Glafkos Clerides had resumed in Geneva as a result of efforts by Kissinger. Meeting with Senator Eagleton and Representatives Brademas, Rosenthal, and Sarbanes, the Secretary reported "some progress." Eagleton, however, was not convinced that this was tantamount to the "substantial progress" now required by law for suspending the cutoff.

On the day before the cutoff was to go into effect, Ankara warned that it would compel Turkey to review its ties with NATO.[29] Two weeks later, the Turkish government informed NATO Headquarters that its forces would not participate in winter maneuvers. Testifying before the Senate Foreign Relations Committee in February, Kissinger reiterated the jeopardy to Allied interests throughout the eastern Mediterranean growing out of Congressional action. In response, the Committee voted out a bill allowing the President to lift the ban. But Congressional wheels grind slowly. Because of the Easter recess, the full Senate did not take it up until April, and it did not pass until May 19. By a hairsbreadth vote of 41 to 40, it authorized the President to suspend the ban if he determined that to do so would contribute to negotiations for a peaceful solution, and if Turkey continued to observe the cease-fire and did not increase its military establishment on Cyprus. The bill also required the President to report to Congress every thirty days on progress toward a negotiated settlement. All the senior Senate leaders—Foreign Relations Committee Chairman John Sparkman of Alabama, Chairman of the Armed Services Committee Senator John Stennis of Mississippi, and Senate Majority Leader Mike Mansfield—had argued strongly in its favor.[30] Ranged against these heavy guns was the array of the rank and file led by the irrepressible Senator Eagleton.

In the House, the Senate bill was not reported to the floor until mid-July, and then only after some important compromises were made in committee in an effort to blunt pro-Greek opposition. Meanwhile, Turkish Foreign Minister Ihsan Caglayangil announced that from July 17, all U.S. military and intelligence-gathering facilities in his country would be placed on "provisional status" and that most would have to cease operating.

Continuing its drive for repeal of the embargo, the Administration organized a meeting on June 19 between President Ford and six leading House supporters of the embargo. Four days later, Ford met again with Representatives Brademas, Sarbanes, Hamilton, and Charles Whalen of Ohio. On June 26, the President conferred with House Speaker Albert and twelve more congressmen. Gone was any claim to the inherent powers of the Commander in Chief. The power of Congress, and its determination to use it, had at last been acknowledged by the White House. In one of the most intensive lobbying efforts ever attempted by any Administration on a foreign policy issue, Ford met on July 9 at a White House breakfast with some 140 legislators. There he called for a total removal of the embargo but agreed that the compromise bill reported out by the House Committee constituted a "fair and equitable solution." Representative Brademas, however, remained unreconciled. "In effect," he said, "they are asking us to capitulate to Turkish blackmail."[31]

The lobbying effort mounted by the Administration appeared, for a time, to hold promise of success. The Turkish Government obliged by suspending plans to take over U.S. installations until after the House vote. Defense Secretary Schlesinger, who had appeared to be at odds with the Administration and to favor a tougher line against the Turks, now testified that the loss of intelligence stations would be a disaster since they were needed to monitor Soviet compliance with agreements limiting strategic arms. He reminded Congress that the stations had provided critical information on such Soviet military movements as the alerting of their seven airborne divisions during the October 1973 Middle East war. Under such persuasion, the *New York Times* reported on July 20 that "many Congressmen have switched to the Administration side."[32]

The compromise came to the House floor supported by virtually all the Congressional leaders of both parties. It continued to deny Turkey grant assistance, but lifted the embargo on $184.9 million in defense purchases made by Turkey before the embargo had come into effect: items that had been bought and paid for but not delivered. It also permitted Turkey to buy freely on the American commercial market for cash. Representative Rosenthal reported, "the Administration's lobbying has been the most strenuous of any that I've ever seen in my thirteen years in Congress."[33]

All to no avail. On July 24, the House defeated the compromise by 223 to 206. President Ford reported himself "deeply disappointed" and warned that the action "can only do the most serious and irreparable harm to the vital national security interest of the United States."[34] To Representative Brademas, however, the result was "a great victory for law and the fundamental principles of American foreign policy."[35]

The next day, the Turkish Government halted virtually all activities at American military installations and ordered the closing of all but one NATO airbase. The closed installations were placed under the "full control and supervision of the Turkish armed forces."[36]

A senior European diplomat called this a self-inflicted wound, adding in despair: "It isn't just the State Department or the President any more. It's Congress now. So you can't sit down with one or two people and work things out. There were fifty Congressmen through here recently, and we all tried to persuade them that it's too dangerous to cut off Turkey's arms supply. But they were only fifty, they don't decide."[37]

The diplomat's views reflected the reaction of many foreign governments to the power revolution that had overtaken the leader of the free world. Nor was their concern cast purely in terms of global politics. No other nation conducts its foreign policy through genuine power-sharing between executive and legislative branches. The sight of legislators actually reversing the U.S. chief of state and his foreign affairs specialists— and in public—was enough to fill all Prime Ministers and diplomats everywhere with the fear and loathing that grips establishments when they hear the guillotine. But beyond such fraternal chagrin, there began to be genuine concern on the part of many friendly foreign governments. Could the U.S. still be counted on to defend the interests of the free world? Now that the revolution had come, would a new leadership, new institutions for wielding power emerge or would a lingering, incapacitating civil war go on indefinitely?

TEACHING THE PRESIDENT A LESSON: ANGOLA

Concern deepened in 1975. In May, Saigon fell. Then, in December, Congress cut off funds and military supplies to two pro-Western factions fighting for control of Angola against a minority Marxist movement supported by almost 20,000 Cuban troops and $400 million in Soviet military assistance.[38] President Ford said Congress had "lost their guts."[39]

But he was wrong. While there were many in Congress who doubted the importance of Angola to the U.S. national interest, it was not neo-isolationism, indifference to Soviet expansion, or loss of nerve that motivated Congress. Rather, it was a fear that the President had embarked on yet another war the United States could not win, and that he had done so covertly, without the Constitutionally required consent of Congress. The parallels to Vietnam were as inevitable as they were misleading.

Again Congress routed the Presidency. One factor in this defeat was the President's utter failure, in Washington's jargon, "to get his ducks in order." Nothing fails like failure. Reeling from a string of defeats at home and abroad, the Executive's foreign policy establishment had become faction-ridden and demoralized. The very person the CIA picked to head its Angola task force believed that "Angola had little plausible importance to American national security and little economic importance beyond the *robusta* coffee it sold to American markets and the relatively small amounts of petroleum Gulf Oil pumped from the Cabindan fields."[40] The Assistant Secretary of State for Africa soon resigned in protest. Key CIA and State Department officials leaked their information and doubts to like-minded members of Congress and the press. Thus Executive disarray, as much as Congressional revolutionary zeal, ensured this Administration debacle.

After the April 1974 military takeover in Portugal, Lisbon had decided to give its Angolan colony independence. The turnover was set for November 11, 1975. A leftist-controlled Junta resolved to tilt in favor of the most Marxist of three Angolan underground factions, the Popular Movement for the Liberation of Angola (MPLA). Off and on for many years, this group had been supported by the Soviet Union.

Opposing the MPLA were two other patriotic groups, the National Front for the Liberation of Angola (FNLA) and the National Union for the Total Liberation of Angola (UNITA). Both groups, like the MPLA, relied primarily on their regional and tribal power base. By late 1974, UNITA had begun to receive considerable support from the Chinese communists. FNLA, which had received token CIA support during the Kennedy Administration, but none from President Nixon, was now also modestly being aided by Peking.

The United States, although for the preceding decade preferring friendship with the Portuguese to the African insurgents, became alarmed at being left out of this emerging contest for influence in Angola. It therefore reactivated its old relationship with Holden Roberto, the leader of FNLA.[41] In January 1975, Roberto—who in the 1960's had been on a $10,000 a year CIA retainer for intelligence collection—was again voted $300,000 in clandestine support by the 40 Committee, the governing body of the CIA. According to one ex-CIA official, the agency had actually begun to make small unauthorized contributions to Roberto as early as the previous July.[42]

The decision to revive the Roberto connection as a way to re-enter the Angolan contest became the focus of considerable controversy within the Department of State and the CIA. Among those most stubbornly opposed was Nathaniel Davis, the new Assistant Secretary of State for Africa. Davis's career had been tarnished, and he had been raked over the coals by Congressional committees, because he had had the misfortune of serving as ambassador to Chile when Allende was overthrown. In August, afraid of being burned again, he chose a quiet transfer to the U.S. Embassy in Switzerland.

Between January and December of 1975, U.S. involvement in covert support for Roberto escalated. As independence neared, it became clear that the projected Angolan elections would never be held, making the civil war a winner-take-all contest. The United States also began to join China in supplying weapons to UNITA. By the end of November, $25 million had been spent for arms and support funds and another $25 million was quietly authorized for further supplies.[43] After that, however, there were no more appropriated funds available for such covert operations. The Administration searched its accounts in the hope of discovering money to reprogram.

Meanwhile, the stakes were rising fast. The Soviet Union had stepped up its support for the MPLA, sending twenty-seven shiploads of military equipment between spring and late autumn and flying thirty to forty supply missions with huge cargo planes between October and the end of November. Then in early December, they dispatched some 200 military advisers. By mid-October, Cuba had begun to send the MPLA large quantities of weapons and troops.

Also in October, South Africa began to introduce at first advisers, then troops, on the side of UNITA: some 3,000 soldiers and fifty armored cars. They swept rapidly through much larger Cuban and MPLA forces,[44] nearly winning the war in November.[45] Then, in early December, Havana began a rapid reinforcement of its 4,000 combat soldiers, soon bringing their total to over 16,000. Also enlisted on the MPLA side were some 3,000 exiles of the former Katangan gendarmerie from neighboring Zaire. They were encouraged to expect that victory would create an Angolan base from which they could attempt to recapture their former homeland. Zaire itself committed two paracommando battalions to fight alongside the FNLA.[46]

Even more important than personnel were weapons. Here, too, the Communists outbid the CIA. Moscow, beginning in March 1975, supplied massive quantities of 24-inch barrel anti-personnel rocket launchers, and tanks firing devastating 122-mm rockets—weapons more sophisticated than any previously supplied other forces by the Soviets. These proved decisive in the pivotal encounter of November 12, outside Luanda. Soon there were Soviet T-54 tanks, manned by Cubans, which easily outmaneuvered American-supplied military hardware consisting mainly of old portable infantry weapons—some of it captured Russian equipment obtained from the Israelis—and anti-tank shoulder-borne missile launchers, all operated by raw Angolan recruits. Russian helicopters airlifted the Cubans and Katangans from battle to battle. While a senior Soviet diplomat in Washington assured the *New York Times* that his people were merely helping MPLA to stay alive with a small commitment no more than equal to that being made by the United States,[47] it soon became quite clear that the Soviet-Cuban commitment was incomparably greater than that being made through the CIA. As a result, the MPLA, which in October had fallen back to defensive positions around the capital of Luanda, was again on the offensive by late November.

A number of things inhibited the CIA and frustrated the side it was supporting. Its 40 Committee, for most of 1975, authorized expenditures of a mere $31 million while sternly forbidding the use of American fighting, or even training, personnel anywhere in Angola. Prohibited, too, was direct supply of weapons to the Angolan forces by Americans. The 40 Committee's limited objective was to create a stalemate conducive to a negotiated settlement, not to win. This roiled the CIA. Its Angola operations chief, John Stockwell, soon came to feel, as had so many military men in Vietnam, that the U.S. should either be intervening decisively or not at all. "It was feasible to rush weapons into Angola, which would decisively win the war," Stockwell wrote later. "I knew that our policy was not designed to win, but I wanted Washington to know that the opportunity existed for total victory, *if we provided* abundant, immediate support"[48] (italics his). He added, "We could give the FNLA and UNITA enough support to win—by going in quickly with tactical air support and advisors we could take Luanda and put the

MPLA out of business before the Soviets could react. Otherwise, if we weren't willing to do that, we would further U.S. interests by staying out of the conflict."[49]

By early December it was apparent that the Russians and Cubans had raised the ante well beyond the CIA's limit and, worse, that the Chinese had decided to abandon UNITA. That decision was based in part on a shrewd analysis of UNITA's prospects and also on the embarrassing fact that the South Africans were now openly fighting on UNITA's side. The presence of these troops from the nation of white supremacy also embarrassed the U.S., even though UNITA leader Jonas Savimbi, a charismatic leader with impeccable freedom-fighter credentials, had invited the South Africans in only after conferring with the Presidents of Zaire, Zambia, Senegal, and the Ivory Coast.[50] Savimbi had argued persuasively that if the MPLA could invite in the Cubans while proclaiming their independence, he, too, as leader of the largest tribal group, was entitled to sup with the devil. The leaders of Zaire and Zambia, the major black nations adjoining Angola, had accepted this explanation and appealed to the United States to increase aid to UNITA. While the Administration debated and improvised, Congress entered the picture.

Most of these events had passed uncomprehended, even unnoticed, by the U.S. public and media, because the Administration had determined to proceed by way of a covert operation, utilizing secrecy and the CIA. This proved a serious miscalculation. The first story of U.S. clandestine involvement in Angola surfaced in the *New York Times* on September 25, 1975.[51] In the immediate aftermath of the fall of Saigon, it was not unexpected that a strong backlash would develop against this new manifestation of Presidential adventurism. Many Americans concluded that the Administration was once more dragging them into a jungle war without benefit of public debate or Congressional authorization. The parallels did not escape the CIA, either. When an idea was floated in the Agency to station fifteen small teams of "observers" in Angola, ostensibly to collect better intelligence on the fighting, a member of its Angola task force responded: "Here we go! It's Vietnam, Laos, and Cambodia all over again! Fifty Americans now, five hundred next month. Fifty thousand next year!"[52] The project was abandoned.

Despite parallels, however, this was not a replay of the secret war in Cambodia and Laos. The CIA's involvement in Angola had been initiated under a set of ground rules that already reflected the systemic transformation worked by Congress. In 1974 the Foreign Assistance Act had been amended, on the initiative of Senator Harold E. Hughes of Iowa and Representative Leo Ryan of California, to require the CIA to brief six Congressional committees "in a timely fashion" on all covert operations. That briefing requirement had been carried out by CIA Director William Colby and by those directly responsible for the conduct of the Angolan operation. In the words of Secretary Kissinger,

> we chose a covert form of response with the greatest reluctance. But in doing so, we were determined to adhere to the highest standards of executive-legislative consultation. Eight congressional committees were briefed on twenty-four separate occasions. We sought in these briefings to determine the wishes of Congress. While we do not claim that every member approved our actions, we had no indication of basic opposition.
>
> Between July and December 1975, we discussed the Angolan situation on numerous occasions with members of the foreign relations committees and the appropriations committees of both Houses that have CIA oversight responsibilities. The two committees investigating CIA activities—the Church Committee and the Pike Committee—were also briefed. Altogether more than two-dozen Senators, about 150 Congressmen, and over 100 staff members of both Houses were informed.[53]

Subsequently, the head of the CIA's Angola task force has disclosed that the CIA lied to members of Congress in the course of these briefings in at least three particulars: in stating, first, that U.S. weapons were not being given directly to FNLA and UNITA; second, that there were no U.S. personnel in Angola with these two groups; and, third, that the CIA was not collaborating with the South Africans.[54] However, Stockwell does concede that the briefed members knew that the U.S. was providing military supplies for its clients in Angola, even if they were led to believe that it was all being routed via the Zaire military, which, in turn, was supplying UNITA and FNLA. Nor does he assert that any CIA personnel fought in Angola in violation of the 40 Committee prohibition, although there have subsequently been suggestions that the Agency may have sent in a few "paramilitary specialists" in the guise of intelligence agents.[55] Finally, cooperation with South Africa appears to have been strictly limited to exchange of intelligence and logistical information. No weapons were sent to, or through, South Africa.[56]

During the first half of 1975, no opposition developed among the members who were briefed. As both U.S. and Soviet-Cuban participation began to increase sharply, however, some Senators and Congressmen began to express doubts, particularly as to the wisdom of extending the CIA's line of credit beyond the $50 million already committed. Senator Clark, who was chairman of the Senate's African Subcommittee, had been briefed by CIA Director Colby. By August he decided he had better go and see for himself. On his return, Clark reported that U.S. Angola policy was alienating the most important African leaders. As a result of his travels he became convinced that the leader of MPLA, Dr. Augustinho Neto, was not essentially more leftist or a captive of the

Soviet Union than someone like Tanzania's Julius Nyerere, with whom the United States had learned to live in mutual tolerance if not affection.

In December, Clark focused his opposition by introducing an amendment to the following year's foreign assistance bill prohibiting all use of funds for covert activities in Angola. The amendment was intended to cover not only monies provided in that bill but also funds made available by other legislation, including CIA funds in the Defense Department appropriation. Given the way CIA funds are buried in various authorizations and appropriations, such a catch-all prohibition was the most far-reaching way to ensure the end of the Angola operation. By choosing as his vehicle the fiscal 1976 foreign aid bill, Clark was deliberately postponing the cutoff until well into the next year, giving the CIA lead time to complete or phase out its operation. (The fiscal 1976 security assistance authorization was not, in fact, enacted until late in the summer of that year.)

It has been reported that a fluke caused the Foreign Relations Committee to adopt Clark's amendment. The CIA's Deputy Director of Operations had testified before it, admitting in questioning that arms were being sent directly into Angola. Later during the same day's session of the committee, another witness, Edward Mulcahy, the Deputy Assistant Secretary of State for African Affairs, was asked the same question. He blandly denied what the CIA had just admitted. According to participants, Senator Clark confronted the hapless Mulcahy with this discrepancy. The CIA's Stockwell concludes that this was the turning point: "Beneath the angry stares of committee members Mulcahy kept his poise, and calmly reversed himself, admitting that arms *were* being sent into Angola. Senator Case angrily denounced the lying. The committee unanimously endorsed Clark's bill."[57]

If that was indeed the basis for the decision of the Committee, it further illustrates the continued priority given by Congress to systemic concerns over foreign relations concerns. How else can one explain punishing the State Department for lying to Congress by cutting off support to Jonas Savimbi fighting Cuban mercenaries for control of his homeland?

On the House side, Clark's growing concern was being echoed by New York Representative Otis G. Pike, who, as chairman of the House Select Committee on Intelligence, struck pay-dirt in sweeping, media-catching denunciations of the CIA and all its works. Democratic Representative Don L. Bonker of Washington announced, on December 15, that he would sponsor the House version of the Clark Amendment.

These efforts to effect a phased termination of CIA involvement were suddenly outflanked by Senator Tunney, not a member of the Foreign Relations Committee but a man with a very urgent problem. The Californian was up for re-election in a tight Democratic primary, pitted against anti-war activist Tom Hayden who was backed by his wife Jane Fonda and the Fonda family fortune. As a lackluster Senator, Tunney was in urgent need of instant visibility and an enhanced dove image. Angola came along like the serendipitous answer to an underdog's prayer.

Two of Tunney's young staffers originated the idea of eclipsing Hayden by projecting the embattled Tunney as the man who saved the U.S. from a secretive Presidency's latest jungle quagmire. Legislative assistant Mark Moran and press aide Bill Coughlin knew Tunney had a playboy's reputation for laziness and indecisiveness. Here was something to refute that charge.

Moran, a 24-year-old whiz-kid known in Congressional halls as the "infant Secretary of State," exemplified the rapidly growing importance of Congressional aides that went hand-in-hand with the increasing power of Congress. Although his Senator was far outside the chamber's inner circle of foreign and military affairs specialists—was not even on any of the committees briefed under Hughes-Ryan—and had shown little prior interest in Africa, Moran prodded Tunney into precipitating another Congressional confrontation with the Executive.

On Friday, December 12, Senators Tunney and Cranston, the two Democrats from California, dined together. The conversation turned to Angola. Where, they wondered, was the CIA getting its money for that operation? In the words of Moran:

> We knew from the Administration's request for a supplement that the contingency funds in the Department of State's budget had already run out. Therefore, whatever funds were currently being used in Angola just had to come from CIA money buried in the Defense budget. But we didn't know exactly where. Then it suddenly occurred to us that the Defense Appropriations bill was just about to come before the Senate. It was exactly the right vehicle to take us where we wanted to go.[58]

Once the decision to go with Angola had been made by the Tunney team, Mark Moran called CIA Director Colby and asked him to "brief Tunney and me. He wanted to know whether I had top clearance and I told him I did." Then, Moran reports,

> I called McCloskey [Assistant Secretary of State for Congressional Relations Robert McCloskey] to get them to brief us. He offered to send Assistant Secretary [for Africa] Schaufele. The next day [Sunday] the CIA called back after checking my clearance. They said they could tell Tunney and me what the Russians were doing in Angola, but not what we were up to. Such garbage! Tunney and I were furious. We became even angrier when Schaufele also cancelled.
>
> If the CIA and State had been relatively frank with us, we might not have gone all the way.[59]

Moran was manning the Angola front on that key weekend while the Senator was in the California trenches. He consulted with Senator Clark about co-sponsoring an amendment to the Department of Defense appropriation. Clark cautiously preferred a colloquy with Tunney during floor consideration of the bill, in which they would build "legislative history" by expressing their belief that Defense Department funds in the bill were not to be used to support the CIA operation—a form of inhibition less binding on the Executive than an actual amendment, which could come later, as part of the foreign aid bill.

On Monday, Moran went with his Senator to the floor. Tunney, Cranston, and Clark were expecting to trigger the colloquy. In the course of the debate, Moran suggested the switch to an amendment, something requiring considerable procedural acumen, given the Senate's arcane rules. "I checked my idea with the Senate parliamentarian," Moran said, "and he said that I could go ahead."[60] Moran then negotiated with legislative aides Marian Albertson (Senator Clark), Mark Schneider (Senator Kennedy), and Bill Jackson (Senator Cranston) at a strategy meeting in Kennedy's private office in the Capitol. In addition to the three Senators and their aides, the group was joined by the Senate parliamentarian Murray Zweben. "I persuaded them. This was the fastest way to get action," Moran recalls.[61] Clark reluctantly agreed, goaded by Cranston who wanted to help out his fellow Californian in distress. "He needs the amendment more than you do" was the argument to which Clark yielded, even though he preferred his own, more phased, approach to extrication.

A last-minute effort to stop Tunney by offering a nonbinding "sense of Congress" resolution was offered by Illinois Senator Adlai Stevenson. It called for, but did not legislate, U.S. withdrawal and the imposition of trade sanctions on the Soviets if they did not reciprocate. Although supported by much of the leadership, it failed to get the unanimous consent necessary for priority over Tunney's motion. Thus, in a sense, the Angola War was lost in the California primary. Thereafter, again in Moran's words, "Schneider and I went off and wrote the amendment and then took it to Zweben who assured us that he would rule that it was in order if there were procedural objections raised when we introduced it on the floor."[62]

On December 19, the Tunney Amendment sailed through by a vote of 54 to 22, a startlingly decisive result. President Ford labeled it "a deep tragedy for all countries whose security depends upon the United States." He asked, "How can the United States, the greatest power in the world, take the position that the Soviet Union can operate with impunity many thousands of miles away with Cuban troops and massive amounts of military equipment, while we refuse any assistance to the

majority of the local people who ask only for military equipment to defend themselves?"[63] In an ABC news interview, Kissinger said:

> If the United States adopts as a national policy that we cannot give
> either military or economic assistance to people who are trying to defend
> themselves without American military forces, then we are practically
> inviting outside forces to participate in every situation in which there is a
> possibility for foreign intervention and we are therefore undermining any
> hope of political and international order.[64]

But it had all been said a few months earlier during the agony of Saigon
and Phnom Penh. Congress had caught the mood of the public and the
media; the executive branch had not. And that was that.

The action now shifted to the House. Meanwhile, events on the
ground moved rapidly. During the week before Angolan independence
on November 11, the forces of the two pro-Western groups, aided by
supplies from the United States and accompanied by a detachment of
South Africans, had succeeded in cutting deep into the territory previously occupied by the MPLA. MPLA defenses had been spread thin
by earlier rapid advances into twelve of Angola's fifteen provinces, made
with the help of Cuban reinforcements and Soviet arms. By November
11, the tables had turned: the FNLA, reinforced by Zaire and U.S.
supplies, had advanced south and west to the outskirts of Luanda.
UNITA, helped by the South Africans, was pressing rapidly north to
link up with FNLA. The 3,000 Cubans, however, were enough to prevent
the capital's fall and this permitted a rapid escalation of Cuban forces.
By late January, there were 16,000 of them and the initiative was decisively reversed once again, this time against UNITA and FNLA.[65] Under
pressure of African and U.S. opinion, the South African troops were
pulled back as the Cubans demolished Roberto's unseasoned forces.
MPLA began to mop up the country. Thus, by the time the House was
considering its version of the Tunney Amendment, it could be argued,
as it had been in respect of continued aid for Vietnam and Cambodia,
that to permit further funding for UNITA and FNLA was to throw good
money after bad, with no prospect of victory. Conversely, it was said
that the failure of Congress to "go the extra mile" with the Administration had cleared the way for defeat of pro-Western forces.

In the House International Relations Committee, a modest version of
the Clark Amendment—one leaving the President some flexibility to
continue aid to UNITA and FNLA providing he did so publicly—was
making its way toward the floor attached to the foreign aid bill that
would not become law until summer. These projections became academic on January 27, when as a floor motion paralleling the Tunney
Amendment was added to the defense appropriations bill on motion by

Democratic Representative Giaimo. Despite vehement opposition by Appropriations Chairman Mahon, it sailed through by 323 votes to 99. President Ford had little choice but to sign the bill which contained the entire $112.3 billion defense budget. The CIA acknowledged defeat—by Congress—and began to withdraw.

The Angolan case once again underscores the disarray of Executive-Congressional relations during this revolutionary period. That disarray became a source of growing unease to observers in America and abroad as they perceived Washington's ability to act decisively being undermined by a third year of unrelenting civil war between the branches of government. Evident, too, was Congress's newfound fact skepticism, its unwillingness to accept as gospel either the evidentiary findings or the strategic assessments of the experts in the Executive departments and agencies. Yet no new system of fact-finding or decision-making was being devised to substitute for the one dismantled by the revolution. It was still each member for himself, as Mark Moran had quickly understood.

To some observers, the Angolan crisis appears, in retrospect, as a unique event, rather than an ominous harbinger of the future. At the time the cutoff was being voted, there was massive public disgust with the waste of lives and funds in Vietnam. The CIA was sinking in a sea of scandal generated by the House and Senate investigations of its myriad illegal and ill-advised pursuits. It was to be expected that Congress would bridle at another war in an area of dubious importance, particularly one conducted in secret by the folks who had failed even to decapillate Fidel Castro.

On the facts as they became known, a serious case can even be made for the proposition that Congress was right over Angola and the Administration's foreign policy experts wrong. By mid-December, even the South African Embassy had begun to assess the situation of the pro-Western forces as hopeless. The equipment being sent to Savimbi was not getting through but being stolen en route. Unseasoned African tribesmen were everywhere being routed by highly trained, better equipped Cubans. In the view of one senior Congressional staff member,

> The only way we could have held out in Angola would have been to have introduced U.S. troops. After the Vietnam debacle, we could hardly be expected to do that. We did look around for mercenaries, particularly among foreign Vietnam War Veterans and in Iran. The CIA simply couldn't get them, and the few they did get were no good and most had no training.[66]

And it may be that it was the Administration, rather than Congress, which ultimately made the ill-conceived choice to wrap up the operation with a law—one which the President, three years later, complained was unbearably restrictive of his policy flexibility. As the situation became hopeless, several senior Senators of both parties went to see Kissinger. They had an offer: if the Administration would phase out the Angolan operation quietly, they would allow a small additional amount of funding and time. There would be no cutoff law. When the Administration refused this offer, even in the face of clear indications that obdurate resistance would assure the passage of the Tunney Amendment, the Senators concluded that Kissinger knew that the operation was a fiasco and simply wanted to shift the blame to Congress.[67]

This view is sharply disputed by senior National Security Council staff members. One such staffer pointed out that on December 9, President Ford had made a formal proposal to the Soviet government through its ambassador in Washington urging that both sides suspend all further Angolan escalation. According to this source, the Soviets responded by halting their airlift to Luanda between December 9 and 24, but went back into high gear immediately after the Senate adopted the Tunney Amendment.[68]

Other bitter arguments marked the Angola post-mortem. Senator Clark and others in Congress argued that the Administration had scant understanding or sympathy for Africa, that the history of African decolonization makes it clear that the new states, even when they call on the Soviets for help, are first and last nationalist and will not permit themselves to be recolonized by any superpower. Sooner or later, he prophesied, Angola would send the Cubans and Russians packing. To this, Department of State area specialists replied that the African states most directly involved by geographic proximity had been far less sanguine, had, indeed, pleaded for continued American aid for UNITA and FNLA. Kissinger argued that, while African nationalism might eventually reassert itself in situations such as those now prevailing in Angola, advice which counsels the long-range view and awaits the verdict of history is no more than a mockery to those who must endure the fate of their country today.[69]

One of the most frequent and persuasive objections to Administration policy voiced in Congress was that the Executive had chosen the covert rather than an overt route. Almost all members of Congress rallied around this procedural issue which went to the heart of the revolution: the Administration must never again be allowed to take secret short-cuts around the constitutional procedure for committing the nation to war. Even were the U.S. role in Angola morally and strategically justified, the procedures had been so wrong as to warrant the cutoff. To this Kissinger replied, "We chose covert means because we wanted to keep our visibility to a minimum: we wanted the greatest possible opportunity for an African solution. We felt that overt assistance would elaborate a formal doctrine justifying great power intervention. . . ."[70] The Secretary felt strongly that it was better to "press the Russians under the table" rather than in a public confrontation that would inevitably involve the global prestige of both superpowers. But even some of Kissinger's own top aides, like Assistant Secretaries McCloskey and Davis, say they were unconvinced by this rationale.

Congress and the Administration also demonstrated a clash of perspectives that was becoming increasingly a part of the revolutionary war between the branches. Congress looked at Angola primarily in regional terms, as a country of little strategical concern to U.S. national or even international interests, located in an inherently unstable continent best left to sort itself out. The Administration saw Angola as a pawn in Soviet strategy to convert America's defeat in Vietnam into a worldwide rout. They saw it as a testing by one superpower of another in full view of the whole uncommitted world. "See," the Russians could now say to the Kaundas and Mobutus of Africa, Asia, and Latin America, "look at Thieu and Savimbi. That's where American alliances get you." This version of the domino theory has not been refuted by subsequent events. Certainly, the leaders of Ethiopia soon concluded that they could expect far better support in their war against the Somalis and Eritreans by shifting sides from America to Russia—and they were proved, resoundingly to be right.

Both sides of these arguments have merit and it is as yet impossible to say with any certainty whether the foreign policies of Kissinger, of Clark, or of Tunney were most clearly in the national interest. Beyond reasonable doubt, however, is the conclusion that it was distinctly not in the national interest to have had disparate sets of officers at the helm concurrently: Ford and Clark, Tunney and Colby, even Moran and Kissinger. In Angola, the United States zigzagged crazily between a logically defensible Executive policy of involvement and a logically defensible Congressional policy of disengagement. But if the United States was to involve itself at all, then it had a duty not to cut off—precipitously and publicly—the lifeline of forces that had become dependent upon it. And if the United States were to disengage, that disengagement should have occurred very much earlier, before U.S. prestige and its reliability as an ally had become so openly committed.

If Angola, as a special circumstance enveloped in special circumstances, teaches few generally applicable lessons, it does pose crucial questions about power-sharing, about the ability of the United States to play a coherent, effective role as a superpower in the new era of Congressional activism.

II

CODETERMINATION:

CONGRESS ALTERS

THE GROUND RULES

3

CODETERMINATION:

Congress Recaptures
the War Power

THE SEARCH FOR SYSTEMIC CHANGE

Cooler heads in Congress, while joining in the legislative revolution to end U.S. involvement in Vietnam, Cambodia, and Angola, realized nevertheless that conflicts over interpretations of Constitutional authority could not become the standard pattern for making foreign policy. Legislators could not make it a practice to "pull the plug"—for example, to deny funds to pay for wars or secret operations after the Executive had already initiated them. The costs to the national interest were too high and the internal divisiveness too great for funding cutoffs to become the routine way to communicate with the President and executive branch on matters of national security. A better way had to be found, one that permitted early, thorough consultation, a sharing of the decision-making process: a system of *policy codetermination*.

Establishing and routinizing this process of codetermination has been the principal accomplishment of these cooler heads: Senators Javits, Clark, Humphrey, Nelson, Cranston, and Representatives Fraser, Bingham, Derwinski, and Zablocki, to name a few. Primarily, their efforts have gone into legislation aimed not at stopping a particular war or ending any single Presidential initiative, but, instead, at creating an entirely new framework of rules for power sharing among the branches of government.

These laws, the new systemic rules of the game, seek to maintain interbranch policy codetermination by establishing a regular procedure that requires the President to report to, and consult with, Congress before committing the nation to a foreign policy position, especially one involv-

61

ing national security interests. They also institute procedures by which Congress can inhibit the President in pursuing a policy opposed by a majority of members, either by using a device known as the "Congressional veto" or by operation of prospective funding prohibitions.

The resultant procedural changes in the ground rules governing the politics of U.S. foreign policy decision-making are of enduring significance. The Cambodian, Vietnamese, Turkish, and Angolan "sub-games" have been won or lost and, while their outcomes will no doubt continue indirectly to influence U.S. foreign relations, they are over. Attention has turned to other crises, different agendas. Firmly in place, however, are the changes, since 1973, in the systemic processes by which foreign relations are conducted, in which realities are perceived and evaluated, and through which choices are made and options exercised.

Of paramount importance among these procedural innovations is the War Powers Resolution of 1973, which transforms the process by which the United States is drawn into military hostilities. Others pertain to oversight over the conduct of CIA operations,[1] military sales,[2] the making of executive agreements,[3] and economic assistance abroad.[4]

The result of all these changes is that Congress, hereafter, means again to be central to decisions as to when and where to use force, to make foreign commitments, and to provide economic and military succor.

This is not a transformation based on one-shot reversals of Presidential policy. Nor has the election of a Democratic President, complementing the Democratic majority in Congress, brought about a restoration of the era of Congressional abdication and Executive paramountcy. While the fortunes of President and Congress have, in the past, been subject to historic swings of the pendulum, Congressional activism may now be here to stay, having been legislated and institutionalized by new procedures of codetermination. The pendulum may have come to rest.

Pride of place in recapturing and systematizing the Congressional role goes to the War Powers Resolution.[5] It is both the first and—politically as well as legally—the most fundamental (and thus controversial) of the new procedural devices for asserting the Congressional right to codetermine the conduct of U.S. foreign relations. It is also the cornerstone in a healthy rebuilding of our adversary democracy. In practice, it has unfortunately also proven a flawed instrument.

The aim of the War Powers Resolution is to restore to Congress the power over the fateful decision when and under what circumstances the nation goes to war. On its face, the Constitution appears quite unambiguous: by Article I, Section 8, it is Congress which declares war and provides a military force to fight it. The drafters did not mean "war" in any technical sense, either, but also meant to give Congress "control of those types of military action short of formal war commonly resorted to during that time."[6]

The drafters also knew that wars cost money, and they deliberately reinforced Congressional control over war-making by giving it—in Article I, Section 9, clause 7—the ultimate weapon: the "power of the purse," as well as sole power "to lay and collect taxes . . . to . . . provide for the common defense. . . ." (Article I, Section 8).

THE DECLINE OF THE WAR POWER

If that is all the Constitution had said about war powers, the supremacy of Congress might not have become the tug-of-war it now is. But the Constitution, like all oracular pronouncements, is anything but simple or straightforward. For example, while declaring war is the prerogative of Congress, it is the President who is assigned the leading role in the conduct of both diplomacy and hostilities. Article II, Section 2, makes him "Commander in Chief" of the army and navy, while Article II, Section 3, instructs him to "receive ambassadors and other public ministers." Successive presidents have enlarged this narrow bridgehead. As early as October 9, 1789, President Washington rather archly answered a letter the King of France had addressed to him and to "Members of the General Congress" by pointing out that the honor of receiving and answering diplomatic communications, by virtue of the new U.S. Constitution "has devolved upon me."[7]

As goes the right to conduct negotiations so, in practice, goes the power to engender hostilities. The inceptive period of U.S. statehood, between 1789 and 1809, was one of recurrent diplomatic maneuvers by Presidents leading to undeclared war. Washington's Neutrality Proclamation of 1793 was made while Congress was in recess. In the "Pacificus-Helvidius" exchange between Alexander Hamilton and James Madison, the latter unsuccessfully argued that the President, acting without Congress, could not use his assigned powers of diplomacy and military command in ways likely to engender combat. Neither Washington, nor the cabinet, nor Congress when it reconvened, accepted Madison's restrictive view of Presidential function, and thereafter Presidents steadily broadened the scope of their power to act in defense of U.S. interests until the Congressional war power was left virtually without meaning.[8] President John Adams, advised by Secretary of War James McHenry, invented the concept of "qualified hostility" or undeclared war, which was approved by the Supreme Court in *Bas v. Tigny*,[9] while Thomas Jefferson, on his own authority, dispatched a U.S. squadron into the Mediterranean with authority to seize, disarm, and sink military—or "pirate"—vessels of the Barbary States.[10] Under President Madison, the Administration plotted and militarily supported subversive movements against Spain in West and East Florida culminating in a form of thinly disguised offensive warfare that Congress had not sanctioned.[11]

"Allow the President," Congressman Abraham Lincoln wrote, "to invade a neighboring nation, whenever *he* shall deem it necessary to repel an invasion . . . and you allow him to make war at pleasure."[12] That has, indeed, been the upshot of the historical experience. President Woodrow Wilson did not deliberately force the Germans to sink U.S. ships in the Atlantic and President Roosevelt did not deliberately provoke the Axis into the attack on Pearl Harbor, but both conducted U.S. foreign relations during a period of neutrality with such a tilt toward the Allied powers as to make it likely that the other side would save the President the trouble of having to persuade Congress to declare war.

Presidential power to use force on his own authority has also been enlarged by arguments based on treaty obligations. If a treaty obliges the U.S. to come to the aid of a foreign power then, the argument goes, the President may act without further Congressional authorization because, by Article VI of the Constitution, treaties are the "supreme Law of the Land." Since the Constitution requires the President—in Article II, Section 3—to "take Care that the Laws be faithfully executed" he may need to employ the military to "execute" a treaty committing the nation to come to the defense of another. Most recently, this justification was used by successive Presidents, citing the South East Asia Defense Treaty to justify U.S. involvement in the Vietnam War. President John F. Kennedy in part justified the quarantine around Cuba during the Cuban Missile Crisis by reference to treaty obligations under the Rio Pact of 1947.

However, it is the "Commander in Chief" power that has become the Presidential trump card. This might surprise the Founding Fathers. Even Alexander Hamilton, in *The Federalist*, Number 69, thought the power "would amount to nothing more than the supreme command and direction of the military and naval forces as first General and admiral of the confederacy" and he contrasted this limited authority to the uncontrolled military powers of the British King, who was free to declare war, raise and regulate the fleets and armies "all of which, by the Constitution under consideration, would appertain to the legislature."

The records of the Constitutional Convention are singularly unenlightening as to what the authors meant by "Commander in Chief"— perhaps itself confirmation that the power was not intended to be of much consequence.[13] Such a conclusion might be inescapable had James Madison and Elbridge Gerry, on August 17, 1787, not moved at the convention to substitute the word "declare" war for "make" in the Congressional War Power clause. The records show that one of the several purposes they had in mind was to remove from Congress, and assign to the President, "the power to repel sudden attacks," whether or not the legislative branch had formally declared war.[14]

Then, too, the drafters of the Constitution—in Article I, Section 10—gave the states authority to use their militias in self-defense or to repel imminent invasion, without waiting for Congress to declare war. Could they have meant to give the President less power than a state governor?

All this indicates that the drafters of the Constitution, in assigning to Congress the exclusive power to *declare* war, were not unaware of the possibility that the United States could become involved in hostilities in some other ways. In these days of nuclear rocketry, locating a stand-by power of instantaneous response in the President is probably a logically imperative way to read the Constitution. Professor Louis Henkin believes it to be self-evident "that the President would have the power to retaliate against a nuclear attack . . . ; probably, he has authority also to anticipate by a preemptive strike an attack he believes imminent."[15]

However, some scholars—and all recent Presidents and their lawyers—have been much less modest, claiming an unlimited Presidential power to initiate hostilities. Their principal support for these claims derives not from the Constitution, but from practice. According to a former State Department legal adviser, Abram Chayes, "even in 1789, the declaration of war was already a decaying formality."[16] Recent studies indicate that even during the century preceding the Constitutional Convention "wars were frequent, but very seldom declared."[17] Thus, it is argued, the power to "declare" war is no more than a role in an obsolete formalistic charade.

Whatever the pre-independence state of legal practice, in the years since *Bas v. Tigny* undeclared wars have, indeed, become commonplace. A chronology prepared in 1972 documents 199 U.S. military engagements undertaken between 1798 and 1972 without a declaration of war.[18] Nor were these mostly trivial or local engagements. Ninety-seven lasted more than 30 days, and 103 took place outside the Western hemisphere. In eighty instances, despite the absence of a declaration of war, Congress provided some other form of authorization. But when, in 1846, President Polk sent American forces pouring into the disputed territory between Corpus Christi and the Rio Grande River, thereby inviting the Mexican War, he acted without prior participation by the Legislature.[19]

In that instance, and in many since, it has been urged by the Executive that funds voted by Congress to support a war constitute retroactive Congressional ratification. There is some authority for this proposition. The authors of the Constitution, according to a recent study by Abraham Sofaer, "did convey a strong impression that a military appropriation, passed for a specific purpose, could constitute legislative approval for the use of force authorized to accomplish the purpose contemplated."[20] But in recent years, Presidents have even claimed that Congress, by merely approving the general annual budget appropriation for the Department of Defense, must be taken to have ratified a Presidential war.

The Senate Foreign Relations Committee has forcefully tried to distinguish between earlier precedents and more recent Presidential usurpations of the war power. "During the 19th century," the Committee reported,

> American Armed Forces were used by the President on his own authority for such purposes as suppressing piracy, suppressing the slave trade by American ships, "hot pursuit" of criminals across frontiers, and protecting American lives and property in backward areas or areas where government had broken down. Such limited use of force without authorization by Congress, not involving the initiation of hostilities against foreign governments, came to be accepted practice, sanctioned by usage though not explicitly by the Constitution.[21]

However, the use of the Armed Forces against *sovereign nations* without Congressional authorization only became common practice in the 20th century.

The report argues that the current trend really originated with President Theodore Roosevelt's use of the Navy to prevent Colombia from reasserting jurisdiction over its rebellious province of Panama, and his interventions in Cuba and the Dominican Republic. Those precedents were reinforced by Presidents William Taft's and Wilson's unauthorized use of armed forces in the Caribbean and Central America culminating in the establishment of American military governments in Haiti, the Dominican Republic, and Nicaragua.

Historian Arthur Schlesinger, Jr., marks 1900 as the watershed year for a "new presidential exuberance in the commitment of armed force to combat."[22] In his view, McKinley set the trend by sending 5,000 American troops to the siege of Peking.

Twentieth-century legislators were notably reticent in the defense of their Constitutional war powers—as long as the President's undeclared wars were won, or at least not definitively lost. Wilson's 1914 seizure of the Mexican port of Vera Cruz to "enforce respect" for the government of the United States, and his having dispatched an armed force under General Pershing into Mexico in "hot pursuit" of the bandit Pancho Villa, were widely applauded even though these acts initiated a war which lasted almost two years.[23] President Harry Truman was seen to be ushering in a brave new world of collective security when he sent U.S. troops into a three-year Korean war. Few objected when he asserted a right to do so in response not to a Congressional mandate but to a decision of the United Nations Security Council.[24] In 1958, there were ripples but no waves when President Dwight Eisenhower sent 14,000 soldiers into Lebanon, this time without authorization either by Congress or the U.N., an example followed in 1965 by President Lyndon B. Johnson with the landing of 22,000 U.S. marines in the Dominican Republic.[25]

Thus it seemed increasingly futile to claim that Presidential war-making is unconstitutional, whatever the text of the Constitution, so regularly has it been practiced without significant challenge from Congress. As late as 1969, Senator John Sparkman, later to succeed William Fulbright as chairman of the Foreign Relations Committee, wrote that the Congressional war power "is steadily diminishing in practical importance. Many people, I think, believe that probably there never will be another declared war; unless a declaration serves to confirm what has already been done." He added that, in his view, the President "has the needed power" to take the nation into hostilities in any "threatening situation" with or without the approval of Congress.[26]

By 1970, however, an undeclared war had begun to go undeniably awry. Some members of Congress, noticing that the Emperor had no clothes, sought to reverse the tradition of Congressional indifference to Presidential war-making. They began to argue that a practice—even a long-standing and relatively consistent one—cannot make Constitutional that which is expressly prohibited by the Constitution.

Paradoxically, this resurgence of Congressional literalism was aimed at President Richard Nixon, who had long prided himself on being a "strict constructionist." Strict constructionism is to the Constitution as Fundamentalism is to the Bible. Yet here was President Nixon on the side of those who would reject sacred text in favor of the secular *Zeitgeist*.

It is almost as paradoxical that this revival of Constitutional orthodoxy was triggered by the Vietnam War, because that conflict was not a particularly egregious instance of Executive usurpation of the war power. In August 1964 at the request of President Johnson, following an alleged attack on American naval vessels in the Gulf of Tonkin, Congress had passed the Tonkin Gulf Resolution.[27] This authorized the President to act in appropriate ways to defend U.S. interests and to take all necessary measures "including the use of armed force" to aid South Vietnam "in the defense of its freedom." Subsequently, Congress had regularly voted the funds for a decade of war.[28]

Still, scale has its own logical imperatives. The Vietnam War came to absorb millions of men over a ten-year period. And it was a military fiasco as well as a human tragedy, making it both inevitable and opportune to re-examine the evolution of a range of constitutional practices and precedents pertaining to the powers of the Commander in Chief. The result has been a Constitutional neo-classical revival, with Congress stripping away two centuries of embossing from the pillars of the Constitution by Presidential initiative and Congressional acquiescence.

REVIVING THE CONGRESSIONAL WAR POWER

In 1969, the Senate adopted a resolution declaring that a national commitment could result "only from affirmative action taken by the executive and legislative branches of the United States Government by means of a treaty, statute, or concurrent resolution of both Houses of Congress specifically providing for such commitment."[29]

This resolution, lacking approval by the House and President, did not have the force of law. But it was the opening round in a tenacious Congressional campaign to win the right to participate with the President in any future decision to commit U.S. forces to war, or to assume treaty obligations to defend allies around the world. The battle for codetermination had begun.

As the Senate pawed the dust, the House, at that time still the President's lapdog, went its own, less militant way. In 1970 and 1971, the Representatives passed bills merely requiring the President to issue reports to Congress *after* sending troops to fight. The Senate scornfully refused to look at these. Instead, it came up with bill S. 2956, a bold attempt to list—and thus limit—the situations in which the President could use force on his own authority: when (1) repelling or anticipating an armed attack upon the United States, its territories and possessions; (2) responding to an attack against the armed forces of the United States, whether at home or abroad, or forestalling an imminent threat against them; (3) protecting U.S. citizens and nationals while they were being evacuated from abroad; or, (4) exercising his discretion under a prior statutory grant of authority.

Even when the President was acting within one of the four permitted categories, the bill allowed him only thirty days of war-making. After that, hostilities could only continue if he obtained the consent of Congress.

Neither House nor Senate bills got enough support on the other side of the Capitol to win passage in 1972. The next year, however, House militancy began to catch up with the temper of the Senate. While the latter proceeded with a new bill (Javits) virtually identical to S. 2956, the House passed H.J.Res. 542 (Morgan-Zablocki), which, while different from the Senate version, was in one respect even tougher. It provided that any Presidential war could be ended by a concurrent resolution of House and Senate.

This ingenious procedural device, also known as a "Congressional veto," takes the form of a clause allowing the President to do something unless or until Congress votes to stop him. What distinguishes such a provision from the ordinary legislative power of Congress is that a concurrent resolution is not a legislative "bill" and so is not presented to the President for his assent under Article I, Section 7 (the "presentation" clause), of the Constitution; he thus does not have the opportunity to veto it. The effect is to allow Congress to stop the President by simple majority vote, rather than by the two-thirds of the total membership of each House that is required by the "presentation" clause to override an Executive veto.

The House also provided that the President's war-making authority would end automatically after 120 days unless renewed by a Congressional declaration of war or other specific authorization. And, in a significant bid to achieve codetermination, it required the President to consult with Congress, when possible, prior to engaging U.S. forces, and to report to Congress within forty-eight hours of the beginning of hostilities. But unlike the Senate version, it did not attempt to enumerate the circumstances in which the Commander in Chief could use force without a declaration of war.

During July, the House and Senate each passed their bills. Then the two went to conference committee. On October 4, a compromise emerged that looked more like the House (Morgan-Zablocki) than the Senate (Javits) version.[30] Gone was the Senate's exhaustive effort to define when the President could use force on his own. Only a watered-down version was left in a preambular paragraph, which, the conference committee explained, would not have binding effect.[31]

The impact of this compromise, in the critical view of Congressional liberals like Tom Eagleton, Patsy Mink of Hawaii, John Culver of Iowa, Elizabeth Holtzman of New York, and Bella Abzug, was to give the President an unlimited license to engage in short wars.

The bill did call for prior consultation with Congress when possible and required reporting within forty-eight hours of any Presidential use of the military. But, in place of a definitive limit on when the Commander in Chief could use force on his own, it opted for the House's approach that limits the period—sixty days plus thirty more for evacuation—during which a President could engage in unauthorized hostilities. In addition, the conference accepted the House bill's provision by which, utilizing a concurrent resolution procedure not requiring Presidential assent, the Congress could terminate any unauthorized hostilities at any time.

This package was passed by the Senate on October 10 by a vote of 75 to 20 and by the House on October 12 by 238 to 123. The House majority was not quite large enough to override the veto ardently promised by President Nixon.

That promise was fulfilled twelve days later. Given the odds against overriding the veto, Representative Clement Zablocki of Wisconsin, the House sponsor quietly prepared a "brave face" statement asserting that, while Congress had "lost an opportunity to restrain growing presidential usurpation," it had clearly signaled the President "that the great majority of Congress wants and expects its rightful role in the decision of war and peace."[32] But the statement was never used because the House did override, by a vote of 284 to 135. The Senate easily followed by an overwhelming 75 to 18.

In the intense campaign to enlist last-minute support, the bill's sponsors made effective use of President Nixon's gathering Watergate troubles, arguing that this was no time to forego the opportunity to hand the President a stinging defeat.[33] Zablocki and his staff pulled out all the stops. They urged what they called "the constitutional purists" among the liberals (Culver, Mink, et al.) to withhold their vote until the very end of the roll call, so as to be able to see whether they could make the difference between Nixon's winning and losing. In the end, most voted to override. Senator Eagleton, one of the earliest sponsors of the war power bill, actually voted to sustain the veto because he accepted the argument that the bill produced by conference was worse than none at all.[34] "What you'll have now," his legislative aide sighed, "is a Pentagon file full of contingency plans for 90-day wars."

Still, it was a victory of sorts. The next day, Representative Zablocki walked into the Democratic caucus to a standing ovation, a rare compliment. Senator Javits sees the bill as his crowning legislative achievement, a monument to his long years in public service. And despite its compromises, the constitutional problems it fails to resolve and the ones it creates, the War Powers Resolution is not to be underrated. The Congress had come up with a seminal formula for Executive-Congressional codetermination in one key aspect of foreign policy. It had devised a way to require the President to pay attention to the legislative branch before, not merely after, committing the nation's forces and resources. And once hostilities begin, it keeps the President on a short leash by giving him a limited amount of time to disengage, as well as by allowing Congress to end undeclared wars at any time without Presidential assent.

Yet there are nagging doubts. Zablocki has wondered, confidentially, whether the Congressional veto procedures in the law are Constitutional.[35] And Senator Church has publicly admitted that he never understood the bill, while former Senator Case later confided that he voted for it only because of his affection for Senator Javits.[36]

THE WAR POWERS LAW IN PRACTICE

The validity of the new procedures can only be tested in practice. They have been in effect for several years, now, and practice confirms that the law is a landmark, while also raising some concern that it will not achieve all that its authors intended. In seven instances since the Resolution was passed, the President has authorized the use of U.S. forces abroad: to evacuate U.S. and other personnel from Danang, Phnom Penh, and Saigon at the end of the Indochina war; to rescue the crew of the *Mayaguez*; to evacuate U.S. and other civilians during civil strife on Cyprus and in Lebanon; and to transport European troops to Shaba province in Zaire during the tribal invasion of that area by the former Katanga gendarmes based in Angola. None of these Presidential uses of force extended beyond the law's 60/90-day grace period. In no instance did Congress attempt to use the concurrent resolution procedure to terminate an operation. Therefore, the most important and controversial provisions of the Resolution are still untested.

Some provisions of the law have been applied, in a fashion, while still others have been evaded, thanks to legislative loopholes and fastidious Executive lawyering. As noted, the law imposes an element of Congressional codetermination by requiring that the President "submit within 48 hours . . . a report, in writing . . ." to both Houses of Congress, whenever, in the absence of declared war, armed forces "are introduced into hostilities or into situations where imminent involvement in hostilities is clearly indicated" or "into the territory, airspace or waters of a foreign nation, while equipped for combat. . . ."[37] That report must set out the circumstances necessitating the intervention, its constitutional or legislative authority as well as its estimated scope and duration.[38] In the case of the Danang, Phnom Penh, and Saigon evacuations, as well as in the *Mayaguez* rescue, the President did report within the required forty-eight hours, but only if the clock is taken to begin to run when the American forces entered foreign space, rather than when the forces were dispatched or when the decision to commit them was made. As a result of this, in each instance, the report reached Congress only after each military operation was already completed. The reporting requirement thus conduced not one whit to Congressional codetermination of whether, when, or how to use force.[39]

In still other instances, there was no reporting at all. President Ford did not report on the use of the military to evacuate civilians from Cyprus or Lebanon. Even in those other instances where he did report, the President carefully added that he was doing so "pursuant to the President's constitutional executive power and his authority as Commander in Chief" and as "Chief Executive in the conduct of foreign relations. . . ."[40] In other words, he reported only because of a spirit of accommodation, motivated by political sensitivity rather than because he felt himself bound to obey the new law.

In the case of the Shaba evacuations, President Carter's legal adviser took the even more startling position that the Act did not apply to the U.S. military airlift of other nations' troops and equipment because they were deposited "more than 100 miles from the site of hostilities. . . ." U.S. forces, the Administration argued, were not introduced into hostilities or into situations where their imminent involvement was indicated, nor were they equipped for combat. "The Zaire airlift," the legal adviser said, was "a limited operation that did not present any threat of United States involvement in hostilities"—a very strained interpretation of the events—and thus did not involve any obligation toward Congress.[41]

In launching the Shaba airlift, Carter had to deal with a particularly relevant provision—Section 8(c)—of the War Powers Act. This made reporting mandatory when U.S. armed forces are dispatched to "participate in the movement of, or accompany the regular or irregular military forces of any foreign country or government when such military forces are engaged, or there exists an imminent threat that such forces will become engaged, in hostilities." On its face, this looks as if it had been written by someone with a premonition of these very events. The legal adviser, however, took the position that flying in the Belgian and French troops to a staging area behind the lines was not covered by the law because those forces were not "engaged" in the fighting as long as the Americans were with them.[42] This view would be a credit to a tax lawyer construing a section of the internal revenue code so as to defend a client's questionable deduction, but scarcely speaks of a new Presidential spirit of accommodation with Congress. It was rather unenthusiastically accepted by the House International Relations Committee's International Relations Subcommittee, with Chairman Zablocki interpreting his own Act as not applicable to the Shaba operation. Several skeptical Representatives concluded, instead, that perhaps the law was just not applicable to Democrats.[43]

If the Presidents have only sometimes and in desultory fashion adhered to the reporting requirement, they have done worse by the Act's requirement to "consult with Congress before introducing United States Armed Forces into hostilities or into situations where imminent involvement in hostilities is clearly indicated by the circumstances."[44] In no case has there been anything approximating meaningful consultation. Again the Resolution itself has several large loopholes, and these the Presidents' lawyers have exploited with alacrity. In particular, the law says that the President need only consult "in every possible instance." In practice, genuine prior consultation has, somehow, never proven "possible."

Obstacles to prior consultation are not wholly imagined or self-serving inventions. President Ford has cited the Lebanon evacuation as a prime instance of difficulties encountered, under conditions warranting urgent action, in finding key members of Congress to consult.[45] In four instances—the three Indochinese evacuations and the *Mayaguez* rescue—Ford did inform Congressional leaders, but only after irrevocable decisions to commit U.S. forces had already been made. The timing of Congressional "consultation" was clearly determined by a concern not to make Congress a real partner in the Administration's decision as to whether or not to act. Commenting on the Danang operation, Representative Zablocki noted "there was a report" but "there was not consultation." He distinguished between "notification, which occurred, and consultation, which did not."[46]

During the Saigon evacuation on April 28, 1975, the President "directed that congressional leaders be notified"—not consulted—"that the final phase of the evacuation of Saigon would be carried out by means of military forces within the next few hours."[47] At 1 A.M. on April 29 a force of 70 helicopters and 865 Marines began to evacuate 1,373 U.S. citizens and 5,595 South Vietnamese. Some fighting ensued.[48] Yet it was only at 11:30 A.M., long after the operation was underway, that the President met with Congressional leaders at the White House for what was described as "a further briefing on the situation in Saigon."[49]

In the case of the *Mayaguez*, the lack of meaningful consultations was even more marked. The first shots were fired by U.S. forces on the morning of Tuesday, May 13. But it was more than twelve hours later, almost at 7 o'clock on Tuesday evening, when William T. Kendall, a Congressional liaison officer for the White House, began to telephone more than a dozen leaders in the Senate and House to inform them of the situation. These perfunctory calls, made over no more than an hour and a half, by all accounts amounted to bare notification, certainly not genuine consultation. Nor were they "prior" to hostilities. "I was not consulted," Senate Majority Leader Mike Mansfield said, "I was notified after the fact about what the administration had already decided to do."[50]

Kendall admitted later that he had been given a prepared statement to read to the Senators on what amounted to a *fait accompli*.[51] But he added, "If anyone had said 'I think this action is inadvisable' I would have written that down and put it in my memo and it would have been seen by the President."[52] According to the White House staff, about half the Senators called had voiced approval of the President's action while the other half simply acknowledged receiving the information.[53]

Even amidst the general jubilation at the success of the Presidential initiative—the White House was inundated with 13,000 overwhelmingly congratulatory letters, telegrams, and calls—Senator Robert C. Byrd (Democrat of West Virginia), then the Senate Democratic Whip, expressed concern over "the failure to ask at least some of the leaders to participate in the decision-making process."[54] The State Department's legal adviser, insisting that there had been consultation, admitted that the "President was extremely apprehensive that there be no breach of security in advance of the time that [the troops] actually were landed, so there were strong arguments for not revealing that information—even to a select group of members—very much in advance of the time it was to occur."[55]

Legal advisers in both the Ford and Carter Administrations pointed to the letter of the law which only requires consultation in instances where U.S. armed forces are being introduced into hostilities, or where their involvement in combat is imminent. Thus, they argued, the President did not need to consult prior to any of the seven operations. The Marines sent into Danang were engaged in a peaceful evacuation. During the April 12, 1975, evacuation from Phnom Penh, 350 Marines were landed to withdraw U.S. personnel and Cambodians, again without encountering resistance. The Cyprus and Lebanon evacuations and the Shaba airlift went off without a shot being fired.

But in the rest of the cases, hostilities were encountered. The April 28 Saigon evacuation, involving 865 Marines, involved sporadic fighting.[56] As for the *Mayaguez* incident, not only did American troops have to fight, but U.S. planes sank three Cambodian gunboats and bombed Ream airfield on the mainland. The Marines who invaded Kho Tang Island suffered at least fifteen killed in action. But casualties after the fact ought not to be the test of whether or not the Commander in Chief should be required to comply with the prior consultation procedures. Even in those operations where fighting proved to be unnecessary, the opportunity for hostility existed and only luck and happenstance prevented it. It is the worst kind of lawyering to interpret the War Powers Act to require prior consultation only when forces are sent into a combat zone expressly for the purpose of fighting, and to refuse to abide by its procedures for codetermination when their involvement in combat is an unintended—but quite probable—consequence of carrying out some other purpose, such as liberating captured Americans.

Such legal interpretation has facilitated evasion by Presidents Ford and Carter. It has made it unnecessary even to try to develop procedures by which codetermination could be made to work. The Administrations' allegations that speed and security would be hopelessly compromised by consultation have never been tested or otherwise faced. In the seven Presidential uses of military force that have occurred since the Act was passed, Congress has been accorded no role except that of spectator.

It can be argued that all these were minor incidents and that none was likely to escalate into serious military involvement. However, several members of Congress have not taken so placid a view. After the Shaba airlift, nine House members—ranging from far-right-wing Republican John H. Rousselot of California to Republican liberals Paul Findley of Illinois and Pete McCloskey—called for public hearings on whether President Carter had violated the War Powers law.[57] "Our primary concern," they said, "is that this is a critical juncture for establishing procedures under the War Powers Act. . . . We do not believe that the War Powers Act applies only when there are U.S. casualties. . . ."[58]

Various proposals have been made to strengthen the reporting and consulting requirements. An amendment proposed by Senator Eagleton would require the President,

> before taking any steps which would firmly commit United States Armed Forces to hostilities . . . in every possible instance [to] discuss fully the proposed decision for his using such Armed Forces with Members of Congress, including but not limited to the majority and minority leaders of the Senate and the House of Representatives, the chairmen of the Armed Services and Foreign Relations Committees of the Senate and the chairmen of the Armed Services and International Relations Committees of the House of Representatives and shall fully consider their advice and counsel before committing the United States Armed Forces to any such proposed decision.[59]

It would solve some, but by no means all, of the problems encountered to date. Basically, the problem cannot be resolved by law alone. Any conceivable formula must leave the President some room to use force at his sole discretion. It does not require much legal skill to translate any small residue of Presidential discretion into a gaping legal loophole, if the President is so minded. The challenge is to convince the White House that loophole-making is not in its own, nor the country's best interest, while the building of workable procedures for codetermination is.

Little is gained by debate over whether the President is constitutionally required to consult. It can be argued, to be sure, that since the Commander in Chief has the absolute, inherent, or plenary power to rescue Americans endangered abroad, Congress cannot require consultation when he is rescuing a *Mayaguez* crew or evacuating Saigon. But such a narrow reading of the law solves nothing and merely conduces to more civil war between the branches with the potential of more foreign policy debacles. Even in the case of a military operation which is solely within the President's prerogative, "Congress could withdraw the means for any such operation . . . even to the point of totally depriving the President of the means for exercising his functions."[60] By the War Powers Resolution, Congress has wisely instituted consultative procedures to avoid future drastic confrontations between its war power and the powers of the Commander in Chief. It is an offer no President, motivated by the national interest, should lightly refuse.

THE WAR POWERS LAW AND THE CONSTITUTIONALITY OF THE CONGRESSIONAL VETO

The reporting and consulting requirements of the War Powers law are the only ones to have come into play so far. However, by far the most powerful weapon in the armory is the Congressional veto over an ongoing Presidential war. Section 5 of the law allows Congress to terminate any use of force, at any time, that has not been authorized by a declaration of war or other legislative authorization. Termination is accomplished by a concurrent resolution passed by simple majority of both Houses.[61] The term "Congressional veto" derives from the fact that such a resolution becomes law without requiring Presidential assent.

That fact is both the advantage of the Congressional veto from the perspective of the legislators and the reason why Presidents—most recently Jimmy Carter—have challenged its constitutionality. Congress likes the device because it facilitates a broad delegation of authority to the Executive while still retaining for itself a very present capacity to participate in determining how the delegated discretion is used. It loosens the reins, but keeps them in a firm Congressional grip. To Presidents, the device violates the clear language of the Constitution's "presentation" clause—Article I, Section 7—which envisions only one way to make laws: by an affirmative vote of a majority in Congress followed by assent of the President, or by two-thirds of each chamber overriding his veto.

When the President asserts the unconstitutionality of the concurrent resolution procedure, he tends toward arguments similar to those used by Congress to resist his usurpation of the war power. In this instance, it is the Executive which complains that no amount of precedent, no record of acquiescence, can alter the plain meaning of the Constitution. Congress, in reply, points out that Presidents have not only accepted, but have actually urged the inclusion of concurrent resolution procedures in legislation when that had served their purpose of persuading Congress to grant them broader discretionary authority.

For example, in 1932 Congress authorized President Herbert Hoover to devise ways to consolidate Executive agencies and functions. It also permitted him to implement reorganization schemes by Executive order instead of by submitting bills to Congress. The law provides, however, that such orders will not become effective until sixty days after they have been transmitted to the legislature for scrutiny. During that period, "if either branch of Congress . . . shall pass a resolution disapproving of such Executive order, or any part thereof, such Executive order shall become null and void . . ."[62]

The effect of this "one House veto" is to facilitate the delegation to the President of broad powers of Executive reorganization. Such restructuring of government departments and agencies is clearly within the exclusive jurisdiction of Congress. Thus, in delegating part of its power to the President, Congress retained the option to exercise a veto in each instance when the President invokes it. It invited the President to draw up blueprints, but retained for itself the power to approve or reject each design. That Congress took its reviewing role seriously is indicated by the fact that the few schemes submitted to it by Hoover in December 1932 were, indeed, vetoed by the House of Representatives.[63]

Similar uses of the concurrent resolution or other veto procedures are incorporated in the Reorganization Acts of 1939, 1945, 1949, and 1977, all passed with Presidential approval. According to a recent Congressional study, there are currently 295 such provisions in 196 laws passed in the last 40 years.[64] Some have been resisted and others welcomed by Presidents. Attorney General William D. Mitchell did advise President Hoover to reject a subsequent "committee veto" provision on the ground that it "violates . . . constitutional principle."[65] But the 1977 Reorganization Act again contains a one-House veto provision, its validity specifically defended by Attorney General Griffin Bell.[66]

Bell, however, distinguishes between that use of the Congressional veto and more objectionable instances. "This power to take no action with respect to reorganization plans should be carefully distinguished," he wrote, "from the situation created by statutes which provide for subsequent resolutions disapproving presidential actions in the administration of continuing programs. . . . Such statutes frustrate the constitutional check of the presidential veto in violation of Article I and infringe on the doctrine of separation of powers."[67]

Only 22 of the 295 provisions for Congressional review of Executive discretion deal with foreign relations.[68] The concurrent resolution was introduced into a senatorial reservation to the Treaty of Versailles. Its effect would have been to give Congress power, by two-House resolution, to withdraw the U.S. from the League of Nations.[69] This contributed to President Wilson's conviction that no treaty at all would be preferable to what the Senate was doing to his crowning achievement.[70]

In 1941, however, President Franklin D. Roosevelt signed the Lend-Lease Act which contained a provision giving Congress the power to terminate the Act by "passage of a concurrent resolution of the two Houses."[71] Before consenting, however, the President had Attorney General Robert H. Jackson prepare a letter which he signed and entrusted to Jackson for publication "some day as an official document."[72] It explains that he had accepted the bill because it was necessary "to meet a momentous emergency of great magnitude in world affairs . . . in spite of the fact that it contained a provision which, in my opinion, is clearly unconstitutional." He added: "A repeal of existing provisions of law, in whole or in part, . . . may not be accomplished by a concurrent resolution of the two Houses."[73]

In *Springer v. Government of the Philippine Islands*,[74] the Supreme Court held that the "Legislative power, as distinct from the executive power" is "the authority to make laws, but not to enforce them"[75] and that "unless otherwise expressly provided or incidental to the powers conferred, the legislature cannot exercise either executive or judicial power; the executive cannot exercise either legislative. or judicial power."[76] This by no means laid the issue to rest. The 1947 Aid Authorization for Greece and Turkey permits termination by concurrent resolution.[77] In 1955, Dwight Eisenhower opposed a rider Congress had attached to a defense appropriation bill which required committee approval before the Department of Defense could close any of its commercial enterprises.[78] Congressional concern had been triggered by the impending shutdown of a Navy rope factory located in Majority Leader John W. McCormack's district of Boston.[79] On the advice of Attorney General Herbert Brownell,[80] Eisenhower signed the bill but announced that he would regard the rider as invalid unless ordered to obey it by a court of competent jurisdiction,[81] whereupon, at the prompting of Congress, the Comptroller General stated that if any executive officer were to sign a check drawing on funds not authorized in accordance with the procedure laid down in the law, he would be personally liable for the amount. The Defense Department prudently decided to adhere to the committee veto provision.[82] The next year the committee veto was dropped from the law.[83]

However, in 1958 Congress was back with an amendment to the Atomic Energy Act of 1954 that permitted a veto by concurrent resolution of cooperative atomic weapon development agreements made with foreign states by the Administration.[84] President John F. Kennedy, faced

with a "lie-in-wait" clause that gave the Appropriations Committees a
veto over reprogramming of economic assistance funds left over from the
previous year, protested against this "attempt to confer executive powers
on the Committee in violation of the principle of separation of powers
prescribed in Articles I and II of the Constitution." But he signed the
bill, adding: "I recognize the desirability of consultations between officials of the executive branch and the committees. It is therefore my intention, acting on the advice of the Department of Justice, to treat this
provision as a request for information."[85] But Kennedy did not cavil
when the Tonkin Gulf Resolution was passed by Congress with a provision for its repeal by concurrent resolution.

Since 1970, the Foreign Assistance Act[86] has provided that any aid
program or project can be compelled to end eight months after Congress
vetoes it by concurrent resolution. Congressional vetoes were included
in the Atomic Energy Act Amendments of 1974[87] and in the Trade Act
of 1974.[88] A one-House veto of base construction on the Indian Ocean
island of Diego Garcia was included in the Military Construction Authorization for 1975,[89] while the Foreign Military Sales Act was amended
in 1976 to give Congress the power to veto exports of major defense
equipment valued at $7 million or more.[90]

The joint resolution by which Congress, in 1975, authorized U.S.
participation in the Sinai early warning system contains a clause that
allows Congress, by concurrent resolution, to withdraw American personnel if it determines that their safety is in jeopardy or that their role
has become redundant.[91] In the same year, as part of a reorganization of
objectives and priorities of the food-for-peace program, Congress gave
itself the power, under certain circumstances, to veto deliveries of food
relief to any country with a per capita income of more than $300.[92] The
same Act also allows Congress to end food and economic aid to any
country "which engages in a consistent pattern of gross violations of
internationally recognized human rights," unless the Agency for International Development can demonstrate that "such assistance will directly
benefit the needy people" of such country.[93]

Even on the basis of this inventory of use, it is difficult to be dogmatic
about the constitutionality of the concurrent resolution procedure, although the Congressional Research Service has argued that "legislative
history suggests [that] constitutionality of the . . . legislative veto . . .
is virtually universally accepted."[94] Its universe evidently excludes the
White House.

The theoretical underpinning of the legislative veto is that, far from
trespassing on an Executive power, it merely qualifies the delegation to
the Executive of a power assigned by the Constitution to Congress. Since
the legislature is under no compulsion to delegate any of its powers, if it

chooses to do so it may surely subject the exercise of that power to any limitations on the way the President exercises this borrowed discretion.[95]

Whatever the merits of this argument, it is not entirely convincing when used to defend the constitutionality of the legislative veto provision of the War Powers Resolution. In at least some instances, when a President uses military force he may be exercising his plenary powers as Commander in Chief—rescuing Americans abroad, or responding to an actual or impending attack against American territory or armed forces— not acting in pursuance of powers delegated by Congress. Yet the War Powers Resolution appears to authorize the legislature to veto *any* Presidential use of force. But when Congress is not the source of the President's power, it is very unlikely that the legislature can interfere in its exercise, except by refusing to vote funds.

The constitutionality of the concurrent resolution procedure in the War Powers Resolution may thus depend upon the circumstances in which it is used.[96] However, this is not a simple yardstick; it does not make the law easier to understand, nor its effects easier to predict.

The uncertainty that surrounds Congressional veto procedures has been compounded by a healthy reluctance to employ it, even after it has become law. According to a recent study, "with the exception of impoundment control, the hundreds of congressional veto provisions have not induced wholesale interventions by Congress in the conduct of administration."[97] Between 1960 and 1975, 351 "veto" resolutions were introduced, more than 100 of them duplicates and only 63 became effective. Most generated "no legislative action whatsoever, not even the introduction of a resolution."[98] The study discloses no instances at all of a concurrent resolution being used to terminate a Presidential foreign policy initiative. Nevertheless, in several instances—particularly concerning human rights and arms exports—the Administration has accommodated Congressional advice in order to prevent a Congressional veto.[99]

Adding to the uncertainty has been the lack of a legal action squarely posing the Constitutional issues. In two recent litigations the federal judiciary was strongly urged to determine, once and for all, the constitutionality of a concurrent resolution device. On both occasions, however, the court declined.[100] Only one concurring opinion—that of Judge Harold Leventhal of the D.C. Court of Appeals, in *Clark v. Valeo*—helped clarify the issue. Leventhal hinted that the constitutionality of the procedure—in that case a one-House veto—might turn on whether Congress was using it to intervene in an Executive action that was essentially "interpretative," and "therefore more aligned with the responsibility of the executive branch" or with an action that was essentially "legislative," that is, which seeks to "implement or carry forward a statutory mandate in ways not specified by the statute, and with respect to which a more substantial congressional role might be proper."[101] By this test, any Congressional veto of a military operation initiated by the President might well be invalid.[102]

It may be that a more definitive showdown can be avoided, at least for the near future. On two occasions, the Carter Administration has endorsed the constitutionality of the War Powers Resolution. At Secretary of State Cyrus Vance's confirmation hearings Senator Javits asked: "Do you challenge [the War Powers Resolution] under the Constitution as to the President's power?" Vance answered, "No."[103] In a telecast, soon after his election, President Carter, too, endorsed the War Powers Resolution as "an appropriate reduction" in Presidential power.[104]

Vance's reply, however, was made in response to a question that focused on the Resolution's requirement for consultation, while Carter was addressing himself to the 60-day war-making limit. It would, therefore, be premature to conclude that there are no storm clouds ahead.

Attorney General Bell has recently taken aim at "statutes which provide for subsequent resolutions disapproving presidential actions in the administration of continuing programs. . . . Such statutes frustrate the constitutional check of the presidential veto in violation of Article I and infringe on the doctrine of separation of powers."[105] On June 22, 1978, President Carter, in a message to Congress, added that "excessive use of legislative vetoes and other devices to restrict foreign policy actions can impede our ability to respond to rapidly changing world conditions. Reasonable flexibility is essential to effective government."[106] He promised to seek to test the constitutionality of concurrent resolutions in a suit before the Supreme Court.

In any such suit, if it arose out of War Powers, the real question would be this: what *are* the Constitutional limits of the Commander in Chief's powers? Years of Congressional neglect have allowed these to expand to the point where President Ford's legal adviser asserted that they embrace not only the right to defend the U.S., its forces, citizens, and territory against attack, and to rescue American citizens abroad, but also to rescue foreign nationals where such action directly facilitates the rescue of U.S. citizens abroad, to protect U.S. embassies and legations abroad, to suppress civil insurrection, to implement and administer the terms of an armistice or cease-fire designed to terminate hostilities involving the United States, and to carry out the terms of security commitments contained in treaties. He added that even this extravagant shopping list was not exhaustive.[107]

Such a definition of Presidential plenary power includes every conceivable occasion for war-making. It would be a President of impoverished imagination who could not fit every contingency into one of these elastic categories.

Congress, in legislation or in litigation, will have to produce a more limited definition of its own, perhaps dusting off the reasonable one included in the Senate version of the war powers bill.

Despite concern about the constitutionality of the legislative veto in the War Powers law, and the unwillingness of successive Presidents to make its consultative procedures work effectively, the law is of major symbolic and institutional significance. It signifies the end of the first stage of the Congressional revolution and ushers in the second. The first stage concerned itself with forcing decisive changes in specific policies already underway. The second began to create machinery for timely consultation and codetermination of policies, wherever possible before they began to be implemented by the President.

The revolutionary zeal that broke up much of Nixon's and Ford's foreign policy now began to be harnessed for building better institutions and instruments of systematic codetermination. The result has been new oversight procedures that have basically altered the rules of the game, although it is too early to know whether Congress will have the diligence, the institutional will, and organizational capability to make effective use of its new powers.

In the balanced view of one seasoned observer,

> [v]iewed in the perspective of history, the changes in the executive-legislative power balance wrought by a single Congress—the Ninety-third—are truly momentous. Ever since the era of congressional government at the close of the Civil War (when Congress succeeded in writing reconstruction policy in defiance of President Andrew Johnson), the flow of power had been all one way, in the direction of the President. In just two years, the trend of a hundred years was dramatically reversed. An extraordinary abuse of presidential power triggered a counter-action equally extraordinary, and the ponderous processes of institutional change were expedited.[108]

The counter-reaction manifested itself in many areas of foreign policymaking. Congress forced the Administration to take into account the human rights record of foreign states in determining whether to provide economic and military assistance—and to share that decision, too, with legislators. It fought for, and won, the right to share with the President key decisions on U.S. arms sales and nuclear exports. It also compelled the CIA to report to Congress on projected covert operations before they were launched, in time to permit Congress to modify or stop them.

In each instance, Congress employed new oversight techniques, including requirements for consultation enforced by the threat of Congressional vetoes, to give itself a codetermining role in key policy decisions. In the midst of the revolution, there appeared signs of a desire for truce, even a whispered hope of partnership.

4

THE NEW OVERSIGHT:

Codetermining Human Rights, Military Aid, and Nuclear Export Policy

THE NEW OVERSIGHT

THE CONSTITUTION assigns to the President, not to Congress, the duty to "take care that the Laws be faithfully executed." Yet throughout the history of the Union, Congress has devised one way or another to look over the President's shoulder to see whether the execution of the laws is being carried out faithfully.

Traditionally, Congress has focused its effort on inspection and has sought to pry out of the Executive the information needed to evaluate bureaucratic performance. This is *investigatory* oversight, based on the shibboleth that information is power. Since March 19, 1790, when a House committee reported on a request by Robert Morris for an examination of his conduct as Superintendent of Finance in order to rebut certain "aspersions,"[1] Congress has never ceased investigating the Administration in order "to insure honesty and efficiency in governmental operations and to promote informed lawmaking."[2] Nor has Congress been inhibited by the fact that the Constitution nowhere authorizes it to engage in such continuing inquiry.

Investigatory oversight has been directed at every level of Government, most frequently to criticize, intimidate, or reform the middle-echelon bureaucracy. The defeat of gout-ridden General Arthur St. Clair by a force of Shawnees, Delawares, and Miamis led by Little Turtle, moved the House of Representatives, on March 27, 1792, to create a select committee to fix blame for what the hapless General himself admitted was "as unfortunate an action as almost any that has ever been fought."[3]

According to Jefferson, the Cabinet "were of one mind" that "the house was an inquest, and therefore might institute inquiries. . . ."[4]

Inquest has continued, ever since, to be a significant part of the legislative function, based on little more than British parliamentary tradition, buttressed by Article II, Section 3 of the Constitution, which requires that the President "shall from time to time give to the Congress Information of the State of the Union. . . ."

The War Powers Act, however, signaled a new kind of Congressional involvement in Executive performance. This "new oversight" is significantly different from the investigative variety. It works by mandating prior consultation, not through the investigation of actions that have already taken place. Its principal object is *decision-sharing*. A new crop of laws requires the Executive to pause before implementing decisions and enlists Congress, or its committees, in the process of deciding. The new oversight tries to involve Congress in shaping, improving, or preventing a decision. Its object is prescriptive and prophylactic.

Investigatory oversight, by contrast, typically seeks information on why or how a decision came to be made—usually after it has already been implemented by the Administration.[5] It often tries to fix blame for a bad decision made without Congressional participation,[6] sometimes generating legislation to prevent recurrence[7] of past mistakes.

The new oversight also differs from the investigatory variety in another respect. It aims at a higher level of authority and impact. Whereas investigative oversight typically involves a Congressional committee monitoring—or harassing—a bureau chief or Deputy Assistant Secretary,[8] the new oversight is focused on the President and his principal cabinet officers. That is because it is concerned with "getting a handle" on the "big issues" whereas traditional investigative oversight is more oriented toward keeping the bureaucracy honest and effective in its daily routine.[9]

Investigative oversight continues to be an important function of the Congress. Since 1973, however, a higher priority has been accorded to developing and implementing the new oversight. Of the various subjects which legislators have subjected to this process, they have had the most success with human rights, arms exports, and nuclear sales. Beginning in 1973, the Congress has gained the right to be consulted in each of these fields *before* key decisions are made or policies implemented.

HUMAN RIGHTS

Since the beginning of the "glorious revolution" on the Hill, Congress—in particular, the House of Representatives—has been determinedly attempting to rewrite U.S. foreign relations priorities to give the human rights factor new and greater importance and to cut themselves into the decision-making process.

In this campaign, Congress was stubbornly opposed by the Nixon and Ford Administrations. Indeed, the House at first received only lukewarm support from the Senate. And in both chambers, the human rights initiatives were originated and pressed by rank-and-file members like Representative Tom Harkin of Iowa and Senator Abourezk, joined by a few veteran members, like Donald Fraser, who had made human rights their specialty.

The top leadership of both Houses tended to regard these initiatives with considerable suspicion: as impractical, unenforceable, counterproductive. They feared the human rights emphasis would occasion further repression in authoritarian countries, and complained that the timing worked at cross-purposes with other initiatives to which the Congressional leadership had already committed themselves, such as arms export controls.

Nevertheless, the human rights campaign succeeded beyond all expectations of its Congressional sponsors. It was enthusiastically embraced by the new Carter Administration when it took office in 1977. That Congress and the Administration now agree on the importance of the human rights factor does not, however, alter the fact that the legislators have acquired a codeterminative role in implementing the new policy.

Beginning in 1973, Congress sent signals to the Administration making increasingly clear its desire to use the nearly 100 U.S. foreign assistance programs to try to improve the standard of recipient governments' conduct toward their own citizens. In that year, the Foreign Assistance Act was amended. "It is the sense of Congress," a new section said, "that the President should deny any economic or military assistance to the government of any foreign country which practices the internment or imprisonment of that country's citizens for political purposes."[10] This provision was not binding on the Administration, but was intended to indicate a distinct Congressional preference.

Early in 1974, a House International Relations Committee subcommittee chaired by Representative Fraser, held public hearings to see whether the preference was being implemented. Fraser's Subcommittee on International Organizations heard testimony on human rights violations in two U.S. clients: South Korea and Chile. The committee then published a report entitled "Human Rights in the World Community: A Call for U.S. Leadership" which complained that the "human rights factor is not accorded the high priority it deserves in our country's foreign policy. Too often it becomes invisible on the vast foreign policy horizon of political, economic, and military affairs."[11] Despite Congress's broad hint, the Administration was still not paying attention to the human rights factor anywhere. On the contrary, U.S. assistance—overt and covert—was buttressing some of the most repressive regimes. And the subcommittee named them. "Our relations with the present Governments of South Vietnam, Spain, Portugal, the Soviet Union, Brazil, Indonesia, Greece, the Philippines, and Chile," it said, "exemplify how we have disregarded human rights for the sake of other assumed interests."[12]

Fraser's report shocked the State Department, which did not think that sovereign governments allied to the U.S. should be subject to such public abuse by an arm of government not authorized by the Constitution to conduct diplomacy. The report warned, however, that if State would not tackle the job of promoting human rights, Congress would take it upon itself.[13] In partial fulfillment of this prophecy, the 1974 Foreign Assistance Act specifically cut economic aid to Chile and ended all U.S. military support.[14] It also imposed a token cut on military assistance to Korea.[15] In another "sense of Congress" provision it declared "the President shall substantially reduce or terminate security assistance to any government which engages in a consistent pattern of gross violations of internationally recognized human rights, including torture or cruel, inhuman or degrading treatment or punishment; prolonged detention without charges; or other flagrant denials of the right to life, liberty and the security of the person."[16]

Although Secretary Kissinger intensely disliked the public "grandstanding" of Congress, which he felt was making it more, not less, difficult for the Administration to influence foreign clients, his Department did take a few steps toward compliance. In January of 1975, a telegram went to all U.S. diplomatic posts requesting a report on "whether those in authority ignore, condone, encourage or direct activities of officials tending to violate" human rights.[17] The Agency for International Development also showed some interest in implementing the advice of Congress, directing its field staff to give priority to projects that show "primary concern" with the human rights aspects of development.[18] By the end of the year, however, these efforts had produced little visible change in U.S. policies.

The next foreign aid authorization focused on new AID priorities for food production, population control, training and upgrading of health and community services. It almost entirely ignored the human rights issue.[19] Polished and marked up, the bill went to the House floor on September 10. But there, once again the leadership lost control. Two or three days earlier, Representative Harkin's legislative assistant, walking down a corridor of the House office building, had run into a lobbyist for the Friends' Committee on National Legislation. She produced an amendment to impose a mandatory human rights test on all aid-receiving states while authorizing either House or Senate to terminate each country's aid program—a "one-house veto"—if the standard were not met. On the spur of the moment, Harkin took his assistant's advice: let's go with it.

Since he was not on the committee reporting the bill, and barely two days were left before it was to reach the floor, Harkin took his case to five veteran committee members who were leading human rights champions. Each thought it was too late, that "this was not the year," that there were too many other important changes in foreign aid already being implemented by the bill.[20] Rebuffed, Harkin introduced his amendment himself, from the floor.

The Harkin Amendment stated that no assistance could be provided to "any country which engages in a consistent pattern of gross violations of internationally recognized human rights" unless the President "determines that such assistance will directly benefit the needy people in such country and reports such determination to the Congress." The amendment also provided that, within thirty days, *either* House of Congress by resolution could override this Presidential determination, thereby cutting off further economic aid to a named recipient.[21]

The decision was a true cliff-hanger. A voice vote was taken, and the amendment was declared lost. However, Harkin had already mustered enough strength to demand a recorded vote. Earlier that day, he had also rounded up some twenty-five of his "freshman class" who owed him favors and arranged to post them at the doors to the Chamber, where they handed out the amendment and lobbied members as they scuttled in to answer the roll call.

Even so, Harkin conceded that he would have lost had Dr. Thomas Morgan of Pennsylvania, the chairman of the committee sponsoring the legislation and its floor manager, taken an active role in securing the amendment's defeat. But Morgan was a tired man near the end of his career. He did not even post committee members at the doors to counteract Harkin's troops. His inactivity allowed the amendment to pass, surprising no one more than Harkin, who found himself suddenly propelled into the front ranks of the human rights movement, a cause with which he had not previously been identified.

Thereafter, in time-honored tradition, Harkin set about trying to sell his amendment to a Senate sponsor. Again, among the Foreign Relations Committee establishment, no one was interested. The Representative felt lucky to enlist two liberals, Senators Cranston and Abourezk, to offer his proposal from the floor.

As expected, the Senate Foreign Relations Committee, in its mark-up of the House bill, snubbed the amendment,[22] preferring a much weaker human rights provision proposed by Senator Humphrey. Humphrey led the attack on Harkin's proposals. "Are we willing and able to make such judgments and to accept such responsibility?" he demanded.[23]

Despite the Foreign Relations Committee's opposition, the floor amendment proposed by Abourezk and Cranston, later joined by Senator McGovern, passed. For Harkin's one-House veto it substituted a concurrent resolution of both chambers. The bill[24] was signed by President Ford on December 20. It was another victory of the rank-and-file revolution.

Once this revolt had succeeded, it generated its own momentum. As committee work on the 1976 foreign aid bill got underway, there was little difficulty in finding sponsors for further human rights provisions[25] which made a human rights test mandatory for most military sales and gifts. The Administration would have been in a much better position to fight these new provisions had it not mishandled Congress so disastrously. After having asked each U.S. embassy to report, the Department did, at last, produce a "Report to the Congress on the Human Rights Situation in Countries Receiving U.S. Security Assistance."[26] But its simplisms merely offended many members. In a letter of transmittal, Undersecretary Carlyle Maw said the Department had "studied these analyses extensively"[27] and had concluded that, while "(s)ome countries present more serious evidence of violation than others. . . . we have found no adequately objective way to make distinctions of degree between nations."[28]

"I find it very difficult to understand," Cranston thundered.[29]

> There may be no objective way to determine the degree of violations—but does the Secretary of State have any subjective feelings about what is going on in Chile, Brazil, Korea, Indonesia, Ethiopia and the Philippines today? And can he give us some examples of where quiet, but forceful diplomacy has made a difference to the people living under those regimes?[30]

What had happened was that the Department had prepared a report to Congress which was country specific, drawing on the field responses to the Department's 1975 request. According to White House sources, Kissinger decided that it was far too inflammatory[31] and ordered the substitution of a laundered version that members contemptuously dubbed the "civics lesson."[32]

The tough new Congressional controls passed easily in this atmosphere of disaffection. Exercising his veto,[33] the President was able to modify the new set of requirements, deleting the power of Congress to terminate any military aid program on human rights grounds by simple concurrent resolution.[34] Congressional advocates of a tough line could comfort themselves, however, with knowledge that the Foreign Assistance Act already had a provision—Section 617—permitting Congress to veto any program upon eight months notice. They could also point to rigorous new procedures and reporting requirements which ensured a major new codetermining role for the legislators.

APPLICATION OF THE NEW OVERSIGHT TO HUMAN RIGHTS

These new provisions in the Foreign Assistance Act require the Administration to promote human rights abroad, to deny security assistance to states that engage in gross violations of those rights, and also end economic aid to violators except where it directly benefits the needy people of the recipient state. To ensure compliance and promote Congressional oversight, the Administration must provide an annual report on the status of human rights in each country receiving economic aid, including a description of steps taken to carry out the mandate of promoting human rights.[35] Additionally, the Department of State must prepare an annual report on human rights conditions in each state receiving military aid or training.[36] House or Senate committees can at any time call for an assessment of the human rights situation in any country receiving economic[37] or security assistance.[38] In the case of economic aid, that report must show whether its continuation will benefit needy people[39] while, in the case of military aid, it must establish whether its continuation is justified by extraordinary circumstances and the national interest.[40]

"Gross violations of human rights" are defined in the Harkin Amendment on economic aid as including "torture or cruel, inhuman, or degrading treatment or punishment, prolonged detention without charges, or other flagrant denial of the right to life, liberty, and the security of person. . . ."[41]

In September and October 1976[42] the House International Relations Committee first utilized this procedure—"just to see whether it would work," according to Representative Fraser. It requested reports on the human rights situation in Argentina, Haiti, Indonesia, Iran, Peru, and the Philippines. State complied, but at first submitted the country reports in classified form, then agreeing to publication under committee pressure. Fraser commented that the reports "are a lot better than I thought they'd be," although he thought the language was often too soft.[43]

Since 1976, there have been increasingly detailed annual reports on all 82 recipient states, running to about 500 pages.[44] They contain documented information on violations of due process and political liberties.[45] Congressional concerns are treated seriously, without "civics lesson"-type platitudes, even as the text tries to balance Congressional faith in exposure of evils with State's own preference for diplomacy.

Despite State's efforts to be tactful, many countries did not take kindly to this airing of their shortcomings, especially after the Administration voluntarily announced some punitive measures for the more serious violators. Military sales credits to Argentina were cut from the $32 million authorized by Congress to $15 million.[46] Military aid was reduced for Ethiopia and Uruguay. Then, in 1977, the Administration cited human rights violations in refusing to sign a new security assistance agreement with Nicaragua.[47]

Argentina's reaction was to blast Yankee interventionism. "No state," the Argentinian government said, "can set itself up as a court of international justice interfering in the domestic life of other countries. . . ."[48] It then rejected further military aid, as did Uruguay. Brazil charged that the State Department report "contained unacceptable and tendentious commentaries and judgments" and "constitutes a violation of the principle of noninterference" leading it to turn down $50 million in military sales credits[49] and to cancel a 25-year-old military assistance treaty with the United States.[50] El Salvador and Guatemala, too, indignantly severed their military aid relationship with the U.S.[51] Most dramatically, Ethiopia demanded the recall of the U.S. military mission[52] and intensified its reliance on the Soviet Union and Cuba for military support in combating Somali and Eritrean secessionist forces. Even some Latin-American opposition newspapers and politicians expressed concern that public attacks on Latin-American regimes would reinforce the xenophobia of a citizenry long conditioned to react against U.S. interference.[53]

While there were efforts by the Administration to comply with Congressional policy, there were also countervailing considerations. The State Department's Coordinator for Human Rights and Humanitarian Affairs noted the need for positive inducements, "rather than to rely too much on aid cuts, public denunciations and other of the more negative approaches."[54] In 1977, the Department told Congress that, because of "overriding security commitments," aid to South Korea, Indonesia, and the Philippines would continue unabated, despite those countries' violations of human rights.[55] Defending this selective policy, Secretary Vance said that the task of balancing human rights with strategic security considerations would be carried out on a country-by-country basis, even if this resulted in unequal treatment that might superficially make the United States appear hypocritical.[56] In an effort to prevent a symbolic cut in aid for the Philippines where negotiations to renew the lease on

Subic Bay military base were underway, Vice President Fritz Mondale called key members and staffers from Manila.[57]

Despite these caveats, many members of Congress seem satisfied that the Carter Administration has genuinely embraced this Congressionally originated new motif in American foreign policy. Having legislated the broad outlines of that policy and established a new and effective oversight, these members are inclined to leave the Executive to implement on a day-by-day, country-by-country basis.

Still, instances arise when Congress and the Executive reach different conclusions as to the seriousness of a country's violations, the weight to be given to countervailing security considerations, or the probable effectiveness of a "get tough" policy. Some members see no reason to accommodate other factors or compromise over something as basic as human rights. They therefore continue to press for further legislation and more rigorous enforcement of existing standards, by Congress if not by the Administration. "Human rights has gotten out of hand in Congress," Representative Fraser has complained. "It is an issue that has begun to attract some pretty odd support."[58]

Both Congressional ultra-conservatives and ultra-liberals have learned to use the popular appeal of human rights to stop U.S. aid to governments of which they disapproved ideologically. Angola, Mozambique,[59] and North Vietnam[60] were targeted by the conservatives; South Korea, Indonesia, Iran, Uruguay, Argentina, Chile, and the Philippines by the liberals.[61] Idi Amin's Uganda was a universally favored target with the result that, in 1978, Congress instituted a total trade embargo over vigorous Presidential opposition—just in time to reap for the U.S. an unaccustomed accolade from the regime which, a few months later, overthrew the dictator.[62] Here Congress was clearly proven more prescient than the White House. Unfortunately, success breeds excess. However, other, less enlightened factions in Congress soon learned to hitch a ride on the human rights bandwagon to try to reach their goal of cutting foreign aid altogether.

But there have also been effective Congressional counsels of moderation. A partial prohibition on military aid to Turkey[63] was lifted by Congress in 1978, subject to some conditions.[64] Many, although not all, of the remaining prohibitions permit waiver if the President certifies to Congress that aid would, for example, help to detach a communist country from subservience to Moscow.[65] In the case of Brazil, El Salvador, and Guatemala, the ban on credits for military supplies[66] was not renewed in 1979, nor was the prohibition on military aid and credits for Uruguay.[67] The prohibition on Angola and Mozambique was deleted from the law at the end of 1978,[68] although military aid may only be extended after the President has certified to Congress that such assistance "would further the foreign policy interests of the United States."[69] In 1978, too, Congress defeated efforts by the ultras to impose new restrictions on aid to Syria, Nicaragua, and Afghanistan.[70]

Congress is also exercising its new responsibilities, cautiously, vis-à-vis the white regimes of Southern Africa: proposing to lift the embargo on trade with Rhodesia after free one-man-one-vote elections are held and the Government makes good faith efforts to negotiate with insurgent groups[71] and banning Export-Import Bank credit to finance trade with South Africa unless the beneficiary business has adopted minimal human rights standards, including integration of facilities and equal job opportunities.[72]

Increasing care and a rejection of precipitous action now also marks Congress's human rights policies toward International Financial Institutions (IFI's). At the height of revolutionary fervor on the Hill, it had been discovered that, while U.S. aid to human rights violators—Argentina, Brazil, Chile, Nicaragua, Indonesia, Thailand, Philippines, and South Korea—had declined from $586.9 million in 1970 to $427.8 million in 1976, indirect aid coming mostly from IFI's in which the U.S. was principal shareholder, had climbed from $1.7 billion to $6 billion.[73] This was perceived as "back door financing" and was decried as a loss of control by Congress, which proceeded to take various steps to make the IFI's adhere more closely to U.S. human rights standards. Representative Harkin, in 1975, succeeded in persuading Congress to require the U.S. governors of the Inter-American and African Development Banks to vote against loans or technical assistance to violators.[74] In 1977 Representative Herman Badillo of New York got this rule extended to all IFI's, including the World Bank (International Bank for Reconstruction and Development).[75]

These efforts were opposed as irresponsible by President Carter, leaders of the Congressional establishment and the heads of the IFI's. World Bank President Robert S. McNamara warned that his institution could not concern itself with "civil rights" because its members do not agree on universal standards, but argued that the Bank, in alleviating malnutrition, sickness, and illiteracy was addressing "the most fundamental of human rights."[76] Nevertheless, efforts continued through 1977 to make the IFI's come to heel. Senator Robert Dole of Kansas[77] and Representative Clarence Long, chairman of the Foreign Operations Subcommittee of the House Appropriations Committee, favored legislation withholding U.S. financial contributions to IFI's to whatever extent the banks voted aid to human rights violators. McNamara announced that the World Bank would not accept U.S. contributions earmarked in this fashion.[78] The effort abated[79] only after President Carter wrote Representative Long promising that he would "instruct the U.S. Executive

Directors in the Banks to oppose and vote against" loans to seven specified "gross violators."[80]

By 1978, sober counsel had reasserted itself. This time the effort by Harkin to deny funds to the banks for use in loans to Nicaragua, the Philippines, Indonesia, South Korea, Uruguay, Chile, and Argentina was buried under a 41 to 360 landslide, as were other efforts to extend the injunction to Mozambique and Angola.[81] A House-Senate conference dropped all remaining country-specific prohibitions, including even those on Vietnam[82] and Cuba.[83]

The making and revising of detailed country-by-country rules is clearly more appropriate to the executive than the legislative branch. But it should be recalled that the momentum of the Congressional *ultras* goes back to the Nixon and Ford Administrations, when government steadfastly refused to implement the general human rights standards established by Congress. It was in that climate of Executive non-compliance that Congress, in some instances, began to administer the program itself. Since the advent of the Carter Administration, few new country-specific laws have been passed and more have been rescinded, usually as a result of the efforts of a new generation of Congressional committee leadership.[84]

THE EXECUTIVE BRANCH AND THE NEW RULES

An extensive reorganization has taken place in the way the Executive makes human rights policy, precisely to ensure that all departments and agencies comply with the spirit of the laws and cooperate with the new oversight. Indirectly, this may have been Congress's most constructive contribution. An Inter-agency Group on Human Rights and Foreign Assistance was created by a National Security Council directive of April 1, 1977. It includes the State Department, which is most directly affected by the human rights provision, and also Defense, Treasury, the Export-Import Bank, and even the Agriculture Department and others.[85]

The Group's mandate is to "examine our bilateral and multilateral foreign assistance decisions as they relate to human rights, to provide guidance regarding specific decisions on bilateral and multilateral assistance, and in general to coordinate the Administration's position in this area."[86] The directive appoints "a representative of the Secretary of State" to chair the Group, which has become known as the Christopher Committee, after Deputy Secretary Warren Christopher who was assigned that function. Representatives of Treasury—usually accompanied by the U.S. Executive Directors of the World Bank and Inter-American

Development Bank—Defense, the National Security Council, and AID always attend; those of Agriculture, Eximbank, Labor, and Commerce only when the subject to be discussed affects them. The Group has been meeting regularly since April 1977.

Before an aid issue goes to the Christopher Committee, it is usually considered at a weekly meeting of an inter-agency subgroup. It is only if they flag a proposal that it goes to the committee for disposition.

Prior to each meeting, the committee receives extensive briefing materials pertaining to the proposals on its agenda, including human rights analyses prepared by State Department's Human Rights Bureau, which describes itself as the "gatekeeper" for assistance projects.[87] Discussions usually begin with an assessment by State's representative of the overall relationship between the U.S. and the applicant state, including U.S. security interests, after which a summary of the applicant's state of human rights is given, with an analysis of trends and prospects. According to a participant, "The Human Rights Bureau, the State Department Regional and Economic Bureaus, the Office of Legal Adviser, Treasury, Congressional Liaison—these do most of the talking. Agriculture, our World Bank Director, and the other agency people tend to talk only if the project directly affects them."[88]

The Group may recommend approval of a project "because human rights conditions in the recipient country are good or are authentically improving or because the assistance will benefit the needy."[89] The Group may also recommend approval conditioned on a diplomatic representation that emphasizes the U.S. government's human rights concerns.

When the Group disapproves a project, it may also recommend a diplomatic *démarche* explaining the U.S. position on rights and calling for improvements prior to reapplication. By mid-1978, the Group had recommended deferral of several AID projects, although the number "is small in comparison to the number . . . recommended for approval."[90] Also, "approximately twenty" IFI loan proposals—six by Argentina, two each by Philippines, Ethiopia, Korea, and Benin, and one each by Chile, Guinea, and the Central African Empire—were redlined by the Group recommending either opposition or abstention by the U.S. voting representative.[91]

Ordinarily, the Christopher Committee functions by consensus. Sometimes, the Deputy Secretary simply makes up his own mind on the basis of the discussion, and, if an AID project is involved, instructs the Agency, which is within his jurisdiction. If the subject is outside his jurisdiction, he must substitute tact for fiat. When the issue is the U.S. vote on an IFI loan, Christopher makes a recommendation to the Secretary of the Treasury. If he and Treasury disagree, as has happened, then the matter may have to be resolved by the President.[92]

That is the theory and, more often than not, the practice. In mid-1977, for example, the Christopher Committee approved its sub-group's recommendation to turn down a proposed credit of $9.6 million for Chilean farmers which would have been used for the purchase of surplus seed and cattle from the U.S. That decision was strongly fought by the Agriculture Department and it sharply divided the Committee. Nevertheless, the Human Rights Bureau's advocacy of a tough line won out.[93]

Then, on May 4, 1978, the Agriculture Department blandly announced a loan, to the tune of 38—not 9.6—million dollars, for almost exactly the same project the Christopher Committee had turned down less than a year ago. While it might have been argued in the Committee that Chile's regime had begun to improve its human rights performance, no such argument was made. "The Secretary of Agriculture just did an end run around us," a member of the committee reports. "He just acted without going through channels. That happens."[94]

It does not happen too often, however, because Assistant Secretary of State Patricia Derian and Deputy Assistant Secretary Mark Schneider are zealous institutional watchdogs who are not easily circumvented. Schneider, a former human rights specialist for Senator Edward Kennedy, has kept his lines to Congress. Immediately after Agriculture's end run, Kennedy attacked them for it in the Senate.[95]

Surprisingly, no machinery similar to the Christopher Committee exists to ensure that human rights considerations are given priority in decisions—again involving numerous departments and agencies—concerning arms exports and security assistance. True, the Human Rights Bureau is represented on the inter-agency Arms Export Control Board; but since the mandate of that group includes all matters pertaining to arms exports, sales, credits, and grants, the human rights factor is very diluted.

This means that military aid decisions are not challenged as early or as effectively within the councils of the Administration as they should be, or as Congress has a right to expect. In turn, that throws a heavier burden on Congress. It was a subcommittee of the House International Relations Committee which had to take the lead in quizzing the Administration about arms deliveries to Indonesia after that country's suppression of self-determination in the former Portuguese colony of East Timor. The same subcommittee had to make waves about the proposed sale of fighter bombers to Morocco for use against those fighting for self-determination in the former Spanish Sahara, a territory Morocco had invaded. Prodded by Congressional hearings, the arguments for suspending delivery of weapons to these aggressor states as required by law had to be made by the Office of the Legal Adviser, since the matter was effectively beyond the reach of the Human Rights Bureau and clearly outside the jurisdiction of the Christopher Committee. In these two instances, House Subcommittee chairman Representative Fraser and the office of the State Department's legal adviser did succeed in persuading the Government that continued arms deliveries to Indonesia and plane sales to Morocco, in the circumstances, would violate the law.[96] But there is need for a Christopher Committee–type inter-agency mechanism to inspect all proposed arms exports for their human rights impact.

Another serious inadequacy is in the Human Rights Bureau's relations with the White House. For example, when Presidential counsel Robert J. Lipshutz drafted the letter by which the President transmitted the Human Rights Conventions to the Senate for ratification, he did not consult the Bureau. Yet the letter contained detailed reservations, understandings, and declarations which the Senate was urged to attach to its resolution of consent. The Bureau, taken aback, seriously considered opposing the "Lipshutz reservations" in public testimony before the Senate. "Disastrous," said an observer of this disarray from his vantage in the legal adviser's office.

Again, in July 1978, President Carter sent a "personal" letter to President Anastasio Somoza of Nicaragua congratulating him for certain human rights improvements. Here, too, the Bureau was not consulted. On the contrary, it was caught by surprise in the midst of opposing a proposed military credit for that country.[97] The President's letter pointed up the failure of the White House to be brought into the interagency process. It also reveals that, even in this comparatively benevolent Administration, the human rights advocates still face an uphill battle.[98]

Nevertheless, compared with the situation prevailing in the executive branch only a few years ago, the climate has improved, particularly in the State Department. Those lonely few who had been relegated to impotence, reviled as "human rights freaks" and "bleeding hearts," have now, much augmented, become a serious institutional force. Secretary Vance, in his 1978 report to Congress, declared his resolve "to give far higher priority to human rights considerations in the formulation of American foreign policy."[99] The Administration has mostly tried to work with, rather than circumvent, its Congressional mandate.

EFFECTIVENESS
OF THE HUMAN RIGHTS POLICY

Congress lit the human rights candle long before it was seized by candidate Carter. It forced a reluctant Executive to join with it in considering human rights as an important part of policy-making. But what was once resisted as a dangerous Congressional trespass on Executive prerogatives has now been recognized as a healthy reform of U.S. policy as well as of Executive-Congressional relations.

Congressional codetermination has also proven a better tactic than had been expected by the practitioners of quiet diplomacy. It is Congress which now draws the ire of foreign dictators, allowing the State Department to appear more understanding in a global game of "good cop-bad cop."

Although the signals have been mixed, there are some indications of success, including a degree of liberalization by the Pinochet dictatorship in Chile. During visits to that country in 1977, the Assistant Secretary of State for Inter-American Affairs concluded that most political prisoners held without charges had been released.[100] In March 1978 the state of siege was replaced by a new, if still rigorous, security law, the curfew was lifted, and some convicted political prisoners were given the option of going into exile.[101]

As the price of ferrying French troops into Zaire's Congo Province the U.S. asked for, and apparently got, President Mobutu Sese Seko to declare amnesty for political prisoners, including the condemned former foreign minister, Karl-i-Bond.[102] In Indonesia, the government announced the release of 10,000 political prisoners, with a commitment to release the remaining 20,000 over the next two years.[103] More political prisoners were released in Haiti, Paraguay, Argentina, and Peru.[104] The military state of siege was lifted in El Salvador[105] and, because of direct U.S. pressure, the opposition was confirmed in its victory after 1978 elections in the Dominican Republic. In Iran, the Shah, before his overthrow, had released a "substantial" number of political prisoners,[106] made a show of cutting back SAVAK, his secret police, and agreed to prison inspection by the International Committee of the Red Cross and the International Commission of Jurists. At least a token release of political prisoners took place in South Korea and the Philippines.[107] El Salvador, Haiti, and Paraguay agreed to precedent-setting inspection visits by the Inter-American Human Rights Commission.

None of these improvements can be traced definitively to the new Congressionally induced policies. Inevitably, costs are easier to attribute to it than gains. Still, the astounding human rights wall posters that flourished in Peking at the end of 1978 suggest that this aspect of American foreign policy has echoed in the common conscience of mankind.

MILITARY AID

In the mid-1970's, control over arms exports became a confrontational issue between Congress and the President. This was not an entirely new area of conflict. In the late 1930's, President Roosevelt's efforts to make the U.S. the arsenal of democracy had encountered the legislative obstacle of the Neutrality Act. Between 1941 and the mid-'70's, however, the arsenal concept had gone largely unchallenged. In the decade between 1963 and 1973, 128 nations acquired $2.5 trillion in weapons and services, the largest part from the U.S. and much of it by grants or on credit. The less developed countries were among the biggest beneficiaries and spenders, in most instances devoting an even bigger percentage of their GNP to military expenditures than the developed nations.

Altogether, since 1950, the United States had given away or sold over $85 billion in military hardware and related services. And the pace was quickening. The volume of U.S. military exports rose to $9.3 billion in 1975. Commercial sales and military assistance grants swelled the 1975 total to $10.6 billion, with clients in seventy-one countries. Then, there was the changing demography of customers. Persian Gulf oil nations, aided by huge petrodollar surpluses, eager to succeed Britain as policeman of the region, raced each other to buy the most recent military technology. Where once the export of arms had been a high-minded part of a global strategy to make the world safe for democracy, now the U.S. appeared to be willing to supply any regime, no matter how unsavory, so long as the customer professed anti-communism and could pay cash.

By 1973, however, the course of the Vietnam War had raised Congressional consciousness about incremental involvements. Some members concluded that arms sales were one path into quagmires. When the U.S. sold high technology defense equipment to a country, it usually contracted to install and maintain it, to train locals in its use, and to provide spare parts. As a result, the U.S. became involved, through the back door, with the purchaser's security. Not surprisingly, there were voices urging Congress to accept responsibility for determining whether and how to make such commitments.

THE NELSON-BINGHAM BILL

As with human rights, Congress began with a simple statement of policy. The "furnishing of economic, military, or other assistance," the Foreign Assistance Act was amended in 1967 to read, "shall not be construed as creating a new commitment . . . to use Armed Forces of the United

States for the defense of any foreign country."[108] This was little more effective than the Surgeon General's warning on cigarette packages. As sales continued to skyrocket in the early '70's, legislators moved to become directly involved in deciding what sales should be made, to whom and under what circumstances.

Until 1974, the law merely required the Secretary of State to report "significant" arms sales[109] semi-annually to Congress. In the summer of 1973, there were reports of a huge sale, including squadrons of phantom jets, to Saudi Arabia. A Senate Foreign Relations staffer tried to interest members of the Committee in establishing a procedure by which Congress could review, and, if necessary, prevent such large sales. As with human rights, however, the establishment was not at first interested. Finding no takers, the committee staffer mentioned the idea to Dr. Paula Stern, legislative assistant to Senator Gaylord Nelson of Wisconsin, a maverick liberal. Nelson thought it was a good idea. Stern and Nelson decided on a reporting "tripwire" of $25 million, the cost of one squadron of F-5E's.

Since no committee sponsor could be found,[110] Nelson proposed his measure as a floor amendment. In the rebellious mood of that era, it passed by 44 votes to 43. The amendment arrogated to Congress the right to examine large proposed arms sales before they were made and, by resolution of either House, to veto any transaction.

In the House, the floor amendment was offered by Representative Jonathan Bingham of New York, and was defeated. The House-Senate Conference met, inauspiciously, at the height of the 1973 Mid-East war and accepted the argument that the President must retain a free hand in supplying arms to allies.

In 1974, as the revolutionary mood of Congress grew in intensity, the attempt was renewed. This time the provision for a one-House veto[111] was replaced by one requiring a concurrent resolution.[112] Despite the threat of a Presidential veto and little support from the Congressional establishment, the rank and file carried the day in both chambers.

The Nelson-Bingham initiative worked a profound transformation in arms export policy. Under the new law, whenever the U.S. government offers to sell any defense article or service costing $25 million or more, the President, before issuing the letter of offer, must send both Houses of Congress a detailed description of the sale's terms and of the weapons involved. The sale may not be made if Congress, within twenty calendar days (later increased to thirty) adopts a concurrent "veto" resolution, unless the President certifies an emergency.[113]

In the first five years of the law's operation, no arms sale has actually been vetoed by Congress. But the law has had very significant impact on U.S. government policy, both on long-range planning and on several major individual sales. It has also affected the approach of foreign arms purchasers.

THE HAWK MISSILE SALE:
THE FIRST TEST

In November 1974 Secretary Kissinger, during a bout of shuttle diplomacy, paid a visit to King Hussein in Amman. The King stressed his country's military vulnerability and argued that lack of modern equipment was draining the loyalty of the Jordanian armed forces.

The Secretary promised the King he would try to help. A month later, the White House directed the Joint Chiefs of Staff to study Jordanian air defenses and to make recommendations.

The Joint Chiefs' survey was completed in mid-February and sent to the White House on March 27. It recommended the sale of Hawks, emphasizing the morale problems of the Jordanian government, and arguing that Hussein would be under pressure to seek alternate sources if the U.S. refused.

The White House thereupon cleared the Defense Department to negotiate the sale of an air defense system. But aware of the criticism the transaction would encounter, it instructed the negotiators to de-emphasize the Hawk missiles and play up various less sophisticated systems such as the Vulcan, Chapparal, and the "Redeye" shoulder-fired anti-aircraft missiles. At least, negotiators were to stretch out the Hawks' delivery schedule. The final package agreed during Hussein's visit to Washington in May provided for fourteen batteries, the first three to be delivered within a year and the remainder within thirty months at an estimated cost of $256 million. The Jordanians also got 100 Vulcans and 270 Redeyes, for a total package costing $350 million. On May 15, the Defense Security Assistance Agency was directed by the White House to begin implementation of the Jordanian request. Congress had still not been informed.

Keeping Congress, and the Israeli lobby, in the dark appears to have been the Administration's deliberate policy throughout this period. At State there was a prevalent belief that key senatorial staff were working hand-in-glove with the Israelis and that the best way to get the deal past Congress was to present it with a *fait accompli*, leaving the Israeli lobby as little time to organize its Congressional friends as possible. A resolution of inquiry moved in June by Representative Rosenthal[114] produced a bland, uninformative reply from White House aide Max Friedersdorff.[115]

Although the Nelson-Bingham reporting requirement had gone into effect the previous year, the White House felt reasonably confident in stonewalling. There had already been twenty-five sales to foreign countries notified under the new procedure. Congress had objected to none. President Ford's advisers were thus inclined to predict that this sale, too, would go through essentially unopposed if they could just keep the lid on until the last possible moment.[116] After all, Congress is a busy place, and it would have only twenty days in which to act.

Friedersdorff's reply also indicated that a letter of offer was being prepared which would be reported to Congress "sometime late in July or early August"[117]—in other words, just in time for the Congressional summer recess, when nothing could be done about it.

This tactic was a serious miscalculation. It permitted the pro-Israeli members to broaden their base of Congressional support by transforming the issue from whether King Hussein should get his Hawks to whether President Ford should be allowed to flout the spirit of the law. Rosenthal, naturally, characterized Friedersdorff's response as "incomplete, inadequate, and inconsistent" as well as "highly suspect."[118] It was the antithesis of the codetermination mandated by law and demeaned Congress.[119]

Finally, on July 10, the Defense Department sent Congress the Army's proposed letter of offer to Jordan. In the House, Representative Bingham, a comparative moderate among the pro-Israelis who had previously expressed some sympathy for Jordan's plight, announced almost at once that he and other members would introduce a resolution to kill the sale.[120] In the Senate, Case introduced a resolution to the same effect.[121]

Hearings were held by the Senate Committee on Foreign Relations and by the International Relations Committee of the House in mid-July. By this time, opponents of the sale had enlisted the support of committee Chairman John Sparkman, and the Administration had reason to be worried, although Assistant Secretary Robert McCloskey still reported that the Administration had the votes to beat the critics.[122] He simply could not conceive of Congress's undercutting a public Presidential commitment to a friendly power. In the wake of the Vietnam evacuation crisis, however, the State Department and the President were not anxious to take chances. Certainly, they were not looking for another fight to the finish. In the third week of July, Secretary Kissinger began domestic shuttle diplomacy—up and down Pennsylvania Avenue.

Actually, it was a three-way shuttle that the Hawk missile crisis initiated. On the one hand, the Secretary began intense negotiations with leading Congressional critics of the sale; and on the other hand, he reopened talks with King Hussein, in an attempt to bring the Congress's and the King's demands closer together.

In an opening gambit, Senator Case and Representative Bingham suggested scaling down the sale to three Hawk batteries, an offer Kissinger found was wholly unacceptable to Hussein. At a later point, the State

Department and the Senate Foreign Relations Committee agreed to try a six battery proposal on the King. On July 24, he reported the King's refusal to a closed session of the Senate Committee. The telegram from Amman read, in part, "This crisis is not of our making. I see no reason why my country should have to provide a face saving formula at our expense."[123]

With the sale thus stymied, Congress took its summer recess. By threatening an immediate pre-recess veto of the sale, Congressional opponents persuaded the Administration to withdraw the notification of offer temporarily. Throughout the recess, intense negotiations continued between the Hill and Foggy Bottom, with Senator Case and Representative Bingham meeting frequently with Kissinger.

In pursuit of compromise, a small team of Congressional staff headed by Senator Case's aide, Stephen D. Bryen, an ex-jet pilot, visited a Hawk missile battalion at Homestead Air Force Base, in Florida, during August. Here they obtained first-hand knowledge of the system's capabilities and limitations. On his return, Bryen recommended several changes in the Hawk model that would lessen its offensive capability, while not interfering with its defensive capacity.

The report recommended that the Assault Fire Command Console, which permits the whole system to remain operational while it is being moved, not be included in the sale package and that the contract exclude training for mobile use of the missiles. Another proposal was to place the missile batteries in concrete configurations known as CONUS (Continental U.S. Implacement). The report, finally, urged that the system's trailer base and wheels be removed.[124]

Kissinger was at first skeptical, but he had also come to suspect that, without some modification, the sale would almost certainly be vetoed by Congress, flexing its new Nelson-Bingham muscle. His task was made easier when the Department of Defense agreed to accept the recommendations, volunteering to tell the Jordanians that they were losing very little because the Hawks, under Jordanian road conditions, were effectively unmovable anyway.

On September 16—after a final flurry of negotiations among State, Defense, the White House, the Jordanians, and Congress represented by Representative Bingham and Senator Case—the compromise was announced: a letter would be sent to Congress by the President containing assurances in "strong language" that the Hawk missiles would be used only for defensive purposes and specifying all the agreed limitations on the weapons system to be offered for sale.[125] As a result of the new assurances, Senator Case and Representative Bingham said they would terminate further action against the sale.[126]

In Congress there was general satisfaction that the President could no longer, on his own, supply large quantities of sophisticated weapons to nations abroad. Representative Bingham exulted: "The watchword of our arms salesmen must now become we'll see if we can sell it to Congress."[127]

Meanwhile, however, all was not well in Amman, where the King was openly hurt and angry at Congress's public inquest into the merits of his regime.[128] After the State Department and Congress had reached their all-too-public compromise, Hussein precipitously called the whole deal off. This denouement, for several months, exactly tracked Russia's petulant rebuff to Congress after passage of the 1974 Trade Act. On that occasion, the Soviet leaders at first agreed to ease barriers to Jewish emigration but finally reneged, after the Congress had made the arm-twisting increasingly public.[129] On this occasion, however, diplomacy—and the dependence of Jordan on clearly superior U.S. technology—were eventually successful in soothing the King's bruised ego.

Nevertheless, these public, often brutal Congressional evaluations of foreign nations seeking to do business with the U.S., tend to have the effect of canceling out whatever goodwill the transaction is intended to achieve. Although the sale was finally consummated, it also demonstrated the weakness of a procedure that encourages the Administration to commit itself to foreign sales in secret, then faces Congress with a choice between acquiescence or the public humiliation of a friendly foreign government. The Hawk crisis showed that the Administration should seek Congressional advice much earlier in the process: *before* a decision is reached on large-scale weapons sales to a foreign government.

The Congress has attempted to address itself to some of these problems. In 1976 it succeeded in lengthening to thirty calendar days the time during which it may consider each sale after notification by the Executive.[130] Although it failed, thanks to President Ford's veto, to place an overall $9 billion annual ceiling on all arms exports,[131] Congress forced the Administration to accept a lowering of the reporting tripwire on major equipment from $25 million to $7 million.[132] It also required the President, at the request of the House or Senate foreign relations committees, to provide more detailed information on each proposed sale, including weapons descriptions, an arms control impact statement, and logistic and strategic analyses.[133]

IMPROVING ARMS EXPORT
CODETERMINATION IN PRACTICE

The present practice in the Senate is to publish in the *Congressional Record* all letters of offer except those that are actually classified. By a "gentleman's agreement" the staff now receives "prenotification" twenty days before the letter of offer is formally submitted. This alerts Congress a full fifty days (twenty days prenotification plus thirty days formal notification) before it must act to stop a sale. Although these prenotifications are not published in the *Record*, a brief notice is inserted indicating the region to which the sale will be made. Staff flag for the Committee those that are likely to be controversial.[134]

In a further effort to become involved in controversial sales before they turn into Presidential commitments to a foreign government, Congress has legislated access to defense requirement surveys[135] while putting foreign states on notice that these "do not represent a commitment by the United States to provide military equipment."[136] In practice, committee staff is now regularly notified whenever a country survey team is to be dispatched,[137] giving them time to canvass members' opinion and report back potential opposition.

During 1975, the Department of Defense issued approximately 17,000 letters of offer for the sale of weapons. Of these, 111 came within the statutory requirement for notification to Congress. After the tripwire was lowered to $7 million from $25 million, the volume increased sharply.[138] Up to August 1976, thirty-nine concurrent resolutions had been introduced in Congress, opposing thirteen proposed sales. Since the Hawks transaction, it has been huge sales to Saudi Arabia that have drawn fire. On September 7, 1976, Senator Nelson alone filed thirty-seven concurrent resolutions to block the shipment of $6 billion worth of U.S. arms offered for sale by the Ford Administration to eleven foreign governments. He was not objecting to the purchaser, Nelson said, but to the volume.[139] Senator William Proxmire of Wisconsin submitted twenty-four resolutions to disapprove $5.3 billion worth of sales to five governments. Public hearings were held on each. The intent was plainly to have a chilling effect on the arms sales industry and the Defense Department. Among the sales targeted by Nelson and Proxmire were 160 F-16 jet fighters for Iran ($3.8 billion) and 850 Sidewinder missiles and 650 Mavericks for Saudi Arabia ($701 million).

The painful experience of inter-branch warfare accompanying the Hawk missile sale to Jordan, together with the tougher new legislation, sent a signal to the State Department that it could not ignore. For example, when it was decided in February 1976 to end the long-standing prohibition on the sale of military equipment to Egypt by selling Cairo six C-130 Hercules military transport planes—a strategically minor but symbolically major policy decision—the Administration began consultations with Congress at an early stage in its discussion with Egypt. In the words of one official, "On sales to Egypt we want Congress in on the take-off as well as the landing."[140] Ultimately, on April 14, Congress allowed the $65 million sale to go through after Secretary Kissinger, at hearings conducted by House and Senate committees, promised that no further sales to Egypt would be made during 1976.[141]

EVALUATION
OF THE CONGRESSIONAL ROLE

While the Executive efforts to face Congress with a *fait accompli* at first caused serious problems in Executive-Congressional relations and strains in U.S. ties to client regimes abroad, the codetermination process has begun to shake down, as everyone—including the foreign clients[142]—is learning to play by the new rules.

On the whole, the Congressional role must now be judged to be distinctively salutary. Hindsight certainly shows Congress to have been right, and the Administration wrong, in connection with the 1977 sale of a 1.2 billion dollar Airborne Warning and Control System (AWACS) to Iran.[143] When, on June 16, Congress received prenotification of the proposed sale, seven Senators, led by John Culver, introduced a veto resolution.[144] A parallel resolution was introduced in the House on June 29.[145]

The AWACS are basically Boeing 707 transport planes equipped with an elaborate dome of radar and communications equipment that monitors and controls air battles over a wide region. It covers very low altitudes not accessible to ordinary radar and represents the best technology in the U.S. arsenal. In a report prepared by the General Accounting Office for six Senators, including Culver, that agency stated: "In our opinion, the justification presented to Congress in support of the proposed AWACS sale to Iran is inadequate."[146] The system was too advanced for Iran's needs; American technicians would have to operate it. And if the system were to fall into Soviet hands, they could quickly overcome the American lead in aircraft detection technology.[147]

As a result of a surprising show of strength by opponents of the sale in both House and Senate[148]—including Representative Don Bonker in whose district AWACS are manufactured—the White House agreed to negotiate a scaling down of the AWACS package.[149] On September 6, President Carter summarized the results of these discussions in a letter to Senator Sparkman which includes a detailed list of gear not to be included in the sale, sets out agreed U.S.–Iranian joint security precautions to protect the equipment, establishes limitations on AWACS use, and details the training of Iranian crews in the U.S. It unconditionally precludes the flying of operational missions by U.S. crews. "The Government of Iran has advised us," the letter says, "that it endorses the assurances which we offer the Congress on AWACS, and that it will assist us to the very best of its ability in applying rigid standards of protection for the AWACS and its subsystems."[150]

As part of the deal made during the summer recess, Chairman Humphrey and Senator Case, the subcommittee's ranking Republican, issued a letter to their senatorial colleagues. It said: "We have concluded that if vigilantly enforced by the President and closely monitored by the Congress, these assurances should provide the increased measure of protection sought by the Subcommittee."[151]

Opinions varied on the effectiveness of these changes in the sales package. The General Accounting Office was unable to certify to Congress that the Presidential assurances would make a difference. It would "depend to a great extent on circumstances occurring after delivery of the aircraft to Iran."[152] Senator Culver and a few of the sharpest critics of the sale remained unreconciled. Fortunately, the AWACS had not yet been delivered as the Shah's rule began to crumble and, in November 1978 the order was cancelled. Once more, however, Congressional instincts had been right, the Executive wrong.

In other instances, too, codetermination has provided occasion for reevaluation and modification of sales policy. When, late in 1976, the Pentagon proposed the sale to Saudi Arabia of 1,900 Sidewinder air-to-air missiles,[153] intense negotiations between members of the Senate Foreign Relations Committee and Secretary Kissinger led to an eventual reduction of that transaction to a "mere" 650.[154]

The most dramatic instance of the new oversight, implementing the Nelson-Bingham procedures, occurred in the spring of 1978. It concerned the Administration's adoption of a new role thrust upon it by the Arab "moderates," Egypt and Saudi Arabia, as "even-handed" arms supplier to them as well as to Israel. The vehicle for this momentous policy shift was a "package" sale of jet fighters to Israel, Egypt, and Saudi Arabia, worth $4.8 billion.

This package clearly tilted toward the Arabs. It consisted of fifty F-5 aircraft (forty-two F-5E and eight F-5F) for Egypt—the first U.S. weapons sale to that country—as well as fifteen F-15C's and seventy-five F-16A's and F-16B's to Israel and sixty F-15's (forty-five F-15A's and fifteen TF-F-15 A trainers) to Saudi Arabia.[155] The Israeli allotment was a sharp rebuke to Jerusalem for what the Administration perceived as its negative response to the peace overtures of Egypt's President Sadat. It offered less than half the planes Secretary Kissinger, on behalf of the previous Administration, had led the Israeli government to expect in return for acceptance of the second Sinai disengagement agreement.[156] Of these planes being sold, the F-15's were by far the most sophisticated, capable of determining the outcome in a conflict with other fighters.

Israel already had twenty-five of them, which left the F-15's score: Saudis sixty, Israel forty. The Administration, knowing Israel's supporters in Congress would try to alter that balance, deliberately presented the sales to Egypt, Israel, and Saudi Arabia as a "package," implying that if the Saudis were denied their allotment—there was no serious problem about the lesser planes destined for Egypt—the President would simply not sell to Israel.

The Congressional liaison specialists in the State Department warned that the linkage tactic would be taken by Congress as a neo-Nixonian effort at compliance by circumvention. It would allow opponents of the sale to transform the debate from one about U.S. Mid-East interests and Israeli security, into a procedural confrontation over the President's duty to obey the Nelson-Bingham law. Congress would again perceive itself to be defending hard-won codeterminational prerogatives against resurgent White House imperium. Instead of a policy debate, Congress once more would have a Constitutional issue.

Secretary Vance actually came to accept this view, resisting the notion of the "package" right up to the time the sales were publicly announced on February 14, 1978. White House advisers, on the other hand, were positively looking for a show-down and successfully insisted that the State Department announcement of the sale use the word "package."[157] Senator Church called that "improper and unintended by the law,"[158] a view echoed by its author, Representative Bingham.[159] Only after Senate Majority Leader Robert Byrd, a supporter of these sales, reported that a majority of his colleagues favored the Saudi sale but would vote against any package on legal grounds[160] did President Carter relent. "There are just times," Byrd told Carter, "when you don't call a spade a spade."[161]

The next morning Carter sent Byrd a draft of a letter Secretary Vance would send to Senator Church "unlocking the package," while still carefully preserving the Administration's option to "review the action taken by the Congress on each of the separate certifications."[162] The letter was, at most, a symbolic concession. But Byrd, by being asked to comment on it before it was sent, was being drawn into the Administration's circle of trusted advisers. In the Senator's opinion, "it was enough to unruffle feathers. 'Package' had become a bad buzz-word, and it had been taken out."[163] Deprived of the "package" issue, opponents of the Saudi sale were forced to join issue on the merits.

To do so, House members on March 10 formed a working group, the core of which consisted of Democrats Benjamin Rosenthal, Dante Fascell of Florida, and Stephen Solarz of New York, and Republican Edward J. Derwinski of Illinois, all members of the International Relations Committee. Fascell was chosen chairman. In the words of the group's quarterback, Representative Rosenthal, "working groups, single-issue coalitions, are used when you don't have access to the levers of power."[164]

In this confrontation, power certainly seemed to be with Administration's Congressional supporters. International Relations Committee Chairman Clement Zablocki and Lee Hamilton of Ohio, the chairman of its Subcommittee on Europe and the Middle East, favored the sale, and Zablocki early informed the White House that he had the votes to kill any veto resolution. Senator Abraham Ribicoff of Connecticut, a prominent Jewish member, endorsed the sale after a January trip to Saudi Arabia, thereby providing protective cover for other liberals favoring the deal but anxious about severing their ties with Jewish supporters. Senator Byrd confirmed to the White House that he had the votes to beat a veto resolution on the Senate floor, should it pass the Foreign Relations Committee. A study prepared by two staffers for the Senate Foreign Relations Committee turned out to be remarkably balanced in presenting the arguments for and against the sale, while implying that the cultivation of Arab friendship was distinctly in America's national interest. (Nevertheless, it revealed that the F-15's could carry up to 18 bombs weighing 500 pounds and thus had a powerful "ground attack capability"—something the pro-Israeli members had been arguing and the Administration soft-pedalling. It also noted that the Administration "had given no thought to the physical security" of the super-secret planes it was going to give the Saudis.)[165] In still another windfall for the Administration, Stephen Bryen, the Senate staffer who had played a leading role in delaying and modifying the Hawks sale to King Hussein, had to be benched by the Senate Foreign Relations Committee while the Justice Department investigated charges by a Michael Saba, former President of the American Arab Association, that Bryen had offered secret documents to an official of the Israeli Defense Ministry while at a table next to Saba's in the dining room of Washington's prestigious Madison Hotel.

On April 28, Congress at last received formal notification of the offer of sale pursuant to Section 36(b) of the Arms Export Control Act.[166] Jody Powell, at the White House, claimed that the President had the votes to beat a veto resolution but reiterated that, if the Saudi sale were blocked, no jets would be sold to Israel, either.[167]

On May 2 the Fascell working group in the House produced its resolution of disapproval.[168] It was signed by an astonishing twenty-two of the thirty-seven members of the House International Relations Committee, and it objected to each of the three country sales. This show of unexpected strength was part bluff, since several signers were not committed to vote for it.[169] Nevertheless, Fascell's group at least signaled that the House would not be a pushover. Their object was not to force a vote but to compel the White House to negotiate.

In this they were successful. A form of compromise was ultimately proposed by the Administration that made the Middle East jet sale acceptable to a combat-fatigued Congress, although it did not go far enough to satisfy the working group. It actually originated with Henry Kissinger, who testified on May 8 before the Senate Foreign Relations Committee. In the course of defending the sale to the Saudis, he suggested committing an additional twenty F-15's to Israel to make a fairer balance. Israel would then have sixty of the planes, the same number as Saudi Arabia and ten more than originally proposed by the Joint Chiefs and Vance. Kissinger put on the table a variation on other proposals to raise the Israeli allotment, rather than cut the Saudi quota, which had at one time or another been floated privately by Byrd, Church, Javits, Howard Baker of Tennessee, Richard Stone of Florida, and Fascell in talks with Vance and Deputy Secretary Christopher. These meetings had explored various formulas, including increased sales to Israel and some modification of the equipment on the F-15's to be given the Saudis.

Later on the day of Kissinger's testimony, Christopher put forward the same idea at a private meeting with the House *ad hoc* group in Fascell's office. He thought he got a sympathetic response. In the evening, Carter convened a meeting in the cabinet room at which he played devil's advocate, resisting one concession after another as if he were the Saudi Government. The meeting ended in agreement: Secretary of Defense Harold Brown would outline the Administration's new proposals in a letter to Chairmen Sparkman and Zablocki.

The next morning at breakfast, Vance met with the Senatorial group and then went off to meet the House and Senate Committees, where he restated the proposed concessions and answered questions. In addition to the increased plane deliveries to Israel, the Administration offered to provide Congress with a series of assurances. Equipment for air-to-ground attacks would not be sold, nor gear necessary for aerial refueling. The Saudis would commit themselves to keep the planes out of Tabuq—a base within striking distance of Israel but which, in any case, was not equipped to handle them—and the rest of the northern region nearest Israel. They would promise not to transfer the planes to another country and not to add to their inventory of combat aircraft until after the last F-15's had been delivered in 1983.[170] Twenty more F-15's would be sold to Israel in 1979 for delivery by 1983–84. "Sympathetic consideration" would be given to a "request from Israel for additional combat aircraft for delivery in subsequent years."[171]

The concessions did not satisfy hard-line opponents, but when, on May 11, Senator Sparkman convened his committee, the veto resolution failed by a vote of 8 to 8. On the Senate floor, it went down to final defeat by a vote of 54 to 44.[172]

Congress had once again participated actively in a key foreign policy decision. Despite the heat engendered by an intensely adversary system, the effect had been beneficial. The country had seen the issues clarified, the terms of the sale improved, and the transaction legitimized by Congressional codetermination. The executive and legislative branches had each consciously tried to learn from earlier mistakes. The President had given Congress far longer notice than the law required in an effort to permit careful consideration. After a psychological false start with the "package," the White House had gone out of its way to retreat from any appearance of non-cooperation. Modifications had been made to appease Congress, while legislators had endeavored to avoid the sort of public discourse that damages relations with the very states whose friendship is being sought.

Senator Stevenson, alone, in the debate on the veto resolution, criticized his fellow legislators for attempting to take over the day-to-day running of foreign policy. "Our founders," he reminded Senators, "reposed responsibility for the conduct of foreign policy in the President. They recognized that the day-to-day protection of U.S. interests in the world required constant attention, a discernible purpose and a deft hand for nuance and foreign sensibilities, as well as a capacity for secret." Congress could provide none of these, he argued. Members were punishing Turkey for invading Cyprus while rewarding the Israelis who had invaded Lebanon. "Traumatized by Vietnam, the Congress had cut off funds for the victims of Soviet-Cuban aggression in Angola, inviting an ancient Russian imperialism elsewhere." Congress, he charged, "has reacted not to history but to the aberrations of history, with such 'reforms' as this. . . ."[173]

Stevenson's speech reflected views not infrequently heard at the White House, even in the Carter Administration. In the summer of 1977, Carter, in signing the foreign aid bill, had expressed "deep reservations" over the constitutionality of the provisions that permit Congress to veto Presidential arms decisions.[174] However, in this latest round, by and large, the White House had resisted the temptation to challenge the new rules of the game; instead, it concentrated on learning to win by playing more effectively by those very rules.

Robert A. Flaten, a key participant in the State Department's campaign to secure Congressional support for the sale, drew the most significant conclusion. The Nelson-Bingham procedures, he said, "are an important and useful addition to the politics of policy-making in Washington. If Congress hadn't forced it on us, we'd have had to invent it. Now, when we send a signal to the Saudis or to Jerusalem, it carries all the voltage of Congress, as well as of the Presidency. The Middle East knows this decision was made by the entire American government, not just by the President."[175]

NUCLEAR EXPORT CONTROLS

Just as the Administration, in the area of arms export policy, has learned to live with—if not inordinately to love—an activist Congress, so Congressional involvement in nuclear power export has been accepted by the Executive, and has—on balance—begun to engender benefits.

The 1974–78 nuclear export debate between Congress and the Administration centered on the policies, rules, and decision-making power that should govern the sale to other countries of U.S. nuclear power plants, nuclear processing technology, and nuclear fuel. The importance of this issue is indicated by the fact that U.S. industry still produces approximately 50 percent of world nuclear technology exports and has a virtual monopoly on the export of enriched uranium fuel. By 1978, fully 42 nations were operating 206 U.S. commercial reactors, with 100 more on order.[176]

Congressional activists shared the view that U.S. nuclear exports were essentially haphazard, governed only by bilateral undertakings of varying strictness and lacking enforcement. They feared that the insufficiently safeguarded technology and fuel could too readily be diverted into nuclear weaponry, a fear underscored by India's diversion of fuel and technology supplied by Canada for peaceful purposes, to produce an atomic bomb.

Opposed to these elements was the U.S. nuclear industry—Westinghouse, Babcock and Wilcox—and its not inconsiderable Congressional support, which argued that stricter safeguards were neither necessary nor effective but would merely drive customers to purchase comparable technology from producers less inclined to meddle. These concerns were shared by the Presidency, which also feared further Congressional intrusions into a field hitherto reserved for flexible case-by-case diplomacy.

The Congressional forces favoring strict regulation clustered around Representatives Jonathan Bingham, Clement Zablocki, and Morris Udall of Arizona, and Senators John Glenn of Ohio, Charles Percy of Illinois, and Abraham Ribicoff. Their first goal was the dismantling of the Congressional guardian of the *status quo*, the Joint Committee on Atomic Energy. In the House, reformers initiated a move after the 1976 elections to strip the Joint Committee of its legislative power.[177] They wanted nuclear export bills transferred to Bingham's Economic Policy Subcommittee of the International Relations Committee. As a member of the

Democratic Steering and Policy Committee, Bingham was in a good position to dispense freshman committee assignments, a valuable item of patronage. On December 8, using this leverage to gather commitments, the reformers handily won in the Democratic caucus by 133 to 97. Thirty-eight votes for reform came from freshmen.[178] The caucus decision was ratified by the full House on January 4.[179] Next, the Senate, in a general reorganization of committees, voted to stop appointing members to the Joint Committee. With that, the Nuclear Committee passed into history.

With the decks now cleared, both the Administration[180] and the reformers[181] introduced draft non-proliferation bills. What emerged was a tough new law regulating nuclear exports and requiring the renegotiation of existing nuclear supply commitments. The first step toward obtaining a nuclear export license is a determination by the Secretary of State that a proposed export of "any production or utilization facility, or any source material or special nuclear material . . . will not be inimical to the common defense and security. . . ."[182] He must act in consultation with the Departments of Energy, Defense, Commerce, and the Arms Control and Disarmament Agency. After that, the Nuclear Regulatory Commission must make its own finding, based—in the case of purchases by states not already making nuclear weapons—on the willingness of an importer to apply International Atomic Energy Agency safeguards against diversion of imports to weapons-production purposes. The Commission must be satisfied that the nuclear export will not be used to make nuclear explosives and provides adequate physical security for the nuclear plant, fuel, and waste.[183]

Whenever the NRC, applying the criteria of the Act, decides not to issue an export license, the President may overrule it if, in his opinion, "withholding the proposed export would be seriously prejudicial to the achievement of the United States non-proliferation objectives, or would otherwise jeopardize the common defense and security. . . ."[184] However, this waiver does not take effect if, within sixty days, it is vetoed by concurrent resolution of Congress.[185]

The law requires all non-nuclear weapons states that import nuclear technology or fuel from the U.S. to accept IAEA inspection of all their nuclear facilities, whether U.S. supplied or not, within eighteen months after the law's coming into force.[186] This requirement, too, may be waived by the President on a case-by-case basis, but such waiver is again subject to Congressional veto within sixty days.[187] Congressional vetoes also apply in several other instances.[188] The law establishes minimal terms for the new safeguard agreements that must be negotiated with importers and makes them, also, subject to Congressional veto.[189]

The Administration objected strongly to the President's discretion being shared with the Congress in this fashion. It also disagreed with the rigorous standards and criteria imposed by the law.[190] For a time there was an effort, focused on the Rules Committee, to prevent the legislation going to the House floor for a final vote and President Carter had to intervene, in September, to overrule those agencies within the Executive which were gearing up to try to defeat the bill on the floor.[191] It passed the House on September 28. A slightly different version was approved by the Senate, in which the House concurred.[192]

At the March 10, 1978, signing ceremony, President Carter called the new law "a major step forward in clarifying our Nation's policy,"[193] but criticized "the numerous provisions in this act which state that Congress may invalidate or approve executive branch action by concurrent resolution. . . ."

The new policy of codetermination was soon put to the test. On April 20, 1978, the Nuclear Regulatory Commission, by a vote of 2 to 2—the fifth seat was vacant—refused to recommend a license for the export of low enriched uranium fuel for Tarapur Atomic Power Station in India. Two commissioners felt that India had failed to meet at least three of the statutory criteria. President Carter overruled that finding on April 27.[194] His message to Congress conceded that India had not accepted the prescribed standard of safeguards, but reported that the Indian Government had promised not to use the enriched uranium for other than peaceful purposes. Carter argued that refusal now would prejudice ongoing efforts to persuade India to accept "full-scope safeguards."[195]

On May 1, Representatives Richard Ottinger of New York and Clarence Long co-sponsored a concurrent veto resolution. It was considered by the House Committee on International Relations, which conducted extensive consultations with the executive branch and the NRC,[196] and held public hearings. On June 14, the Committee overwhelmingly adopted a motion proposed by Representative Bingham, that rejected the veto resolution.[197]

Premier Morarji Desai showed his understanding of the new rules of Congressional codetermination in highly effective appearances before House and Senate Committees, where he candidly discussed the issues. Equally refreshing was the decision of the Administration not to challenge Congress's right to use its veto in carrying out its new oversight responsibilities. Testifying before the Senate Foreign Relations Committee, a Presidential spokesman characterized the new procedure of Congressional review as "wise."[198] Instead of battling the right of Congress to participate, the White House focused on helping the legislators understand the issues, obtain information on current negotiations, and thus enabled them to come to the right decision. At last it had been understood that it is better, in practice, to discuss the merits of a serious national issue with Congress than to meander into a debate on Constitutional theology in pointless defense of dubious Presidential prerogatives.

The involvement of Congress—whatever its inconvenience to those who prefer to exercise anonymous, unfettered power from somewhere in the precincts of the White House—has actually become a substantial boon to the U.S. negotiators in their talks with India. Although the Senate Committee, like its House counterpart, decided to permit the 1978 shipment,[199] it sent a clear, tough signal.[200] "The executive branch and the Indian government," it wrote President Carter, "should base their discussions on the anticipation that, if full-scope safeguards are not achieved" by the end of eighteen months, "it is highly unlikely that a waiver allowing continued exports would be acceptable."[201]

Similarly, the legislation sent a hard-nosed message to western Europe. The U.S. nuclear cooperation agreement with the European Community has twenty more years to run, but the new Act requires its renegotiation within eighteen months in order to implement new safeguards. Critics of Congress prophesied that the law would provoke and alienate these allies—which, to some extent, it did.[202] Nevertheless, on July 10, the European Community announced that it was ready to talk about standards of security for its U.S.-supplied uranium. Since U.S. imports account for half the Community's total fuel needs and 95 percent of its research-grade ore,[203] the Europeans, too, chose to address the legitimate global security concerns raised by Congress,[204] rather than stand on legalism.

5

CONGRESS TAMES
THE INTELLIGENCE COMMUNITY

THE BACKGROUND OF
CONGRESSIONAL ABDICATION

By far the most widely publicized and controversial of the new Congressional initiatives to establish procedures of control over Executive discretion has occurred in the field of U.S. intelligence activities. Revelations of significant abuses by the Central Intelligence Agency, the FBI, the Internal Revenue Service, and the intelligence community of the Department of Defense led Congress, in the post-Watergate era, to reexamine its control of intelligence activities.

Prior to these most recent developments, most members of Congress knew virtually nothing about U.S. intelligence operations, nor did they wish to know. The conventional wisdom was that intelligence activities involved necessary but unappetizing ventures which members could neither expect to understand, much less control. It was, therefore, best not to know what could not be altered.

After the National Security Act, passed in 1947, established the CIA, an informal arrangement developed that left its funding and oversight to a few members of the Appropriations and Armed Services Committees. The foreign relations committees, despite the obvious foreign policy implications of CIA operations, were not allowed to participate.

Jurisdictional "turf wars" over the CIA were less a problem, in this period, than Congressional insouciance.[1] It was less a matter of eager committees competing for control than of the members' virtually universal reluctance to get their hands dirty. That reluctance was reinforced by the lack of political payoff for work that had to be done out of the public limelight. In the words of one observer, it "takes a U-2 incident or a Bay of Pigs to interest Congress in intelligence."[2]

That most traditional instrument of oversight, the power of the purse, was largely unused. The Central Intelligence Agency Act of 1949[3] excuses the Agency from seeking regular appropriations, and uniquely endows it with the right to receive monies of unstated amounts by way of secret transfer from the appropriations of other agencies.[4] These transfers are left to the discretion of the Office of Management and Budget acting in accordance with instructions of the chairmen of House and Senate Appropriations Committees: a cozy arrangement that made it unnecessary for the CIA to defend, or even present, a budget to Congress. Congress— with the exception of a handful of members—therefore had no basis whatever for reviewing the policy, or judging the performance, of the Agency.

There was reason to conclude, in these circumstances, that the most successful covert operation of the CIA was getting its funding from Congress. The President's annual budget document, which contains a detailed analysis of itemized expenditures, rivals in size the largest metropolitan telephone directory.[5] Yet, nowhere in this maze of data does one find a mention of the Central Intelligence Agency or, for that matter, of its brethren: the National Security Agency, the Defense Intelligence Agency, or the intelligence agencies of the armed services. Instead, proposed spending for intelligence purposes is hidden among the budget requests for other agencies' programs.

The CIA, while thus largely unsupervised, at least operated under laws enacted by Congress.[6] The rest of the intelligence community was spared even this modicum of control. The Defense Intelligence Agency was established in 1961, on the authority of the Secretary of Defense, and the key National Security Agency was the creation of a Presidential directive in 1952. That directive, which describes NSA's authority and responsibility, remains highly classified.[7]

According to a Congressional staffer's study,

> It is obviously impossible for the Congress to determine if DIA has succeeded in coordinating Defense intelligence programs if the scope and magnitude of these programs are unknown. It is equally impossible for the Congress to debate the cost-effectiveness of NSA's COMSEC (communications security) and SIGINT (signals intelligence) operations if the Agency's organization and even the number of employees are a closely guarded secret.[8]

Yet Congress has specified that it will not require "the disclosure of the organization or any function of the National Security Agency, of any information with respect to the activities thereof, or of the names, titles, salaries or numbers of the persons employed by such agency."[9]

The Vietnam War began to reveal the costs of such benevolent neglect. Congress discovered that the CIA had acquired the capacity for running its own military operations even in countries such as Laos, with which the United States was ostensibly at peace. Earlier, a trickle of information about the Bay of Pigs paramilitary operations, financed and directed by the CIA in Cuba, had hinted at this capability. However, it was not until the publication of the Final Report of the Senate's Church Committee, the first Congressional investigation of U.S. intelligence activities, that the broad powers asserted by the Agencies abroad—and, even more alarming, at home—became fully known.[10]

REFORMING INTELLIGENCE OVERSIGHT

As noted in Chapter 2, the revelation of an unauthorized, clandestine CIA war in Laos caused Congress to pass the Hughes-Ryan bill, in 1974, which became Section 622 of the Foreign Assistance Act.[11] In a revolutionary shift from its prior policy of *laissez-faire*, Congress now prohibited the use of any funds by the CIA for operations in foreign countries except for intelligence-gathering activities, "unless and until the President finds that each such operation is important to the national security of the United States and reports, in a timely fashion, a description and scope of such operation to the appropriate committees of the Congress. . . ."[12] The President may waive the reporting requirement only "during military operations initiated by the United States under a declaration of war approved by the Congress or an exercise of powers by the President under the War Powers Resolution."[13]

The Hughes-Ryan Amendment imposed the first real Congressional control over covert activities. Yet, it was considerably less stringent than a version passed by the Senate, which would have required the President to report all covert activities to the relevant Congressional committees *prior* to their commencement. Prior notification was modified, at the insistence of the House, to a vaguer obligation of "timely reporting."[14]

In adopting Hughes-Ryan, the Senate also rejected, by a vote of 17 to 68, a far more radical amendment proposed by Senator Abourezk that would have prohibited any agency of the Government engaging in "any activity within any foreign country which violates, or is intended to encourage the violation of, the laws of the United States or of such country."[15] The effect of that would have been to terminate all covert and clandestine activities of every intelligence agency.

Under the Hughes-Ryan formula, six committees and subcommittees had to be given "timely" information on covert activities: in the Senate, the Armed Services Central Intelligence Subcommittee, the Appropriations Intelligence Operations Subcommittee, and the Foreign Relations Committee; in the House, the Armed Services Special Intelligence Subcommittee, the Appropriations Defense Subcommittee, and the International Relations Committee.

Although this was a radical break with the past, it was not enough. When the Church Committee reported its findings at the end of April 1976 it found that "Congress had failed to provide the necessary statutory guidelines to ensure that intelligence agencies carry out their missions in accord with constitutional processes. Mechanisms for, and the practice of, congressional oversight have not been adequate." It also condemned "Congress' failure as a whole to monitor the intelligence agencies' expenditures" and found that this failure "has been a major element in the ineffective legislative oversight of the intelligence community."[16]

Questions about the adequacy of the Hughes-Ryan procedures were raised in connection with the CIA's covert war in Angola. Members who had been "deep-briefed" felt themselves constrained by their commitment to those briefing them, and tended to keep silent about an escalation the wisdom of which they increasingly came to doubt.

Even earlier, on December 22, 1974, the *New York Times* had exposed a large, illegal CIA domestic intelligence operation against the anti-war movement and other dissidents, including break-ins, wiretapping, and surreptitious mail opening. The Executive responded by appointing an eight-member Presidential Commission headed by Vice-President Rockefeller, while the Senate and House each voted to create their own investigations into the entire intelligence network, including the FBI.[17] Senator Church headed the Senate Select Committee and Michigan Democratic Representative Lucien N. Nedzi that of the House.

The Church Committee was organized into four task forces dealing, respectively, with the FBI; the Pentagon; the CIA; and with the White House, National Security Council, and Department of State. Each Senator appointed to the Select Committee was allowed to designate one staffer to the Committee and these were then allocated among the four task forces. In practice, the staff was divided between a group headed by F. A. O. Schwarz, Jr., which dealt mainly with domestic abuses, and another concerned primarily with foreign operations, under the direction of William Miller. The Schwarz group, however, also looked into CIA assassination of foreign leaders and, because of its tough lawyers' tactics, were nicknamed the "investigators" while Miller's staff were called the "scholars."

While the Senate's committee got off to a fairly fast start, its House equivalent stumbled. Its chairman, Representative Nedzi, came under concerted fire from the left because he had previously been briefed by the CIA on the very matters now to be examined. Three-and-a-half months into the investigation he quit, to be replaced by New York Democrat Otis Pike. The right wing got its revenge by nailing another member of the committee, Representative Michael Harrington of Massachusetts, for allegedly using his access to leak "secrets" to the media. He was widely believed to be the press's source of classified information on the CIA's role in the overthrow of Chile's Marxist President Salvador Allende.

By the time the House committee got itself reorganized,[18] the Church Committee had already cornered most of the more newsworthy issues and Chairman Pike seemed determined to overcome this handicap through sheer stridency. Much of this was directed by the members and staff at each other.

From the beginning, the Pike Committee was under attack from its own members for "horrible staff work." In the words of one veteran of the Committee, this was partly because Pike's staff "were a Watergate-seasoned crowd who had learned too much about confrontational tactics. They were all young, wildly inexperienced, with no feel for politics."[19] For one thing, they established highly inadequate security procedures. Members also complained that, while Pike was open enough to suggestions on topics for investigation, he was not a bit interested in sharing operational control or taking advice on tactics.

Talking about the lack of collegiality developed under Pike, one legislator reported that committee members, running into colleagues on the floor, would be reduced to asking each other "What's happening?" And, he added, no one would know. There was virtually no consultation and few meetings. Several members complained that they had had no input into the writing of committee reports which were being prepared entirely by the staff. As a result, they were unwilling to fight for the product when it came under attack.

Most damaging, however, was the uncontrolled leaking from some members and staff which soon antagonized the rest and sealed the controversial decision of the full House to suppress the committee's final report. On January 29, 1976, the House, by a ratio of 2 to 1, voted to halt its publication. In the words of Democratic Representative Samuel Stratton of New York, "there has been from these investigations a steady hemorrhaging of our intelligence secrets and our intelligence procedures. That hemorrhaging has certainly damaged the reputation of Congress, and . . . it has also damaged the ability of our intelligence operations to function. This, I believe, was why the House voted [to halt publication] . . ."[20]

To some extent, the ill-fated Pike Committee was also a victim of bad timing. Its activities never caught up with those of the Senate Committee. Chairman Pike's explosive confrontation with Secretary Kissinger over access to the Boyatt memorandum, for example, came too late to take advantage of the Executive's Watergate-induced weakness. As Representative Aspin has correctly pointed out, "Timing is everything." In this instance, Pike had demanded to see a memo in which Thomas B. Boyatt, a middle-echelon State Department career officer, had expressed disagreement with Kissinger's 1974 Cyprus policies. The Secretary had refused to produce it, instead accusing Pike of trying to destroy the confidentiality essential to all frank exchanges with a government department. The chairman replied with a threat to cite the Secretary for contempt.

But, says Aspin, the tide was already running against the investigation.

What had turned it was the attempt on President Ford's life and the assassination of Agent Welch, the CIA man in Athens, by a leftist. Welch had been killed just after leaks from the Pike Committee had enabled various little publications to publish lists of CIA agents overseas. His funeral, in December, was carefully staged to make the point that something must be done to curb those nuts who are trying to destroy the CIA. They used the Welch thing to the hilt. The air transport plane carrying his body circled Andrews Air Force Base for three quarters of an hour in order to land live on the Today Show.[21]

The Pike Committee fiasco, Aspin concluded, teaches three lessons.

Hire people who are more experienced and have a better balance between energy and wisdom; develop techniques for collegial decision making among the members, particularly as regards investigatory tactics; and don't try to develop oversight through a temporary select committee. The temporary select committee was the wrong tool for that sort of investigation. It had a fixed termination point and no budgetary control over the agency it's investigating. So those being investigated knew they didn't have to be responsive, that if they just kept stonewalling, the mandate of the committee would run out.[22]

The Senate's Select Committee, however, did not seem to suffer from such terminal malady. On balance, it seemed to operate quite effectively in an area where the national security interest inevitably collides with democratic process and values. Those who served on the committee, both staffers and Senators, report the experience as one of effective collegiality, especially for a committee formed at short notice, for a brief term and with a limited purpose. There were tensions between the "investigators" and the "scholars" as well as between two members of similar persuasion but conflicting Presidential ambitions: Church and Mondale. But the committee produced revelations and recommendations that were responsible and constructive, while proving that the Senate, if it had the will, could conduct effective intelligence oversight.

In only two instances did committee members violate the ban on publicity by leaking the work of the committee while an investigation was on. The first breach was committed by Mondale when, in a speech at a small university, he inadvertently let slip that the U.S. intelligence community had been engaging in a deliberate program of assassination of foreign leaders. The next day, Mondale began the committee session by making an immediate and intense apology. Nevertheless, members were moved to express their anger at Mondale in terms one participant described as "extreme."

The second breach was by Chairman Church, in a speech graphically characterizing the CIA as a "rogue elephant." Again committee members were irritated and Church had to apologize. Otherwise, according to a participant, "everyone was very responsible" notably including Senator Gary Hart of Colorado, who was generally believed to be the most anti-Agency of the members. Hart led the attack on Church's "rogue elephant" remarks and took a particularly hard line against leaks. He also voted with Senator Goldwater to have closed executive sessions on the "shamrock" operation—a secret program in which the three U.S. global telegraph companies[23] cooperated with the CIA to monitor private messages.

One of the reasons why the Church Committee worked as well as it did was probably because, although its groups met frequently, Senators were rarely directly involved in the actual gathering of information, except at hearings. Even then, staff prepared the hearing books, briefed the Senators, and suggested the lines that interrogation should take. Virtually all investigation was carried out by staff working with the middle-echelon bureaucracy. This had the advantage of keeping most disputes over access to data, security, and release of information at a relatively low level. Senator Church, CIA Director William Colby, or Secretary of State Kissinger would be drawn in only on the rare occasions when a dispute could not be resolved at the middle level, or by the committee's General Counsel and Staff Director. In this way, relations between the Senators and the top Executive officials did not become poisoned. By contrast, on the House side, Chairman Pike personally involved himself in all significant negotiations over access, thereby rapidly generating an intense mutual antipathy between himself and Ford, Kissinger, and Colby.

Between them, the Senate and House committees managed to compile an impressive list of transgressions and folly on the part of the intelligence community. That list includes evidence that the CIA illegally monitored and intercepted mail of U.S. citizens, including members of

Congress.[24] Among those watched were Senators Kennedy, Humphrey, and, most embarrassing, Church, together with approximately 1,300 other individuals. The committees also examined the role of the CIA in plots to assassinate various foreign leaders—Premier Fidel Castro of Cuba, President Rafael Trujillo of the Dominican Republic, General Rene Schneider of Chile, Prime Minister Patrice Lumumba of Zaire, and President Ngo Dinh Diem of Vietnam.[25] Congressional investigators uncovered a substantial U.S. role in the "destabilization" of Chile up to 1973[26] and brought to light the activities of the National Security Agency in scanning the telegraph and telephone traffic of U.S. citizens, without judicial supervision.[27]

The investigators also scrutinized the quality of intelligence being generated by the community,[28] the allocation of intelligence gathering and evaluating functions, and the command structure within which policy control is theoretically exerted over the agencies.[29]

The Senate Select Committee published a detailed blueprint for reform. It featured a proposal for a "permanent intelligence oversight committee of Congress" charged "to provide firm direction for the intelligence agencies" and to draft "new statutory charters" for them "that take account of the experience of the past three and one-half decades."[30]

In response, Senator Church and seven colleagues introduced a bill to establish a Standing Committee of the Senate on Intelligence Activities.[31] In amended form, this became Senate Resolution 400: another major victory in the Congressional revolution and the source of more new oversight rules to ensure Congressional participation in the foreign relations process.

Having once decided that they wanted a say in intelligence operations, the Senators had to resolve four important operational questions: (1) What should be the composition, jurisdiction, and tenure of the oversight committee? (2) Should the committee demand prior notification of all intelligence operations, or merely "timely" (i.e., *post hoc*) notification? (3) If they were to opt for prior notification, should the committee, or even the Senate as a whole, have a veto over proposed operations? (4) How should the committee provide the security needed to protect intelligence secrets?

The Church bill provided for the establishment of a regular standing committee with a membership of nine, five to be appointed by the majority leader of the Senate and four by the minority leader. It limited service of each member to six years, in order to minimize the danger, apparent in the activities of committees exercising jurisdiction over the armed services and defense, that prolonged involvement in oversight breeds cooption of the overseers by the overseen. As ultimately established by S.Res. 400, the oversight function was assigned to a Select

Committee composed of fifteen members, eight from the majority and seven from the minority, with two members each from the Committees on Appropriations, Armed Services, Foreign Relations, Judiciary, and seven appointed from the Senate at large. Service on the committee was ultimately limited to "eight years of continuous service."[32]

The new committee was given exclusive legislative jurisdiction in respect of the CIA and the Director of Central Intelligence, while the Appropriations Committee's Intelligence Subcommittee was allowed to retain the appropriations power. Legislative jurisdiction over other intelligence agencies and components of the intelligence community, such as the Defense Intelligence Agency and FBI, is shared "sequentially" by the new committee with the Armed Services and Judiciary Committees. The new committee was given broad oversight jurisdiction, shared, in the case of the CIA, with the Foreign Relations Committee.

According to a senior staff member of the Church Committee, this is a second-best answer to the problems it had identified. "The ideal solution would have been to assign all intelligence oversight and legislative responsibility to the Senate Foreign Relations Committee. Control of overseas intelligence operations belongs in the broader context of U.S. foreign policy supervision."

Desirable as this would have been, it proved unfeasible because neither the Armed Services Committee nor the Appropriations Committee's intelligence subcommittee was willing to surrender its jurisdiction to another existing, rival committee—"however scandalously little they had exercised it in the past."[33] Therefore it became necessary to create an entirely new committee on which Armed Services, Appropriations, and Foreign Relations committees could all be represented equally and also to leave bits and pieces of important jurisdiction with the older committees.

Even more difficult and important was the question of how much control Congress should exercise over sensitive operations. The Church bill spelled out *prior* notification of "any significant covert or clandestine operation in foreign countries" except for operations intended "solely for collecting necessary intelligence."[34] According to staff members, a deliberate distinction was made between notification and clearance. "No Senator wanted the new committee to be required to give prior *approval*."[35]

In practice, this is approximately where things have ended up, although that is not so apparent on the face of the legislation. After vociferous objections from such key conservatives as Senators Howard Cannon of Nevada, Harry Byrd of Virginia, Stennis, and John Tower of Texas, the strong and specific prior notification requirement in the Church bill gave way in intense bargaining to a Mansfield-sponsored compromise which states "the sense of the Senate that the head of each department and agency of the United States should keep the select committee fully and currently informed with respect to intelligence activities, including any significant anticipated activities. . . ."[36] The "fully and currently" test does not appear tantamount to a prior consultation requirement. However, a section-by-section analysis of the compromise, which is an important part of the resolution's legislative history, specifies that the "requirement extends to briefing the committee in advance of any significant anticipated activities. . . ."[37] Senator Baker, the senior Republican negotiating the compromise, added, "the intent . . . is to require prior consultation between the Committee and the intelligence community. . . ."[38]

S.Res. 400, as well as the Baker statement and the legislative history, also make it clear that the committee is not given a veto over Executive decisions to institute covert or clandestine intelligence activities. But it must be informed before an operation is launched. In the words of Senator Mansfield, hereafter the committee "should be in on the takeoff . . . so that if, despite the judgment of the Senate committee . . . an operation . . . went ahead, it would at least have made its position clear. . . ."[39] Senator Church added that notification, together with Congress's power of the purse, would effectively discourage any activities of which the oversight committee disapproved.[40]

In addition to its power of the purse, the Senate armed itself with the ultimate weapon of disclosure.[41] Section 8 of S.Res. 400 provides that the committee may vote to disclose any information in its possession. If it votes to do so, and the information is classified, it must first notify the President, giving him five days in which to object in writing. If he does, the committee may take the matter to the full Senate, meeting in secret session, for final determination.[42]

To protect secret information, S.Res. 400 provides that "no member of the select committee shall disclose any information, the disclosure of which requires a committee vote, prior to a vote by the committee on the question of the disclosure of such information or after such vote except in accordance with" the provisions for disclosure set out in S.Res. 400.[43] Unfortunately, there is no provision for enforcing this injunction beyond the normal power of the Senate to censure, expel, or try at its bar. Moreover, the Constitution probably precludes imposing criminal penalties on a member of Congress who discloses classified information in Congress itself.[44]

What of unauthorized disclosures by staff? The question was briefly considered during senatorial hearings on the Resolution. In an exchange with Senator Percy, Senator Church indicated that the sole recourse would be "immediate dismissal," adding, "We were not in a position to pass a criminal law."[45] S.Res. 400 does provide that committee staff will receive security clearance "as determined by such committee in consultation with the Director of Central Intelligence."[46] Staff are also required to sign a contractual agreement that they will not disclose classified information.

THE NEW OVERSIGHT IN PRACTICE

Given the complexity of the global issues and the institutional practices of the agencies being overseen, the new Senate Select Committee has found it difficult to recruit a staff of the level of expertise necessary to these tasks. Senator Daniel Inouye of Hawaii, the first chairman, was under pressure to proceed rapidly, particularly with the writing of new legislative charters for the intelligence community. Accordingly, he had little choice but to select his staff primarily from among persons already working for the Church Committee. "They were already cleared," he said. "It would have taken at least six months to get a new team access to top secret information." But the more aggressive "investigators" had gone back to their law firms, so Inouye inherited primarily the "scholars," many of whom, it turned out, had previously worked with the intelligence agencies.[47]

Senator Inouye has reported that he had particular difficulty finding staff able to oversee the intricate intelligence budget, asserting that there were perhaps fifty people in the entire country who understood the subject sufficiently to be able to do effective analysis. It was also difficult to recruit experienced intelligence evaluators. "On the other hand," the Senator has observed, "if you hire people without prior experience, they are going to be too dependent on the information and analysis that the agencies are only too willing to provide."[48]

Nevertheless, the committee has managed to improve the quality of senatorial oversight. It functions through four subcommittees which are concerned with writing agency charters, protection of civil rights, budget, and the quality of intelligence and operations. Review of covert operations is conducted by the committee as a whole.

To implement S.Res. 400, the CIA agreed to give the committee forty-eight hours notice before commencing a covert operation, after the proposed operation has received the approval of the President.[49] This, Inouye found, provides "a reasonable time to confer."[50]

While the committee does not approve operations, in Inouye's words, it "certainly does have a *disapproval* function."[51] After the committee is notified of a proposed action, "if there is any controversy, the Director of Central Intelligence (DCI) is invited to state the case for the proposed operation and respond to members' questions. It is up to him to convince us." According to Inouye, "in some instances we talked for six hours before being convinced that the risks were small enough and pay-off sufficiently great. Even then, there were still one or two who remained skeptical, but when the committee voted, they went along."[52]

If a majority were to decide against a proposed covert action, the chairman would communicate this decision to the DCI. If the director were to persist, the committee chairman could ask the President to intervene. Should he refuse, the committee could call the Senate into executive (closed) session. The Senate could then pass a secret resolution opposing the proposed operation. If that failed to get results, the operation could be debated in open session. "That," Senator Inouye commented, "would make it a public covert operation."[53]

An elaborate system of communications and security applies to the committee. The chairman can be reached by the DCI at all times. In the United States, he is invariably provided with access to a "secure telephone" and, when abroad, uses the military communications network. All other members of the committee must likewise be within reach of urgent conference calls. So far this system has worked smoothly, belying the common assumption that members of Congress cannot be part of a policy-making process that requires rapid decisions.

In the House of Representatives, the establishment of an oversight committee proved more difficult after the trauma of the Pike Committee. On January 29, 1976, Pike's suppressed report was given to the *Village Voice* by TV newsman Daniel Schorr who had obtained it in violation of the House vote. The Representatives then charged the Committee on Standards of Official Conduct to investigate,[54] thereby generating still more heat but little light.[55] In all this, the Pike Report's relatively modest recommendations were all but forgotten.

One recommendation was to establish "a standing Committee on Intelligence of the House of Representatives"[56] rather similar to the one established by the Senate. However, a bill to this effect introduced by Representative Pike on June 4, 1976, became mired in the Schorr controversy.[57] Reintroduced by Pike the next spring,[58] it still failed to win support.

Not until July 13, 1977, did the House Rules Committee give its imprimatur. But no sooner had it recommended setting up a permanent select committee than the House was plunged into bitter debate over its composition and powers. Among the reasons was the Democrats' decision to allot 9 of the 13 places to themselves instead of using the more generous 8 and 7 formula of the Senate.[59] The final vote, in the summer of 1977, divided the members along strict party lines.[60]

The House Select Committee differs in several other respects from its

Senate counterpart,[61] although its basic jurisdiction is very similar. Members are limited to six-year terms[62] while the Senate term is eight. The agencies are required to provide "informed and timely" intelligence reporting as against the Senate's requirement that its committee be kept "fully and currently" informed.[63]

In conformity with the Administration's wishes, the House empowered the Select Committee to make regulations governing and restricting access to its files by "any other committee or any other Members of the House"[64]—an innovation, because in the House, unlike the Senate, every member ordinarily has access to all records except those of the Ethics Committee. Procedures to deal with unauthorized disclosure are established, consisting of an investigation by the Committee on Standards of Official Conduct which may recommend to the House "action such as censure, removal from committee membership, or expulsion from the House, in the case of a Member, or removal from office or employment or punishment for contempt, in the case of an officer or employee."[65] Four subcommittees are established, on oversight, evaluation of performance, legislation, and budget.[66]

Because the House was still haunted by the memory of the Pike Committee, the Select Committee on Intelligence was given a distinctly conservative membership, including its first chairman, Democrat Edward P. Boland of Massachusetts. The two exceptions are Democrats Norman Mineta of California and Les Aspin. Even more than its Senate counterpart, the House committee has been staffed by persons recruited from the intelligence community, some of whom continue to have close personal ties to the Agencies.

According to a staffer, members have been convinced by constituent mail and home-town newspaper editorials that anti-intelligence feelings of 1974–76 have now abated, that opinion has swung to favor a stronger intelligence capability in the face of growing international danger. "Most Americans think we've picked on the CIA too long and too much. They want us to lay off," he reports.

Committee Chairman Boland has arranged to be briefed on all covert operations 24 to 48 hours before they begin. While the committee has given its chairman discretion as to whether the DCI reports to the whole membership, a subcommittee, or even the chairman alone, ordinarily it is the full committee that is briefed.

In his briefings, the DCI, Admiral Stansfield Turner, has been very candid, according to a participant, deleting only the names of individuals connected with an operation. As in the case of the Senate, the House committee may express its opposition to a pending operation by secret resolution, or in person to the President. During its first year, no votes were taken on covert operations. According to an observer, "although questions asked in connection with an operation have indicated some reservations on the part of a few members, none has so far taken that concern beyond asking sharp questions."

If strong opposition to an operation were to arise, and it were communicated to the DCI or the President, a staffer explained, "we assume the proposed operation would be stopped or at least modified to meet our concern." If the DCI or President did not reconsider in the light of active Committee opposition, "we would call for a closed session of the House, at which a resolution of prohibition would be discussed. But by then, of course, the whole thing would be in the press."

Besides keeping an eye on covert operations, the House and Senate committees have undertaken the task of writing comprehensive legislative charters that would establish standards of performance and bring the entire intelligence community under legal controls. In this, the Executive has been faster off the mark than Congress. President Carter's Executive Order 12036 of January 26, 1978, makes an effort to prohibit, or at least supervise more rigorously, some of the dubious activities identified by the Church and Pike Committees. That order, promulgated by the President after consultation with the committees, also tries to reduce security over-classification, cuts back the number of agencies and officials with authority to classify, terminates the classification of most documents after six years, and establishes a classification monitoring system run by the General Services Administration. Restrictions are put on intelligence surveillance of U.S. persons or domestic groups.

However, Presidential orders are not law, and can be revoked or amended at the chief executive's discretion.[67] Thus work on the legislative charters has continued. The Senate Select Committee's draft was published[68] early in 1978 to be greeted by fire from both right and left.[69] It proposes to make illegal such activities as the overthrow of democratically elected governments, payments to journalists or clergy, and covert support for books and journals. The National Security Agency (NSA) is brought under law for the first time.

The White House and DCI worked with the Senate subcommittee to prepare this draft,[70] but the House Select Committee was kept at arm's length. "They sent us copies of the bill at the eleventh hour," a House staffer said, "about the time they sent it to law professors for comment. We didn't contribute a thing," he said, "so we'll be taking a long, hard look. In all probability, our committee won't buy it. We'll want to write our own."

In fact, however, by the end of 1978 the House committee had produced nothing. Members of both House and Senate were beginning to express concern that "the moment for action has slipped by." The only legislative harvest so far has been a law to control electronic counter-espionage surveillance by requiring a judicial warrant in most instances.[71] Even this modest reform, however, was initiated by Judiciary, not Intelligence, Committees.

A useful outcome of the mid-1970's tumult has been the institution of new budget control procedures. While the Select Committee shares with the Armed Services Committee jurisdiction over Defense Intelligence and National Security Agency budgets, it has exclusive jurisdiction over that of the CIA. Despite the difficulty in developing the necessary analytical expertise, it is here that the Select Committees do their most significant oversight. According to a former staffer,

> In most instances it is just unrealistic to expect the agencies' conduct to be affected by legislation or even case-by-case oversight. There are limits to how much the behavior of agents and bureaucrats can be regulated by statute, or by Congress looking over their shoulders. The real pressure point is the ability of Congress to punish those responsible for fiascos. And that leverage is essentially budgetary. The behavior of bureaucrats is most likely to be affected if they believe that they, or their agency, will be held accountable for conduct the outcome of which meets the disapproval of Congress. It is this "chilling effect" which modifies behavior most efficiently, much more than a statute, a review process or an investigation. Ultimately the committee's power depends on making the Executive reluctant to pay the price of non-cooperation.[72]

A former Deputy Director of the CIA has added:

> The mere fact that the Committee now requires the agency, as part of its annual funding authorization, to prepare a congressional presentation document in support of its request means that the agency has to sort out priorities, plans, objectives, even values. Whatever the benefit of this exercise for the Committee, the very act of supervising the preparation of the presentation adds immeasurably to the power and control the Director of Central Intelligence can exercise over his fiefdoms. He can use the occasion to knock heads together and to compel coordination and planning. That, in itself, makes the process worthwhile—regardless of whether they read the document at the other end.[73]

SECURITY AND COOPTION

Two continuing problems for the committees are security and cooption. To improve control over classified information, the Church Committee has proposed that, with the creation of the Select Committee on Intelligence, the Congress should repeat the procedure established by the Hughes-Ryan Amendment that requires Agency briefing of six other committees. But S.Res. 400, being a Senate rule of procedure, not a law, left Hughes-Ryan unaffected.[74] Thus what was intended to consolidate actually proliferated the briefing requirement. Senator Goldwater has complained: "The Hughes-Ryan amendment which requires six committees of the Congress to receive notification of covert action has all but destroyed this capability. Under its provisions nearly 50 Senators, over 120 Congressmen, and numerous staff receive this highly sensitive information. Disclosure to the press is the inevitable result."[75]

Requiring the Agencies to deal with so many members does aggravate the security problem, but it reduces the chances of Congressional cooption. How this trade-off is viewed depends on who the observer is. A senior European intelligence official has complained that the need to brief eight Congressional committees or subcommittees keeps most of his American counterparts unavailable for anything else.[76]

President Carter has joined his predecessors in complaining, repeatedly, that Congressional leaks of classified information are damaging national security and that reliable intelligence sources are drying up because they fear the leaking of confidential information they supply.[77] In response, there has been some effort to tighten up procedures for access. The House Intelligence Committee rules now sharply limit access of members not on the committee to secure information. A request must be made to the committee in writing, after which the committee "must determine by recorded vote whatever action it deems necessary in light of all the circumstances of each individual request."[78] Understandably, few apply.

A tougher line has also been taken by the Administration to all but the Intelligence Committees. Recent efforts by the International Operations Subcommittee of the Senate Foreign Relations Committee to obtain highly classified CIA information on intelligence operations of Iran's secret police in the United States were rebuffed. This information, the CIA said, had already been given to the Intelligence Committee. The Foreign Relations Committee should address its request to them.

This tougher policy has caused new difficulties in Executive-Congressional relations. In the summer of 1978, the CIA charged that Cuban forces in Angola were behind the invasion of Zaire's Shaba province. The Senate Foreign Relations Committee asked to see the data on which this conclusion was based. The request was denied, although DCI Admiral Turner agreed to brief the committee.[79] The White House told Chairman Sparkman that it had supplied the data to the House and Senate intelligence committees, but would give it to no one else. Sparkman had to write Intelligence Committee Chairman Birch Bayh to get an assessment of the data's probity, a procedure that seems sensible only to those not familiar with senatorial sensibilities. By making the Intelligence Committee the selective retailer of its secrets, the Foreign Relations Committee charged, the CIA was turning the intent of Congress on its head. After hearing Admiral Turner, the committee got its revenge by reporting that the "Administration had failed to produce conclusive evidence to support its charges" against Cuba.[80]

More criticism of procedures for dealing with unauthorized leaks came recently from a Senate committee studying the Committee System. It found "deficiencies in Senate rules relating to unauthorized disclosures" and added that many committees other than the Intelligence Committee "routinely handle classified and confidential documents," making it impossible "to identify the source of a disclosure." For these reasons it concluded that "responsibility in this [security] area should be broadened and consolidated in a single committee."[81]

Oddly, the Congress, in 1978, did enact criminal penalties—a maximum of one year in jail and $10,000 fine—for disclosure by U.S. government employees, or former employees, of trade secrets pertaining to insecticides, fungicides, and rodenticides.[82] But nothing comparable has been enacted to discourage the retailing of intelligence secrets except when actual espionage can be proven.

A 1978 CIA survey of Congressional security procedures concluded that only those of the Senate Select Committee on Intelligence adequately protect classified data. The Senate Foreign Relations Committee, House International Relations Committee, and even the House Permanent Select Committee on Intelligence were deemed "not secure." As a result, the Executive uses different procedures in dealing with each. Secret executive agreements—which, by law, must be reported to the foreign relations committees—are shown to the Senate committee's chairman, senior minority member and chief of staff but are then sent for safekeeping to the Select Committee on Intelligence. In the case of the House International Relations Committee, they are shown to the same three officials, then returned to the CIA.

Critics of the Administration's "get tough" policy point out that, even with Hughes-Ryan still in effect, "the total increment in those entitled to full information on a 'need to know' basis is likely to be quite small."[83] They also note that the Executive, not Congress, is the prime source of leaking. A good example is the CIA's own batting average. In November 1978, for example, it discharged an employee who had passed highly sensitive top-secret CIA reports on the Strategic Arms Limitation Talks to a staffer of Congressional SALT critic Senator Henry Jackson of Washington.[84] About the same time, a twenty-three-year-old clerk hired by the CIA was arrested for having sold a spy satellite manual to the Russians which he had purloined without it even being missed.[85]

Much of the Agency's leaking, moreover, comes from senior officials who selectively feed information to Congress and the press to advance their interests.

The second problem is cooption. Senate committees face an unenviable dilemma when they attempt to oversee government secrets. If they expect to get data, the Agencies will expect discretion in return. However, if they are unwilling to share their information with other committees and members, they are suspected of having been coopted. If they fail to make secrets available to the media, they may find themselves attacked while those who leak are rewarded with favorable coverage.

Citing unidentified Congressional sources, newspapers have reported that the committee has become "almost as secret as the agencies it monitors." The *New York Times* complained, "Almost no information has come from the committee" and it added, "there have been so few outward signs of its activity that some critics have charged that the committee has been coopted by the agencies it is supposed to monitor."[86]

In May 1977, as if to disprove the *Times*, the Senate Intelligence Committee turned down a plea by President Carter not to release a staff study containing secret Agency information. It revealed the embarrassing fact that the CIA had been monitoring representatives of the Micronesian independence movement with whom the State Department was negotiating, in order to "produce information bearing on the status of negotiations."[87] Although the effort had been "wholly unproductive"[88] the committee noted that "such a highly intrusive technique" would "warrant appropriate Congressional consultation" in future and is "appropriate for use against an armed adversary" rather than "against a people under U.S. administration and protection."[89]

While these revelations earned the committee an unaccustomed amount of favorable attention by the media, it obviously caused serious strains with the community being supervised, as well as with the White House. Other tensions arose when it was revealed that Chairman Inouye had asked the FBI to monitor selectively the activities of members and staff, a policy committee member Senator Hart called "an outrage."[90] On June 17, Senator Inouye announced that he would resign as chairman of the committee at the end of 1977, adding that he was doing so voluntarily, in accordance with his belief that the chairmanship should rotate every two years.[91]

This prompted a brief truce all around. Soon, however, the leaks and the countervailing cries of cooption were again in evidence. In June 1978 the *New York Times*'s Seymour Hersh wrote about two covert operations the Intelligence Committees had authorized the previous fall. With that, it was no longer clear that those on the Committees who disagreed with an operation were necessarily playing by the rules. At least one leak, that intelligence had supplied Egypt's Anwar Sadat with communications equipment to monitor his own military chiefs, could have been distinctly damaging to U.S. interests.[92]

Replying to renewed charges of cooption and laxity, the new Senate Intelligence Committee chairman, Birch Bayh of Indiana, wrote that his group "reviews in detail every covert-action activity, and each activity is voted upon by every member of the committee after deliberation and discussion."[93] He also indicated that the Carter Administration was fully honoring its commitment, in Executive Order 12036, to give the committee all relevant information. Representative Boland, calling the renewed allegations of cooption "misleading," asserted that his committee "has gone into the C.I.A.'s covert action program in great detail," adding that the budget subcommittee also "examined the risk and policy implications versus cost of each of the C.I.A.'s covert action programs." According to Boland, "Congressional oversight . . . is vibrant, thorough and continuous."[94]

That may be putting it rather too strongly, but Congressional oversight of intelligence activity, despite serious problems and deficiencies, has now become a significant factor in the Agencies' operational policy-making.

By April 1977 the Senate's intelligence committee had become involved in detailed analysis of the intelligence budget, the first time a Congressional committee had attempted such a thoroughgoing review of intelligence programs and expenditures. Inevitably, the overall amount of the budget request was leaked to the press—$6.2 billion—even as the committee, the President, and the agencies were engaged in a discussion as to whether the figure should be made public.[95] Four weeks later, the Carter Administration announced that "it would not oppose public disclosure" of the total figure which had already appeared extensively in the press.[96] The release of those figures had been vigorously opposed, however, by Admiral Turner, who felt that such disclosure, which in turn might well lead to further unveiling of individual items in the budget, would not be without risk and, if carried to the point of public line-by-line disclosure, could do "irreparable harm to our country."[97]

Congressional budget control has already effected a sharp reduction in covert operations personnel. Whether the resultant decline in the agencies' capacity for "dirty tricks" proves to be in the national interest, remains to be seen. Those, including the committees and the DCI, who have favored this retrenchment, have argued that the U.S. needs better intelligence gathering and evaluating, which can best be achieved by pruning the thicket of covert operations that had overgrown the CIA.

However, if success in intelligence production is a fair measure of the effectiveness of this new approach, enthusiasm must be reserved. President Carter had occasion, at the end of 1978, to deplore the quality of information the intelligence community has been providing.[98] Even as he did so, the Senate Intelligence Committee leaked a faulty CIA evaluation of the Shah of Iran's prospects and announced that it would investigate the inadequacy of this reporting.[99]

Aides to the House Committee, not to be upstaged, said they planned to launch a similar study, soon.[100]

6

TREATIES, AGREEMENTS, AND COMMITMENTS:
Putting "Advice" Back into Advice and Consent

OF THE VARIOUS foreign relations initiatives open to a country, the most crucial are the making of war and the undertaking of solemn commitments. The U.S. Constitution clearly provides that both functions shall be exercised through Executive-Congressional codetermination; yet, in recent years, both became effectively a Presidential monopoly. In the War Powers Resolution, Congress created a framework for reasserting its share of responsibility for the international use of force. However, efforts to create a similarly comprehensive process of codetermination for the making of international commitments have eluded Congress. The result is continued warfare between the branches. Disarray in this area of foreign policy is a very serious problem for a superpower whose ability to speak clearly, decisively, and credibly, is the linchpin of the international system.

THE DECLINE OF ADVICE

The Constitution provides that the President "shall have power, by and with the advice and consent of the Senate, to make treaties, provided two-thirds of the Senators present concur."[1] This represents a compromise, for the original draft of the Committee of Detail had assigned the treaty power exclusively to the Senate.[2]

As conceived by the drafters, the Senate was to play two parts: it was to advise on the negotiations and it was to consent to the final document.[3] John Jay did not think the advice function amounted to much,[4] but most delegates agreed with Pierce Butler of South Carolina that it meant treaties should "be gone over, clause by clause, by the President and Senate together, and modelled."[5] Indeed, acting on this assumption, President Washington on August 21, 1789, sent a message stating: "The President of the United States will meet the Senate, in the Senate Chamber, at half past eleven o'clock, to-morrow, to advise with them on the terms of the treaty to be negotiated with the southern Indians."[6]

The Senate, as it so often does, referred the matters raised at that meeting to a committee, forcing the President to come back a second time. Although that particular in-person consultation proved mutually embarrassing,[7] and was not repeated, Washington continued to seek senatorial advice by other, less direct means. On February 9, 1790, he sent a message asking for detailed advice on a wide range of U.S.– British boundary disputes prior to entering into treaty negotiations, declaring it "advisable to postpone any negotiations on the subject, until I shall be informed of the results of your deliberations, and receive your advice as to the propositions most proper to be offered. . . ."[8] The Senate responded in writing on March 24.[9]

The vitality of the advice function continued. In the 1790's the Senate was asked to approve the appointment of treaty negotiators[10] and to advise on their negotiating instructions.[11] Jefferson had occasion to warn Washington not to begin talks with Algiers without first consulting the Senate, since that body might otherwise withhold its consent to whatever was eventually agreed.[12] The President took that advice, asking Senators whether they would be likely to approve a ransom scheme for the release of U.S. captives.[13]

By 1794, however, slippage had begun. That year the Jay Treaty became the first agreement negotiated without prior senatorial advice. The Senate responded by amending its Article 12 as part of the process of giving its consent.[14] With that, a new practice came on stream. Presidents now rarely consulted the Senate on the terms of a treaty before, or during negotiations, while the Senate, cut out of its "advisory" role, retaliated by making extensive changes in the finished text of agreements as part of its "consent" function.

This new practice vastly annoyed the parties with which the U.S. was negotiating, as it still does. In 1803, British Foreign Secretary Lord Harrowby, denouncing the practice "of ratifying treaties, with exceptions to parts of them" angrily rejected the King-Hawkesbury Convention from which the Senate had amputated Article 5.[15] Presidential officers were no less vexed. Secretary of State John Hay, after the Senate had altered the Hay-Pauncefote Treaty of 1900 concerning a proposed canal through the Panama Isthmus, wrote that "it never entered into mind that anyone not out of a madhouse could have objected"[16] to its terms. In view of the Senate's changes, the British rejected that one, too.

In still other instances, senatorial changes have caused Presidents to abandon fully negotiated agreements. "I think that this amendment makes the treaties shams," President Theodore Roosevelt wrote Senator Henry Cabot Lodge in connection with some arbitration conventions to which the Senate had consented with major changes, "and my impression is that we had better abandon the whole business rather than give the impression of trickiness and insincerity which would be produced by solemnly promulgating a sham."[17] Hay added, a "treaty entering the Senate is like a bull going into the arena; no one can say just how or when the blow will fall—but one thing is certain—it will never leave the arena alive."[18] President William Taft, similarly embarrassed by amendments, wrote of putting the treaties[19] "on the shelf . . . in the hope that the Senators might change the Senate—instead of which they changed me!"[20]

Yet Presidents seem to prefer embarrassment and even defeat of their treaties to the Constitution's injunction to seek timely senatorial advice. There were exceptions, of course. President Andrew Jackson in 1830 asked the Senate for negotiating help before entering into talks with the Choctaw Indians[21] and, in 1846, President James Polk consulted the Senate on pending negotiations with Britain over the Oregon Territory[22] because, he said, he understood that, in this way, "the President secures harmony of action between that body and himself. . . ."[23] That he was being less than candid is made clear, however, by the fact that a mere six days elapsed between his request for advice and the presentation of a fully negotiated treaty for senatorial consent.[24] The prevalent attitude was that of Secretary of State Richard Olney who wrote a British diplomat in Washington about an agreement just negotiated: "the Senate is now engaged in asserting itself as the power in national government. . . . The Treaty, in getting itself made by the sole act of the executive, without leave of the Senate first had and obtained, had commited the unpardonable sin. It must be altogether defeated or so altered as to bear an unmistakeable Senate stamp. . . ."[25] Yet Olney, correctly analyzing the mood of the Senate in attempting to assert its Constitutional prerogative, preferred defeat to power-sharing.

Thus, as Presidents gradually abandoned efforts to seek advice on pending negotiations, the Senate increasingly responded by rewriting treaties—some 167 to 1,046 submitted up to 1944 were amended and 104 more were rejected or shelved.[26] Instead of retracing their steps in an effort to revive the advice function at an early, constructive stage in the negotiations, Administrations have increasingly tried to deal with what they perceive as senatorial obstructionism by two devices: *cooption* and *circumvention*.

COOPTION

Senators like to dabble in diplomacy. John T. Morgan, the chairman of the Senate's Committee on Interoceanic Canals, busied himself with canal negotiations involving the Colombian Minister in Washington at the very time the Senate was frustrating Secretary Hay's canal treaty.[27] Senator William Borah of Idaho, chairman of the Foreign Relations Committee, opened direct negotiations with the President of Mexico on oil expropriations that ran contrary to State Department efforts, while Senator Henry Cabot Lodge, another Senate Foreign Relations Committee chairman, carried on an extensive correspondence with European leaders behind President Woodrow Wilson's back throughout the Versailles Conference. He used to read the letters to his committee.[28] At one point, a resolution offered in the Senate Foreign Relations Committee sought to mandate the addition of eight Senators to the U.S. team at Versailles.[29] It was defeated,[30] but only after a waggish member had interjected an amendment enlarging the senatorial delegation to ninety-six.

Exploiting this senatorial penchant for diplomacy, Presidents have taken to appointing Senators to their treaty negotiating delegations. Far from making the system of checks and balances work, this approach merely circumvented it. Instead of giving the Senate a more functional role, it enhanced Presidential control behind a façade of selective senatorial participation. Nor was the tactic limited to treaties or to the Upper House. Presidents, perceiving themselves unable to control the Congress in its assertion of an independent foreign relations role, began appointing key members of both Houses to a broad range of Executive foreign relations policy–making positions. In return for such honor and preferment, the members were expected to ensure the passage of the resolutions or legislation necessary to give effect to the Executive policy of which they had become a part.

The drafters of the Constitution had expressly sought to protect against this tactic. Article I, Section 6, paragraph 2, provides:

> No Senator or Representative shall, during the time for which he was elected, be appointed to any civil office under the authority of the United States, which shall have been created, or the emoluments whereof shall have been increased during such time; and no person holding any office under the United States shall be a Member of either House during his continuance in office.

This was plainly the minimum demanded by public opinion. As one historian has observed, the "people at large, distrustful of delegated power, favored insistence upon this ineligibility."[31] Significantly, those men who, after having been privy to the drafting of the Constitution, later became President, did strictly honor the intent of this clause, even when they ignored other aspects of the separation of powers. Several members of the judiciary, including Chief Justices John Jay and Oliver Ellsworth, were quickly drafted for diplomatic service,[32] yet no members of Congress were appointed to diplomatic roles during this inceptive period.

With only a few trivial exceptions, during the first three-quarters of the 19th century, Presidents continued to avoid appointing sitting members to diplomatic functions. The occasional member offered an appointment invariably resigned from the legislature. For example, at the close of the War of 1812, President James Madison selected Senator James A. Bayard of Delaware to serve with John Q. Adams and Albert Gallatin in negotiating a peace treaty with Britain. Similarly, Henry Clay, then Speaker of the House, was appointed a commissioner for the conference at Ghent. Both men immediately left Congress.[33]

On November 3, 1892, however, the rule was broken when President Benjamin Harrison appointed Senator William B. Allison of Iowa and Representative James B. McCreary of Kentucky Commissioners to the International Monetary Conference to be held in Brussels later that month. They did not resign from Congress. On June 6th of the same year, Harrison appointed Senator John T. Morgan of Alabama an arbitrator, under the U.S.–British treaty of February 29, 1892, to determine the jurisdictional rights of the United States in the waters of the Bering Sea in connection with the preservation of fur seals.[34] He, too, did not vacate his seat.

The holes Harrison's appointments had made in Constitutional principle and practice were enthusiastically enlarged by President William McKinley, who had been "schooled in dealing with Senate opposition by many years of observation in the House."[35] On April 14, 1897, McKinley appointed Senator Edward O. Wolcott of Colorado, no stranger to the silver industry, "special envoy to France, Germany, Great Britain, and other countries to seek an international agreement to fix the relative value between gold and silver under the act of March 30, 1897."[36]

The following year, in July 1898, McKinley appointed three sitting members of Congress to the Joint High Commission established to resolve disputes concerning fisheries, fur seals, commercial reciprocity, and the Alaskan boundary that troubled relations between the U.S. and Canada.[37] He also appointed three members commissioners to recommend legislation that produced annexation of the Hawaiian Islands.[38] At this point, however, the Senate became restive, declining to confirm the nominees, on the ground that their appointment violated the Constitutional prohibition.[39] Members warned they would no longer agree to the use of sitting legislators to negotiate treaties. Republican Senator George F. Hoar of Massachusetts thundered against appointments, "that would put an improper temptation in the way of the legislator to induce him to become a tool of the Executive will."[40]

McKinley, however, was not easily deterred. On September 13, 1898, he appointed the two senior Republican members of the Senate Foreign Relations Committee, Cushman K. Davis of Minnesota and William P. Frye of Maine, and Senator George Gray of Delaware to negotiate a peace treaty with Spain. This action, coming on top of the earlier appointments, led to severe criticism in the Senate. Bills were introduced to prohibit the practice altogether, some of which were referred to the Committee on the Judiciary.[41] But McKinley, it turned out, had already thoughtfully appointed three Senators on the Judiciary Committee to the International Water Boundary Commission. Nevertheless, Senator Hoar was sent by the Senate to tell McKinley "that they hoped the practice would not be continued."[42]

McKinley protested that shrewd negotiators were hard to find outside Congress,[43] a patently absurd argument so characterized by Hoar.[44] As if to underscore the Senate's concern, the treaty's annexation of the Philippines passed with just one vote to spare. That margin was provided by Senator Gray, one of the negotiators, who had earlier wired Secretary Hay, "I cannot agree that it is wise to take Philippine Islands in whole or in part."[45]

After the Hoar-McKinley confrontation, the practice of appointing members to diplomatic negotiations appears to have lapsed until the 1920's.[46] But then came the Treaty of Versailles debacle. President Warren Harding, who succeeded Wilson, had observed it from his place at the table of the Senate Foreign Relations Committee. He concluded that Wilson's error had been in not appointing Senators to negotiate at Versailles.[47] He eagerly compensated by a return to the Senate-handling tactics of McKinley. At first he failed to interest several Senators in joining the negotiations for a U.S. peace treaty with Germany.[48] There was a better response for the Washington Naval Conference of 1922. Among the delegates named were the two party leaders, Senators Lodge and Oscar Underwood. Harding successfully coopted both men, who supported in the Senate that to which they had agreed in the conference.[49] As a result, there were no long committee proceedings, the debate was short, and no complicating amendments were proposed.[50] The press, with a few exceptions, viewed the appointment of Lodge and Underwood as an excellent tactic, comparing it favorably with Versailles,[51] while in the Senate itself no objection was raised when the nominations were announced, although there were protests during the ratification debate by Senators Hiram Johnson and Joseph Robinson.[52]

Later, Harding named Senator Reed Smoot, the chairman of the Senate Finance Committee, and Representative Theodore E. Burton, to the Foreign Debt Commission.[53] Opposition to those appointments led to a floor debate[54] and to a decision to ask the Judiciary Committee "to inquire into and report to the Senate" on the propriety of the appointments in the light of Section 6 of Article I of the Constitution.[55] The Committee's report concluded "that the gentlemen named are ineligible"[56] and emphatically rejected the contrary legal case submitted by the Attorney General. Yet, despite this clear verdict, the "club" blithely confirmed Smoot's and Burton's appointment by 47 to 25,[57] a triumph over the spirit of the Constitution by its most persistent enemy, *noblesse oblige.*

The practice of appointing Senators to represent the President in diplomatic negotiations, while now less frequent, still continues. In 1930, President Hoover named Senator Robinson—who had attacked Harding's appointment of Lodge—a delegate to the London Naval Conference.[58] Between 1930 and 1960, 252 places on U.S. delegations to international conferences were doled out to members of Congress. Most were to ordinary meetings of international organizations,[59] but fifty-two were to major negotiations[60] with forty members serving as accredited delegates.[61]

The effect of this is not to solve the "advice" dilemma but to make it worse. Members who serve as delegates of the executive branch are rarely asked to advise but, instead, are given instructions which they have little or no part in composing. They are not free, either, to share their confidential negotiating experiences with their Congressional colleagues. The result may be to secure the member's support for the agreement when it comes before the legislature for action, but the practice merely compounds the tension between the branches by adding a violation of the Constitution's Article I, Section 6, to the violation of Article II, Section 2.

CIRCUMVENTION

Instead of seeking the cooperation of the Senate in joint exercise of the treaty power, Presidents have found it more convenient to by-pass the legislature through the device of the executive agreement.

The executive agreement is an undeclared treaty which, like an undeclared war, seeks to avoid paying its Constitutional dues by changing its name. It is, simply, an agreement between the President or his subordinates and a foreign counterpart, which, because it is not called a treaty, is not submitted to the Senate for its advice and consent. In many ways, far from being a solution to the problems of Executive-Congressional relations, this short-cut has become a paradigm of the problem itself.

The treaty process established by the Constitution is cumbersome and stressful. But, as the Panama Treaty experience amply illustrated, it does ensure a full, public consideration of just exactly what kind of commitment we are assuming. When the President takes a short-cut, the nation can no longer be sure what obligations are being assumed, and foreign nations cannot be sure the obligations will be considered binding by Congress and the people.

In the fall of 1975, for example, after Egypt and Israel had signed the second Sinai disengagement agreement, Secretary Kissinger asked Congress to authorize the stationing of 200 U.S. technicians between Israeli and Egyptian forces to run an early warning system.[62] As the Congress considered this straightforward request, it learned that, although the U.S. was not, itself, a party to the Egyptian-Israeli agreement, Kissinger had made various commitments to each party in order to induce them to compromise. Some of these were public and some secret. A few agreements contained obligations binding on the U.S., others were looser commitments to "consult" or to take steps in an indefinite future contingent on prior approval by Congress. But none of these commitments was presented to the Senate for approval because they were not treaties, only "undertakings." Yet they imposed on the U.S. obligations of great importance to Israel and Egypt.

Section 10 of the Israeli–U.S. secret Agreement E was the most controversial. It states that if "a world power" (i.e. the Soviets) were to threaten Israel, the United States would "consult promptly with the Government of Israel with respect to what support, diplomatic or otherwise, or assistance it can lend to Israel in accordance with its constitutional practices."[63] Although, literally, this does not obligate the U.S. to do more than talk, the Senate Legislative Counsel[64] correctly observed that the clause is almost identical to the assurance provided by the U.S. in various mutual defense agreements with such allies as the Philippines,[65] Australia, New Zealand,[66] and the Republic of Korea.[67] Yet each of these was considered a solemn enough obligation to warrant being put in treaty form.

Section 10 obliges the U.S. to consult with Israel in a crisis on what "assistance" or support, "diplomatic or otherwise," the United States might give Israel. While the meaning of "diplomatic support" was clear enough and "assistance" presumably meant military supplies, what, Senators wanted to know, did "or otherwise" mean, if not the dispatch of U.S. combat forces?[68]

Congress was never invited to participate in making these commitments, but only to authorize the stationing of the 200 U.S. technicians in the Sinai.[69] In the process of doing this, however, the Senate Foreign Relations Committee expressed its anger over the corner-cutting methods of the Administration by releasing the text of the secret understandings Kissinger had given both Israel and Egypt. In addition, Congress demonstrated its independence by tinkering with Kissinger's commitments. For example, while authorizing the stationing of the technicians, it provided that they could be withdrawn, by vote of a simple majority of both Houses.[70] More important, Congress specified that it did not approve any of the other, secret agreements, understandings, or commitments made by Kissinger, such as the controversial Section 10 of Agreement E.[71]

The severe mauling the State Department took in securing Congressional approval of its Sinai package underscored the renewed determination of the "revolutionary" Congress to play an important part in the negotiation of international commitments, by whatever name called. Having been consulted neither as to the form or content of agreements with Israel and Egypt, members retaliated. They refused to abide by the secrecy classification imposed on some of the "understandings" transmitted to the committees in confidence. They altered fundamental expectations by inserting Congress into the process for withdrawing the technicians. They all but disowned the secret "understandings" that had induced the parties to sign the accords.

This short, unhappy interaction between the executive and legislative branches was merely another chapter in the battle of Congress—and, particularly of the Senate—to gain control over the President's freewheeling use of the executive agreement as a device for evading the need to obtain advice and consent. The executive agreement has become the focus of a battle to force the international commitment process back into a codeterminational mode and to reestablish Constitutional fundamentals.

The Constitution provides but one way in which the United States can enter into international commitments: via treaties made "by and with the Advice and Consent of the Senate. . . ." Still, it is undisputable that, before and after the adoption of the Constitution, Presidents occasionally signed international arrangements, not called treaties, which became binding without advice and consent. These early executive agreements were mostly made pursuant to legislation or joint resolution of Congress. For example, in 1784, Congress specifically authorized amendments to a treaty of amity and commerce with France by means of executive agreement[72] and, in 1792, it asked the Postmaster General to enter into international agreements for reciprocal delivery of mail.[73]

Executive officials, nowadays, cite these early precedents to conclude that long "years of congressional practice have established the legitimacy" of this procedure.[74] But earlier Presidents seem to have had doubts. Monroe, on the strength of a law permitting him to sell or lay up naval vessels on the Great Lakes, entered into the Rush-Bagot executive agreement of 1817 with Great Britain, limiting naval armaments on the Great Lakes.[75] But then he began to have doubts and sent the text to the Senate for its consent.[76]

Such doubts are appropriate. If the drafters of the Constitution had intended to permit serious U.S. commitments to be made *either* by and with the advice and consent of two-thirds of the Senate *or* by a law passed by a simple majority of each House, why was only the first, more onerous process debated and agreed to? The answer is that the drafters wanted important international commitments made by a process requiring a higher degree of consensus than is needed to pass an ordinary law. The convention thoroughly aired a proposal, advanced by James Wilson and Gouverneur Morris, to have international commitments made by the President and a majority of both House and Senate. It was decisively rejected.[77] Yet Presidents have increasingly come to treat the two processes as interchangeable. The annexation of Texas was accomplished by executive agreement supported by a joint resolution after the Senate had refused the two-thirds majority necessary for a treaty.[78] Most recently, President Carter has indicated that if he could not secure the support of two-thirds of the Senate for a SALT agreement, he might recast it as an executive agreement and seek its implementation by ordinary legislation. And, he added, if the legislation failed to secure a majority in each chamber, well, he would conclude SALT as an executive agreement based solely on his plenary powers as Commander in Chief.[79]

In support of his power to act alone, it has been noted that the "early practice by the framers of the Constitution also reveals that executive agreements might be authorized not only by statute, but by the Constitution itself."[80] This argument asserts that, since the Constitution gives a President some unfettered plenary discretion—as Commander in Chief, for example—he must, in those areas, also have the power to enter into what might be called "pure" executive agreements with foreign states to give his powers effect.

In the early days of federal history, however, such "pure" executive agreements were rare and of very limited scope. In 1799, President John Adams did settle the private claim of an American against the Netherlands by an agreement that had not been authorized by Congress and was not submitted for the "advice and consent" of the Senate. But Adams's was little more than a consular action to protect a citizen and, as such, would fit even the most limited definition of the President's diplomatic prerogatives. Larger money claims against a foreign state by groups of citizens, on the other hand, were consistently resolved, during this period, by treaties submitted to the Senate.[81] Again, in 1813, President Madison concluded an executive agreement with Great Britain for an exchange of prisoners of war, a minor exercise of his inherent plenary powers as Commander in Chief.[82]

Beyond small indemnity or prisoner exchange agreements, however, there is little in early Constitutional history to confirm the allegation that the President may act on his own to commit the U.S. Twentieth-century history, however, abounds with successful assertions of very wide power. The high-water mark came with Franklin D. Roosevelt's executive agreement recognizing the communist regime in Moscow, and transferring title to certain Russian property in the U.S. to compensate U.S. citizens who had lost investments in Russia. The Supreme Court held this executive agreement Constitutional because, the court said, it was essentially an exercise of the President's plenary power to recognize foreign governments.[83] Again, on September 2, 1940, in an exchange of letters between Secretary of State Cordell Hull and the British ambassador, fifty U.S. destroyers and unspecified weapons were transferred to England in return for ninety-nine year leases on base sites in the Caribbean, Bermuda, and Newfoundland. The agreement was merely transmitted to Congress for informational purposes but was not authorized by law or consented to by two-thirds of the Senate.[84] This tendency has generated alarm among legislators. "Clearly, the power to enter into executive agreements is not expressly granted under the Constitution," Senator Sam Ervin said, "and the most cursory reading of the constitutional history reveals the intention of the Founding Fathers that the President was to be precluded from engaging in the making of any substantive foreign policy without the advice and consent of the Senate. For most of our earlier history, this restraint was honored and virtually all of our foreign commitments were entered into by formal treaties."[85] Ervin pointed out that in 1930, the United States concluded twenty-five treaties and only nine executive agreements, while in 1968 it made only sixteen treaties but 266 executive agreements. By January 1, 1972, there were 947 treaties as against 4,359 executive agreements.[86]

The counsel of the Senate Foreign Relations Committee has complained that while many crucially important commitments, including base agreements, have been made by executive agreement, trivial agreements—governing the status of three uninhabited coral reefs in the Caribbean; regulating shrimp fishing off the coast of Brazil; and setting rules to prevent collisions at sea—have been transmitted to the Senate as treaties.[87]

CODETERMINATION OF INTERNATIONAL
COMMITMENTS

Neither cooption nor circumvention any longer frees the President from Constitutional constraints. Congress, and the Senate in particular, have become anxious to reclaim their share of the international commitment power. It was a tactical blunder for President Carter to threaten to implement a Strategic Arms Limitation Agreement without the consent of the Senate. Only five short years after Watergate, does the Presidency again need to be reminded that the primary objective of American foreign policy is to preserve our Constitutional system?

While codetermination has not yet been effectively established in the making of commitments, there have been a few steps in the right direction. This has been partly a matter of trying to recapture the ephemeral spirit of bipartisanship and inter-branch accommodation that was last seen during the conception, negotiation, and enactment of the Marshall Plan in 1947 and the North Atlantic Treaty in 1948–49. After Secretary of State George C. Marshall's trial balloon was floated at the 1947 Harvard Commencement, it was a House of Representatives Select Committee under Christian Herter which was encouraged to conduct hearings in Europe. Its findings were taken seriously by the Executive which credited it with securing the Plan's Congressional approval.[88]

On the Senate side, similar close consultation and credit-sharing was the rule, with Senator Arthur Vandenberg, Chairman of the Foreign Relations Committee, being involved in advance at every step of the way. According to a study by Richard Neustadt, Vandenberg was invited to

> frequent meetings with the President and weekly conferences with Marshall. He asked for an effective liaison between Congress and agencies concerned; Lovett and others gave him what he wanted. When the Senator decided on the need to change financing and administrative features of the legislation, Truman disregarded Budget Bureau grumbling and acquiesced with grace. When, finally, Vandenberg desired a Republican to head the new administering agency, his candidate, Paul Hoffman, was appointed despite the President's own preference for another.[89]

And Marshall, calling Vandenberg his "full partner" said, "I was his right-hand man, and at times he was mine. . . ."[90]

During the 1948–49 negotiations leading to the North Atlantic Treaty, the Executive encouraged the impression that Congress was the initiator. The legislators obliged by passing Senate Resolution 239, some of the language of which was incorporated into the Treaty.[91] In the debate on ratification, a content Senator Vandenberg said, "Indeed, I would not know what I was asking for on that historic day last June if this Pact is not it."[92]

For years these models of codetermination and credit-sharing went unemulated. In very recent times, however, another model has emerged. Instead of either coopting or circumventing legislators, the Executive has begun to invite them to negotiations as advisers informally representing Congress. In this capacity, Senators and Representatives have attended the Law of the Seas Conference, the United Nations Conference on Trade and Development, and the Assembly of the Organization of American States.[93]

At times, Congress has even mandated its advisory participation. The Trade Act of 1974 requires the Speaker of the House and the President *pro tempore* of the Senate each to name five members, not more than three from the same party, "who shall be accredited by the President as official advisers to the United States delegations to international conferences, meetings and negotiation sessions relating to trade agreements."[94] Under this arrangement the selected members and designated staff of the Senate Finance Committee and House Ways and Means Committee have access to almost everything pertaining to the negotiations. "We see about eighty percent of cable traffic here," a staffer reported.[95] All government position papers are circulated to designated committee staff as are negotiating instructions, although usually three to ten days after they are dispatched to the negotiators.

In 1978, Presidential arms control negotiator Paul Warnke took the initiative to invite the House Speaker and Senate presiding officer to name "several" members to serve as "advisers" to the U.S. delegation negotiating the Second Strategic Arms Limitation Treaty with Russia. In making his request, Warnke explained that his purpose was "to facilitate Congressional knowledge and involvement and to increase public understanding of the objectives of these negotiations." Distinguishing between the Congressional "advisory" role and that of the diplomats, Warnke pointed out that "the actual negotiating would have to be done by the Delegation itself" but that Congressional advisers could attend plenary meetings as observers and would participate in all U.S. delegation meetings "where their comments and advice would be solicited."[96]

According to one Congressional appointee, Representative Thomas Downey of New York, one of Warnke's purposes was to enlist key Congressional support on his side in disputes with other agencies over negotiating strategy. "For example," Downey reports, "in a particularly contentious matter Warnke has asked us to come up with a draft of what we thought might be acceptable both to Congress and to the Russians. He then used that to convince others in the Administration who wanted to hold out for something tougher."[97]

Members who have served in this capacity report that they play a triple role. They advise the American negotiators about the mood of Congress and the probable reception, there, of various possible negotiating outcomes. With the encouragement of the State Department, they also speak informally to the foreign negotiators, communicating to them the Congressional constraints under which the U.S. negotiators were operating and, on occasion, quietly initiating behind-the-scenes compromises. Finally, they interpret to Congress the difficult and complex realities of the negotiations without laboring under the cloud of cooption.

"We get the communications, instructions, memos. Even though we can't speak there, we can attend all the negotiating sessions," Representative Downey has reported from his SALT experience. "But we have plenty of opportunity to talk within the delegation and, in the corridors, to the Russians. That's where the real work gets done, anyway." But, Downey adds, "we're there on behalf of Congress, not the State Department."[98]

This is a viable strategy for reviving the advisory role of legislators. But it will work only if both sides want it to. So far, the Executive has not employed it widely. And busy members are reluctant to commit the time necessary to be effective advisers. A staffer of the Senate Finance Committee noted that, in 1978, four Senators did go as advisers to the Geneva trade negotiations, but stayed only for two days. "It's difficult to get Senators interested in an agreement that's still at least six months down the road," he explained, adding that while committee staff regularly brief the "few Members who really care, no Senator has ever asked to see the documents or the cable traffic." On the House side, the somewhat less harried members' interest is a little higher.

If this is so in respect to trade negotiations, a comparatively bread-and-butter subject with domestic political resonance, the problem of getting members' attention is likely to be greater when the subject is less politically sensitive. "We really do have a handle on the advice function, at least on an experimental basis," a Senate staffer concluded, "the problem is getting the Senators involved."

It may well be that as members are routinely named advisers to U.S. conference delegations, they will need to make their presence felt primarily through staff. An experienced legislative aide to a key Senator, a veteran of the House International Relations Committee's core staff, would probably be in as good a position as any member to predict Congressional attitudes and provide early warning of Congressional pitfalls. Through assiduous shuttling between negotiations and the Hill the staffer should be able to serve as broker, facilitator, and briefing agent, communicating and informing—in both directions. Such appointees would make liaison between Executive and Congress a two-way street.

While legislators are exploring new ways to structure a timely role during the negotiation of treaties, they are also seeking a way to exert some control over the Presidential penchant for executive agreements. The difficulty, here, is that the interests of the Senate do not coincide with those of the House of Representatives. Both chambers are alarmed by the growing frequency with which the President enters into "pure" executive agreements on the basis of his inherent or plenary Constitutional powers. But the Senate is opposed equally to the growth of the other kind of executive agreement, while the House has benefited historically from the practice of authorizing executive agreements by resolution or statute. Representatives, who are excluded from participation in the "advice and consent" process, become the equals of Senators in enacting laws authorizing foreign commitments. The House, therefore, is not particularly concerned with cutting back on those, but with exercising greater direct control over their content. For the House, in other words, the issue is less one of Constitutional purism than of Congressional oversight.

Despite these divergent perspectives, the House and Senate were able to agree, in 1972, to enact one measure designed to increase Congressional surveillance over executive agreements. Co-sponsored by Senator Case and Representative Zablocki, it requires the Secretary of State to "transmit to the Congress the text of any international agreement, other than a treaty, to which the United States is a party as soon as practicable after such agreement has entered into force with respect to the United States but in no event later than 60 days thereafter." Where a disclosure of a secret agreement is believed by the President to be "prejudicial to the national security of the United States" the agreement, instead of being given to all Senators and Representatives need only be given to the foreign relations committees of the two Houses "under an appropriate injunction of secrecy to be removed only upon due notice from the President."[99]

The law is not retroactive and so does not cover the more than 4,360 pre-existing international agreements to which the U.S. already was a party. But it does apply to all the approximately 200 new agreements now made every year.[100] In reporting the bill to the floor of the House, the Foreign Affairs Committee made it clear that "The Congress does not want to be inundated with trivia. At the same time, it would wish to have transmitted all agreements of any significance."[101] Even "pure" executive agreements must be sent over. The Committee, citing its interest in legislation "necessary and proper" to carrying out Executive functions—Article I, Section 8, of the Constitution—concluded that "the Congress clearly has the power to require the disclosure to itself of the texts of *all* international executive agreements."[102] In the first three years of the new law's operation, 657 executive agreements were sent to Congress and 30 classified agreements were made available to the committees. However, in February 1976 the General Accounting Office, after an investigation, found that thirty-four agreements between U.S. and South Korean intelligence agencies had not been transmitted.[103] It also turned out that they had not been shown to the State Department. By a subsequent amendment to the Case Act, all executive agencies are now required to consult with the State Department before entering into any international agreement.[104]

Making the Executive at least notify Congress is a useful first step in reasserting some surveillance over the use to which the executive agreement is put. However, the Case-Zablocki law gives Congress no power to alter or reject executive commitments to foreign states. Neither does it limit the President's freedom to choose whether to make commitments by treaty or to use the executive agreement short-cut. The continuing differences between House and Senate have so far made it impossible for Congress to agree on curbs with teeth.

After 1972, the House did consider several versions of a bill to allow Congress to veto "any executive agreement concerning the establishment, renewal, continuance or revision of a national commitment" within 60 days after it is transmitted.[105] One draft defines "national commitment" as "the introduction, basing, or deployment of the Armed Forces of the United States on foreign territory" or "the provision to a foreign country, government, or people," of "any military training or equipment, . . . and nuclear technology, or any financial or material resources."[106] The Senate has blocked such legislation, pointing out that these national commitments should be made by treaty, not by executive agreement, and has come up, instead, with a proposal to block funding for carrying out any executive agreement making a "significant political, military or economic commitment."[107] In the words of its originator, former Senator Clark: "If the Executive Branch submits as treaties agreements which in the opinion of the Senate ought to be so submitted, then the Senate will join the House in funding them. If the Executive Branch does not submit those agreements as treaties, then the Senate will not join the House in funding them."[108]

The Clark resolution was strenuously opposed by the State Department, joined by the House. With the House and Senate thus divided on how to deal with proliferating executive agreements, the Executive, aligning itself now with the Senate, now with the House, has been able to keep its options wide open.[109]

Meanwhile, however, the executive branch went through a reevaluation of its own strategy. Out of this came a decision to move some way toward voluntary compliance with the Senate's demands. In an exchange of letters in July, Foreign Relations Chairman Sparkman had asked that his committee be consulted on what form a proposed agreement would take.[110] Assistant Secretary of State Douglas Bennet, Jr., replied that his department would supply the committee periodically with lists of "significant international agreements" to be negotiated, describing the subject matter and indicating whether they would be in the form of a treaty or executive agreement. This early-warning procedure was a large step away from the past policy of keeping Congress in the dark for as long as possible. "I suggest," Bennet added, "that the committee in turn advise the Department of any listed agreement as to which it desires to consult concerning its form. Then we would proceed with the actual consultation."[111]

Commenting on these significant new procedures, Chairman Sparkman said that the Senate Committee "expects that in implementing this procedure, consultation—not notification—will occur at any time an option is opened or foreclosed to use the treaty or executive agreement form. . . ."[112] Thus, for the first time in this century, a procedure has been established for getting the advice of the Senate Foreign Relations Committee, before and during negotiations, on the form, although not the substance, of a proposed foreign commitment.

In return, Senator Sparkman, on behalf of the Senate Committee, appears to have accepted the State Department's criteria for guiding the choice between treaty and executive agreement form.[113] These are set out in State Department Circular 175 and are (1) the extent to which the agreement involves commitments or risks affecting the nation as a whole; (2) whether the agreement is intended to affect State laws; (3) whether the agreement can be given effect without the enactment of subsequent legislation by the Congress; (4) past United States practice with respect to similar agreements; (5) the preference of the Congress with respect to a particular type of agreement; (6) the degree of formality desired for an agreement; (7) the proposed duration of the agreement, the need for prompt conclusion of an agreement, and the desirability of concluding a routine or short-term agreement; and (8) the general international practice with respect to similar agreements.[114]

There can be argument about the appropriateness—let alone the relative weight to be accorded—these various criteria. But at least the "bottom-line" decision, which had previously been made by the Executive alone, would now be made by joint consultative process and before the beginning of negotiations. This can be a felicitous move in reviving the Senate's advisory role.

RECIDIVIST TENDENCIES

But the temptation to take short-cuts will not easily be extirpated. In mid-1977, the Carter Administration found itself in a dilemma. The second Strategic Arms Limitation Agreement had not yet been hammered out and was taking longer than expected. Meanwhile, the first five-year SALT agreement, made in 1972, was due to expire at the beginning of October. The Russians had indicated a willingness to extend SALT I until SALT II was ready. However, the law authorizing the current round of disarmament negotiations states that any new agreement must be made "pursuant to the treaty-making power" or "by further affirmative legislation."[115] On the basis of this, the Senate Foreign Relations Committee advised the Secretary of State "that some form of Congressional approval would be necessary for an extension"[116] of SALT I.

Over the summer, however, the Administration found a better way, a device that would make Congressional approval unnecessary. Instead of a U.S.–Soviet agreement to extend the moratorium, a unilateral statement would be issued by each country indicating a willingness to adhere to SALT I ceilings as long as the other did likewise. Such parallel statements, the State Department legal adviser said, would not constitute an "agreement" and, therefore, required no Congressional or senatorial consent.[117]

Such a mutual exchange of Parallel Unilateral Policy Declarations (P.U.P.D.) was made on September 23, ten days before the expiration date of SALT I.[118] Secretary Vance informed the Senate Foreign Relations Committee, but argued that this move required no action by the Committee.[119] The tactic could scarcely have been more ill-conceived. The New York Times observed that the exchange of notes, while achieving a sensible purpose, was designed to "circumvent" the law and was an "evasive procedure" likely to generate the very ill-will that might provoke the Senate later to reject SALT II.[120] Confirming this prognosis, Senator Case spoke heatedly of the need to prevent "a precedent for any extension of any constitutional authority" of the President.[121] Senator Cranston called for "the final interment of the Parallel Unilateral Policy Declaration doctrine, a doctrine that has the potential of constitutional excess even beyond that displayed by past administrations through the misuse of executive agreements in foreign affairs"[122] and Senator Jackson dismissed P.U.P.D. as a new short-cut to an agreement "contrary to the established statutory and constitutional procedures for concluding such agreements."[123]

To the Administration's credit, while still insisting that an exchange of unilateral commitments did not constitute a binding agreement,[124] it began to look for a way out. A week before P.U.P.D. was to become effective, chief SALT negotiator Paul Warnke conceded that a Congressional resolution of approval might be useful after all.[125] A few days later, Senator Jackson raised the matter with President Carter, indicating that any circumvention of the law could create serious future difficulties. Carter replied, "Well, I don't know anything about all that. This is the first I've heard of the problem. But, as far as I'm concerned, we'd be delighted to have Congress pass a joint resolution approving the Administration's initiative." About the same time, Senator Cranston's legislative aide, Allyn Kreps, reported that his former law partner, Undersecretary of State Warren Christopher, had also indicated that a resolution of approval would be welcome.

The P.U.P.D. caper illustrates the folly of an insistence on short-cuts, on going it alone. But the story, alas, does not end happily with the Congress passing a resolution authorizing the Executive to extend SALT I until the end of SALT II negotiations. Now it was the Senate's turn to prove that it could not be trusted to share power responsibly. A resolution of approval did make its way to the floor, but only on October 3, the day SALT I was to expire.[126] The chairman of the sponsoring committee, Senator Sparkman, was unavailable to lead the debate due to a dentist's appointment. Majority Leader Byrd had allotted thirty minutes for floor debate. Soon the resolution was mired in procedural maneuvers and amendments. One required reports by the President to Congress, every six months, on "the exact status of negotiations for . . . SALT II. . . ."[127] Another, moved by Idaho Republican Senator James A. Mc-Clure, provided that nothing should be construed to prevent or inhibit weapons "development, procurement or deployment" authorized by Congress.[128] While the amendments did not succeed, a point of order did. Senator McClure claimed to have information that the resolution had been reported by the committee while lacking a quorum.[129] Sheepishly, Senator Church admitted the error, but noted that the entire committee had subsequently been polled and that the "committee then met a second time, this morning, a few minutes ago, on the floor of the Senate, . . ."[130]

To no avail. Senator James Allen of Alabama, the Senate's master of procedure, wanted to know whether the committee had obtained the permission of the leadership before meeting on the floor, and noted that the rules require a day to pass before a bill voted out by a committee could be debated.[131] In the ensuing parliamentary chaos, Senator Mc-Clure managed to make quite a long speech in support of the B-1 bomber, the cruise missile, and even a naval base in the Indian Ocean at Diego Garcia.[132]

Through it all, Senator Church tried to press the obvious point that it "is very important that we act . . . the interim agreement expires to-day."[133] At one point, he expressed a willingness to accept the tabled McClure Amendment if McClure would withdraw his point of order concerning the quorum. That deal failed when other Senators began to demand the same for their own pet amendments.

So the effort to involve Congress in codetermination failed, as the time allotted to the subject was used up in wrangling. It was frustrated not by the Executive but by the Senate's inability to deliver, to act effectively on the basis of committee deliberation and recommendation.

The resolution was recommitted, and an opportunity was lost to establish a precedent, however flawed, closing the P.U.P.D. loophole. Instead, the October 3 deadline for Congressional participation passed. In the House of Representatives, International Relations Committee Chairman Zablocki, without consulting his Senate counterpart, sent a letter to the State Department approving the P.U.P.D. In a reversion to the days before the Congressional revolution, Zablocki's letter had actually been drafted by a senior aide to the Secretary of State. By February 1979 President Carter was threatening to use a P.U.P.D. for SALT II if the Senate were to withhold consent.

Senator Javits had the sad last words: "I have been in the Senate 21 years," he said,

> and I have spent all that time trying to bring Congress into a real partnership with the President on foreign policy. Mr. President, why have we not been successful? Precisely for this kind of a performance. It is unbelievable that 100 responsible men cannot do something on time, and it discredits us completely when we say we should be full partners in a foreign relations effort.[134]

A FOREIGN POLICY
OF LAWS, NOT MEN?

CONSTITUTIONAL THEOLOGY OR
POLICY PRAGMATISM

REVOLUTIONS are the ultimate triumph of politics over law. The Congressional revolution, paradoxically, was the defeat of politics by law.

This is an inevitable concomitant of Congressional ascendance. The Presidency is capable of enunciating "doctrines," but it usually speaks through pragmatic, non-normative, flexible policy initiatives and responses. Congress, on the other hand, normally speaks through statutes and debates intended to make "legislative history." It is by legislation that Congress has insinuated itself into a foreign policy partnership with the executive branch. During this revolutionary period, the passing of laws became Congress's way of expressing its policy preferences.

The past six years have seen an exponential growth in foreign policy by legislation and a commensurate shrinkage in unfettered Presidential discretion to conduct foreign relations case-by-case. Reflecting the suspicions of the public toward the Presidency, Congress sought to clip the Executive's wings, using legislation as its instrument. Subjects that have hitherto been handled by the White House, State Department, Defense Department, or Treasury, exercising their pragmatic judgment to meet the challenges of international politics, have increasingly been subject to the preferences of members of Congress expressed by passing laws and overseeing their implementation. Top State Department bureaucrats, long accustomed to making policy and conducting negotiations without a thought to the statute books—at most, taking a few sympathetic legislators to cursory lunches in the Secretary's dining room—now find them-

selves chained to detailed statutory policy directives and complex reporting requirements.

If it was the genius of the U.S. Constitution to conceive a government
of laws, not men, then the revolution carried out by Congress from 1973
to 1978 has restored the Constitution's reach to embrace the conduct of
foreign relations.

The sharp, decisive victories in the revolution were won by passing
laws forcing the Administration to stop doing something: Congress
halted air support for the anti-Communist forces in Cambodia and military aid to Saigon. It prohibited military deliveries to Turkey and covert
operation in Angola. But Congress also began to use law to initiate
policy: requiring the government to negotiate nuclear safeguard agreements, limit arms exports, push for human rights, and revise foreign
assistance priorities, downgrading infrastructure and emphasizing pov-
erty-abatement, rural development, and population planning.

It is not so surprising that law, as a foreign policy instrument, should
be in the ascendant over "seat of the pants" pragmatism. The United
States has always perceived itself a nation governed primarily by laws. It
has been argued, however, that this proposition does not apply to foreign
affairs. In the famous *Curtiss-Wright* case,[1] Supreme Court Justice
George Sutherland approved a very broad delegation of foreign policy
discretion to the President by Congress, urging that such a concentration
of authority in the hands of the nation's Executive officers is the proper
and best way for a sovereign state to conduct parlous foreign relations.
But even Sutherland, long a devoted advocate of Presidential management of international affairs,[2] did not argue that these powers were
inherent in the Presidency—merely that it was meet and proper for Congress to bestow them by law from time to time on the Chief Executive.

Although, in this fashion, Congress has given Presidents very broad
powers in wartime and other periods of emergency—and has even allowed Presidents to appropriate what was not formally bestowed—the
nation has never felt particularly comfortable with Sutherland's proposition that such a concentration of power ought to be the ordinary, not
merely the extraordinary state of affairs in the conduct of foreign relations. This lingering resistance to the bifurcation of the Constitution—
one set of principles governing the distribution of power over domestic
affairs, another for foreign relations—finally seemed to fade in the period
between 1941 and 1973 because, in an age of perpetual nuclear confrontation, the boundary between emergency and normalcy became indis-
tinct. By the early '70's, most Americans may still have felt nostalgic
loyalty to the separation of powers and governance by laws, but, of
course, they also recognized the overweening need for strong, decisive
leadership in a crisis. And the crisis had become perpetual.

The fiasco of the Vietnam War tested the proposition that extraordinary times require management by extraordinary men endowed with extraordinary powers. That war was conducted by an executive branch vested with virtually unlimited power and, until 1973, largely immune to checking and balancing by a complaisant Congress. Yet the nation's unprecedented investment in its policy elite purchased neither victory nor wisdom. Such a concentrated dosage of power merely affected the leaders' vision, widening the gap between reality as they perceived it, and as it really was. By 1974, crisis or no, the United States was ready for a sharp turn toward structured, law-bound governance in place of faith in the free-wheeling wisdom, discretion, and common sense of a policy elite.

Critics of the Congressional revolution say it has gone too far. They charge that the legislators have destroyed the nation's ability to act decisively and have mired policy-making in a legal morass. But, while it is easy to come up with instances of legislative overkill, the general proposition has not been proven, despite a growing campaign by the White House to rid the President of "debilitating constraints."

That campaign has been something of a comedy of errors. In mid-1978, during a brief Cuban-backed Angolan war against neighboring Zaire, President Carter spoke angrily to members of Congress of the intolerable legislative constraints tying his hands. When it was pointed out that the only option foreclosed by law was a covert U.S. attack on Angola, Carter quickly backpedalled. That had never been in his mind, he said, disowning Admiral Stansfield Turner, who, taking his cue from Carter's complaint, had gone to see Senator Clark, chairman of the Africa subcommittee of the Foreign Relations Committee, to ask whether that law might be lifted. (Clark had emphatically said "no.") Next, the Carter Administration prepared a list of the "intolerable legislative restraints"—only to withdraw it a few days later when it turned out that some of the cited laws had already expired while others had simply been misconstrued. Then, during the January 1979 Iranian crisis, the White House let it be known that its toothless action of sending to the region a squadron of F-15's stripped of all weapons was necessitated by the War Powers Act. Even a cursory reading of that law makes it clear that the President could have sent the entire navy and air force to the Gulf, providing only that he made a reasonable prior effort to consult with Congressional leaders. It is perhaps unavoidable, but regrettable, that heirs to the once-imperial Presidency should still confuse a requirement to consult with a prohibition on action.

If these serio-comic ambushes are the best the Administration can do by way of counter-attack on the Congressional revolution, it would be well to call the whole thing off and concentrate on establishing a *modus vivendi*. But, for Presidents, Constitutional theology seems to exert as irresistible a call to battle as did Jerusalem for the crusading princes of Europe. Whatever else, each President appears determined to retire with the power patrimony of his office undiminished and, if possible, enhanced. Thus, beginning with Washington, chief executives have squandered their efforts on battles with Congress turning less on issues of the national interest than on arcane questions of each branch's Constitutional prerogatives.

Richard Nixon and his lieutenants seemed to spend more time proclaiming and defending his inherent right as Commander in Chief to bomb anywhere, anytime, than in making a logistic case for continuing air support of the blighted Lon Nol regime.[3] More recently, President Carter gave notice terminating the 1954 Mutual Defense Treaty with Formosa while Congress was in recess, without consulting the Congressional leadership. He acted in the face of a law signed only a few months earlier that called for Congressional consultation prior to such action.[4] In explanation, the President cited his Constitutional powers—which, in the matter of treaty termination, were rather unclear—and thereby provoked a lawsuit by Senator Goldwater and a dozen Congressional draft resolutions designed to provide new mandatory protection for Taiwan. Much of this could have been avoided by a little judicious consultation.

Carter, in treating Congress thus, was acting to enhance the Presidency, not his Taiwan policy—which would have had an even better reception in a generally sympathetic Congress, had there been some effort to consult. But he was determined to demonstrate that the President didn't *have* to consult—an important point to have scored in the game of Constitutional theology, comparable to the Pope's suppressing an outcropping of the Albigensian heresy.

The decision to join issue over the respective Constitutional rights of executive and legislative branches, rather than on the merits of a foreign policy initiative, is symptomatic of what has become almost a national disease: a preoccupation with Constitutional theology, with its concomitant neglect of real questions of comparative advantage. Nixon approached the Cambodian air war and Carter the Mutual Defense Treaty as if the future of the Presidency, not Phnom Penh or Formosa, were at stake. As a result, intricate national policy decisions were made largely as fall-out in a battle over Constitutional prerogatives. Similarly, Congress would rather defend its Constitutional prerogatives than discuss the merits of policy options. Thus, in voting to end the Cambodian aerial war, Senator Javits said, "At issue is the question of legal and constitutional authority and not a question of the correctness of policy. . . . What we seek to assert . . . is the rule of law, and not a rule of man."[5] Thus did a decision to accelerate the fall of Cambodia to the Pol Pot clique come about in a debate essentially about U.S., rather than Cambodian, freedom.

It would be better for the Presidency and Congress to suspend the theological debate and accept that, because of the institutional transformations chronicled in these pages, foreign policy will continue to be made, as the Constitution intended, through the joint, competitive, or complementary effort of Congress and the Executive. This means that it will be a policy of laws *and* men. There is now in place a statutory basis of American foreign policy which establishes procedures for consultation, outlines criteria for assessing options and, in some instances, mandates certain objectives and prohibits others. The time has perhaps come when Congress and President should stop arguing over the Constitutional theology of the separation of powers and begin to examine its functional implications.

WHEN BY LEGISLATION?

Legislation is a means to a foreign policy end. As such, its utility in any particular instance should be calculable in terms of its ability to advance the policy it seeks to implement. As an instrument, legislation has qualities—as does a trowel or scalpel—which are likely to be conducive to certain effects and not to others.

In a democracy, legislation is the most public of foreign policy–making processes, arrived at in the spotlight of open debate and controversy, broadcasting its intentions and proclaiming its predictions of future behavior and consequences. Its most prominent characteristic is *publicity*.

A second characteristic is *legitimacy*. When a bureaucrat issues a ruling, or even when the President makes a speech, the voice of an individual—albeit a powerful one—is heard. When Congress writes, and the President signs, a law, it speaks in a chorus of the nation. The act of legislating endows policy with a dignity, validity, and authority attained by no other product of the governmental process.

The third characteristic of legislative mandate is its *immutability*. Legislation can be amended, or repealed, but it is a difficult and time-consuming process in any parliamentary democracy, particularly as glacial a one as ours. Thus what is set out in a law is less likely to give way to momentary change, intellectual trend, or strategic fashion, than policy based on mere pronouncements of public officials.

A fourth quality is *comprehensiveness*. Policy statements, even treaties, may deliberately engage in vague generalities. Legislation, because its concern is with enforcement, attempts to foresee most eventualities and makes provision for them, leaving as little as possible to chance or man.

A final quality of law is its *universality* of application. A law may, of course, distinguish between those to whom it applies and others who are exempt. But, ordinarily, laws apply equally to all, and in every circumstance. It is this inexorable, immutable certainty of effect in anticipated future contingencies that most clearly distinguishes a policy of laws from one administered by officials vested with open-ended discretion to do "whatever seems best at the time."

Publicity, legitimacy, immutability, comprehensiveness, universality: these characteristics of legislation can be highly functional or dysfunctional to the policy being pursued, depending on the circumstances.

For example, the highly visible, public pursuit of human rights that is the consequence of the 1975 and 1976 human rights laws on balance has probably done more to help than hinder the achievement of the human rights policy's objectives. The high priority human rights have attained in U.S. foreign policy is a departure from the past, one which may have required publicity to become credible in foreign capitals. Publicity also has helped mobilize private interest groups here and abroad. It has transformed human rights from a U.S. diplomatic concern into a global popular issue. It can be argued that the educational and mobilizational benefits attendant upon publicity have outweighed the systemic costs of openly antagonizing some of our allies.

On the other hand, where the success of a policy depends upon discretion and deniability—getting the Soviets to agree to a larger emigration quota, for example—the publicity attendant upon the legislative process has proven highly dysfunctional.

Publicity given by Congress to the process of deciding whether or not to permit the sale of F-15's to Saudi Arabia may have disturbed the government in Riyadh; but not very much, for they had learned to play by the new rules, and probably felt it was worth it to get the benefit of Congressional commitment to the arms sales policy. The publicity costs, in other words, were more than offset by the legitimacy gains.

So, too, with treaties. Secret agreements may be faster made and less likely to cause inconvenience or embarrassment. But the United States is not really behind a commitment that has not been openly arrived at, debated, and willingly accepted, by the people's representatives. A foreign government will usually be well advised to pay the costs of publicity for the benefits of legitimation.

Immutability, the resistance of law to change, is a quality of great value in assuring allies that our policy commitment to them is more than transitory. Such assurance is essential when states are asked to exchange a present advantage for future commitments. It was in this context that Israel insisted on legislation, not a Presidential policy statement or written agreement, establishing the U.S. observer force in the Sinai as part of the price for a pull-back of Israeli forces. Similarly, if the purpose of a U.S. policy is to deter an enemy, its embodiment in legislation is convincing evidence of the nation's determination to stand fast. Unlike a Presidential policy statement, or even an agreement, laws cannot be readily changed or abrogated. When a commitment is locked into law, foes are placed on notice that our steadfastness is unlikely to diminish. The nation, in a sense, deliberately makes itself hostage to its pledged word. Deterrence may be made significantly more credible in this fashion, by embedding aspects of national resolve in the immutable concrete of legislation.

When, on the other hand, flexibility, rather than immutability, is more likely to achieve the desired policy objective, legislation becomes a dysfunctional instrument. The legislative prohibition on the use of force in, over, or off Indochina that began the Congressional uprising may have been justified in the historic context. But it created dysfunctional certainty where policy interests might better have been served by flexibility. The certainty that America would not respond, no matter what North Vietnam did, ensured the failure of the Paris accords and needlessly gave Hanoi a green light to proceed with renewed invasion of the South. And the inflexible law ultimately faced President Ford with an unacceptable choice between violating it, or abandoning thousands of Americans and pro-American Vietnamese in collapsing Saigon. The law had not, of course, been written with a view to preventing the use of U.S. forces in such circumstances. Yet that is precisely what it did, and the legislative process could not be geared up to change it in time to take care of the unanticipated emergency.

A rule of thumb might be that legislation should not be used to prohibit Presidential initiatives in unforeseeable circumstances. That rule has been embodied in the War Powers Resolution, which allows the President great latitude of response but then requires him, after a short time, to obtain Congressional endorsement.

Similarly, the legislative quality of comprehensiveness can be useful in advancing a policy where the contingencies are essentially foreseeable: economic assistance, nuclear exports, trade. The new Congressional guidelines for foreign aid–worthiness, for example, shade from the comprehensive into the petty, but they have successfully reoriented the economic development priorities and behavior of the U.S. donor agencies as well as of recipient governments. On the other hand, comprehensiveness is a burden when a policy has to operate amidst unforeseeable contingencies. A Congressional effort to tell the President exactly how many military attachés the Saigon embassy could have, or an effort to legislate the percentage of Soviet emigrés to be drawn from urban areas illustrates the folly of over-specificity into which legislative foreign policy can be tempted.

A prominent distinguishing attribute of law is its universality of application. "The law," in the words of the common law maxim, "is no respecter of men"—by which is meant that it applies to all without regard for who they may be. This quality can be very useful if it has been decided that a policy shall be applied to all states, regardless of the circumstances or our relations with the country affected. Once such a decision has been made, it becomes less damaging to U.S. relations with another country to cut off its nuclear fuel, to refuse to continue to supply arms or economic aid, or to impose a countervailing tariff, if we can show that we are merely applying a clearly stated rule which is consistently employed.

But if a rule is not to be applied consistently, then it is far better the policy not be embodied in law. To the Turks, it would no doubt have been distressing to be denied U.S. arms regardless of the circumstances. But it must have been doubly enraging to be informed that the law required them to be placed under an embargo for violating the rule against using U.S.–supplied weapons for offensive purposes, when they knew full well that the law had conspicuously not been invoked against other violators such as Israel and Greece.

Law is an efficacious means for universalizing policy. It is ill-employed when a policy is to be applied selectively.

The debate over the role of Congress in foreign policy has too long proceeded solely on the basis of Constitutional theology. The great boundary issues of our system have spellbound officials and scholars. But in focusing too exclusively on them, we have forgotten that the separation of powers has conduced to the growth of two separate, but not necessarily antagonistic, foreign policy capabilities—one executory, the other normative. Each has special utilities. The task is to learn to employ them to best advantage. The final and most important function of law may be to create a flexible, but not ruleless, framework—as the new oversight does—for determining in indeterminate future circumstances *when* to proceed by the majesty of law and when by the wisdom of men.

III

WILL THE CONGRESS
COME TO ORDER?

8

THE NATIONAL INTEREST
AND THE SPECIAL INTERESTS:
Congress and the Foreign
Relations Lobbies

ONE OF Congress's most serious problems in retaining and using the power it has acquired as a result of the 1973–75 revolution and of the institution of foreign policy codetermination is the negative way in which it is perceived by the public. There is a fairly widespread impression that our basic representative institution cannot be trusted, that members are only interested in reelection, not in the national interest, that they are for sale to the highest bidder.

To some extent this negative perception is shared by the members themselves. House International Relations Committee Chairman Zablocki has said, "Congress is too responsive to the lobbies of ethnic and special interests in the U.S. to be able to take the lead in foreign policy-making without endangering the national interest."[1] This view is seconded by inveterate Washington-based columnist James Reston, who has recently commented that "the 'goodness' of the American people is overwhelmed by the special interest lobbies"[2] operating through Congress.

Such concerns are given weight by some empirical evidence. In a survey of 114 Washington lobbyists, 54 percent thought Congressmen, their assistants, and committee staff to be their most effective contacts; 63 percent also reported them to be their best sources of unauthorized information.[3]

These are disquieting observations. If Congress is, indeed, the vulnerable branch of government, then its increasing codetermination of foreign policy may be tantamount to the subversion and corruption of the national interest.

THE KOREAGATE SCANDAL

Certainly, sensational press reports on the Korean Intelligence Agency's buying of members have done much to cause the public to be apprehensive about Congressional susceptibility to lobbies. Consequently, that episode requires careful scrutiny, for its import has been extraordinarily misunderstood.

It all began on December 8, 1973, when a South Korean businessman returning to his home in Washington, D.C., underwent a luggage search at Anchorage, Alaska, his plane's first touchdown on U.S. soil. The customs official reportedly discovered a paper which the Korean traveler, Tongsun Park—or Park Tong Sun—attempted to snatch out of his hand, thereby drawing extra attention to it. Mr. Hazelton, the customs inspector, reported that "I encountered strong resistance from Mr. Park. He used both hands to grab my arm and hand in an attempt to stop me from opening the folder." It turned out to be a list of names of seventy to eighty members of Congress with columns headed "Name," "State," "Party," "Committees," and "Contribution." In time the customs report found its way into the press. It stated that "amounts shown on the list ranged from 5 to 50. . . . When asked, Mr. Park stated that the figures represented hundreds of dollars."[4]

This incident only came to light more than three years later, as a House subcommittee took a searching look at Korean human rights violations, including Korean Central Intelligence Agency (KCIA) activities in the U.S. Testimony was heard on alleged bribery, espionage, intimidation, extortion, influence peddling, and various other illegal practices in the precincts of Congress by the Koreans. That triggered widespread reports by the media of "corruption of the national interests" by the KCIA operating through Mr. Park and others.[5] There followed further investigations by the House Committee on Standards of Official Conduct, headed by Democrat Flynt. A number of other committees in the House and Senate, the Departments of Justice and Internal Revenue followed suit.[6] Soon the press was enthusiastically featuring leaks from the various committees and agencies which suggested "that at least 115 Congressmen or former Congressmen were involved."[7]

The stakes were high and the unraveling plot made juicy rapportage: an attractive naturalized Korean "hostess" planted in the office of Speaker of the House Representative Carl Albert; top-level defections of Korean intelligence agents just as they were being recalled by Seoul; and the escape beyond the reach of U.S. jurisdiction of the alleged star witness, Tongsun Park. Most important of the stakes was the relationship between South Korea and the United States, forged in the Korean War and now involving the presence of 42,000 American troops and a large air force contingent. There was also an annual aid package of about $200 million a year in military credits and about $100 million in food-for-peace subsidized exports of agricultural products.[8]

The future prospects of U.S. military and economic assistance programs to South Korea became parlous as inferences were drawn that they were mired in corruption. On December 6, 1976, the *New York Times* reported that

> Five years of lobbying in the United States Congress by South Koreans, some of it legal, some of it questionable and some of it allegedly illegal, apparently paid off last spring with passage of a military assistance bill from which provisions unfavorable to the Koreans had been deleted. . . . [O]f the 241 Congressmen who voted for the pro-Korean position, 60 are known to have received one favor or another from the Korean lobbyists.[9]

Among the Representatives named were Clement J. Zablocki, William S. Broomfield of Michigan, Edward J. Derwinski, all senior members of the International Relations Committee. Also specified were the top Democratic leaders: Representatives Carl Albert, Thomas P. "Tip" O'Neill, Jr., and Whip John J. McFall of California.[10] The thrust of the story is that South Korean agents succeeded in illicitly influencing these leaders to bring about the defeat of proposals which would have cut back aid to Korea in retaliation for Seoul's restrictive policies on human rights.

No evidence whatsoever substantiated that assessment of the lobby's effectiveness. Instead, on closer examination, the allegations against these senior members of the House turn out to cover rather a variety of sins, ranging from pride and imprudence to venality. Zablocki, in the *New York Times* story, is accused of nothing more heinous than serving on the Advisory Council of the Korean Cultural and Freedom Foundation which was headed by a man "reportedly" a KCIA agent,[11] of having been "warmly welcomed while on trips to Korea," and of receiving an honorary degree at a Korean university.[12] Broomfield also received an honorary degree while Derwinski "has been decorated by President Park, entertained by Korean diplomats and members of the National Assembly and is a friend of Jhoon Rhee, an owner of karate gymnasiums who has said his duty here is to improve Korea's image."[13]

More seriously, it was alleged that Carl Albert "has a Korean-born woman," Sue Park Thomson, on his staff who "has been identified by Korean and American sources as a KCIA agent. . . ." But allegations that O'Neill "has been a favorite" of Tongsun Park were supported by little more than that the Korean "has twice given elaborate birthday parties for him." It was also reported that, after the House had voted in favor of Korean aid, "many of the Congressmen who had fought for the Korean position helped jubilant diplomats and lobbyists celebrate at a party given by the South Korean Embassy."[14] The implication was that men like Zablocki, Albert, and O'Neill supported U.S. aid to Korea because of the job lobbyists had done in undermining their ethical autonomy.

McFall's case was different. He had already admitted accepting $3,000 from Park in October 1974 and depositing the funds in his office account.[15] But the same net had caught persons who had accepted money payments, recipients of honorary degrees, and gregarious party-goers.

By spring of 1977, newspaper reports were alleging that Park had spent "between $500,000 and $1,000,000 a year in cash, campaign contributions, gifts and lavish entertaining to influence congressional action on legislation affecting South Korea."[16] It was asserted that more than twenty Congressmen, both Democrats and Republicans, accepted "large amounts" of cash, "expensive gifts" of furniture, jewelry, vacations, airline tickets, and "lavish entertainment."[17]

There were gifts in money and "gifts in kind." In the latter category were lumped together the merely bizarre, the marginal inducements, and illegal influence-buying. Some sixty-four members of Congress had visited Seoul in the twenty-two months preceding mid-1976, "some of them several times." On such visits, the *Times* reported, "after-hours accommodations with kisaeng or salon hostesses can sometimes be arranged"[18] for the susceptible. Representative Bonker reported being offered a $200 digital watch and "an attractive Korean woman who would be pleased to meet with the congressman on matters of mutual interest."[19] The *Washington Post* said that in the two years preceding 1976 "dozens of U.S. congressmen and congressional staff aides" accepted "questionable" all-expense-paid trips to South Korea and Taiwan from two private organizations "with close ties to those governments"[20] which were conduits for the kinds of favors—free travel and living expenses—that members can no longer accept directly from foreign governments under a 1974 ethics committee ruling.[21]

Yet such trips are allowed. Indeed, tax exempt (and thus government-subsidized) U.S. foundations have frequently paid to bring foreign officials and parliamentarians to our shores, as has the U.S. Government's "leadership grant" program. Sauce for the foreign goose need not necessarily be sauce for the American gander, of course, but if members of Congress were prohibited from traveling abroad at the expense of subsidized non-governmental organizations, their capacity to learn would be curbed along with their capacity to be influenced. Rightly or wrongly, most members are convinced they could successfully withstand the blandishments of a trip to Asia, and some even return from sponsored visits to places like the Republic of South Africa or Korea better informed about, and more distressed by, the human rights policies of those regimes.

Then there is the ubiquitous honorary degree. Opinions here, too, vary. "I regard it as a form of bribery," Representative Fraser has said, a view not widely shared among members. More typical is a sense of its not being worth the sheepskin it is supposedly written on.[22] Representative Leo J. Ryan reported refusing an offer of an honorary degree from the South Korean President after he was startled to be asked to "select the university" from which he would prefer to have it.[23] On the other hand, New York Democratic Representative John M. Murphy, a Korean War veteran, led a delegation of seven members of Congress to South Korea in October 1975 to commemorate the anniversary of the Korean War and to receive honorary doctorates from a Korea University. The recipients were all staunch supporters of the Republic of Korea, before, as well as after, the degree granting ceremonies. There is a certain amount of cavil in the criticism of degree-gathering. When a Jesuit school receiving U.S. funding awarded an honorary degree to Representative Zablocki, Representative Otto Passman of Louisiana let it be known that the ethical implications troubled him in his capacity as chairman of the House Appropriations Subcommittee on Foreign Operations.[24] Later, Passman himself was charged with receiving large sums of money in connection with rice sales to Korea,[25] charges which he denied[26] and of which he was ultimately acquitted by a home town jury.

Whether a member accepts or rejects an honorary degree is surely within an ethical grey area. Accepting payments from a foreign government, however, is not. Rather, it is illegal and unconstitutional. The U.S. Criminal Code makes it an offense, punishable by $5,000 fine and five years in prison, for any candidate for office knowingly to solicit, accept, or receive any contribution of money or valuables from an agent of a foreign government or indirectly through any other person.[27] The Constitution prohibits any "person holding any office of profit or trust" from taking a present or emolument of any kind from a foreign State.[28] House and Senate rules also prohibit the acceptance of gifts worth over one hundred dollars from anyone having a direct interest in legislation. Finally, bribery of legislators to influence legislation and the receipt of bribes is also criminalized by Title 18 of the U.S. Code.

The instances of violation of these laws, however, do not quite live up to the touching popular faith in widespread political mendacity. During January 1976 the *Washington Post* reported that the Korean Government took money from American defense contractors selling military equipment to South Korea and channeled it back to members of Congress and other officials to influence their votes.[29] The *Post* also found that Tongsun Park had been made the Korean President's designated commodity purchaser in the U.S. with the understanding that some of his profits would be used to buy a favorable legislative climate in Congress.[30] There followed frequent reports of impending widespread indictments. Two Representatives, Joseph P. Addabbo and Robert L. Leggett of California, were said to be under investigation by the FBI on suspicion of having accepted bribes.[31] John E. Nidecker, a former special assistant to President Nixon, volunteered that a South Korean National Assemblyman, Chin Hwan Row, whom he had met at a White House prayer breakfast, had offered to answer several members' prayers with campaign contributions in the 1974 election.[32] By October of 1976, the media said, the FBI and a federal grand jury were investigating reports that more than twenty U.S. Congressmen had received cash and gifts.

Little came of it, however. Certainly there was evidence of payments and/or attempted payments. As the investigations progressed, a spokesman for Representative John Brademas acknowledged that Tongsun Park had made three contributions totaling $5,150 between 1972 and 1974.[33] In November, Representative Richard Hanna of California reported that he had received between $60,000 and $70,000 over a three-year period as a "silent partner" in the rice business of Park Tong Sun. Representative McFall admitted accepting $3,000 for his office fund and a wristwatch from Park while he was Democratic whip.[34] Kansas Republican Larry Winn, Jr., said that a man he had met at an embassy reception told him, "We'd like to help your office," and handed him an envelope that turned out to be stuffed with $100 bills.[35] Alaska Senator Ted Stevens recalled getting a large check—at least $2,500—from a U.S. fish processing company during his 1972 re-election campaign with an accompanying note: "Your friends in Korea asked me to send you this."[36] Stevens said he had returned the money. Representative John M. Murphy accepted $500 in campaign contributions from Park,[37] as did Illinois Representative Melvin Price, chairman of the House Armed Services Committee, and Tom Foley of Washington, chairman of the Agriculture Committee.[38]

However, all denied that the contributions had purchased their favor. More important was the fact that such contributions were not illegal, since Tongsun Park's connections with the Korean government were disguised. Recipients were not "knowingly" accepting funds from a foreign government agent. "I just knew the guy as a rice salesman," Representative McFall said, noting that he represented a major rice growing district.[39] On the other hand, businessman Park was not soliciting favors for his rice trade, either. He appeared as just a Korean national passing out contributions to sympathetic members. In only a few egregious instances was there evidence that the contributions had been accepted with the understanding that they would influence legislation. Only after 1974 did it become illegal for a foreign national (other than a resident alien) to make a campaign contribution to Congressional candidates,[40] and almost all the contributions had been prior to that date.

However, a different set of allegations was made in November 1977 by a key KCIA defector, Sohn Ho Young, who testified to the existence of a 1976 KCIA plan for spending $750,000 on about 140 different operations in the U.S. to sway American policy in favor of South Korea. These included campaign fund contributions, money for members of Congress and staffers, and, perhaps most bizarre, an item of $1,200 "for utilization of Jewish lobbyists."[41] While the ubiquitous Mr. Park continued to insist that he had acted as a private Korean businessman, Young's charges implicated Korea's former Ambassador to Washington, Kim Dong Jo, in direct payments to Congressmen. Again, the smell of blood was in the air. At least ten present members had accepted money from Ambassador Kim, the *Washington Star* indicated.[42] Such payments by a known foreign official would fall squarely within the criminal law. The House Ethics Committee, after a false start marked by bitter squabbling between members and staff, hired Leon Jaworski to investigate, and Congress threatened to cut off military and economic aid if South Korea did not produce Ambassador Kim to testify.[43] The Justice Department pursued its own quest for indictments.

The results of these investigations do not sustain the dire expectations raised by the early stories. After three years' search, the Justice Department had obtained the conviction of one former Representative (Hanna) and the indictment of one other (Passman). In the instance of no sitting Congressman was there evidence to warrant going to trial. Representative McFall's party denied him the job of Majority Leader, for which he had been next in line. As a result of Jaworski's investigations, the ethics committee voted to bring disciplinary proceedings for accepting money in violation of House rules against McFall and three other sitting Representatives.[44] That was about all.

As the investigations drew to a close, it became increasingly apparent that Tongsun Park's big payments had, at most, encompassed the $260,-000 to former Representative Hanna, an alleged $221,000 to former Representative Cornelius Gallagher of New Jersey, and another alleged $247,000 to former Representative Otto Passman. All were in one way or another asserted to be rice trade-related. Payments to sitting members who favored aid to Korea had been petty—in the $100 to $5,000 league, over a five-year period. The latter was money Park, at that time, was legally entitled to contribute and which members could lawfully receive. And while the payments had apparently been made to about thirty-one Representatives, only twelve were still in Congress when the investigations were concluded.[45]

In the trial of Hancho Kim, another Korean conduit, the Government did not assert that any of the $600,000 the defendant had received from the Seoul regime had actually gone to members of Congress. Instead, the prosecutor suggested that Kim had probably kept most of it for himself.[46] The evidence, incomplete as it was, could not sustain another conclusion. Ex-Ambassador Kim, of course, was not talking. But Tongsun Park had been interviewed at length by Justice Department officials in Korea and by the House ethics committee in Washington. It seemed that Park, too, had probably inflated his reports to Seoul in order to account for a large budget which had gone into deals having no foreign relations impact, and into lavish entertaining.

While the susceptibility of many in Congress to such entertainment may point to looseness in the institution's rules of ethics, or even in the law, it does not begin to approximate early press estimates that 115 legislators were involved in bribery. According to Jaworski, these accounts were "terribly exaggerated by the media."[47]

This is not to say that the Korean influence-buying scandal does not point to a significant problem, nor that the law is yet sufficiently responsive to the dangers of corruption in a sensitive legislative process involving some 17,500 members and staff. However, the scales must be carefully balanced. Efforts to further tighten the laws are desirable, particularly in respect of unauthorized disclosure of information helpful to lobbyists. But it is also necessary to realize that lobbying is an unavoidable, important, and constitutionally protected aspect of the individual's right to approach his or her member in search of support for a cause or redress of a wrong. Intrusive police methods, unacceptable in a democracy, would be required to protect against all abuse of this right, because the difference between harmless and venal giving so much depends on the states of mind of donor and recipient.

Three kinds of legislation have attempted to curb abuses of legitimate lobbying activity without creating new ones: general laws to regulate lobbying, particularly through disclosure; laws requiring registration of foreign lobbyists; and campaign contribution limitations.

LEGAL CONTROL ON LOBBYING ABUSES

A representative assembly, wrote John Stuart Mill, should be

> at once the nation's Committee of Grievances, and its Congress of Opinions; an arena in which not only the general opinion of the nation,

but that of every section of it . . . can produce itself in full light and
challenge discussion. . . . A place where every interest and shade of
opinion in the country can have its cause even passionately pleaded, in
the face of the government and all other interests and opinions.[48]

One has but to compare a citizen's unimpeded access to the corridors of
the U.S. Capitol, the Congressional office buildings, and the legislators'
suites with the impenetrable barrier erected to keep citizens out of the
halls, offices, and meeting rooms of the British Parliament, to realize
that it is in the U.S., not in his native England, that Mill's vision has
been realized.

Undoubtedly, the Founding Fathers were conscious of the various
abuses that would accompany such open access by citizenry to legislators.
Indeed, James Madison, in essay Number Ten of *The Federalist*, argued
that the proposed political process would attract "citizens . . . who are
united and actuated by some common impulse of passion, or of interest. . . ." He recognized in the openness of the system a means to
channel and control the violence associated with faction. With this in
mind, the right to petition the government was guaranteed in the First
Amendment to the Constitution, becoming to lobbies what freedom of
speech and press became to the media. Inevitably, each of these First
Amendment rights is vulnerable to abuse and must be weighed against
countervailing Constitutional rights. But the validity of the concept,
with its roots in the *Magna Carta* of 1215, has been proven by experience
beyond reasoned challenge.

Lawmakers, realizing this, have been reluctant to enact legislation
which could pierce the Constitution's protective veil. Efforts to regulate
lobbying have therefore focused primarily on disclosure, rather than on
prohibition or constriction of activity. It is generally agreed that effective
disclosure strikes a reasonable balance between the citizen's right to petition and the right of the public to know who is trying to influence their
government.

While individual states have had statutes regulating lobbying activities
for over a century, Congress has come up with little such legislation, although, as far back as 1852, the House of Representatives prohibited the
use of reporters' seats on the floor by anyone who was employed to influence claims pending before the Congress.[49] But not until 1913 were there
demands for systematic controls on organized "petition." These grew out
of a Congressional investigation of the National Association of Manufacturers' tariff lobbying. The House panel turned up evidence that the
NAM controlled several members of Congress, kept the chief page of
the chamber on their payroll, and successfully influenced assignments to
strategic committee posts. After the clamor died down, however, the
only clear result of the probe was the resignation of one House member.

A "control of lobbying" bill was introduced in 1928, but not passed. Then, Senator Hugo Black's 1935 revelations of lobbying abuses by the utilities and financial institutions led to the Public Utilities Holding Company Act,[50] the Merchant Marine Act,[51] and the Foreign Agents Registration Act,[52] each aimed at imposing registration and reporting requirements.

The first comprehensive lobby-control law, the 1946 Federal Regulation of Lobbying Act,[53] was written by the Joint Committee on the Organization of Congress (the La Follette-Monroney Committee). The FRLA defined as a lobbyist any party whose "principal purpose" was to "influence, directly or indirectly, a passage or defeat of any legislation by Congress." Lobbyists were required to register with the Secretary of the Senate and the Clerk of the House and to file quarterly financial reports listing total receipts and expenditures, including detailed accounts of any contributions over $500 and any expenditures over $10. Failure to comply with any of the law's provisions was classified as a misdemeanor, punishable by imprisonment for one year and/or a $5,000 fine.

Soon after its passage, the scope and constitutionality of these regulations were challenged. A Select Committee to investigate the efficacy of the law called for records of various groups, including a list of bulk purchasers of the groups' publications. In *U.S. v. Rumely*,[54] the Supreme Court held that this fell outside the investigation of "lobbying." Under the First Amendment, Congress could only investigate "representations made directly to the Congress, its members, or its Committees."[55] One year later, in *U.S. v. Harriss*, the Court affirmed this narrow construction as the price of upholding the law's constitutionality. The *Harriss* case set three prerequisites for regulation. First, the lobbyist must have solicited, collected, or received contributions. Secondly, one of the main (non-incidental) purposes of the lobbyist or the contribution must be to influence legislation. Thirdly, the intended method of influencing must involve direct communications with members of Congress. So construed, the majority said, the FRLA does not violate First Amendment guarantees.[56]

Chief Justice Earl Warren defended the principle of regulation, stating, "Present day legislative complexities are such that individual members of Congress cannot be expected to explore the myriad pressures to which they are regularly subjected. Yet full realization of the American ideal of government by elected representatives depends to no small extent on their ability to properly evaluate such pressures. Otherwise the voice of the people may all too easily be drowned out by the voice of special interest groups seeking favored treatment while masquerading as proponents of the public weal. This is the evil which the Lobbying Act was designed to help prevent."[57] The Court thought this public interest in protecting its legislative process took priority over First Amendment rights offenders by the disclosure requirement, as long as the lobbying being regulated is confined to "direct communication with Members of Congress."[58] Such direct lobbying, however, while primarily defined to include traditional person-to-person communication with members, was also expanded to include one "grass-roots" activity: the "artificially stimulated letter campaign."[59]

The dissenting opinions of Justices William Douglas and Hugo Black suggest qualm about this balancing of self-protection and First Amendment rights. Moreover, the Court's majority opinion found the law Constitutional only by construing it as a very low hurdle. It does not cover lobbying by groups or industries that do not solicit contributions but spend their own funds. Nor does it apply to lobbies which can show that they are only influencing legislation incidentally to some other function. Not covered, either, are most lobbyists who influence Congress by influencing the public—so-called "grass roots" lobbying—or who lobby the executive branch. The law is also vague as to the kinds of contacts with Congress that constitute lobbying. Individuals or groups can still claim they are merely disseminating information, not seeking to influence members.

The law also does not lay down rules for determining expenditures attributable to lobbying, leaving this effectively to the lobbyist's discretion; neither does it provide for investigation or enforcement. As a result, there were only five investigations by the Justice Department in two decades since the *Harriss* case.

The 95th Congress, reacting to "post-Watergate morality," intensified efforts to pass a more effective disclosure law. A subcommittee of the House Judiciary Committee produced a bill[60] covering oral or written communications intended to influence not only members of Congress but also their staff and certain senior bureaucrats of the executive branch. Registration and quarterly reporting requirements were applied to any business, organization, or person spending $2,500 per quarter to retain outside help in making oral or written communications or which spent $2,500 in lobbying while employing one or more individuals who, in aggregate, spent thirteen or more days per quarter in lobbying. Exemptions are granted for communications with the members of Congress representing the interest's area of origin, for communications by individuals expressing a personal opinion, for communications made on the public record (a newspaper advertisement, for example), and for communications by way of periodic publications that are primarily unrelated to lobbying.

The registration and reporting requirements of the bill are quite exacting. Information on financial, personnel, procedural, organizational, and policy matters, including names of principal contributors, must be filed. New and more severe penalties—a $10,000 fine and two-year imprisonment—are provided. The General Accounting Office is given authority to implement the law, and promulgate rules and advisory opinions, subject to Congressional veto.

This bill (now HR 8494) was approved by the House in late April 1978 over opposition of both conservatives and civil liberties–oriented liberals. A companion bill before the Senate Governmental Affairs Committee, sponsored by Senator Ribicoff, was at first expected to be tougher.[61] However, in committees, weakening amendments introduced by Senators Charles Mathias of Maryland and Edmund Muskie of Maine, with strong support from business, labor, and the American Civil Liberties Union, so gutted the bill that no action was taken before adjournment.[62]

In addition to existing registration requirements, a tax law affects lobbying. Section 501(c)(3) of the Internal Revenue Code provides that organizations claiming tax exempt status as religious, charitable, or educational institutions may lose that exemption if a "substantial" part of their activities are directed to propaganda, attempts to influence legislation, or intervening in any political campaign.

In addition to these controls on lobbying in general, the law has imposed more comprehensive limitations and requirements on propagandizing or lobbying for foreign governments. The Foreign Agents Registration Act of 1938[63] grew out of a House investigation of Nazi propaganda in the United States. In reaction, Congress passed FARA (the McCormack Act), primarily to curb enemy agents. It requires all agents of a foreign power to register with the Justice Department unless they are diplomatically accredited. Between 1938 and 1944, nineteen indictments and eighteen convictions were obtained under the FARA, all relating to propaganda rather than lobbying. Between 1944 and 1964, there were only ten indictments and five convictions.[64]

In 1966, amendments, first proposed by the Senate Foreign Relations Committee, significantly modified FARA to accord with a shift in concern from secret enemy agents to lobbyists, often retained by friendly governments. The new law placed "primary emphasis on protecting the integrity of the decision-making process of our government."[65] These new provisions were inspired by hearings chaired by Senator William Fulbright that painted a picture of "secret campaign funding, buying [of] the media, disguising lobbying expenditures."[66]

FARA, as amended, requires every foreign agent[67] who engages in political activity for, or in the interests of, a foreign principal[68] to register with the Justice Department. Exemptions are provided for diplomats, foreign government officials, persons engaged in bona fide commerce, humanitarian fund-raising, or solely in religious, scholastic, artistic, or scientific pursuits.[69] The President may grant further exemptions "vital to the defense of the United States. . . ."[70] The Act requires detailed reporting of activities, sources of income, expenditures, and contributions. Records must be kept and be available for inspection.[71]

In a memorandum to the House ethics committee, its controversial special counsel, Philip A. Lacovara, pointed out that under the Foreign Agents Registration Act, if members were induced by Tongsun Park to lobby other members on behalf of South Korea, they, too, could be considered foreign agents and liable for criminal penalties, including a $10,000 fine and two years in prison for failing to register. "Since a member of the House is elected to represent the interests of his voting constituents and of the people of the United States as a whole," Lacovara wrote, "any finding that he actually acted as an agent of a foreign government could justify severe punishment, whether or not the acts were themselves corrupt."[72]

Despite such fang-baring, FARA has not been nearly as effective as was originally hoped. It has not brought about full disclosure, nor has it been properly enforced.

To begin with, the very language of the FARA produces a negative image not conducive to voluntary compliance, due in part to the odious association of the term "foreign agent" with subversion and espionage.[73] This stigma is reinforced by the fact that the Registration Unit remains part of the Internal Security Section of the Justice Department's Criminal Division.

Besides, the Registration Unit has been understaffed and underfunded. As its workload has increased, its staff has decreased. Even if properly supported, however, the monitoring of compliance would present practical difficulties. When there has been compliance, it has often been nominal. A review by GAO of the files of forty-five randomly selected foreign agents revealed that 67 percent of registration statements, and 33 percent of reports were not received within the prescribed time limits. In addition, 70 percent of the supplemental statements lacked the requisite detail.[74] Nevertheless, since these deficiencies were pointed out in 1974, there has been an upsurge of Unit activity with at least 180 inspections of books and records.

A third line of legislative regulation of lobbying concerns limitations on campaign contributions by private interests. The 1966 amendments to FARA include a criminal prohibition on foreign principals making any contributions to candidates for public office.[75] In 1974 this was tightened to include all foreign non-resident nationals.[76]

None of these laws can be totally impervious to evasion. A Washington lawyer engaged in buying an embassy for a foreign government, not so incidentally, may also discuss a zoning waiver with a staffer or member of the District of Columbia Committee. If challenged as an unregistered agent, he will probably take the position that he is acting as lawyer, determining the feasibility of a purchase, not as a lobbyist. He will argue that to impose a reporting requirement on such activity violates the lawyer-client relationship.[77]

Or, suppose a partner of a law firm collects $100,000 from a client government for legal services, then contributes $1,000 to the Congressional campaign of a legislator known to favor aid to that government. How is the Justice Department to prove that the lawyer is merely a conduit for the foreign government's contribution to the Congressman, that the fee was really only $99,000, with the additional $1,000 earmarked as an illegal campaign contribution?

Nevertheless, lawmakers continue to chip away at the problem. The Federal Election Campaign Act of 1971 requires candidates to reveal political contributions and expenditures.[78] But this has given rise to First Amendment problems similar to those occasioned by the 1946 FRLA. In litigation based on these provisions, the Supreme Court recently said, "we have repeatedly found that compelled disclosure, in itself, can seriously infringe on privacy of association and belief guaranteed by the First Amendment."[79] However, the Court found redeeming public interest in disclosure where the object is candidates' political committees, noting that disclosure of major contributors appears to be "the least restrictive means of curbing the evils"[80] of unwarranted influence and corruption in the political process.

On the other hand, some similar requirements imposed by the law on "issue groups" whose main purpose is not the nominating or electing of candidates, or which are not engaged in advocating the election or defeat of a clearly identified candidate, was held unconstitutional by the Court of Appeals in the same case.[81] This part of the judgment was not appealed to the Supreme Court. It held "that groups seeking only to advance discussion of public issues or to influence public opinion cannot be equated to groups whose relations to political processes is direct and intimate." The Court adopted the earlier distinction of the courts between "representations made directly to Congress" as opposed to "indirect efforts to influence legislation by changing the climate of public opinion."[82]

The most direct effort to curb the power of the private purse has taken the form of limits on the amount individuals and organizations—businesses, trade unions, social organizations—may contribute to candidates; limitations on the amount any individual may contribute to a Congressional candidate or member; and proposals for public financing of Congressional campaigns. While such private campaign contributions have traditionally aimed at influencing Congress on domestic issues, there has been a large increase, in recent years, of campaign spending to affect foreign policy.

Under a new law, individuals may only contribute up to $1,000 in the primary and $1,000 in the general election to each candidate for the House or Senate and may give no more than a total of $25,000 to all federal candidates in any calendar year.[83] Organizations or groups of fifty or more donors organized to contribute to five or more candidates— Political Action Committees (PAC) of businesses, professions, or unions—may contribute up to $5,000 in the primary and $5,000 in the general election to each House and Senate candidate.[84] An individual may contribute up to $5,000 per election to a PAC and up to $20,000 to a political committee of a national political party.[85]

Taking advantage of these provisions, labor unions, corporations, dairy committees, professional associations, and other interest groups legally contributed more than $23 million to Congressional candidates in 1976. By the 1978 elections this had soared to more than $60 million[86] per election. The contributions—up to $5,000 per candidate—raised from union and professional association members, corporate executives and stockholders, presumably went to curry the favor of incumbents and to help candidates supporting the best interests of the contributing group. The *New York Times* called this "a legalized form of genteel bribery" that accords "the Washington representative of the union or corporation" making the contribution "a claimed access to the lawmaker, to a small share of his attention."[87] Moreover, the system, in practice, is heavily skewed in favor of incumbents and, currently, toward Democrats.[88] On the other hand, no single contribution is likely to exceed about 4 percent of a Senator's, or 10 percent of a Representative's campaign budget.[89] More important, the contributions are a matter of public record, reported to the election commission by both the donor and the recipient. Anyone can now find out the extent to which, for example, the chairman of a Congressional energy subcommittee is indebted to oil and gas companies.

However, one important aspect of this most recent attempt to limit campaign contributions has run into the First Amendment again. It has been successfully argued that the contribution of an individual's own funds to a political campaign constitutes an aspect of free speech.[90] The only way to balance the effect of personal wealth on election campaigns, and, thus, on the law and policy-making process, is through a public funding of Congressional elections, a step for which most members have not been ready because it would end the fund-raising advantages of incumbency.

There are, then, things the law can do, and things it may not, or should not, do, to limit the power of domestic and foreign special interests. Unless a genuine threat to the system can be demonstrated, the Constitution welcomes lobbying as an integral part of the First Amendment's delicately balanced mobile of fundamental freedoms.

FOREIGN GOVERNMENTS AS LOBBIES

It is useful, in weighing the impact of lobbies on the judgment of Congress in the foreign relations field, to distinguish among foreign governments' lobbies, ethnic interest, public interest, and economic interest groups.

The activities of the KCIA, the Korean Ambassador, and Tongsun Park in Washington are by no means the only activities of foreign governments to influence Congress. Although only one other regime has been accused of making direct payments to a legislator in recent years[91]— that of Haiti's Duvalier—many governments, realizing the growing role of Congress in matters of direct interest to them, seek, and with increasing frequency obtain, direct access to members and their staffs.

Most foreign governments do not have to resort to such desperado methods to cultivate a favorable climate and understanding of their concerns. They employ highly regarded former legislators, ex-cabinet members, or partners of the most prestigious firms to give them the best possible representation in dealings with the Executive and, increasingly, with the Hill. Advocacy, not bribery, is their method.

Under FARA, which is reaching only the tip of the iceberg, the number of registered agents has grown from 160 in 1944 to over 600 today. Washington lawyers may be retained only to purchase an embassy or help draw up an air landing rights agreement; however, they are not infrequently also hired to persuade legislators in matters before Congress. During the first six months of 1977, sixty-seven law firms, earning $3.5 million in the process, registered with the Justice Department as foreign agents.[92] Many of these lawyers have themselves served in the U.S. Government and are hired, at least in part, for their access to officials and legislators: men like former Secretary of Defense Clark Clifford, retained by Algeria, former Secretary of State William Rogers representing Iran, former Deputy Attorney General William Ruckelshaus for Greece, and former Attorney General Richard Kleindienst for Algeria. Frederick G. Dutton, a former Kennedy administration official who is a registered agent for Saudi Arabia, has reported, "I advise the Saudis on legislation—who is pushing it, and what can be done. Until lately, the Arabs didn't even know where the Hill was."[93] Former chairman of the Senate Foreign Relations Committee, J. William Fulbright, is a registered agent for the United Arab Emirates and Saudi Arabia.

All this is lawful and above-board. Yet it is clear that Senator Fulbright is not your ordinary American citizen when it comes to access to the staff he hired and the friends he developed in his many years at the helm of the committee.

Foreign governments also hire public relations specialists, who, through the mass media, try to establish the public image desired by the client country. This activity, while substantially aimed at the Congress, is the equivalent of "grass roots" lobbying. Other strategy is more direct. The Saudis employed a public relations firm headed by Crawford Cook, a friend of John West, the U.S. Ambassador to Saudi Arabia, to help clear the Saudi purchase of sixty F-15 fighters,[94] and hired Michael Moynihan, New York Senator Daniel Moynihan's brother, for other lobbying activities. Jordan hired John O'Connell, the former station chief of the CIA in Amman.[95]

Many governments also maintain advocacy offices in Washington that are more or less independent of their embassies, but are nonetheless under the foreign government's control. Some take the form of trade councils, staffed by Americans, but with close ties to ministries of foreign trade in the client country. The United States–Japan Trade Council is a particularly active example, representing U.S. and Japanese business firms and actively campaigning—mainly in the United States, of course—for free trade. In this it deploys publications, testimony before Congressional committees, and direct contact with legislators and officials. Its director, Nelson Stitt, has stated that although "the Japanese government supports us . . . it does not dictate our policies . . ."[96]

It is groups similar to the U.S.–Japan Trade Council which sometimes arrange Congressional travel to their countries for members and their staffs, thus circumventing the House rules which prohibit members from traveling at the expense of a foreign government. More important, they marshal the support of prominent U.S. businessmen for causes before Congress, another form of "grass roots" lobbying. This is not a new development, although the number of countries in a position to use such business ties has increased as has the range of U.S.–foreign business connections. The role in Congress of the U.S. Chamber of Commerce in the 1978 campaign for increased foreign economic and military assistance has been credited by White House aides with saving those programs from their customary maulings on the House floor.

Among those actively engaged in business with Middle East oil-producing states are the traditional oil companies as well as prominent former political figures like Bert Lance, John Connally, and Spiro Agnew. According to the *New York Times*, "[a]ll, in one way or another, become lobbyists for Arab views."[97] During the controversy over the U.S. sale of fighter planes to Saudi Arabia, several large U.S. firms with business interests there—Bechtel Corporation and Computer Science Corporation[98]—joined the plane manufacturer in lobbying Congress for approval.

Not infrequently foreign business interests, with or without their government's direct subsidy, lobby actively. The South African sugar growers, seeking favorable import treatment, recently admitted providing free trips to South Africa for three key Congressmen and the wife of Representative John Flynt.[99]

Affluent foreign governments have also invested heavily in academia, endowing professorships and establishing centers at Harvard, University of Southern California, Georgetown University, and elsewhere.[100] These, at very least, ensure that senior teaching and research appointments are given to persons of recognized expertise who are sensitive to the views of the countries concerned, and who may use their eminent positions to provide advice and testimony to Congress on matters relevant to the region.

Besides hiring agents and supporting semi-autonomous but sympathetic groups, most foreign governments actively engage in Congressional politics through their embassies. Among the most active and influential in recent years have been those of Israel, Canada, Britain, Argentina, Egypt, and Saudi Arabia.

With increasing frequency, foreign governments now address themselves directly to Congress, in word or deed. The Turks communicated by deed when they closed U.S. bases in protest against the Congressionally imposed embargo on arms exports to their country, and in words when they held out the prospect of reopening them if the ban were repealed. All four national leaders involved in that dispute—Turkish Prime Minister Ecevit, Greek Prime Minister Caramanlis, Turkish-Cypriot leader Rauf Denktash, and Cypriot President Spyros Kyprianou—met with the International Relations Committee in the summer of 1978, as the vote to repeal the arms embargo approached. When the Senate Foreign Relations Committee staff began drafting the amendment that conditionally lifted the embargo, the Greek minister in Washington called frequently on the drafter. At first he argued against the repeal, but later prudently shifted to suggestions for improving the text to make it more acceptable to Athens. Some of his proposals were incorporated in the law.

It has become quite common in the past four years for foreign leaders or their envoys thus to approach Congress directly. This was virtually unheard of, previously, when foreign governments, at least formally, communicated only with the President and his officers. As early as January 1796 the Senate debated the propriety of its being in direct communication with the government of the French Republic. Two years earlier, the Committee of Public Safety had addressed Congress directly. Its letter was transmitted to both chambers by the President, and Congress, in turn, instructed the President on the contents of an appropriate reply. On the later occasion, after heated debate, the Senate voted to make no reply but merely to inform the President that the French Government's communication had been received "with the purest pleasure."[101] Senator Oliver Ellsworth argued forcefully that "Nothing could be found in the Constitution to authorize either branch of the Legislature to keep up any kind of correspondence with a foreign nation. . . . A correspondence with foreign nations was a business of difficulty and delicacy. . . . The people who sent us here placed their confidence in the President in matters of this nature. . . ."[102]

The first major break in this tradition in recent years was widely regarded as a failure; yet the foreign head of state secured essentially what he wanted. On August 25, 1975, during the height of Congressional opposition to a proposed sale to Jordan of 14 Hawk missile batteries, all 100 Senators and 50 key Representatives were startled to receive a personal letter from King Hussein.[103] Describing his country and people as "true friends of America," and "for two decades the only supporters the United States had in the Arab World," the King reminded members of Jordan's "moderate non-aggressive policy" and of its contribution "to maintaining stability and moderation in our area" adding that he had "cooperated very closely with your government, at considerable cost to my country and its people, in our common search for a just and lasting peace in the Middle East."

After arguing that the weapons were essential to Jordan's protection, would be defensively emplaced, and would not upset the overwhelming weapons superiority of Israel, Hussein concluded,

> The matter is in your hands now. If your decision to provide Jordan with the urgently needed fourteen batteries of Advanced Hawk missiles is a positive one, then no one will be more pleased or satisfied than I, your old and traditional friend.
>
> But if your decision is a negative one, I regret to inform you that I would have no other choice but to seek the best comparable system, which is available only in the Soviet Union. . . . As a friend, allow me to say that such a development will not only affect your interests in the Middle East but also incur irreparable damage to the United States credibility and reliability, not only in the Arab World, but perhaps throughout the world.

According to a legislative aide, "Here was a moderate asking for a modest amount of equipment. Hussein felt he had good relations with the United States and with many of Israel's strongest supporters in Congress. But now other Arab leaders were saying to Hussein, 'You've always been America's advocate in this region. Look what it gets you.' "[104]

At first, however, the reaction to the letter in Congress was overwhelmingly unfavorable. Representative Bingham spoke for many when he said he was particularly upset by Hussein's "threatening" tone, adding "is this kind of blackmail any proper basis for our Nation's foreign arms sales policies? I cannot believe that it is and I hope that the Congress will quickly reject it."[105]

Still, as we have seen, after some modification of the weapons' specifications, Congress did vote Hussein his missiles. On balance, the letter probably did more good than harm in influencing undecided votes. It also set a precedent for direct contacts with Congress to which the Administration could scarcely take exception since they were also pushing for quick approval of the sale.

Today, such direct contact by foreign leaders is almost usual. Several heads of state in Washington for President Carter's inauguration made a point of visiting the foreign affairs committees of House and Senate. So heavy has the traffic become that the House International Relations Committee has actually hired a protocol officer with functions comparable to her State Department counterpart. The House has provided a special budget—$55,000 in fiscal 1978—for entertaining and escorting these visitors.[106]

Whereas, in the past, Congress has had ceremonial meetings with foreign leaders or, on rare occasions, been addressed by them, the new interaction is in the form of working meetings, comparable, at times, to a diplomatic negotiation. These are now even prompted by the State Department, which wants the foreign leader to convince the legislators of a position the executive branch has already accepted. It was at State's suggestion that Prime Minister Morarji Desai went to both House and Senate committees in the summer of 1978 to persuade them—successfully—not to veto the President's decision to sell India enriched nuclear fuel.[107]

During the Administration's battle with Congress over the 1978 sale of F-15's, three Royal Saudi Princes—Bandar Bin Sultan (military aircraft specialist), Turki Faisal (chief intelligence officer), and Saud (foreign minister)—came to Washington, making their rounds of Capitol offices under the benign eye of the Carter Administration. "I have been told by members of the Saudi royal family," said Brian Atwood, the Deputy Assistant Secretary of State for Congressional Relations, trying to nudge Congress to act, that "a delay is just as bad as a rejection."[108]

Not only did the Saudi visitors go around encouraging their Congressional supporters and trying to convince waverers, but they even visited hard-core opponents. Like an experienced tactician, Prince Bandar met with New York City Representative Rosenthal on April 24, at the height of the jet sale debate, less in search of a compromise than to demonstrate that the Saudis bore no ill-will toward American Jews.

Perhaps the most fruitful visits of friendly persuasion by a foreign head of state were those of President Anwar el-Sadat of Egypt. Sadat met with both House and Senate committees in 1977 and again in 1978. These encounters are widely credited with playing an important part in turning Congressional opinion to accept the sale of U.S. jet fighters to his country, and in preventing Congressional opposition to the Carter Administration's increasingly tough line toward Jerusalem. On the other hand, Israeli Defense Minister Moshe Dayan, more effective with Congress than Prime Minister Menachem Begin, was equally busy. In April 1978 he himself convened what a participant described as a "private rump session of the Senate Foreign Relations Committee" to discuss strategy for blocking the sale of fighters to Arabia. An outside observer of all this coming and going mourned for the days "when there were rules and even manners about what was permissible in the conduct of foreign relations."[109]

In the summer of 1978, Senators were lobbied for an amendment proposed by Republican Senator Jesse Helms of North Carolina to repeal the trade embargo on Rhodesia. What was surprising was that the very effective lobbyist operating out of Helms's office was none other than Bishop Abel Muzorewa, a leading cabinet member of the new multi-racial Rhodesian Government. Later the same year, Senators Helms and Hayakawa invited Rhodesian Prime Minister Ian Smith to Washington. During that visit, Smith made one newsworthy announcement. He agreed to meet with leaders of the Patriotic Front fighting a guerrilla war against his regime "without preconditions"—a concession the State Department had long sought. Significantly, Smith did not reveal this shift during his meeting with the Department but reserved it for an informal gathering of the Senate Foreign Relations Committee.[110]

In a few short years, it appears, foreign regimes have learned to play Congressional politics in much subtler ways than those employed by the hapless Koreans. But it has become a reciprocal ploy. Congressional visitors to Cuba are always assured a statement by Fidel Castro, containing vague but tantalizing promises, calculated to gain the visitors, as well as Castro, headlines in the U.S. Some U.S. legislators and foreign leaders are developing a symbiotic relationship, using each other to hunt headlines and cadge support in Congress and among the public. The Somali government, once a Soviet client, used the visit of four Congressmen to invite U.S. warships in the Indian Ocean to consider using its Russian-built naval base.[111] Part of the strategy is to make legislators who are friendly to the foreign government appear responsible for a good-will gesture or concession. The government of Vietnam informed Senator Kennedy and his Subcommittee on Refugees—not the State Department—of a 1978 decision relaxing emigration rules. "As proposed by Senator Kennedy," read the message, "the Government of Vietnam has agreed to authorize the children having U.S. passports to travel, with their mothers, to the U.S. to join their relatives."[112] A senatorial party visiting Peking early in 1979, headed by Senator Sam Nunn of Georgia, was given a public assurance regarding the future of Taiwan by Deputy Prime Minister Teng Hsiao-ping that went well beyond anything the State Department had been able to produce in the exchange of communications with the Chinese Government announcing the decision to establish full diplomatic relations. Teng also extended a conciliatory public invitation to Senator Barry Goldwater, the leader of Congressional opposition to the new policy of "normalization."

Conversely, it had become not unusual for foreign governments to attack individual legislators, or even Congress in general. Moscow had publicly blamed Congress for lack of progress toward a strategic arms limitation agreement after a bruising visit to the Hill by a delegation led by the Politburo's Boris N. Ponomarev.[113] *Pravda* reserved its bitterest scorn for Senator Henry Jackson, a SALT specialist and critic, calling him "an archenemy of detente."[114]

THE ETHNIC LOBBIES

Foreign regimes that retain professional help in Washington, or whose top officials tramp the halls of Congress, are often attempting to balance an advantage enjoyed by those few fortunate governments which can leave the lobbying process primarily to mass movements of U.S. citizens. Fortunate is the state that can mobilize the vestigial ethnic loyalty of a sizable group of U.S. voters and campaign contributors.

By far the most effective citizen-ethnic lobby is the American Israel Public Affairs Committee (AIPAC), which was founded in 1951. During the crisis over the sale of Hawk missiles to Jordan, it was AIPAC, rather than the Israeli government or Israeli Embassy in Washington, which carried the ball with Congress. According to a pro-Israeli senatorial staffer who had worked on the campaign to stop the sale, we never had any help from the Israeli Embassy. To my knowledge we had no expression of views from their ambassador or staff. Senator Humphrey, at meetings of the Senate Foreign Relations Committee, kept saying, "If this is so important to the Israelis, why hasn't [Ambassador] Dinitz called me?" The answer was that the Israelis prefer to have AIPAC do the running for them.[115]

Since Jordan was then Israel's least hostile neighbor, Jerusalem preferred to appear almost neutral. Besides, AIPAC, with its lines to Jewish voters and fund raisers, had far more clout with Congress than the embassy.

AIPAC is responsible for funneling the policy preferences agreed upon by the representatives of organized American Jewry to decision-makers in Congress.[116] It has a small, but highly efficient, professional staff of twenty-one, only three of whom are registered lobbyists. None is registered as a foreign agent. It maintains extremely close relations with key legislators and staffers, particularly on the House side, and is headed by Morris Amitay, a former legislative aide to Senator Ribicoff.

While AIPAC is widely believed to be the most effective of ethnic groups—in 1975, one of its leading lobbyists was quoted as saying, "We've never lost on a major issue"[117]—it is by no means alone in the field. There are, from time to time, very active Greek, Irish, Chicano, Hungaro-Romanian, Chinese, and other lobbies. Efforts are also underway to mobilize black Americans into an Afro-American lobby which, potentially, could be the most powerful of all.

AIPAC is supported by 11,000 dues-paying members and has the presidents of virtually all major U.S. Jewish organizations on its executive committee. It operates almost entirely on issues affecting Israel, using a budget of less than a million dollars a year. A different Jewish-American organization, the Conference of Presidents of American Jewish Organizations, deals with most other issues of concern to Jews, as do groups like the American Jewish Committee and the Anti-Defamation League of B'nai B'rith. However, when AIPAC speaks to Congress on issues affecting Israel, it is almost always specifically endorsed by these other groups.

To AIPAC, its most important asset is early access to a remarkable range of information leaked to it from inside Congress and the Executive. This permits it to be fast off the ground. Amitay knew about the proposed Hawk sale to Jordan long before most members of Congress.[118] The earlier the leak, the longer AIPAC has to mobilize opposition. In such mobilization, the unit is at its best. Amitay, for example, very early received a top secret copy of the report of the Chiefs of Staff, based on the military survey mission, recommending only six missile batteries for Jordan, not the fourteen agreed by Kissinger. As a result, he was able to alert the Foreign Relations Committee, even helping to formulate the embarrassing questions asked when the chairman of the Joint Chiefs came to testify. General George Brown's public admission that the Joint Chiefs had, indeed, favored a much smaller arms transfer than the one actually concluded, almost induced the Committee then and there to pass the veto resolution.

Another value of this sort of lobby is its research capacity, which makes it helpful to legislators who do not have the staff resources to prepare their own issue papers and speeches. Over the first weekend after the Hawk sale was made public, AIPAC's research staff prepared an authoritative two-page memo describing its background, scope, and implications. It drew on Israeli defense intelligence, and argued that the improved Hawk system, far from being merely defensive, was capable of providing cover for offensive operations by Jordan against Israel. Every member received this fact sheet on Monday morning, long before anything came from the State Department, and it set the theme for the ensuing debates.

Meanwhile "instructions" went to Jewish communities in 197 major cities and 200 smaller communities throughout the country. In a demonstration of effective indirect or "grass roots" lobbying, AIPAC mobilized various Jewish national organizations including the American Jewish Committee, B'nai B'rith, Jewish War Veterans, National Council of Jewish Women, and the Union of American Hebrew Congregations: 397 local chapters. Within twenty-four hours, members were besieged with telephone calls, telegrams, and mailgrams from Jewish constituents urging them to oppose the sale of Hawks. The "Jordan Desk" of the State Department's Bureau for Near-East and South Asia Affairs was deluged with phone calls expressing opposition—so many, in fact, said one official, that the callers had to be referred to the State Department's Bureau of Public Affairs for answers "so we could get some work done."[119]

AIPAC also began an immediate roundup of sympathetic non-Jewish interest groups, including the Americans for Democratic Action and the AFL/CIO, organizations in which Jews were prominent or for which Jewish organizations had done favors in other lobbying efforts. In the words of one pro-Israeli Congressional staffer, "George Meany unleashed the Communications Workers on our side."[120] Amitay also provided statements to the House subcommittee during hearings on the sale, assisted in securing other friendly witnesses, and testified before the Senate Committee on Foreign Relations. According to one official of the House subcommittee, Amitay is "young, aggressive, and given to operating through new mass media techniques which are different from the low-keyed informal and personal touch used by his predecessor. The Hawk missile crisis was his first major congressional campaign and he saw it as a crucial test of his abilities and methods."[121]

In the campaign to enact the Jackson-Vanik Amendment, which tried to force the Soviets to make concessions on Jewish emigration in exchange for more trade and credit, lobbying was coordinated by a coalition of interests called "the Washington group." This included both professional lobbyists such as June Silver Rogul (then head of the Washington office of the National Conference on Soviet Jewry, later with AIPAC) and such Congressional staffers as Richard Perle, Dorothy Fosdick, and Tina Silver of Senator Jackson's Permanent Subcommittee on Investigations; Mark Talisman, an administrative assistant to Representative Charles Vanik of Ohio; and Morris Amitay, then still with Senator Ribicoff.[122]

It was to the National Conference on Soviet Jewry—an umbrella organization including B'nai B'rith, the American Jewish Committee, thirty-two other national Jewish organizations and at least 200 local Jewish agencies—that Senator Jackson announced his proposed amendment linking trade with emigration. Immediately, the campaign to enlist Congressional co-sponsors for the Senator's amendment got under way, led by staffers Perle and Talisman. A simultaneous grass-roots effort was organized by the National Conference. Letters were dispatched to about 1,000 Jewish leaders by the executive vice-chairman of AIPAC. Soon these efforts yielded a steady influx of mail from constituents. When Vanik introduced his amendment in February 1973 an astonishing 259 members had signed as co-sponsors.

George Meany and the AFL/CIO were enrolled almost from the beginning, in part out of the leader's inveterate anti-communism but also because they perceived an opportunity to undercut legislation aiming at expanding free trade, a cause labor had begun to oppose selectively. Some Christian leaders and such non-Jewish ethnic groups as the Lithuanians and Latvians also joined the lobbying coalition because, of course, the amendments called for free emigration in general, not for Jews only.

The lobbies rallied support and they kept waverers in line. At one point, the White House, utilizing President Nixon's assistant for liaison with American Jews, Leonard Garment, as well as Henry Kissinger, attempted to negotiate with a group of Jewish leaders. But as soon as it appeared that Senator Jacob Javits might support a compromise, the *Jewish Press* ran a critical editorial and pressure was exerted by the Greater New York Conference on Soviet Jewry. He retreated, again taking his stand squarely on the Jackson Amendment.[123]

Near the end of the tortuous negotiations between Jackson and the White House, the word went from the National Conference to about twenty-five top officers of major Jewish organizations to send telegrams to President Ford expressing outrage in the strongest possible terms. At another point, however, the National Conference leaned on Jackson to be more flexible in his negotiations with Kissinger and Ford, placing themselves behind a new compromise worked out by Senator Javits. As the debate dragged on, the Jewish lobby became a key independent actor in a global transaction involving the Soviets, the President, and members of Congress and their staffs.

The effectiveness of the Jewish lobby has attracted growing notice and criticism. Senate Majority Leader Mansfield told President Ford of his concern that a precedent had been set during the Jackson-Vanik negotiations which could make the future conduct of foreign relations unmanageable.[124]

During the AIPAC campaign to block the 1978 jet sales to Egypt and Arabia, this sort of criticism became widespread. Members resented the intensity and frequency of the pressure being applied as well as AIPAC's open participation in the legislative caucus organized to oppose the sale. That participation extended to attending caucus meetings, drafting the resolution to disapprove the sale, and questions for committee hearings.

Indeed, the very hard-sell lobbies generally court a backlash. Voting for the Saudi jet sale, Senator Mike Gravel of Alaska said that this "kisses away all kinds of financial support" and added, bitterly, "I think this will be a watershed year for Jewish influence in this country. . . . When you deliver an ultimatum once, you cannot deliver it twice or three times" because the victim has "broken away into what becomes a total independence."[125] Speaking of another (non-Jewish) pressure group recently, Senator Culver told his colleagues, "I am sick and tired of that kind of politics. I am sick and tired of it."[126]

Some in and around Congress openly worry about "the overall ethnicization of foreign policy."[127] A Congressional relations specialist for the White House has argued that new Congressional tendencies to intervene in the daily administration of foreign policy, together with the members' vulnerability to special interest group pressure, was "imparting an ethnic hue to an increasingly broad spectrum of American diplomacy."[128] He argued that, by comparison, the Executive bureaucracy and the President are better insulated against these kinds of ethnic pressures.

However, this is probably too dark a picture of reality. AIPAC lost its 1978 campaign to persuade Congress to veto the Middle East arms package precisely because members proved jealous guardians of their independence and tended to react as much against, as for, repetitive pressure tactics. Also, lobbies tend to generate counter-lobbies, producing a creative, competitive balance. The Arab states, lacking a domestic U.S. constituency, found other ways to inform and influence the Hill. While professional lobbyists are the core of this counter-lobby, there has also come into existence the National Association of Arab Americans, the American Palestine Committee, the Action Committee on American-

Arab Relations headed by the outspoken Dr. T. M. Mehdi and the American Near East Refugee Aid.

In addition, a key variable is the White House. The success of President Carter in defeating the Jewish lobby in 1978 is but one of several recent demonstrations of the importance of that variable. Thus, while lobbies are increasingly important, they are also increasingly offsetting each other, thereby escalating the intensity of each foreign relations debate—and better informing it, in the process—but no foreign policy lobby is instrumentally determining the outcomes.

Next to the Jewish lobby, and often in conjunction with it, the most effective ethnic interest group to influence foreign relations on the Hill in these past six years of Congressional ascendance has been the Greek-American lobby. Greek-Americans have long been adept at forming effective community organizations: at first dedicated primarily to the church, education, social, or athletic activities. The Greek-American Progressive Association, formed in the early 1920's and consisting of about 10,000 members, has striven to preserve Hellenic culture; the American Hellenic Educational Progressive Association (AHEPA), with some 25,000 active members and more than 400 chapters, was organized to promote Americanization and effective upward social mobility.[129]

Gradually, Greek-American organizations began to develop the art of political pressure, particularly after 1940, when Greece's heroic stand against the Italian Fascists and German Nazi forces began to evoke considerable sympathy in the United States.[130] After the war, American Greek organizations rallied for the Marshall Plan and in support of the Truman Doctrine, taking their case to Congress as well as to the White House.

In the 1950's these efforts shifted to support for the Greek community of Cyprus, first against British colonial rule and in favor of the island's union with Greece, later in opposition to perceived threats by Turkey against Cypriot independence. American Greek and Cypriot organizations played a role, in 1964, in influencing President Johnson to write Turkish President Ismet Inonu warning him against use of "any United States supplied military equipment for a Turkish intervention in Cyprus. . . ."[131]

The biggest and most successful effort of the Greek organizations and churches was in persuading Congress to punish Turkey after its 1974 invasion of Cyprus. That attack began on August 14; by August 30, Democratic Majority Leader Mansfield was complaining publicly of the avalanche of telegrams from Greek-American organizations urging Congressional action to stop the flow of U.S. arms transfers to Turkey.[132] That an embargo was imposed by Congress against the advice of the President and almost all Congressional leaders of both parties testifies to the effectiveness of a campaign coordinated by Father Evagorus Constantinides and implemented in the House of Representatives by a handful of members of Greek origin who are highly respected for their ability and political acumen.

Father Constantinides, himself born in Cyprus, was from the Congressional district of Representative Ray J. Madden of Indiana, then the chairman of the powerful Rules Committee. The Madden connection turned out to be crucial, particularly in repelling efforts, in 1975, to repeal the embargo. Madden simply pocketed repeal legislation, preventing it from being reported to the floor. Although eventually outvoted by his committee, the delay helped ensure that action could not be taken before the House adjourned for the summer. Explaining his conduct, Madden, with Father Constantinides in the front row of spectators, openly and appreciatively discussed on the floor of the House the intensiveness of the efforts by which Greek organizations had persuaded him to block the bill.[133]

In subsequent years, as each successive administration fought to lift the embargo, a Greek professional lobby emerged in Washington somewhat self-consciously modeled on AIPAC. The American Hellenic Institute (AHI) was formed three days after the second Turkish offensive on Cyprus. An organization started with just over 200 members, it first focused on recruiting influential Greek-American businessmen and civic leaders to appeal directly to their representatives in Washington in support of the Turkish embargo. For lobbying purposes, it established the American Hellenic Institute Public Affairs Committee (AHIPAC), on March 25, 1975, under the chairmanship of Eugene Rossides, a former Assistant Secretary of the Treasury, supported by one full-time lobbyist, Leon Stavrou. For grass-roots appeals, AHIPAC continued the use of AHEPA.[134] Between them, AHIPAC and AHEPA were able to mobilize avalanches of letters, cables, and telephone calls to every member each time there was a Presidential attempt to get the embargo lifted. In a mass-mailing letter to international law and foreign relations teachers, following Congress's lifting of the Turkish embargo, Rossides complained of the lack of scholarly interest in, and writing on, the Greek case and included lists of possible research topics as well as a bibliography.

A few members like Senators Claiborne Pell of Rhode Island and Edward Kennedy were subject to influence by sizable Greek blocs of voters among their constituents. But the Greek-American population is not so large—estimates range from 600,000 to 3,000,000—so coherent, or so affluent as to be able to affect the political fortunes of many in Congress. The success of the Greek lobby thus depended in considerable part on a handful of tactically skilled Greek-American members of Congress and on alliance politics that forged a common front with other "ethnics."

Representative Lester Wolff of New York, for example, represents a constituency with very few Greek-Americans but a substantial Armenian-American population. The latter were prodded to urge Wolff's taking a hard line against Turkey. The Jewish-Greek alliance, led by Representative Benjamin Rosenthal—whose district has a substantial Greek-American component—and by AIPAC's Morris Amitay, was particularly effective.

There were those who criticized this alliance tactic. The Israeli Embassy even warned Rosenthal "with much feeling" that his leadership of the pro-embargo forces had caused Ankara to threaten a breach of diplomatic relations with Jerusalem.[135] Undersecretary of State Carlyle Maw concluded that AIPAC "really miscalculated in their decision to support the Greeks."[136]

Neither Rosenthal nor Amitay agree. They see the ethnic alliance as benefiting both Israel and the Greek Cypriots. Certainly it seemed to pay off for a time, helping to rally support for a wide variety of Jewish and Greek aims: keeping the Turkish embargo in effect, impeding the sale of sophisticated weapons to Arab states, criminalizing U.S. business compliance with the Arab boycott of Israel, blocking the new U.S. base agreement with Turkey. Even after the alliance began to lose some battles such as the sale of F-15's to Saudi Arabia, the core of the coalition[137] continued to command an impressive loyalty. After a trip to the Eastern Mediterranean in mid-1978, Senator Javits confided to a friend, "I know we have to repeal the Turkish ban, but how can I vote against Paul [Senator Sarbanes] when he's been so far out front on the Middle East jet sale package?"

As with AIPAC, so the early success of AHIPAC has engendered counter-lobbying. Some of this, judged remarkably ineffective by Congressional staff, has come from the Turkish Government; much more from the White House. But other groups also weighed in. By August 1975 the American Legion, galvanized by military concern at the disintegration of the key Turkish link in NATO, passed a resolution that strongly urged "Congress immediately to lift the embargo on military aid to Turkey." The Veterans of Foreign Wars, condemning "this Congressional blunder," also called for repeal, as did the Airforce Association.[138] These cumulative pressures balanced those of the ethnic coalition. When Congress reconvened, in October, the boycott was partially lifted and in August 1978 it was effectively repealed.

This counterposition of opposing lobbies is an aspect of the democratic system's infinite capacity to develop resistance to a new pathology. Not that most members vote solely on the basis of a pressure meter. But to the extent such pressures are—and should be—felt by the people's representatives, the push in one direction is seldom unchallenged by a pull in another. This creates, for most members, the systemically desirable, if personally uncomfortable dilemma known as free choice (or, "I'm damned if I do and damned if I don't").

OTHER FOREIGN POLICY LOBBIES

Industry lobbies differ little from the method of operation used by foreign governments and ethnic groups. Once free to hand politicians huge direct contributions—Gulf Oil in 1975 admitted that it had maintained a $12 million "slush fund" for politicians over a thirteen-year period[139]— the corporations are now closely monitored and limited in the campaign contributions they can make to any one member. Consequently, they, too, have ventured into direct and grass-roots lobbying.

The work is done by such senior executive groups as the 200-member Business Roundtable, by broadly based interest associations like the U.S. Chamber of Commerce, and by research-oriented teams of professional Washington influencers. Many firms also have their own staff of house lobbyists. Altogether, more than 500 corporations operate Washington lobbies, a five-fold increase in the past decade. In addition, more than 1,500 national trade and professional associations now have headquarters in the capital, at least in part to promote access to government.[140] Even ex-spies have their lobby, an Association of Former Intelligence Officers.[141]

The most influential of the industry and business lobbies is the Chamber of Commerce, with 2,500 local affiliated chapters, 1,300 professional and trade associations, and 68,000 corporate members.[142] The Chamber in 1977 took up 61 legislative issues, utilizing a finely tuned grass-roots lobbying system based on 1,200 local Congressional Action Committees with 100,000 members. Its computerized communications system and research publications speed an "action call" to seven million people,[143] producing the desired siege of calls and telegrams to legislators. At six regional offices, the Chamber studies the habits and associations of that area's members of Congress, identifying and cultivating "key resource people" who have special influence on them: college roommates, law partners, relatives or friends, campaign fund-raisers. Although they are not primarily involved in foreign relations operations, the Chamber has been highly effective in rescuing the U.S. foreign aid program and in encouraging continued commitment to U.S. allies abroad at a time of post-Vietnam lassitude.

In the foreign relations field, the Emergency Committee for American Trade (ECAT), consisting primarily of businesses favoring trade liberalization, has been described as representing "forty percent of our

GNP."[144] In the 1974 campaign for the Trade Reform Act, ECAT, with the League of Women Voters, was able to marshal 1,200 leading corporate figures for a last-minute lobbying drive in the halls of Congress. Individual industries active in lobbying for trade protection include the American Iron and Steel Institute, the chief research and lobbying arm of the steel industry. Its chairman, Edgar B. Speer, is the head of U.S. Steel.[145]

In the early 1970's the bulk of the U.S. fisheries industry—led by the Atlantic States Marine Fisheries Commission,[146] the National Coalition for Marine Conservation, the Maine Sardine Packers Association, and even the Yakima Tribal Council—lobbied Congress to establish a 200-mile wide exclusive fisheries zone around the U.S. This met strong opposition from the State Department, then engaged in a world-wide negotiation for a comprehensive Law of the Seas treaty. The Department argued that a unilateral move by Congress on one of the key subjects of the negotiations would damage chances for a global agreement. Nevertheless, the legislation passed in 1975,[147] pressed by such otherwise-ardent internationalists as Senators Edward Kennedy and Claiborne Pell, both of whom come from states with large fishing populations. As usual, lobbies were ranged on the other side of that issue, including the American Shrimpboat Association and National Shrimp Conference, and the Tuna Fishery Boat Association. These strenuously opposed the 200-mile zone because they fish in waters off foreign states which could be expected to reciprocate.

Mining companies such as Kennecott Exploration, Standard Oil of Indiana, Lockheed Missiles and Space Co., and Deepsea Ventures have pressed Congress to enact legislation permitting them to explore and exploit mineral resources on the deep seabed, another subject of international negotiations.[148] In 1978, the U.S. beet sugar industry succeeded in having the Senate Foreign Relations Committee hold up U.S. ratification of the International Sugar Agreement, holding it hostage to Presidential agreement on higher subsidies for their own product.[149] They were able to enlist the support of two key Committee chairmen, both from sugar beet producing states: Church of Idaho and Russell Long of Louisiana.[150] In the absence of a countervailing White House and consumer-group lobbying alliance, Church was able to bottle up the treaty in his Foreign Relations Committee.

The most important foreign relations–related single-industry lobbies are those maintained by oil and aerospace. Indirect lobbying takes the form of helping the cause of oil-producing countries, and aiding Middle Eastern and pro-Arab interest and research groups. Direct lobbying is the task of the American Petroleum Institute (API) representing 350 corporations. While chief executives of major U.S. oil companies also do their own lobbying, they frequently retain prominent law and public relations firms in the capital. API and Standard Oil of Indiana each pay Washington public relations specialist Tom C. Korologos—a former Congressional aide—about $100,000 a year.[151] It is, of course, energy policy that has occupied most of the oil industry's effort, although companies have also fought against anti-boycott legislation and for arms sales to Arab countries. They constitute another formidable counterweight to the Jewish lobby.

Since the arms industry employs over one thousand former Defense Department officials and numerous ex-Congressmen, it does not lack connections. But it is too concentrated and competitive to permit any but the most general causes to be pursued through its trade group, the National Security Industrial Association. Most persuading of Congress is done by the individual firms, and the result is a lobby which is often at cross purposes with itself. In the words of Representative Aspin, himself a former Defense official and chief critic of the industry, the lobby is "powerful but not cohesive. Nobody orchestrates because all of its members are out fighting for their own piece of turf."[152]

On the other hand, a particular industry can have a virtually commanding effect on the member in whose district it is located. For example, Congress and the Administration have continued production of the F-18, even though the Navy had serious doubts about its usefulness. Since none of the Armed Services is inclined to oppose weapons production gratuitously, the insistence of Congress in foisting the unwanted F-18 on the Navy requires some explanation. This lies in the fact that its engine is made by General Electric in Lynn, Massachusetts, the home district of House Speaker O'Neill. With O'Neill and Senator Kennedy in full-throttled support of the plane, continued production was an offer the Navy could not refuse.[153]

It should be noted that General Electric's clout is due not to some secret source of influence but to the fact that 5,000 or more jobs are at stake. The unions, local commerce, and housewives together provided the letters and telephone calls, with General Electric merely the leading spokesman. In a politically responsive system, it is appropriate for O'Neill to answer to such pressures, even when he doubts their wisdom. Politics in a democracy is no guarantee of the national interest except insofar as the highest national interest is itself democracy.

Nevertheless, such issues create crises of conscience for the sensitive legislator. Democrat Thomas Downey, a liberal member of the key Armed Services Committee of the House who represents a district on New York's Long Island that has a sizable aerospace industry, felt strongly enough to vote against production of the B-1 bomber. "Its cancellation cost my district 1,500 jobs. The aircraft industry and the unions

really put the squeeze on me. I can't go on voting my conscience on
arms questions and expect to get reelected." Downey's pragmatic answer
was to request transfer to another committee. "Every time a pressure
group comes to see me," he said, "it's always a matter of life or death:
whether it's tax credits for tuition, abortion or blocking arms sales to
Saudi Arabia. That's why so many members are quitting. They're finding
they just can't stand the heat."[154]

A prime source of heat is the labor movement. Unions, much like business, work through massive information and education programs aimed
both at Congress and at voters. They spend large sums on research and
publication, contribute to sympathetic candidates through lawful Political Action Committees, and maintain large Washington offices in part
to engage in direct lobbying of Congress. To the extent its grass-roots
efforts have succeeded, organized labor has brought liberal legislators to
Congress; many of these now find themselves under strenuous labor pressure to vote against their consciences for protectionist amendments to
trade legislation or in favor of Congressional vetoes intended to reverse
Presidential denials of special protection to industries hard hit by more
cost efficient foreign producers of steel or shoes. Labor also opposes another liberal cause, the extension of a General System of Preference to
permit third world manufactured products to enter the U.S. at reduced
tariffs, and has distanced itself from liberals over arms limitation agreements with Russia.

Fifty individual unions maintain their own lobbying offices in Washington. Most powerful of these is the Teamsters, in impressive offices
facing the capitol. In addition, the umbrella organization, the AFL/
CIO, employs a 300-member staff at its headquarters near the White
House. It is in alliance with other lobbying groups such as AIPAC that
labor tends to win its principal victories in international matters. Thus,
the strong support of the AFL/CIO for the Jackson-Vanik Amendment
tying Soviet trade preferences to freer emigration was a success of sorts
for the unions, if not for the Jewish groups that initiated the effort, because, while it did not achieve unrestricted emigration from Russia it
killed Soviet trade privileges. The AFL/CIO also made common cause
with some Jewish organizations to persuade the U.S. Government to
withdraw from participation in the International Labor Organization.
Labor's objection to the ILO stems from the Organization's recognition
of captive unions manipulated by totalitarian regimes; the Jewish groups
resented the ILO's anti-Israeli resolutions and projects.

Finally, there are various so-called public interest, citizens' or single-
issue lobbies. These include organizations like the Sierra Club which,
though mainly concerned with domestic environmental issues, was actively represented at the Law of the Seas Conference and lobbied there

and in Congress for rigorous national control over a wide coastal zone to enforce stringent conservation and anti-pollution standards. It was joined in these campaigns by the Environmental Defense Fund, the Environmental Policy Center, Friends of the Earth, and the National Audubon Society.[155]

An Emergency Coalition To Save the Panama Canal served as an umbrella organization for many groups opposed to the "give-away." The American Legion, Veterans of Foreign Wars, American Conservative Union (ACU), American Security Council, Young Americans for Freedom, the Conservative Caucus, Citizens for the Republic, Committee for the Survival of a Free Congress, and the National Conservative Political Action Committee all registered strenuous opposition on the Hill. Richard Viguerie, leading direct mailer of literature for conservative causes, called this the biggest "grass roots" effort to influence Congress ever undertaken by American conservatives.[156] He estimates that anywhere from five to ten million letters were mailed by his operation before spring 1978.[157] Republican leader Senator Howard Baker, as early as November 1977, had already received 22,000 letters on the issue, only 500 in support of the treaties.[158] An unprecedented media blitz begged: "Don't let President Carter give it away."[159] Viguerie predicted that his people would "do an awful lot of punishing next election,"[160] and there is evidence that the issue did play a role in the defeat of some liberal members in 1978.

An impressive coalition of forces was ranged on the pro-treaty side, centered at the White House, which enlisted help from both George Meany and the U.S. Chamber of Commerce. James Reynolds, the President of AIMS, the American Institute of Merchant Shipping—a principal canal user—testified that the U.S. must recognize that the era of colonialism is over.[161] The AFL/CIO's Committee on Political Education (COPE), headed by Lane Kirkland, generated grass-roots support as did actor John Wayne, a conservative who also happened to be an old friend of Panamanian President Omar Torrijos. The Panamanian Government was encouraged to use professional lobbyists in dealing with the Senate,[162] who counselled him to launch his campaign for U.S. grass-roots support with a political pilgrimage to Israel.

To press its case for the Canal treaties, the White House opened a speakers' bureau, starring Chief of Staff General George Brown. Civic leaders from around the country were flown to Washington for Presidential briefings. In a calculated ploy, invitations were issued by the President on behalf of the local Senator. An aide said, "We made it look like the Senator had personally arranged for the invitation. That way, even if we failed to convince the guest, we still picked up points with the Senator."

The Congressional campaign for human rights, discussed in Chapter 4, had its origins in—and to some extent continues to be pressed by—a Washington agglomeration of citizens' human rights lobbies: one of a new phenomenon of "single issue" lobbies that are the ideological equivalent of a one-finger typist. The Human Rights Working Group of the Coalition for a New Foreign and Military Policy which unites forty religious, labor, professional, and social action organizations in an effort to demilitarize U.S. policies, is generally considered to be the Washington-based umbrella organization for human rights lobbying. The Americans for Democratic Action have also recently become active. Research and information is generated by London-based Amnesty International, which opened a modest but effective office in Washington in 1976.[163] The Geneva-based International Commission of Jurists, with representation in New York, also provides data on human rights violations. Amnesty and the Commission can count on about fifty members to give currency to their investigations, and both are frequently consulted by Congressional committees.

As an antidote to the "single issue" approach, several prominent Americans, including Robert McNamara, Rev. Theodore Hesburgh, Norman Cousins, John W. Gardner, Cyrus Vance, Margaret Mead, and Jack T. Conway got together toward the end of 1976 to organize New Directions (ND), hoping to emulate the successful citizens' lobby, Common Cause. They resolved to focus on global solutions to hunger, environmental deterioration, war, and violence.[164] However, progress has been slow. National membership, after two years, remained below 10,000. In 1979, respected former liberal-Republican Representative Charles Whalen took over the ailing organization, enhancing its prospects.

In tandem with proliferating activity by lobbies, members of Congress have organized numerous caucuses that respond not to party but to regional, ethnic, professional, and other special interests. These in-house lobbies range from the high-minded Members of Congress for Peace Through Law to the urban caucus, steel caucus, rural caucus, and even a blue collar caucus, among many others. One liaison official in the State Department has observed that these groups have quickly become more important pressure points than the formal committees. According to Charles Whalen, this is the most remarkable change in Congress over the past decade. "There are so many single-issue caucuses in Congress now," he said, "that you can't even count them."[165] All of which may merely verify that, in this post-revolutionary period inside Congress, the members share the general public's aversion to established institutions and prefer adversarial groups that delineate, rather than paper over, differences.

These developments need not be dangerous for democracy. There are many who regard them as salutary. Nor need they subvert Congress's new foreign relations role. In the ongoing process of defining the national interest in the context of specific issues, it is essential for Congress to know the facts; and, most important of these, is a realistic appraisal of how the different publics are ranged. This cannot be judged solely in plebiscitary terms, that is, by how many voters favor or oppose a policy. It is equally important to know how deeply different groups feel, and how organized, tenacious, and determined they are in defense of their feelings.

From the adversarial confrontation of intensely held feelings may come a realistic sense of what is possible, an important stage in the process of understanding what is desirable. Lobbies, all kinds of lobbies, can be useful indicators of intensity and tenacity. And when they intersect in Congress, that body plays its unique Constitutional role as sociopolitical cauldron, where heat tests, tempers, and, sometimes, alloys ideas to mold a polity. This is admittedly a more complex, and certainly more stressful, process for defining and applying the national interest than a Secretaries' meeting on the seventh floor of the State Department. But it is also one less likely to lead to another self-inflicted disaster through insufficient understanding of the complexities of American reality, of how national self-interest is defined by different segments of the society.

Essential to this confrontational model of consensus-building are boundaries and equilibrium. That there must be limits to the lobbying activities is already recognized by laws prohibiting some and compelling disclosure of others. These regulations can be tightened and better enforced. Equilibrium, however, is the enforcer of last resort. If the lobbies focusing on an issue are in approximate balance, legislators benefit in rather the way a judge and jury do when the parties are each represented by excellent lawyers. If they are not, the national interest is likely to suffer.

THE INTEREST CONFRONTATIONAL MODEL: ANTI-BOYCOTT LEGISLATION

In a recent instance, Congress went far in the direction of recognizing the role of a creative balance in generating a consensus. After more than a year of wrestling with the drafting of a law to prohibit U.S. business from cooperating with the Arab League's boycott of Israel, key legislators and the President, in effect, told the adversary Jewish and business lobbies to work it out between themselves.

The Arab boycott of Israel became a domestic issue in the mid-'70's as sales to Arab lands rose from 2.4 percent of total U.S. exports in 1973 to almost 6 percent in 1976. This made the Arab countries America's fastest growing foreign market, accounting for sales of $6.9 billion.[166]

The Arab boycott of Israel operates on primary, secondary, and tertiary levels. The primary boycott consists, simply, of Arab refusal to trade with Israel. The secondary boycott operates through Arab refusal to do business with firms and individuals that do business with, or in, Israel. The tertiary boycott requires foreign business, as the price of trading with Arab countries, to promise not to subcontract with, or use components of, firms violating the primary or secondary boycott.

In 1976, both the House and the Senate, under strong lobbying pressure of the American Jewish Congress and the Anti-Defamation League of B'nai B'rith, passed bills to criminalize participation in the secondary and tertiary boycotts. The Ford Administration strongly opposed this on the ground that it would invite Arab retaliation against other U.S. interests and divert purchases to Western Europe.[167] In the dying moments of the 94th Congress, the bill failed to pass because Senator Tower invoked a procedural technicality to prevent the appointment of a conference committee. Nevertheless, a "shadow" conference convened unofficially and produced a compromise between House and Senate versions which supporters in both bodies were ready to introduce at the beginning of the 95th Congress.

However, the issue was marked by considerable reticence all around. Most business was reluctant to antagonize the U.S. Jewish constituency for fear of setting off a retaliatory consumer-investor boycott. The White House and most legislators were not happy to be forced into a public choice between business interests—potentially allied with labor groups fearful of the loss of half a million Middle East-related jobs—and the Jewish positions cast in moral and nationalistic terms.[168] Jewish groups, mostly headed by business leaders, were reluctant to be insensitive to the interests of business, or to court head-on confrontation with forces known to be both powerful and, ordinarily, friendly to Israel.[169]

Nevertheless, the issue could not be wished away. Candidate Carter made it clear that business would no longer be able to hide behind the coattails of the White House,[170] calling the boycott "an absolute disgrace" and promising to do "everything I can as President" to stop it.[171] It was a badly kept secret that Carter's campaign position had been drafted by Representative Rosenthal's office.[172] Business, sensing its back to the wall, geared up for battle as the Congress reconvened to begin consideration of S.69, the bill reported out of the "shadow" conference, now sponsored by Senator Stevenson, as well as a still tougher measure, S.92, proposed by Senators Proxmire and Harrison Williams of New Jersey and the parallel House bill, H.R. 1561, introduced by Representatives Rosenthal and Bingham.[173]

These brought a drove of industry lobbyists to the Hill to spread the alarm. The Petroleum Equipment Suppliers Association predicted the loss of more than 100,000 jobs per year for the next five years in its industry alone. The major oil companies jumped in with both feet, Mobil Oil Corporation, as usual, in the exposed lead. The National Association of Manufacturers and the Chamber of Commerce played a cooler role, reflecting the mixed views of their constituents. They professed agreement with the principles of anti-boycott, but concluded that existing laws and regulations were adequate to deal with any problems. Jewish groups perceived an "avalanche of industry groups" burying their position in Congress, and sounded the tocsin.[174]

With the respective sides shaping up for the lobbying donnybrook of the decade, the White House decided to try to formulate a policy of its own. But an inter-agency committee consisting of representatives of Commerce, State, Justice, and Treasury, however, were able to agree on little more than vague guidelines. This left the Executive with no agreed position of its own to present to Congress. In the words of one senior aide, "we knew what we didn't want, which was the pending legislation. We also knew we had to back off the forward position taken by Carter during the campaign. Yet, we didn't want to be seen doing it. So we cast about for some way to support a more moderate anti-boycott position without actually initiating it."

Unbidden and unexpected, a strange but serviceable vehicle for achieving just that hove into view. It came at precisely the propitious moment, launched by a chance encounter between Irving S. Shapiro, chairman of E. I. duPont de Nemours & Company and chairman of the Business Roundtable, and Benjamin R. Epstein, national director of the Anti-Defamation League (ADL). At an ADL dinner, on November 30, 1976, these two antagonists—both Jewish—commiserated that the emerging struggle between them could tear apart the carefully built ties between business and the Jewish community.[175] Shapiro observed that these ties helped build up Israel's economy through American investments. "You're going about this in the wrong way," he told Epstein, "if you're taking on a major fight with the American business community."[176]

Also present at the dinner was Burton M. Joseph, chairman of the ADL and president of the I. S. Joseph Company, a Minneapolis grain concern. Epstein called Joseph over. In the ensuing discussion, Shapiro proposed that representatives of the Business Roundtable and the ADL sit down together in an effort to reach an agreement. Burton Joseph agreed on the spot, and with that a new departure in foreign relations lobbying was born.

The meetings began on January 28 in the executive dining room of the Seagram Building in New York with twelve representatives, each, of ADL and the Roundtable. Besides Shapiro, the corporate officials included chairmen of Exxon, General Motors, General Electric, Bechtel, FMC Corporation, and Federated Department Stores, as well as high executives from Citicorp, Chase Manhattan Corporation, and Mobil, accompanied by a senior member of Charles Walker Associates, lobbyists.[177]

Throughout February, much of the actual negotiating was carried on by lawyers. On March 2, a Joint Statement of Principles emerged, a sort of consensus, although three members of the Roundtable expressed reservations and one, Rawleigh Warner, Jr., chairman of Mobil, dissented. Although ADL had kept other leading Jewish organizations—the American Jewish Committee and the American Jewish Congress, in particular—informed of the negotiations, they were not asked to adhere to the Statement.[178] Not to have insisted on this proved a tactical error for the Roundtable.

The parties had agreed that U.S. business should not be free to comply with the boycott by discriminating against U.S. persons furnishing information helpful to the boycott, nor by boycotting Israel or U.S. businesses on the Arab blacklist.[179] It was agreed that a violation of the above principles "may be implied by a course of conduct."[180]

But it was also agreed that there could be significant exceptions. No U.S. business selling to an Arab country should be prevented from complying with its laws prohibiting import of goods from Israel. Business should be free to reveal to the Arab Governments information concerning an export's country of origin, name of carrier, route of shipment, and name of suppliers connected with the product,[181] and to comply with Arab laws governing the choice of carrier.

Most important was an exception for "unilateral selection." This means that an Arab official, or a U.S. business representative in an Arab country, can designate as part of the sale, which suppliers shall provide component goods and services, including manufacturers, subcontractors, insurers, carriers, bankers, or freight forwarders.[182] Somewhat ingenuously, the parties agreed that these exceptions "are not designed to violate the intent of the principles."[183]

Congress and the White House were delighted to be off the hook. Already on February 9, President Carter, in announcing the formation of the Joint Committee, had committed the White House to support whatever set of agreed rules it could produce.[184]

Unfortunately, no sooner had the Statement of Principles been published than it began to unravel. Although the Statement seems clear enough on its face, the commercial subject matter is so complex that subsequent disagreement over its meaning was not altogether surprising. On March 8, 1977, Alfred Moses, chairman of the Domestic Affairs Commission of the American Jewish Committee—itself not a party to the negotiations but a group which had been kept informed by the ADL and was believed by the Roundtable to be "on board"—testified to the House International Relations Committee. "These principles," he said, looking at Representative Rosenthal, "are embodied in the language of H.R. 1561, for which we are most grateful to you and your colleagues on this committee, Mr. Chairman."[185]

To the Roundtable and other business leaders, this came as a shock. Their purpose in negotiating had certainly not been to embrace Rosenthal's H.R. 1561. During committee questioning, Moses acknowledged that some changes would be needed in light of the agreed principles and exceptions, but argued that these differed from the Rosenthal-Bingham draft "only in some minor respects and nuances. . . ."[186] Discussing the unilateral selection exception, Moses defined it in a way that would have prohibited most of what the Roundtable thought it had gained.[187]

On March 10, Irving Shapiro wrote to President Carter and Senator Adlai Stevenson objecting strongly to various aspects of the Moses testimony. It is essential, he said, that a U.S. person engaged in business in a foreign country be free to honor his buyers' selection of services and components. As the Roundtable understood the Agreed Principles, "it would be permissible for a U.S. exporter to honor the selection by a national or a resident of a foreign country of specific manufacturers of components (e.g. tires by A, batteries by B, and so on) to be included in, for example, a tractor to be supplied by that exporter."[188]

These disagreements became face-to-face confrontations on March 15 at a hearing before the Stevenson subcommittee at which both Shapiro and Joseph testified. Although Irving Shapiro and Burton Joseph had prepared and even presented joint testimony before the committee, their common front collapsed under Stevenson's cross-examination. In reply to a rather general question from the Senator, Shapiro committed the error of specificity.

"Let me be quite precise," he said.

> Suppose that Saudi Arabia, of its own volition, said we want to buy trucks, but we do not want DuPont tires on trucks that come into Saudi Arabia.
>
> Under the principles that we have proposed, there would be no legal liability for an American shipper in respecting that request.
>
> On the other hand, if, because of this request by the Saudis, the American shipper changed his line of suppliers, and stopped putting DuPont tires on trucks going elsewhere, then one would have a right to infer that he had associated himself with the boycott, and a jury might very well conclude that there was an implicit agreement in violation of the law.
>
> . . . Second, you have the case of an American resident in the boy-

cotting country. Suppose an engineer, who knows of the practice of that country, knows that no matter what you do, DuPont tires will not be admitted. So when he places a requisition for materials in the United States, he says don't put DuPont tires on that vehicle.

We think that is the same as the first case, because otherwise you are asking the resident American simply to go through a useless formality of going to the Government and saying "put it to me in writing, so I won't have any trouble with the law."

Senator Stevenson then asked Mr. Joseph, "Does the ADL accept that proposition?" to which he replied, "No; not at all. If the reasons are boycott related . . . that is out."[189]

Stevenson complained that the principles "go all over the lot and get in the way of each other."[190] Everyone, including Senator Stevenson, left the room mad at everyone else.[191] Both Jewish and business representatives felt betrayed, and strong voices in both camps urged a return to active lobbying.

With the unraveling of the agreement, the two Congressional committees reverted to the bills before them. On March 31, the International Relations Committee reported a revised version of H.R. 1561.[192] Introduced by Representatives Hamilton and Whalen, it slightly softened the criminal anti-boycott provisions by requiring the prosecution to prove that the law had been violated "willfully."[193] A form of unilateral selection was also allowed, but not "in any case in which the United States person has actual knowledge that the sole purpose of the designation is to implement the boycott."[194] A new section made it a crime for a U.S. business to use "a foreign person, including a subsidiary or affiliate, in order to circumvent" the law.[195]

The Hamilton-Whalen bill also granted the President the power to permit case-by-case exemptions "from any requirements of the rules and regulations" of the law.[196] This had been inserted as a result of strong pressure by the White House which had been persuaded by State and Commerce Department arguments that a tough bill would jeopardize diplomatic and trade relations with the Arab world.[197] Jewish leaders were particularly distressed because the White House seemed to be going back on an "understanding" reached at a March 12 meeting between the President's coordinator on anti-boycott, Stuart Eizenstat, and Jewish leaders.

Meanwhile, on the Senate side, the Banking Committee considered amendments to S. 69 that had been written by the White House and, according to one senatorial participant, "peddled from door to door." He added, "They finally talked poor old Sparkman into offering the thing. When he eventually came to understand what it was all about, he ended up voting for the substitute."

That substitute was a compromise proposed by Senator Stevenson. Like the Administration's version, it permitted unilateral selection by the boycotting country, but only of sub-contracted items that are "identifiable by source." Stevenson sought to illustrate the difference by an example: tires on a tractor are easily identifiable, he said, because they can be seen but the pistons on a tractor are not.[198] In the midst of these committee maneuvers, Saudi Arabia's oil minister, Sheikh Ahmed Zaki Yamani, hosted a persuasion breakfast for sixteen key Senators.

With compromise bills reported out of the House and Senate Committees—both providing exceptions for unilateral selection and compliance with host country laws[199]—supporters of the tougher legislation favored by the Jewish lobby promised to take the battle to the floor of each chamber, where they had reason to expect more support.

When Congress adjourned for the Easter recess on April 7, battle plans for the floor fight were being drawn up by both Jewish and business groups. According to one participant, oil company lobbyists were circulating a nine-point list of "Minimum Changes Required To Permit Continued U.S.–Arab Trade Relations." The National Jewish Community Relations Advisory Council (NJCRAC) summoned its member agencies to organize a gigantic grass-roots campaign for a floor amendment to the Senate bill barring any unilateral selection known to be made primarily to implement the boycott. The Chamber of Commerce, the National Association of Manufacturers, and the Emergency Committee for American Trade scheduled a joint meeting in Washington for April 18 to urge its 300 member groups to lobby against any boycott legislation or, at least, to demand further watering down. The next day the Israel lobby, AIPAC, began its annual meeting, bringing some 600 delegates from across the country to lobby for a tougher version of the Senate bill. According to a participant, "emotions ran high. The divisiveness in prospect was something neither side wanted."[200]

In a last-ditch effort, Stuart Eizenstat, on April 9, again met with Jewish leaders: Moses, Paul Berger of AJC, and Max Kampelman, a member of the ADL's national board. He told them: "The President wants this resolved."[201] The same message was passed to business leaders. On April 13, Shapiro called Kampelman, a Washington attorney and former aide to Senator Humphrey. Was a meeting to find a compromise still in the cards? Kampelman promised to find out. Two days later, twenty representatives of the principal Jewish agencies, meeting under the chairmanship of Burton Joseph at the Harmonie Club in New York, agreed to resume negotiations. The Roundtable named a team of four lawyers headed by Hans Angermueller, the General Counsel of Citibank. The Jewish organizations selected Berger, Kampelman, and, this time, Moses.

The negotiators understood that the clock was running out. The House bill was passed while they talked. Senate floor action was due in about two weeks. According to participants, both sides now showed surprising flexibility, once the doors were closed. The Business Roundtable offered to use the Senate bill as the basis of discussion rather than the weaker House version. A Jewish negotiator understood that "the unilateral selection exception as it then stood in the Senate bill would have required the Aramcos and the like, resident in the Arab world, to take their business away from U.S. companies." He acknowledged this was neither necessary nor desirable and agreed to deletion of a key restriction in the unilateral selection exception.[202] In return, the Roundtable agreed to a narrowing of the exception for compliance with the laws of the host country as well as to tightening certain anti-evasion provisions.

The lawyers' negotiations took approximately one week. Within the three Jewish groups, some felt more could have been gained by taking the case to the floor of the Senate. An AIPAC aide found it particularly difficult to accept one compromise and staged a stormy hallway confrontation with the Jewish negotiators. He backed down after being promised that the negotiations would not be allowed to drag to the point where they could make a floor fight impossible.[203]

The business side, too, had its hardliners. On April 25, end runs around the Conferees to Secretaries Cyrus Vance and W. Michael Blumenthal were attempted by dissident business leaders, just one day before the end of the negotiations. Mobil, again the loner, persisted in lobbying the White House. Its president, William P. Tavoulareas, on April 22, published a letter in the *New York Times* predicting Armageddon-like Arab trade retaliation, oil price increases, and restrictions on oil exports if Congress dared enact any anti-boycott law, while reassuring readers that "Mobil enjoys many business relationships with Jewish firms. . . ."[204]

On Tuesday, May 3, the President announced the negotiators' agreement and placed the Administration's support behind it. Drafted as amendments to the Senate bill, the agreement was endorsed by Senator Stevenson and introduced by Senator H. John Heinz of Pennsylvania. It was adopted without dissent.[205] In the House-Senate conference committee, the House receded entirely in favor of the Senate. The Business-Jewish negotiating text became the new legislation.[206] Alfred Moses allowed himself an accolade: "In a little more than two weeks the Jewish organizations and the Roundtable had achieved something unique— agreement on legislative language enacted without change by the Congress. . . ."[207] Irving Shapiro tactfully demurred that "corporate executives are not elected to office . . . they must leave public issues in public hands."[208]

The effect of the new compromise was partially cosmetic, for it transferred to the Commerce Department the job of making sense of the law by promulgating the regulations giving it effect. This task was assigned to Stanley Marcuss, a Stevenson aide who had written one of the bill's first drafts but who had since been translated to Deputy Assistant Secretary of Commerce. As passed, the law permits a U.S. person to comply with a boycotting country's unilateral and specific selection of carriers, insurers, suppliers of services to be performed within the boycotting country and of specific goods which, in the normal course of business, would be identifiable by source in the state in which they are supplied to the buyer.[209] The law also permits a U.S. person resident in a foreign country to comply with the laws of that country with respect to activities exclusively in that country.

Perhaps as important as the provisions themselves is the process by which they were conceived. Senator Heinz noted that his amendment was "a compromise which is the result of prolonged negotiations between the two major forces that have concerned themselves with this bill. . . ." and added that "it is somewhat unusual for us to consider intact actual language developed outside the Congress, but in this case I believe the circumstances clearly warrant it."[210] As if to reassure his colleagues that they had not waived the right to legislate, he added: "It is not simply a behind-closed-doors agreement of various lobbyists. It is a fundamental understanding of how far we will go in enforcing the principles of nondiscrimination and it is an understanding developed by the two most clearly affected parties."[211] But Heinz also read into the record an even more unconventional item: a memorandum of agreement among the negotiators stating their belief "that there is reason for concern that the over-all benefits . . . may well be lost if the bill is subject to wholesale floor amendments. We do not believe that the beneficial aspects of this vital legislation or the national interest are well served by extended confrontation and divisive floor debate."[212] In other words, the lobbying interests had not only written the bill, they had also sent it to the floor with a closed rule barring floor amendments.

According to an aide, that day a draft of Senator Heinz's speech had been gone over carefully by a lawyer for the ADL to make sure that it would make the right kind of legislative history.[213]

It was left to the perennial spokesman for Jewish interests to criticize this procedure. "None of the Jewish organizations or the representatives of the Roundtable were elected to the U.S. Senate," Senator Javits said, adding, "Senators have an obligation to stand up and speak out on the issues."[214]

The incident illuminates what has recently been happening to the profession of lobbying. Foreign policy has become increasingly the business of Congress. In a decentralized Congress, the serious lobbyist tends to be welcome and has many more opportunities for input than are available when he or she approaches the executive branch. But the power of the lobbyist has also been increasingly circumscribed by law and by the proliferation of other rival lobbies. The lobbyist can no longer expect to operate in an atmosphere of "anything goes," unregulated by law. Nor are there many lobbyists still running in a wide open field. In most instances rival counter-lobbies now square off against each other. They add intensity and complexity to the ordinary clamor surrounding an important issue, yet the ultimate decision is likely to be a compromise or consensus.

In one sense, the role of the lobbies in making an anti-boycott law is unusual, in that Congress and the President were so willing to let the lobbies work out the consensus among themselves. Of the participants in the anti-boycott episode—White House, business, Jewish groups, legislators—none believes that this aspect is likely to be replicable. Reconciling, compromising, and, ultimately, choosing among rival concepts of the national interest must be, in virtually all cases, the painful responsibility of all the representatives of all the people. Ordinarily, this responsibility cannot be delegated, not even to those well-organized publics most intensely affected.

9

UP THE HILL, SIDEWAYS:

Congress in Search
of a Delivery System

THE UNWIELDY FLOOR

NOT ONLY has the Congressional revolution seized a large terrain but, in the process, it also badly mauled the instruments and structure through which Congress traditionally exercises power. The rank and file battered the repositories of Congressional power because they stood too close to the principal target—the White House—but also because the Vietnam and Watergate experiences were themselves great levelers, destroying the mystique of power and revealing its underlying sham.

Leadership and followership became indistinguishable as governance by floor amendment replaced Presidential fiat. Yet revolution requires organization. If Congress cannot introduce an effective institutional infrastructure into its newly occupied territories, if it fails to organize an effective delivery system, then it will inevitably begin to lose the ground it has gained.

What Congress had sought, in its revolution, was the right to codetermine foreign policy. Codetermination assumes the ability of each branch to exercise its share of power efficiently, in the national interest. That, in turn, requires each to have procedures, structure, delegation of authority, expertise. Unless Congress can organize itself to deliver informed, timely decisions, codetermination will become synonymous with non-determination. Paralysis would yield a harvest of new foreign policy defeats and send the power pendulum shuddering back in the direction of the Presidency.

Yet Congress is finding great difficulty developing structure commensurate with its new power. In an August 1978 editorial headed "435

210

Secretaries of State," the *Washington Post* commented on the widening disenchantment among Americans with the continuing revolution of the Congressional rank and file. The editorial pointed "to the readiness of the House to legislate on the floor without sifting proposals through the committee system."[1] Referring to a House vote to cut off economic aid to Syria in response to that country's month-long shelling of Christian communities in Lebanon, the *Post* added, "Members tend to slough off both committee discipline and party discipline" and to go off "half-cocked."[2] The same week, Harvard Professor Stanley Hoffmann, writing in the *New York Times*, complained that "Since Vietnam and Watergate, individual members of Congress insist on having their own policy on every issue."[3] Evidently, Congress could no longer count on the automatic support of the media and academia—as in the Vietnam days—for its tilts against the Commander in Chief.

In fact, the Congress has not acted so capriciously as all that. Aid to Syria was restored before the bill left for the White House. At that, the House action had accurately caught the anguish of Americans, not least those of Lebanese Catholic origin, at the month-long rain of fire visited by Syrian artillery on the Beirut Christians. And there were many instances, even at the height of the resolution, of sober Congressional responsibility. During the spring and summer of 1978, sixty-eight Senators had approved a Panama Canal Treaty in a vote that was clearly not motivated by political self-interest. Congress also allowed the President to persuade it to approve the sale of huge shipments of our most sophisticated arms—despite the determined opposition of a once-invincible Jewish lobby—to Saudi Arabia: again, hardly the actions of a venal rabble bent on self-aggrandizement. In 1978, Congress repealed its Turkish arms embargo and modified some of its earlier strictures against foreign aid to countries with poor human rights records—such as Mozambique and the Philippines—in deference to policy considerations advanced by the Administration. None of these votes was politically popular; none an example of individual members "doing their own thing."

Still, some whiff of the post-revolutionary anarchic euphoria lingers. It hung in the air during a recent Senate debate: nominally about troop withdrawals from Korea but, really, a contest for power between Senators who specialize in foreign affairs and those who do not, yet will not defer to those who do.

The problem arose in mid-1977, when some Senators, including Majority Leader Byrd, expressed doubt about the Carter Administration's decision to withdraw all 36,000 U.S. troops from South Korea by 1982. Byrd eventually engineered a compromise between those, like Senator Robert Dole, who wanted to prohibit U.S. withdrawal altogether, and the White House, which had insisted on a free hand. This was embodied in an amendment to the State Department authorization bill which said: "United States policy toward Korea should continue to be arrived at by joint decision of the President and Congress."[4]

When the compromise came to the floor, Senator Nunn explained that it meant Korean troop withdrawal would be closely watched by his Armed Services Committee. While we "do not specify by statute where the troops are deployed," he said, his committee, which writes the Defense Department's annual spending authority, would make sure it was consulted.[5] That, he thought, would protect the legislators' interest, making it unnecessary to vote actually on the numbers to be withdrawn each year.[6]

But this did not suit the rank and file. Senator Allen spoke for them: "It would not be a decision of the Congress if the President has a breakfast meeting with a couple of committees and, at that meeting, they say they agree to a withdrawal of 10,000 troops from Korea. . . ." He reminded Nunn that there were many in Congress not on the Foreign Relations or Armed Services committees. "I do not feel that is Congress speaking when committees meet with the President."[7]

In this exchange, Allen, the Southern conservative, placed himself at the head of revolutionary populists against the elite, railing against cozy arrangements between coopted committees and the executive branch. In the new order of things, every member has an equal say.

And Allen won his point. After a spirited exchange, in which he threatened to filibuster Byrd's compromise, the Alabaman maneuvered the hapless Nunn into agreeing that his committee would not presume to speak for Congress in dealing with the President. Instead, the committee would provide a legislative vehicle—a bill or resolution—that would permit Congress as a whole to become involved and, ultimately, to decide. Triumphantly, Allen had the last word: "In other words this action [future troop withdrawal] could not take place unless the House and Senate approved it, which is a far cry from what has been said before, that if the committees agreed to it, then it could be done. Now it is being said it takes a specific vote by both Houses. If that is the legislative history, that is fine."[8]

Fine for Allen and the rank and file, but hardly the arrangement the President had in mind and a sharp rebuff to the Armed Services Committee. The next year, the Security Assistance Act stipulated that "further withdrawal of ground forces . . . may seriously risk upsetting the military balance in that region and requires full advance consultation with Congress."[9]

Senator Nunn's hasty retreat before the forces of senatorial populism is in sharp contrast to the confident elitism expressed only a quarter of a century ago by Representative James P. Richards, chairman of the

House Foreign Affairs Committee. "The committees of the two Houses have a rather unique function in the policy-making process," he said. "They are the links between the Executive with its specialized knowledge, and the House or Senate as a body with generalized knowledge or lack of knowledge."[10]

That link has been much weakened, of late. The Korean colloquy points to a serious disorder in Congressional management of foreign policy. It is probably wrong for Congress, in the name of codetermination, to insinuate itself into troop logistics; but it is certainly impractical to try to decide such questions *on the floor.* A matter of such sensitivity, requiring prolonged immersion in the details and nuances, cannot usefully be left to 435, or 535, Secretaries of State.

Yet that is what has been happening. A key indicator is the increase in, and changing patterns of, traffic on the floor. For example, during the 91st Congress, there were only thirty-nine floor amendments offered in the House to thirty bills and resolutions sent forward by the Foreign Affairs Committee. Most of these amendments—69 percent—came from dissenting committee members. Even so, only fourteen were adopted (35.9 percent). By contrast, in the revolutionary 94th Congress, 112 floor amendments were moved to 42 committee bills and resolutions, of which 51 were adopted (45.9 percent), even though most (74 percent) came from the rank and file who were not members of the committee.[11]

While these statistics do not distinguish between trivial and important amendments, they do illustrate the trend towards greater rank and file participation in initiating law from the floor of the House and a lessening in the deference previously shown to the work and advice of the committee.

Two quite separate tendencies have come together recently. One is the growing interest of Congress in the management of foreign affairs; the other is a widespread inclination on the part of the members to perceive themselves as chiefs, not Indians. This combination distinguishes the current Legislative-Executive confrontation over foreign relations from earlier ones. In the past, the Congress has generally been led into battle by its captains. On this occasion, many of the captains were, themselves, deposed. The force behind the drive for power came not from a powerful chairman like Senator Borah or Henry Cabot Lodge, but from large numbers of members, most not even connected with the Congressional foreign policy establishment.

While both Congressional reassertiveness vis-à-vis the Executive and rank and file resurgence vis-à-vis the legislative establishment may be equally salutary, it is the confluence of these two trends that has created a crisis in the "delivery system." The other participants in the game of foreign relations—the President and foreign states—have found it difficult to know how to relate to this new kind of Congress, with whom to consult and bargain, even how to get its attention. Yet, as communicating with it has become more difficult, it has also become more important. Greater Congressional participation in policy-making has been confounded by the concurrent trend toward wider, democratized participation. Even those *Verligte* in the Administration who see the need to share power with Congress, ask, "with *whom?*"

In the period beginning in 1978, one began to hear whispers in Congress—and loud murmuring in the precincts—that the delivery system is in need of overhauling, that populism has gone too far in scattering its thin mulch of power indiscriminately over the terrain. In part, the imperatives of power were becoming clearer. In part, too, the demands of power were exhausting the desire for it. Members were beginning to weary of the innumerable roll-call votes that forced them to take public stands on intense, "no-win" issues which would only be remembered by those their vote had offended. A more effective delivery system, it was being argued in the halls and cloakrooms, would let the specialists handle some of these matters quietly and would relieve the rank and file of having to stand up and be counted quite so often.

If, indeed, there is a will, a way can be found. There are at least three candidates for rebuilding an effective Congressional delivery system, for marshalling the Congressional foreign relations power: (1) the House and Senate leadership, (2) the party caucus, and (3) the committees and their subcommittees.

LEADERSHIP FROM THE LEADERSHIP

In the 1975 Murphy Commission study of the organization of government to conduct foreign policy, a key research paper chose to pin its hopes on the party leaders.[12] In a rather arbitrary Hegelianism, it calls leadership "in large part a matter of will."[13] But then it suggests institutional ways to strengthen it, such as appointing the Majority and Minority Leaders *ex officio* to the foreign relations committees.[14]

This prescription is rejected in a more recent study prepared for the Senate Select Committee on the Committee System which concludes that the days of strong party leadership ended—at least in the Senate— with Lyndon Johnson. They are not likely to be relived in the foreseeable future, the study argues, because Senators won't stand for it. "Johnson provided centralized policy guidance with a vengeance."[15] In his heyday, the caucus "would be convened just once or twice during the session, usually to hear the majority leader's State-of-the-Union message or some similar Johnsonian pronouncement."[16]

Johnson's personal style of leadership power, however, depended on more than his personality or will to rule, important as that was. He functioned at a time when the Democrats enjoyed the sort of narrow majority that makes for cohesiveness. Then the 1958 elections suddenly converted the party's two-seat majority into a thirty-seat landslide. A largely Northern and liberal freshman class proved less amenable to the personality cult, or to the decorous traditions of the "club." The study observes, "Lyndon Johnson left the Senate majority leadership, probably in the nick of time, to become Vice President. His successor, Mike Mansfield, viewed the Senate from a very different perspective. . . ."[17]

It was the new leader's style to disperse power among his colleagues and, in particular, to the committees and subcommittees which flourished and multiplied during the Mansfield decade-and-a-half. But the devolution of power, its dispersal, went beyond committees. The party conference met with greater frequency, and the party's policy committee began to pass resolutions on substantive issues. Thus, the Senate became "a far more independent and assertive place than it was when Mansfield assumed the majority leadership. Individual Senators are more accustomed to pursuing a broad range of legislative interests. . . . And there is a reduced capacity by the majority party leadership to control the handling of legislation in committees and on the Senate floor."[18]

By the end of the decade, the "Senate floor had changed from a place where the majority leader's intricate strategies were almost always consummated to an arena where parliamentary surprises and unforeseen outcomes were a common occurrence."[19]

The Senate study neatly poses the resultant problem: "when everyone gets into the act, how do you get any action?"[20] It rebuts the notion that aggressive leadership is the answer. A muted style and wide delegation of power are almost inevitable, now that the 7 P.M. television news has made aspiring media stars of most Senators and just beneath each senatorial media star lurks a candidate for the Presidency.[21] Certainly the successive election to the Presidency of three ex-Senators (Kennedy, Johnson, and Nixon) has done nothing to cause members of that chamber to bridle their egos, a necessary prerequisite for a strong party leadership and discipline.

Probably an even stronger factor in the modulation of leadership is the widespread use, particularly in the House, of the electronically recorded vote. Previously, tellers simply reported the numbers voting for or against an amendment. Many members took advantage of this anonymous system to seek the shelter of their office when the division bells rang on a controversial matter. Others simply voted with the leaders, knowing that their vote would be observed by them, but would be anonymous to the outside world, which would learn only the totals. Now, however, detailed voting records go into the hometown newspapers and, in the words of one member, "everyone scurries to vote on everything." Having lost anonymity, they vote with their eye on the constituency, not on the leaders. The result is that the leadership has far less control over the outcome.

Then, too, members now have staff resources that make it much more difficult to argue for modesty based on an implied assumption of ignorance. Whatever the reason, it is unlikely that the party leadership can again become *the* focal point for creating a Congressional foreign policy. True, Senator Byrd and Representatives O'Neill and Jim Wright of Texas have already demonstrated a zest for brokering, if not actually commanding, power. But their control over members is limited, and there is no reason to believe that they will wish to expend most of their credits on foreign affairs. While Senator Mansfield did serve as a member of the Senate Foreign Relations Committee, Senator Byrd does not; nor does Speaker O'Neill sit on the House equivalent. There is inherently no reason why they should. Indeed, the leaders can better play their role as brokers-of-last-resort—as with the Panama Canal treaties—if they are not too closely involved in committee politics.

LEADERSHIP FROM CAUCUS

The Senate study backs a different candidate for the restructured delivery system. Noting that the "electorate's willingness to endure 4 years of nitpicking between a Democratic President and a Democratic Congress is likely to be limited," it discerns a yearning to return to a "more centralized, integrated and responsible focus to the policy process."[22] To resolve this paradox between "senatorial individualism and policy integration" the study recommends that power devolve on "party-based institutions" such as the Democratic Policy Committee.[23]

One problem with this solution is that it is not at hand. The Senate Democratic Policy Committee, the Steering Committee, and caucus, are essentially housekeeping instruments of the Majority Leader. Each leader has used them differently, but only in very rare instances are they tools for creative policy-making. The last time was when the Democratic caucus of each House voted to end aid to Indochina. Nowadays, Senator Byrd uses the Policy Committee mostly for scheduling. It has an excellent staff, each employee being assigned responsibility for keeping the leader informed in a designated subject. But it is essentially an extension of the leader's own office.

Caucus is an equally inappropriate instrument for marshalling power or mounting a delivery system. In the Senate, it tends to be convened primarily for informational, procedural, or organizational purposes. On the House side, equally, caucus concerns itself almost exclusively with procedural and organizational issues.[24] Members are leery of any attempt to introduce aspects of the British parliamentary system, in which, according to Gilbert's *Mikado*, the caucus prods members to vote "at their party's call" while "never thinking for themselves at all."

Another problem with this approach is that the members of the policy committees of the parties have neither the expertise nor the attention-span necessary to master complex international issues. They cannot conduct arms control or human rights policy negotiations with the executive branch. What is needed is manifest expertise on the part of a manageably small group of persons in each chamber who make the commitment of time necessary to master most aspects of foreign relations, and follow up with the necessary studies, negotiations, and button-holing to become an effective delivery system.

Yet expertise is not enough. An effective delivery system depends on a delegation of power to a group which, in addition to being coherent and specialized, is also seen by the rest of the 535 to be legitimate. This means that the rank and file must perceive it as being cross-sectionally representative and chosen by an open, credible process.

LEADERSHIP FROM COMMITTEES

What, in Congress, is coherent, specialized, legitimate, and capable of leadership? The answer is committees, probably—but only quite recently. Historically, committees have been distrusted and untrustworthy.

Congress's attitude to its own committees is now properly skeptical. Although committee power has reached great heights at various periods, it is a delivery system with which legislators have never been comfortable. Members hate to surrender their autonomy. If Congress had a motto, it might well be the old legal maxim: *Delegatus non protest delegare*— the delegate cannot delegate. And well they might be cautious, for when committees and subcommittees have blossomed, as in most of this century, they have tended to become unrepresentative and unresponsive repositories of inexpert, personalized power.

The early Congresses emphatically preferred to exercise their authority through Committee of the Whole or through select committees, created to expire at the end of one Congress. Although select and standing committees were known to the British House of Commons and such colonial assemblies as those of Pennsylvania and Virginia,[25] the rules adopted by the House of Representatives, when it convened for the first time in the spring of 1789, provided for the existence of only one standing committee: on elections.[26] In 1794, the House established the standing Committee on Claims and, in 1795, the Committees on Interstate and Foreign Commerce and on Revisal and Unfinished Business (which later became the Committee on Ways and Means).[27]

Early in the nineteenth century, however, the House seemed to overcome this reluctance to delegate, under the prodding of Speaker Henry Clay, until, to quote a recent House study, committees became the all-powerful "nerve ends of Congress—the gatherers of information, the sifters of alternatives, the refiners of legislation."[28] By 1825, the end of Clay's tenure, the House had established many of its most important committees: Interior, Post Office, District of Columbia, Judiciary, Veterans' Affairs, Government Operations, Agriculture, Foreign Affairs, Armed Services, and Public Works.[29] Their jurisdiction, then, was much as it remains today.

Since, committees have grown in number,[30] influence, and prestige. "Increasingly they became autonomous in their operations."[31] Concerted attempts were made, periodically, to rationalize jurisdiction and cut back. Yet they continued to proliferate. By 1905 there were no less than sixty-one standing committees. The Legislative Reorganization Act of 1946 combined forty-eight committees into nineteen, bringing the number close to its present level. However, no less than seventy-seven different committees have existed in the House at one time or another.[32]

The 1946 Reorganization Act produced a new instrument of proliferation: the subcommittee. By 1975, the total number of House standing committees (or equivalent) was still only twenty-three,[33] supplemented by five Joint Committees of both Houses; but these twenty-eight parent bodies have spawned fully 150 subcommittees.[34]

There seems little prospect, now, of retrenchment. The House rules currently do not limit subcommittee proliferation. On the contrary, they provide that each "standing committee of the House of Representatives, except the Committee on the Budget, that has more than twenty members shall establish at least four subcommittees."[35]

Historically, the Senate followed the House lead, but, being a small club, was at first even more reluctant to delegate power. As in the House, the early tendency was to establish only select committees to deal with specific subjects for the period of one Congress.[36] Gradually, their mandates came to be renewed almost automatically at the beginning of each Congress, while new subjects were sometimes added to their jurisdiction. Nevertheless, until 1816, very few Senate standing committees were formally established. These were limited to "housekeeping" matters: to look after "enrolled bills" (1789), "engrossed bills" (1806), and "contingent expenses" (1807).[37]

In 1816, however, the Senate followed the lead of the House. It organized twelve permanent or standing committees that did not need to be renewed by successive sessions. Seven of these are still in being: Armed Services, Commerce, District of Columbia, Finance, Foreign Relations, Interior, and Judiciary. Thereafter the number grew to twenty-seven by 1844, forty-nine by 1899, and seventy-four by 1921. In 1921, these seventy-four standing committees were consolidated into thirty-four, and with the Legislative Reorganization Act of 1946, there was a further reduction to fifteen. Between 1947 and 1976, three more were added, as well as several permanent special, select, and joint committees, most with power to conduct investigative oversight but no legislative authority.[38] As in the House, however, the radical reduction in committees effected by the 1946 Act did not reduce proliferation but merely diverted it into subcommittees. Altogether, in 1976, there were in the Senate thirty-two standing, select, special, and joint committees, which had a total of 171 subcommittees.[39]

According to a recent Senate study, between 1947 and 1976 the average member's standing committee assignments increased from 2.1 to 2.56 while subcommittee assignments rose from 2.4 to 11.4, or 14.3 if subcommittees of joint, special, and select committees are added. "Counting all the committees, subcommittees, party committees, panels, studies, and boards to which Senators are assigned," the report found, "there are 1,999 positions to be filled by 100 Senators—or an average of nearly 20 assignments each."[40] It is notable that the Senate, although underpopulated compared to the House, and a late starter in delegating authority, has of late shown an even greater tendency to proliferation than the other chamber.

In 1977, the Senate passed S.Res. 4 which once again overhauled the committee system. By reduction and consolidation, it got the number of standing committees down to only 15, with three Select Committees (Intelligence, Small Business, and Ethics), two temporary committees (to be phased out), and one Special Committee (Aging). These committees had 112 subcommittees. S.Res. 4, with a few exceptions, limits each Senator to service on two major and one minor committee, to three subcommittees of major and two of minor committees.[41]

Along with the abating of resistance to committees in both chambers came an unchecked accrual of committee power and, ultimately, autonomy. This power increasingly came to be used for corrupt or, at best, idiosyncratic ends by members who had been anointed not by their peers but, at first, by a leadership cabal and, ultimately, by the dead hand of seniority.

Professor Nelson Polsby's study of Congressional committees has divided their history into four periods.[42] The first extends through the Washington Presidency and reflects Alexander Hamilton's preference for coordinating Executive-Legislative policy-making through liaison with the Committee of the Whole and a suspicion of standing committees. The second era extends through the Jefferson Administration and is characterized by Presidential use of committees to guide Presidential programs through Congress and disseminate data supporting the Administration's legislation.

The third period's tone was set by Henry Clay who became Speaker of the House in 1810. As a Whig, Clay espoused legislative independence and supremacy. He shaped the committees to reflect these ideas, using the Speaker's power of appointment. Under Clay, the committees resisted cooption by the Executive. They became, at first, bastions of Congressional independence and, ultimately, of virtual autonomy.

The fourth phase began in 1910–11 with the House rebellion against the autocracy of Speaker Joe Cannon. When the House stripped him of the appointment power, substituting the seniority system, committees "won solid institutionalized independence from party leaders both inside and outside Congress."[43] One Representative at the time observed, "Congress is a collection of committees that come together in a chamber periodically to approve one another's actions."[44] Woodrow Wilson, even before his tenure in the White House, fulminated against committees that "rule without let or hindrance."[45]

There is, now, a fifth phase which features the democratization and legitimation of committees in the 1970's, with their powers diminished and their effectiveness reduced under attack by the rank and file.

Today, the committee again represents the best hope for restoring an effective Congressional delivery system. But in rebuilding an element of committee power, a warning is in order. We have but recently emerged from a period of committee and subcommittee autocracy, of government by tenured idiosyncratic chairmen and their cronies, of near-terror-by-oversight.[46] It was a time to be remembered by those who now complain of excessive Congressional atomization and decentralization of power.[47] Martin Dies, chairman of the House Un-American Activities Committee, as well as Representative Hamilton Fish and Senators Patrick McCarran and Joseph McCarthy, became synonymous with the use of committee power to harass individual bureaucrats unable to defend themselves in situations that had gone from inquest to inquisition. In addition, Appropriations Committee power was used ruthlessly to cut back particular units of government for reasons that had to do more with vendetta than good government.[48] This was truly power run amok.

Obversely, there developed disturbingly cozy relationships between powerful senior members of certain committees and their counterparts in the bureaucracy. This created chaos in the executive branch, with bureaucrats owing their first loyalty to Congressional satraps rather than to cabinet officials. Even more distressing was the erosion of the adversary system. By the time of Vietnam, most key committee leaders had become inextricably tied to Executive policy, and so they remained—long after the mood of the rank and file had turned hostile.

For these contradictory sins of excessive vendetta and uncritical co-option, the committees became early casualties in the mid-1970's crossfire between the Hill and White House. Yet there is no viable alternative to delegation, to the committee system, if Congress is to exercise power effectively in the foreign relations field. Recognizing this, Congress, during the past five years, has reconstructed the committee system, from top to bottom, in an effort to make it both representative of the rank and file and yet justify a leadership role based on merit.

RECONSTRUCTION

Reform of committees has had to address itself to three related elements of institutional power: selection and tenure of committee and subcommittee chairmen; selection of committee members; and, finally, the power of committees to control the flow and determine the fate of legislative proposals.

Initially, committee members and chairmen were chosen anew by each Congress through plurality votes of each chamber.[49] While there developed a tendency to reelect the same members to each committee, changes in selection did occur quite frequently.[50]

Between 1823 and 1846, the Senate experimented with various other methods of selection. First, the presiding officer was given the appointing power. Then Vice-President John C. Calhoun actively assumed the Presidency of the Senate and used that post to make committee appointments. The Senate reacted by reasserting collegiality. It voted to revert to electing its committee members and chairmen.

By 1846, party organization had developed sufficiently to facilitate selection of committees by majority and minority caucuses. Every member had a say, at least in theory, but once selected, the caucus slates were then accepted pro forma by the Senate as a whole.

It soon became apparent, however, that the Senate caucus was becoming tightly controlled by a small leadership group. Next, the power of selection in both parties passed from caucus to a small Committee on Committees which Senator Albert Beveridge called a "veiled legislative autocracy."[51] But, once a member was selected, seniority became the decisive factor. He remained unless defeated or he chose to leave. If he stayed, he advanced automatically towards the chairmanship or senior minority member's post as vacancies occurred, quite regardless of whether his politics accorded with the prevalent mood of the public. Indeed, seniority was a hedge: both against democratic whim or electoral fashion and against leadership power. It filled the more important committee posts with veterans from states that stuck loyally with one candidate.

Not surprisingly, under this system, conservatives enjoyed disproportionate strength in the powerful committees controlling the budget, taxation, health and welfare policy, military policy, and the internal legislative processes of Congress.[52]

In the House, as in the Senate, the process of choosing committee members and chairmen was essentially subterranean, a mixture of seniority, log-rolling, and elitism. The problem was compounded by the fact that, since 1911, the House Democratic Committee on Committees was made up exclusively of the party's members on the Ways and Means Committee, itself a bastion of seniority, conservatism, and political longevity.[53] The consequences of that system were predictable. At the time of the 1973 Congressional revolution, the average member of the House Ways and Means Committee had sixteen years of service; this meant that he "had come to Congress in a different era" and "reflected the conservative views prevalent in the House" when the appointment was made.[54]

At the beginning of every Congress the member of this Committee undertook to fill all vacancies on all standing committees. Naturally, they tended to manage things in such a way as to insert like-minded persons in key vacancies. Each Ways and Means Committee member had jurisdiction over candidates from his geographic zone. The selection took place in closed session and was formally ratified by a complaisant caucus.[55]

On the Republican side of the House, the system was slightly more democratic. Committee assignments were made by a Committee on Committees consisting of one member elected by each state's Republican delegation. Yet here, too, seniority has tended to play the decisive role.[56] Each member cast as many votes as there were Representatives of the party from that state, thereby concentrating power over assignments in the hands of the large state delegations.[57]

In both chambers, too, the party leaders have tended to keep a close eye on the selections and they usually clear potential appointees with the chairman of the recipient committee.[58] This, too, has helped make committees small, like-minded, self-perpetuating fraternities.

The committee selection process thus positively flaunted its distortive qualities. This scandal was compounded by the tendency of powerful committee chairmen to thwart the majority in their own committees whenever their absolute control was threatened. Increasingly, chairmen alone determined the times and frequencies of committee meetings, set the agenda, scheduled hearings and decided on the list of witnesses. The size, composition, and work of the committee staff came within the chairman's discretion. So did the choice of subcommittee chairmen. Most autocratic of all was the chairman's power to prevent a bill from coming to the floor for a vote.[59] By pocketing a draft bill, and simply refusing to refer it to a subcommittee, the chairman could simply block consideration. In miniature, these authoritarian practices were emulated by subcommittee chairmen in their domains.

Undemocratic committee practices were of far more than passing importance. A study for the Murphy Commission in 1975 noted: "Who sits on a committee may, in many instances, determine what emerges from that committee."[60] And who sat on a committee came to have almost nothing to do with the democratic representative process. As this system perfected itself, it became evident that it must yield to reform, just as it had originally, itself, been the instrument of a reform that had restricted the autocratic powers of the House Speaker and Senate President. The current revolt of the rank and file thus was a healthy reaction to a committee system that had lost its capacity to respond to rapidly changing national and Congressional attitudes.

The first changes came in 1971, when the House Republican Conference—the party caucus—decided to give itself the power, by secret ballot, to pass on the committee assignments made by its Committee on Committees. This meant, among other things, that the ultimate power over the naming of the ranking minority member of each committee—who becomes chairman in the event of a Republican majority—devolved on the rank and file in caucus.

The same year, the Democratic caucus made a more timid change. Whenever ten members so requested, the nomination of a committee chairman by the Committee on Committees was subject to secret ballot. Skeptical members dubbed this the "kamikaze plan." Two years later, the House Democrats went much further, making all chairmanship appointments subject to ratification by a majority vote of the caucus at the beginning of each Congress. A secret ballot could be requested by 20 percent of the members. Finally, in December 1974 the caucus went all the way, deciding to subject all committee chairmanships to secret ballot of the caucus in every instance.

Immediately—in January 1975—the caucus implemented its new powers by rejecting three sitting chairmen: Representatives W. R. Poage of Texas (Agriculture), Hébert (Armed Services), and Wright Patman of Texas (Banking and Currency). The retirement of these formerly all-powerful totems was a momentous victory for committee accountability. Unquestionably the new procedures make committee chairmen and, thereby, the committees themselves, more responsive to the rank and file.

Even more significant was the decision to transfer the selection of committee members as well as of chairmen from the party's members of the Ways and Means Committee to a far more responsive forum: the caucus's 24-member Steering and Policy Committee. This is composed of eight Democratic House leaders (the Speaker, Majority Leader, Whip, Caucus Chairman, and the Deputy Whips), three members appointed by the Speaker, twelve elected by the regional sub-caucuses, and one freshman member selected by lot.

In addition, the House voted to clip the wings of its chairmen by deciding that no member may chair more than one legislative subcommittee. By another innovation, subcommittee chairmen must now be selected, not simply by seniority, but by vote of all members of the majority party in the committee.

Most remarkable of all was a new rule stripping committee chairmen of the power to pocket bills. They must now be referred to subcommittees within two weeks of receipt. All committees were also required to establish at least four subcommittees—a rule directed at the Ways and Means Committee which had operated without subcommittees throughout most of the sixteen-year one-man rule of Wilbur D. Mills. In still another curb on the arbitrary power of chairmen, committees were required to establish written rules.

The House has also decided to require all committees to meet in public, unless a session is closed by a public vote of the members. Open sessions are the rule even when "marking up" a bill, so that the public may now follow that vital, hitherto secret, process by which the content of legislation is negotiated, clause by clause.

These inordinately significant changes in selection and organization of committees all were made by the House between 1971 and 1975, the same period in which the Congress was seizing control over foreign policy.

Meanwhile, similar reforms were being made in the Senate. At the beginning of 1975 the Democratic Conference (caucus) agreed to a proposal by Senator Dick Clark to require election of committee chairmen by secret ballot, whenever one-fifth of the members so request. In practice, a list of those nominated for chairmanships by the Democratic Steering Committee is now distributed to all Democratic Senators at the start of each Congress. They anonymously check off the names of the nominees they want subjected to secret ballot. Whenever at least 20 percent so indicate, a secret vote is held two days later. On November 5, 1975, the Senate also approved a rule, similar to that of the House, opening committee meetings to public scrutiny.[61]

In the words of a recent Senate self-study, "Senators have been making it more difficult for committee chairmen or a determined minority to frustrate the exercise of majority opinion—a recognition of a certain obligation by the Senate to act more responsibly on policy questions. . . . [A] chairman who consistently ignored a majority opinion on his committee or in the full Senate would be in trouble."[62]

By S.Res. 4, adopted by the Senate in 1977, good committee appointments are also more widely accessible. Each Senator is now limited to service on two major committees and one minor, and every member must be given at least one subcommittee appointment before anyone receives a second. A chairman of a committee may hold only two subcommittee chairmanships and other Senators only one, per committee.[63]

The legitimacy of delegated authority in a Congress innately skeptical of delegation depends on two elements: the specialized expertise and the democratic representativeness of those exercising delegated authority. The reforms recently instituted in the House and Senate have undoubtedly made the committee system more genuinely representative, responsive, and open, in both fact and appearance. This was accomplished at a time when better educated members, supported by augmented professional staff, have enhanced their claim to be Congressional "specialists."

The seniority system, however, is not completely dead. It still applies to tenure on a committee, making it difficult to prune deadwood. Yet, Senate Majority Leader Byrd defends seniority, while acknowledging that there may be a few committees—the Intelligence Committee is one—in which there should be rapid turnover to guard against cooption. On balance, however, he argues that the "advantages of seniority usually outweigh the disadvantages," and that there are insoluble problems—like the common cold—for which remedies "are ineffective, if not worse than the problem."[64]

Nevertheless, compared to a decade ago, the committees have been democratized and opened up. Their legitimation, in recent years, entitles them to respect. Certainly, a committee bill or resolution deserves a rank and file presumption in its favor if it was written after careful study and research of the issue by members who are both specialists and representative of—and responsive to—their peers. Once committees are again able to marshal sufficient prestige to give Congress a delivery capability, the abuses of past periods of committee ascendance might reemerge; but only if the rank and file let slip their effective new checks on committee chairmanship, membership, and procedures.

A responsible, responsive, and respected committee structure is essential to continued Congressional participation in foreign policy codetermination. There will be crises and extraordinary occasions when the party leadership, in each chamber, will have to become actively involved in rescuing—or quashing—a foreign relations initiative such as the Strategic Arms Limitation agreement, or the Panama Canal Treaties. But the new oversight calls for day-to-day Congressional participation in many other issues of considerable importance that cannot expect to draw on the attention of the leadership. For the ongoing process of advancing the national interest, primary responsibility in Congress must fall on those who make a career of the management of foreign relations, the committees assigned that role by the Senate and the House.

10

EXPERTISE:

Powering the Congressional Delivery System

THE STAFF EXPLOSION

COMMITTEE legitimacy, and the capacity of committees to provide an effective delivery system, depends not only on *democratization* but also on *expertise*. The rank and file, if they are once more to adopt a presumption in favor of committee recommendations, must be convinced that the product is authoritative.

The need for expertise was first perceived as part of the unequal struggle between the Congress and the President, with members coming to understand that they could not share power in the foreign relations field if they did not develop "a way to follow closely what the President was doing."[1] This, until recently, they did not have, certainly not in the field of foreign policy. A Senate foreign relations staffer freely concedes, for the period up to 1974, "the executive's dominance of operational information, or to put it another way, the Senate's failure to develop the independent resources to secure the information which it needed."[2]

The Murphy Commission found that by 1974 this inferiority had begun to trouble Congress.[3] During the unraveling of U.S. policy in Vietnam, the Administration's analyses and prognoses were repeatedly proven wrong, not by Congress but by events. Thus the inability of Congress to provide a viable alternative system of assessments, estimates, and options could no longer go unnoticed. Representative Richard Bolling of Missouri was appointed chairman of a Select Committee to reform committees, including their information systems. His conclusions pointed to the same expertise gap.[4]

Challenged by events, by Executive failures, and by perceptive critics in its ranks, Congress has begun to improve its capacity to make informed policy decisions. At the heart of this effort is the foreign relations committees' enhanced capacity to gather and analyze data. Part of the answer is being found in the use of new technology.[5] But the main thrust has been in the direction of more and better staff, in the words of one study, to "redress the balance and help restore independence and higher status to the legislative units."[6]

To close the expertise gap between itself and the executive branch, Congress has equipped its foreign policy committees and its members specializing in international affairs with augmented staff. This has had the important secondary effect of widening the expertise gap between the specializing committees and the rank and file.

Staffing is the key to committee effectiveness—a truth as inevitable and as unpalatable to many inveterate loners in Congress as that committees are the key to Congressional efficacy. Since 1954 Congress has more than tripled its personal and committee staffs. These now exceed 17,000 persons—more personnel, for example, than the Department of State. If the Congressional research agencies are also counted—General Accounting Office, Congressional Research Service, Office of Technology Assessment, Congressional Budget Office—the total exceeds 23,000. Students of Congress are finding that these "dramatic increases in the numbers of professional staffers give Congressmen the ability to dig more deeply into a wider range of issues. . . ."[7]

The term "staff" inexactly describes six different categories of Congressional employees, each performing different functions, operating under somewhat different rules, and pursuing separate purposes. Closest to most members of Congress are the *personal staff*. The next concentric circle around the Senators (the House has no equivalent category) is made up of the *S.Res. 4 staff*, specialists hired to facilitate the Senators' work on assigned committees. Next are the *committee staffs* and *subcommittee staffs*, who, at least in theory, are at the disposal of all members of the units that hire them, with a few hired specifically by and for the minority party members. Then there are the *staffs of select or temporary committees*, frequently persons on leave for short periods from law firms, universities, and other committees, who have been hired to carry out a single investigation or participate in a short-term assignment. Finally, there are the *research support staffs* of the General Accounting Office, the Congressional Research Service, and the Office of Technology Assessment, and the Congressional Budget Office. Each of these categories has shared in the phenomenal recent growth of staffing. And the foreign relations committees, as well as members specializing in foreign affairs, have been among the principal beneficiaries.

As the staffs of Senators have grown to accommodate specialists hired not to answer mail but for their knowledge of one, or several, of the subjects for which the member has assumed committee responsibility, as committees' staffs have expanded exponentially not merely to arrange meetings and secure the interests of the chairman but to undertake detailed study of aspects of committee responsibility, so has the credibility of Congress grown in policy confrontations with the Executive. Specialization has become inextricably linked with expertise, and expertise with staffing and committees.

Few generalities are equally applicable to each of these six categories of Congressional employees. However, it is broadly true that as their number has increased in the past two decades so, commensurately, has their power to influence various outcomes. However, while the power of this "invisible third chamber" is growing—and that growth makes controversy and jealousy inevitable—it is also generally correct that staff growth has led to an increase, not a decrease, in the power of Senators and Representatives, especially in the area of their committee assignments. These legislators are now supported by incomparably better research, saved from time-consuming public relations obligations by press- and case-work specialists, and plugged into an effective, trouble-shooting staff network. That network connects not only the offices of key members and of the multiple committees with related jurisdiction, but also provides an open line between Congress and the middle-echelon bureaucracy. Most members thus find themselves better coordinated and organized to cope with the increasing complexities of their role. Critics say they also have more time to harass the executive branch.

Inevitably, however, members have achieved this greater public effectiveness at the cost of having to share their power with a growing legion of unelected specialists. The legislative branch, in the 1970's, has undergone a bureaucratization comparable to that of the executive branch during the 1930's.

Personal staff of all Senators grew from 39 in 1891, to 1,749 in 1967, then shot up to 3,251 in the next decade. On the House side, as recently as 1914, each legislator received a staff allowance of $1,500. In 1930, staff stood at 870; by 1967 it was 4,055 and in 1976 it reached 6,939.[8] Much of this personal staff is still involved in the traditional chores, the care and feeding of constituents, answering mail, resolving citizens' problems with the federal bureaucracy, meeting with lobbyists and citizen-advocates. But most personal staffs now also include a growing core of assistants who are legislative specialists. In 1965, Representatives employed only 111 legislative assistants while Senators employed 82. By 1977, the figure for Representatives had risen to 752 while that for Senators was up to 349.[9] A new Senator may have only two or three such subject-specialists on his staff, while more senior—or more affluent—

Senators like Ted Kennedy can muster what a staffer working for a rival has described as "his own personal State Department."

In the Senate, where fewer members are stretched thinner over more committee and subcommittee appointments, personal staff has been augmented by a reform voted on June 12, 1975. This provides each Senator public funds sufficient to permit him "to hire staff for the purpose of assisting him in connection with his membership on one or more committees on which he serves. . . ."[10] The member is allowed one free staff specialist for each major standing committee assignment. These "S.Res. 4" staffers are allowed to participate in all sessions and have access to all files of the committee for which they are responsible.[11]

With the passage of this new staffing rule, the public purse opened to afford Senators far more expert help with committee assignments than hitherto. It also created a new category of staffers, enjoying most of the benefits and few of the disadvantages of two other categories: personal staff and professional committee staff. Like personal staff, the S.Res. 4 staffers enjoy close, intimate contact with their Senator and can wheel and deal with the authority that comes from easy access and direct responsibility. But the S.Res. 4 staff, unlike other members of a Senator's personal entourage, can also expect to devote time almost exclusively to a designated area of specialization without being pulled away to deal with other chores. Like a committee professional staffer, the S.Res. 4 staff has access to classified documents and privileged communications but is not subordinate to the committee's chief of staff. While the S.Res. 4 staffer may choose to focus attention on a single project of the committee, he or she can neither be compelled to do so nor be excluded from any aspect of the committee's work.

Whereas the professional staff of committees must make an effort at professional objectivity, S.Res. 4's can combine specialization with open policy advocacy in the name of their Senator. It is therefore hardly surprising that these S.Res. 4 posts have become highly prized. Carl Marcy, a retired Chief of Staff of the Senate Foreign Relations Committee, has remarked that the S.Res. 4's were the ones who "are getting the real action" because they "can deliver Senators and therefore other Senators rely on them to negotiate the contents of bills being drafted and involve them in the process of putting together the groups of sponsors for legislation."[12] Marcy reports that the S.Res. 4's "are forming a kind of liberal caucus that constitutes the most important single network on the Hill."[13]

Within a year after the position was created by the Senate, members had hired 291 S.Res. 4 staffers.[14] At least one appointee turned down a highly prized offer to join the Senate Foreign Relations Committee's core staff in order to be in "the S.Res. 4 caucus," believing it to offer the best prospects for that aphrodisiac of the Hill, "impact."

This assessment may not do justice to the growing power of recently augmented and professionally up-graded committee staffs. Their growth in numbers and influence has been at least as phenomenal as that of the S.Res. 4's. Congressional committees have had the assistance of "clerks" for about 125 years, but it was only with the enactment of the Legislative Reorganization Act of 1946 that the Congress created the basis for a core of permanent committee professionals. Under that scheme, each standing committee of the Senate and House was authorized to appoint "by a majority vote of the committee not more than four professional staff members in addition to the clerical staffs on a permanent basis without regard to political affiliations and solely on the basis of fitness to perform the duties of the office. . . ."[15] These staff were to serve "the chairman and ranking minority member of such committee. . . ."[16] A numerical exception was made for the Committee on Appropriations of each House which was authorized to make as many appointments as its members "determined to be necessary."[17] Top salary was set at $8,000.[18] It was also provided that no committee staff member "shall be eligible for appointment to any office or position in the executive branch of the Government for a period of one year after he shall have ceased to be such a member."[19]

In 1970, the number of professionals per committee was raised to six.[20] That reform also added two professional staffers to be selected by and for the minority members of each committee.[21]

Since then, committees' staffs have grown even more rapidly both in numbers and quality. Top salaries now run to $50,000, with many above $35,000. In 1974, the Bolling Committee on Committee Reform, recognizing that core staff provides "administrative support and policy expertise" and thus enable the House to form judgments "independent of the executive branch," proposed a further increase from six to eighteen per committee, with the Appropriations Committees still exempt from any limit.[22] Bolling's recommendations on staff expansion were adopted in October 1974[23] just in time for the revolutionary Congressional confrontations with the President. At the beginning of 1975, the House International Relations Committee staff tripled.

The Senate Foreign Relations Committee staff formally remained at six.[24] However, at about the time the House was acting on the Bolling Report, the Senate also specifically authorized additional staff hiring by the Committee on Foreign Relations.[25] It also authorized the borrowing of Executive personnel "on a reimbursable basis." By the end of 1974, the Foreign Relations Committee's staff had grown to 58.[26] Since adoption of S.Res. 4, approximately another dozen professionals have been added.

The core staffs of the Senate and House foreign affairs committees are further augmented by additional professional staffers hired for several subcommittees. In the case of the Senate, subcommittees are staffed by persons on loan from the core committee. A significant exception was the Subcommittee on Foreign Assistance of the Senate Foreign Relations Committee which, from January 1976 to its abolition in January 1979, had the clout to hire its own staff director and six professionals. With the death of its chairman, Senator Humphrey, the subcommittee lost its engine, and most of its staff were absorbed by the core committee.

In addition, the Senate committee has added staff each time it set up a special subcommittee to investigate a topical issue, such as the allegation that U.S. multinational corporations were engaging in bribery and subversion of foreign regimes. A recent report by the Stevenson Committee on Committees notes that approximately 305 employees, one-fourth of all Senate Committee staff in the 94th Congress, were funded under twenty-seven separate "special investigative subcommittee" resolutions.[27]

Separate subcommittee staffs constitute the rule, rather than the exception, in the House of Representatives. The House International Relations Committee, in 1978, had a complement of sixty-one professionals, of whom twenty-five worked for the core committee and the remainder for nine subcommittees. Each subcommittee chairman has a staff director and three assistants able to focus on such subjects as "international security and scientific affairs," "Europe and the Middle East," or "International Organizations."[28] In addition, the minority in each subcommittee is entitled to one professional staffer. Between 1976 and 1978 the number of International Relations subcommittee staff specialists actually doubled (from eighteen to thirty-six).

There are differences of opinion as to whether the approximate tripling of professional staff in the decade 1967–1977 has provided the foreign affairs committees with sufficient expertise. Jack Brady, the Chief of Staff of the House International Relations Committee, believes that the optimum has been reached or even exceeded.[29] In the Senate, the Stevenson Committee reported: "permanent staff sizes are still unrealistically low; they do not begin to correspond to the workloads of many committees."[30]

STAFF EXPERTISE

Already, the growth of staffing has done as much as has committee democratization to legitimize the long-resisted and even longer-abused Congressional system of delegation and specialization. The House International Relations Committee rules state the aim: "The Committee staff shall . . . provide a comprehensive range of professional services in the field of foreign affairs. . . ."[31] This has been achieved. Chairmen, and even individual members, are now more often in a position to challenge Administration officials with independently obtained facts and statistics as well as with their own informed analyses of the facts' significance for the national interest.

This has as much to do with the level of staff competence as with numbers. The Rules call for "persons with training and experience in foreign affairs who have a variety of backgrounds and skills so as to make available to the Committee services of individuals who have a first-hand acquaintance with major countries and areas and with major aspects of U.S. overseas programs and operations."[32] This objective, too, is being met. On December 31, 1977, the House received a demographic study of its employees, the Obey Commission Report, which found that the "work force is extremely well-educated" with almost 61 percent being college graduates and one-third having attended graduate school.[33]

Among professionals, almost all recruited in the past decade, are college graduates, and a majority have advanced academic training. A recent study by Fox and Hammond concludes that 45 percent of their sample of 313 committee professionals holds law degrees, while a further 24.8 percent holds masters degrees or doctorates. A sampling of House International Relations Committee professionals suggests an even higher concentration of specialized graduate training—Ph.D.'s, M.A.'s, and J.D.'s—than among committee staff professionals in general.[34] And more than a third (34.9 percent) are graduates of a different sort, having previously held positions in the executive branch.[35]

Much the same holds true for members' legislative assistants. Figures compiled by Fox and Hammond for Representatives' legislative assistants show fewer lawyers (25 percent) and doctorates (2.1 percent) but more Masters degrees (19 percent) and B.A.'s (47 percent).[36] Their Senate figures are very similar.

Considering that staff professionals are predominantly young, they, too, are well paid. The Congress can compete for the best with the private sector. As of July 1977 the top salary for Senators' staff specialists was $49,993; it was $47,500 for Representatives' aides.[37] Committee professionals' salaries are somewhat higher than are those of members' personal staffers. To salary must be added the fringe benefit of impact—the sense of direct influence on significant events—as well as excellent prospects in the executive branch, law firms, and industry.

Congress has thus given itself a counter-bureaucracy that attracts a very high level of excellence and ambition, and in doing so, has given the committee system new validity.

In some other respects, the staff system leaves room for improvement. Jobs continue to be filled by a process that has failed to turn up significant numbers of blacks, other minorities, or women.[38] Recruiting, far from an open merit-based competition, is by an informal process that emphasizes "whom you know on the staff" or, in the words of the Obey Commission, just plain "being around."[39] One veteran staffer describes it thus: "People on the hill hire entirely by network. Someone knows someone, or someone knows someone who knows someone." David Aaron, Deputy Director of the National Security Council and once legislative aide to Senator Mondale, described the hiring practices of the Church Committee to investigate the intelligence agencies as turning on a "network of friendships, neighbors, ex-colleagues, that sort of thing."[40]

The first rung on a staffer's ladder may thus be a Congressional internship or a summer research, or even clerical, appointment to a committee or member's staff. At a more senior level, staffers are handed on by retiring or defeated members to newcomers. It seems far less important that a specialist legislative assistant actually be from the member's state or district than that he or, rarely, she be known personally by someone already on the staff.

One recent, although not entirely new, hiring practice has proven a boon. An important source of recruitment for the foreign affairs committees is the State Department's Foreign Service. Several young Foreign Service Officers have recently made the leap from relatively humble Grade 5 to a Deputy Assistant Secretaryship via a detour of work for Congress. These "dopplegängers" bring Congress an insider's experience in dealing with the State Department as well as skills gained in service abroad.[41]

STAFF INFLUENCE

Congressional staffers derive their power from three sources: (1) close association with key members; (2) recognized expertise and political sensitivity; (3) being part of a staffer's network.

The close relationship of personal staff to members derives initially from the process of mutual selection. It needs constant reinforcement through effective performance. A senior staffer must be able to function as alter ego to the member, knowing when to be present, when assertive, when diffident, when and where to be bold in committing their member and when to hold back and consult. Personal aides, at the request of their members, are frequently "given the privilege of the floor" in the House and Senate. They can be seen hovering nearby when their member is speaking, whispering, passing sheets of paper or running to make a deal with other staff in the cloakroom. According to Senator Mark Hatfield of Oregon, every legislator knows that when a staffer says of his member, "He'll go along, after I explain it to him," it does not actually commit the Senator, but means, "I think I can deliver."[42] A National Security Council official observed that staffers frequently reject proposals without consulting their member. He added, ruefully: "If I can just get past the staffers to the Senators themselves, I often find they take positions considerably softer than those of the aide. But several Senators on the Foreign Relations Committee are really under their staff's control."[43]

The power of staff in relation to their member becomes particularly obvious when the buzzer sounds to call members to the floor for a vote. During such a vote call, staffers can be seen milling about the doors of nearby elevators waiting to meet their principals. In the thirty seconds it takes to sprint from the banks of elevators to the floor of the chamber, the staffer delivers a rapid-fire summary of the issue in an upcoming vote. How he characterizes that issue and the recommendation he makes frequently determine the member's vote. If the issue is not one of profound interest or concern to the legislator, this briefing may be the first and only time the member focuses on that subject.

In the words of Senator Hatfield, "There is a growing dependency on staff, almost to the point of [an aide] saying, 'I think you should vote this way.' " Senator Robert Morgan of North Carolina has put it more strongly, charging that this "country is basically run by the legislative staffs. . . ."[44] Such hyperbole is an inevitable concomitant of the increase in professional support service to members: they become more effective but also more dependent. Senators' attitudes toward certain problems and constituencies have been known to change noticeably after a new legislative assistant joins the staff.

Given the unmanageable workload of all Senators and, to a lesser extent, of Representatives, it is not surprising that they have become so heavily staff-dependent. But the phenomenon is easily exaggerated, not least because some staffers' egos match—and merge with—those of their principals. Most staffers, however, cannot transform dependence into role-reversal. Members very rarely become instruments of their aides, even though it may occasionally look that way to outsiders. When, as is frequently the case, the staffer is more liberal than the member, the aide must still be governed by the legislator's philosophy and, even more, by considerations of constituency politics. A defeated member usually means an unemployed staffer. And while a member may sometimes permit the aide to "get ahead of him" on an issue, he or she will not be forgiven if the result is an unfavorable home town editorial and deluge of angry mail.[45] Staffers also are unlikely to survive if they draw the spotlight away from their employer.

Assistants who do "get out in front" take a calculated facilitator's risk. They may find their principals publicly disowning them. When that happens, the staffer loses credibility not only with his member but with the whole network on which his or her efficacy depends. In 1976, for example, one of Senator Kennedy's legislative assistants negotiated a hard-fought compromise with Justice Department lawyers on the kind of writ that would be required in new legislation Kennedy was introducing to regulate counter-espionage wire-tapping. When the bill came before the Committee, however, Kennedy failed to defend the compromise against senatorial critics. The aide lost caste when it became apparent that he could not "deliver" his Senator. On the other hand, Senator Tunney's aide, Mark Moran, seemed to have been given a genuinely free hand to negotiate with the State Department, the CIA, even the Government of Luanda during the 1975–76 crisis over Congressional termination of covert operations in Angola.

An effective staff member must combine expert specialized knowledge of subjects for which a member or a committee has assumed special responsibility with an ability to work with the relevant lobbies and grass-roots interest groups. He or she must combine elements of Vance, Brzezinski, Jordan, and Rafshoon, preparing data, analyzing options, making connections, and generating public support. When Congress was considering the Jackson-Vanik Amendment on Jewish emigration from the Soviet Union, the legislative aide to Representative Vanik, Mark Talisman, undertook a sixteen-hour-a-day campaign to contact every one of 435 Congressional offices, cajoling key staffers to secure the co-sponsorship of the amendment by their principals. He called some offices as many as fifteen times.[46] And it was Talisman who conducted most negotiations with Jewish lobbying groups. Similarly, Representative Tom Harkin has acknowledged that the human rights issue was of little interest to him until Rebecca Switzer of his staff handed him the fully drafted amendment to that year's foreign assistance authorization that became the first mandatory human rights legislation.[47]

The committee staff are in a different role from members' personal aides. Their power derives from an ability to speak and act on behalf of the committee as a whole. In some instances, the system of the 1950's still applies: that is, the committee staff works for the chairman. This is not the case, however, in the two foreign relations committees, where the majority and minority staffs serve the whole committee.[48]

The power of committee staff derives not only from professionalism and a degree of independence from each member that comes from being the servant of all, but also from the important areas of discretion that are ordinarily assigned to them. In the case of the House and Senate committees dealing with foreign relations, it is the staff which organizes and conducts most oversight investigations, decides who shall be asked to testify, writes the first drafts of most legislation, deals with, or fends off, professional lobbyists and public interest groups, and carries on day-to-day communications between the committee and government agencies. Staff propose the witnesses to be heard, and brief Senators on the issues likely to arise at hearings, supplying questions to be asked of witnesses. They conduct staff mark-up sessions, participate in committee mark-up, and write the reports that accompany every bill to the floor.

In preparation for hearings, staffers research the witnesses' briefs. One staffer reported, "The International Development Agency, which we oversee, would draw up a list of projects they said were implementing the guidelines mandated by Congress. It would be my job to look into these and then to write a memorandum tearing their written testimony apart. I'd try to show that these projects were only window dressing, that they didn't really implement the law."[49] Another complained that committee members did not have the depth of information necessary for follow-up questions after the witness's first, often "soft" answer. "The foreign affairs committees ought to allow staff to do most of the cross-examining," he said, "because then we could really hone in on the witness who was feeding us a line."[50]

These are broad responsibilities and even wider aspirations. In the words of a recent study, whether "a legislative proposal originates with a Senator, a staff member, or a lobby group, the responsibility for translating it into legislative language, and nursing it through the committee process, rests largely with the staff. Indeed, the success or failure of a piece of legislation often depends upon whether a Senator is a member of the committee involved, and thus has a committee or subcommittee staff member who can be considered an 'insider' by others on the staff, and give the legislation regular attention."[51] A senior Administration aide has complained that legislation, and legislative history, are becoming increasingly complex because of the enthusiasm of committee staffers for drafting bills and reports to cover every eventuality. "I remember participating in a meeting with Kissinger and [Senator] Humphrey," he said, "at which they were trying to work out some differences over a foreign assistance bill. But its procedures were so incredibly complicated that we had to give up. Neither Kissinger nor Humphrey, whose bill it was, could understand what the thing was trying to say. We had to call in the staffers because only they knew what it all meant."[52]

In recent years, committee staff have even begun to join U.S. delegations to international conferences as observers. Part of their job may be to advise on how a line of negotiations with foreign countries is likely to influence Congressional support for a projected agreement.

When staff have become too encrusted, or are insufficiently supervised by their committee chairman or by the members, a Congressional bureaucratic autocracy can result, rivaling any at the other end of Pennsylvania Avenue. It can frustrate the democratic process and recreate, at the staff level, the climate of personalized tyranny that earlier brought committees into disrepute. One example, a professional staff member of the powerful Foreign Operations subcommittee of the Senate Appropriations Committee, has taken to speaking as imperiously as any seniority-encrusted solon. When consulted by bureaucrats, as he constantly must be, he approves or vetoes ideas on the spot, apparently confident that he need not consult his chairman. A senior Presidential aide has said, "One of the advantages of being in the White House, rather than at an agency, is that I can get past that S.O.B. to the chairman, who we find very courteous and helpful." Less fortunate bureaucrats who do have to deal with the staffer report that "we know the kinds of projects that bother him, so we don't do them, even if they're worthwhile. That way we don't have to go over there to be castrated."

This, however, is an exception. As Chairman Zablocki of the House International Relations Committee has said, "when decisions are made, staff will not make them. Members will make them."[53]

Still, it is the staffers that design the issues and lay out the options. That makes them vulnerable to attack by those who think the committee made a wrong decision. In order to protect themselves against such charges, most committee staff carefully cultivate their professional image. While most actually are less blatantly political than the members' personal or S.Res. 4 staffers, committee professionals do tend to be identified with a new kind of partisanship. Even when they are not clearly identifiable as Democrats or Republicans, they tend to belong to the "activist party" which enthusiastically believes that social problems are tractable rather than inevitable, and that, in all probability, the answer lies with Government and the law. Representative Morris Udall has observed that the staff explosion has set off a legislative explosion that is threatening to clog the system. In a recent study of committee staffs, Professor David E. Price characterized these staffers as "policy entrepreneurs,"[54] men and women who, on their own, seek out social problems in their area of expertise, investigate them, listen to advocates for relevant causes, assign them priorities, produce a legislative focus for reform, and then sell the project to key members of their committee. Increasingly, the professional committee staffers tend toward this "policy entrepreneurial" prototype. Young, well paid, highly educated, but with little experience in business, agriculture, labor, or industry, the activist committee staffers tend to confirm the conservative's stereotype of big-government–loving liberals who generate facile, interventionist solutions.

According to one Senator, himself a former legislative aide, "staffers work faithfully for you all year. Then the day comes when they tell you they've got a really great idea for a bill. You just don't have the heart to turn them down. Next thing you find yourself on your feet in front of the presiding officer with this piece of legislation in your hand. And you're saying to yourself, 'How did I get into this?' "

On occasion, when a committee professional has a good solution to what he perceives to be a pressing social problem, yet cannot find a sponsor among his own committee's members, he may offer it to a friend working for a member not on the committee or for some other committee. That, as we indicated in Chapter 4, is how Senator Nelson came to sponsor the Arms Export Control law, after none of the members of the Foreign Relations Committee proved willing to adopt it. However, such staff entrepreneurship, extending outside the confines of the committee, is unusual. For the most part, committee specialists find a ready market in their own committee. Indeed, members of Congress crave ideas, preferably embodied in printed bills that bear their names.

This is subject, of course, to the vagaries of political fashion. If liberal interventionism comes to be replaced by a conservative policy of benign neglect, members will rein in their staffers or be less responsive to an entrepreneurship that has lost its popular appeal. If so, members might prefer the style of an older generation of staffers, like the recently retired Pat Holt, a former Chief of Staff of the Senate Foreign Relations Committee, who is out of sympathy with the current crop of "policy entrepreneurs" on committee staffs. In Holt's words, "staff forget that they don't represent a single U.S. voter."[55] Yet under Holt, key staffers such as Richard M. Moose and James G. Lowenstein had extraordinarily wide discretion to make field investigations of war conditions in Vietnam and of political conditions in Saigon, engaging in exposés by press release from abroad, even before returning to Washington. These activities were encouraged because they enhanced the visibility and credibility of committee Chairman Fulbright in his lonely battle against U.S. policies in Vietnam.[56] Similarly, the Symington Subcommittee sent its own investigators to twenty-three countries; their headline-hunting investigations were perceived by the chairman to be advancing his policies and, incidentally, doing no harm to his national reputation.[57] It is probable that if legislative entrepreneurship becomes unfashionable, it will be replaced not by inactivity but by other kinds of activism: cutting back on government activity or encouraging more participation in policy execution by non-governmental groups.

For the present, a committee staff appointment presents one of Washington's best opportunities to cut through inertia, red tape, and bureaucratic rivalries to effect new policies. Charles Paolillo, after work in the Agency for International Development and the Overseas Development Council, joined the House International Relations Committee to implement policies he had failed to promote through a bureaucracy hobbled by imaginative constraints and preoccupied with jurisdictional turf-wars. Through the committee he was able to promote changes in foreign aid priorities that emphasized direct-impact assistance to the neediest over large capital-intensive infrastructural projects. Paolillo's idea came to be nicknamed "trickle up," to distinguish it from the kind of traditional big-project capital-intensive aid which was expected to— but rarely did—trickle down to the poor. Another specialist on the same committee, George Ingram, became the proponent of industrial "miniaturization," a way to translate mass production technology into forms adaptable to the needs of smaller markets in less developed countries.

On the Senate side, economist Karin Lissakers, a monetary and trade expert, has given the committee a new role in the domestic dialogue over the international lending policies of private U.S. banks. Robert Mantel, an arms sales specialist recruited by the Humphrey subcommittee from the Office of Management and Budget, organized the systematic review of foreign military assistance and sales by Congress necessitated by the Nelson-Bingham Amendment. It is the staffers, not the members, who read every letter of intent filed with the committee before an arms sale. And it is the staffer who decides which of the numerous proposed transactions should be brought to the attention of busy Senators. In the House International Relations Committee, too, it is staff which performs the "flagging" function and so determines what arms exports are merely routine and which require more careful scrutiny.

The third basis for staff influence is membership in a "network" connecting a few key legislative assistants, S.Res. 4 staffers specializing in foreign policy, the core committee staff, and a few subcommittee specialists, as well as upper-middle echelon bureaucrats in the White House, National Security Council, CIA, Department of Defense, and Department of State. This network derives, in part, from shared interest and similar specialization, as well as from the extraordinary mobility that keeps staffers hopping from job to job in Congress, and from one branch to the other and back. It spans, and often transcends, the hallowed rivalries between personal staffs and committee professionals, and even modulates the war between the branches.

The staffers' network is kept in place by an elaborate system of reciprocal cooption. The advent of the Carter Administration was the occasion for what amounted to a mass migration in both directions. From the Senate, Richard Moose moved back to State as Assistant Secretary for African Affairs after a period as director of the staff of the Foreign Assistance Subcommittee. His successor, Robert Mantel, soon followed him to Foggy Bottom, becoming a senior official in the Bureau of

Politico-Military Affairs. Brian Atwood, a legislative aide to Senator Eagleton who played key roles in the Vietnam and Turkish arms cutoffs, was appointed by the Carter Administration to be Deputy Assistant Secretary of State for Congressional Relations. Atwood, too, had once been a State Department foreign service officer. As Deputy Assistant Secretary he works under Douglas Bennet, another former senatorial staffer. In the same mode, Madeleine Albright left Senator Muskie's staff to join the National Security Council, while a Mondale and Intelligence Committee aide, David Aaron, became its Deputy Director. Dan Spiegel, who had been Senator Humphrey's S.Res. 4 staffer, joined Secretary Vance as special assistant. On the House side, Jack Sullivan, who had been a senior staff consultant of the International Relations Committee, became Deputy Administrator of the Agency for International Development while the Committee's Chief of Staff, Marian Czarnecki, went to the Inter-American Development Bank. Moving in the opposite direction, Sam Goldberg, Henry Kissinger's Deputy Assistant Secretary, became legislative assistant to Republican Senator John Heinz upon his election in 1976.

The network mitigates the severity of the war between the branches and the jurisdictional clashes between House and Senate as well as among overlapping committees because staffers know and understand one another and each other's jobs. Most respect the constraints of their servitude, and are less harried and more accessible than their principals. Experienced legislators know that it is best, whenever possible, to keep inter-committee, inter-house, and inter-branch relations at the staff level, bringing in members only as a last resort. This saves the principals time and keeps them in reserve as an appellate tribunal to handle the toughest cases. During the Executive-Congressional confrontation over covert CIA intervention in Angola, for example, negotiations between Senate and State Department were often at the level of specialist staffers—"the Afrika Korps"—and Department bureaucrats.

Recognizing this, the Carter Administration has made a point of organizing regular staff briefings on foreign policy issues at the National Security Council. These shows are put on by top-flight casts: senior officials of NSC, State, and Defense, in recognition of staffers' importance and influence. Additionally, a program "posting" State Department officers and Congressional staffers for a tour of duty in each other's precincts has been developed.

Sometimes the network works too well. House International Relations Committee staffers have been criticized for being too close to the bureaucrats of the Departments of State and Defense. Cooption, this time at the staff level, is a charge once more being leveled—albeit still quietly— at committees. On the other hand, there are counter-tendencies. Some staffers went to Congress to get away from disillusioning experiences in the foreign service. A State Department official has complained that his former colleagues, when they get to the Hill, "tend to be particularly hard on us. They often left here under circumstances of mutual disillusionment and are getting even." A former member of Congress who joined an Executive agency observed that "former staffers who come here are not good at handling Congress. They still suffer from staffers' disease, an irrepressible contempt for Members. As legislative assistants they learned to manipulate us, and it's a lesson some of them just can't seem to forget."

Despite these caveats, the network does operate and, on balance, is another important benefit of the current staff expansion.

THE INFORMATIONAL SUPPORT SERVICES

The expertise which increasingly supports the foreign relations committees' claim to leadership in their areas of specialization derives not only from increased and better staffing, but also from several important support services that augment the committees' own staff work. Three agencies created by Congress have a research capability that extends to foreign policy data and analysis: the General Accounting Office (GAO), the Congressional Research Service (CRS), and the Congressional Budget Office (CBO). A fourth, the Office of Technology Assessment, also sometimes deals with foreign relations–related problems. All have foreign affairs specialists.

GAO, as of September 30, 1977, had 5,332 employees, of whom just over 4,000 were professional staff.[58] Organized by Congress in the 1921 Budget and Accounting Act, it was given added responsibility in the 1970 Legislative Reorganization Act, and again by the Congressional Budget and Impoundment Control Act of 1974. It was originally designed to check the government's books, but now seeks out data about Executive agencies' operations, including critical evaluations of program efficiency and efficacy: Is an experimental program working as Congress intended? Are new solutions generating unexpected problems? The GAO's task is to assist Congress with surveys, reviews, and studies mandated by legislation or requested by Congressional committees and individual members. It may also assign staff members to work directly with a Congressional committee.[59]

GAO has ten principal units, one of which is the International Division, consisting of fully 134 professionals: a highly qualified group. All have doctoral or master's degrees in such fields as political science, international relations, or international economics.[60] In fiscal 1977, the

Division wrote twenty-eight reports, nineteen of them at the request of Congressional committees. They dealt with such subjects as implementation, effect, and violation of U.S. sanctions against Rhodesia; the capacity of Egypt to absorb U.S. assistance; an analysis of U.S. base negotiations with the Philippines; and a critique of U.S. forces' deployment in Korea.

While GAO rejects its popular image as the investigative arm of Congress, preferring to be thought of as management consultants, the International Division, alone of Congressional units, maintains its own listening posts abroad: in Panama, Bangkok, Frankfurt, and Honolulu.[61] It frequently sends investigative teams to other parts of the world.

The Director of the International Division, Kenneth Fasick, has said, "We try to produce knowledge for Congress. . . . We maintain continuous relations with the major committees in the international field. . . . We attempt to stay abreast of new developments in a wide range of subjects: trade and finance, balance of payments, mutual security, nuclear proliferation. . . . We try to phase ourselves so we'll be ready when a committee turns to a new subject. When suggestions come from Members' or Committee staff, ninety percent of the time we've already got the subject under scrutiny."[62]

In addition to preparing studies and conducting investigations, GAO specialists regularly testify before Congressional committees, between 100 and 160 times a year, on subjects ranging from the effect of a proposed embargo on Ugandan coffee to assessment of the effectiveness of an AID project in the Sahel. Frequently, GAO, on its own or at the request of a committee, will study a draft bill, analyzing its provisions in terms of existing legislation and will assess its probable impact. Teams sent abroad may report on the political, social, and economic context of a problem on which Congress is legislating. Such a field survey of Saudi Arabia was undertaken in connection with arms sales offers lying in wait before the foreign affairs committees.

GAO personnel maintain close contact with Congressional staffers, first to get ideas of "hot" topics and issues "coming down the pike" but also to negotiate the terms of any requests sent by members or committees. The way a request is made, or its terms of reference set out in the letter of request, may affect the outcome of GAO's study. Therefore, its formulation is often the subject of intense bargaining between the members or staffers originating a request—who usually already know to what conclusion they want the GAO to come—and the Division's staff which seeks to protect its independence and objectivity.

The Congressional Research Service of the Library of Congress was established by Congress in 1914 with the limited primary purpose of preparing law indices and digests.[63] That mandate has been vastly broadened, beginning with the Legislative Reorganization Act of 1946 which authorizes direct assistance to committees and members on legislative proposals. The 1970 Reorganization Act emphasized an even wider role in policy research and analysis. In the five ensuing years the staff grew from 323 to 778, 565 of them professionals.[64]

CRS provides reference library–like services, answering questions on every conceivable subject. It prepares "Issue Briefs," summaries of bills, operates computer information services, and drafts speeches for members. Its professional personnel can be lent to Committees for work on a project. The Service also prepares lists of programs under the authority of each committee, indicating which ones require reauthorization in the next session.[65]

CRS has a Foreign Affairs and National Defense Division, currently manned by fifty professional researchers,[66] twice as many as two years ago. A short-term unit meets members' requests for drafts of speeches or simple information. This is not popular work with the staff who prefer to be policy analysts, like everyone else, but it is a valuable service to busy legislators. As a result of recent reorganization and augmentation, however, this aspect of CRS's work has been cut back. The professional staff, which previously spent 80 percent of its time on short-term requests, now expends only about 15 percent on such relative trivia. Instead, more "depth" analysis and middle-range projections are being undertaken. "We have changed the image of the Congressional Research Service," a senior official says, "from that of a legislative reference service to an organization doing serious research. We have demonstrated we can do professional analysis and no longer are relegated to the role of mere reference librarians."[67]

Some recent studies done by CRS for the Senate Foreign Relations Committee have analyzed arms control impact statements submitted in connection with the Administration's annual budget requests,[68] and have looked critically at Presidential policy on conventional arms transfers.[69] A report for the House Committee surveys all U.S. military aid and sales programs and the legal requirements and Congressional controls applicable to them.[70]

Newest of the supporting service units is the Congressional Budget Office, which is the Congress's fiscal scorekeeper. Congress now requires every bill reported out of committee to be accompanied by a CBO estimate of what it will cost to implement over five years. Even earlier, working with the staff of the foreign affairs committees, CBO informally estimates the costs of almost anything members or staffers suggest for possible inclusion in a bill. This information is provided before the bill goes to committee mark-up. Thus, members can see price tags as they consider what to include. According to the CBO's foreign affairs cost accountant, this process cannot help but have policy implications. "Nowadays, when a subcommittee realizes early enough what the cost implications of a proposal are going to be, and that the cost estimate will become public when the program does, they sometimes change their mind about it, or reduce its scope."[71]

CBO also gives the foreign affairs committees an independent assessment of what a program proposed by the Administration is likely to cost, often coming up with figures quite different from those of the "feds."[72] It also monitors fiscal aspects of arms deliveries under the Foreign Military Sales Program and Export-Import Bank credits and repayments.

Two additional professional staffers of CBO are assigned to longer-range foreign policy analysis, with emphasis on fiscal implications. Thus CBO in 1978 entered the debate over withdrawal of U.S. troops from Korea with a study demonstrating that it could be more expensive to deploy the same forces in the United States.[73] Inevitably, not every member of Congress is delighted when a study such as this comes up with information undermining a policy espoused by the member. Another controversial study quantified the U.S. cost savings on weapons development resulting from foreign military sales by the Defense Department.[74] These essentially fiscal analyses inevitably affect, though they probably do not often determine, how Congress thinks about such subjects as pulling U.S. troops out of Korea or restricting U.S. arms sales abroad.

It is readily apparent that in the past five years there has been an expertise explosion in Congress. It is the committees, newly democratized and legitimized, which have been the principal beneficiaries. Busy members cannot be expected to read everything generated by their burgeoning "think tanks"—any more than do the Executive's Secretaries and Undersecretaries. Still, salient points in the better studies enter the dialogue that precedes the making of decisions, usually via the personal and committee staffs. Consequently, the House International Relations Committee and the Senate Committee on Foreign Relations have vastly enhanced their credibility in dealing with the Executive and, one hopes, in once more giving leadership to the Congressional rank and file.

YOUR PLACE OR MINE?: TURF WARS
UNDERMINE COMMITTEE CREDIBILITY

The legitimizing reforms in committee structure, together with specialized expertise achieved by augmented staffing, have begun to re-establish the committees' capacity for leadership, for research, informed negotiations, reasoned interaction, compromise, and decision. All this is lost, however, when the allocation of committee jurisdiction is so dysfunctional that wrong committees are seen to be making key decisions. When responsibility for important aspects of foreign policy is vested in committees whose members and staff are not specialists in that subject and who have no continuing familiarity with it, then there is no reason for the rank and file to defer. To refer crucial foreign policy choices to committees not manifestly equipped by commitment, experience, and staffing, is, inevitably, to invite extemporaneous floor action by the rank and file. When none is in charge, all are equally in charge.

Jack Brady, the Chief of Staff of House International Relations Committee, says, "I spend about half my time protecting the jurisdiction of this committee and its subcommittees."[75]

Turf wars are endemic in Congress. The Barbour Resolution of 1816 established the first ten standing committees of the Senate.[76] Since it headed that list, the Committee on Foreign Relations is frequently referred to as the "ranking committee." But its *ad hoc* predecessor, a select committee on foreign affairs appointed for one Congress at a time, had been stripped in 1812 of its jurisdiction over army and naval matters. These went to a new select committee on military affairs.[77] This truncated concept of foreign relations has survived to the present, nullifying much of the beneficial effect of recent staff augmentation.

Jurisdictional fragmentation has managed to create, in the midst of an expertise explosion, something approximating government by the least qualified. Committees other than the one assigned to specialize in foreign policy deal with such important aspects of the subject as foreign intelligence operations, monetary policy, military preparedness, arms limitation negotiation, international energy policy, and multi-lateral trade negotiations. Congress continues to be organized somewhat as if U.S. foreign policy not only were, but ought to be, merely the incidental sum of a gaggle of random, independent integers.

There have been many efforts in both chambers to concentrate foreign policy jurisdiction, all to little avail. In 1975, the Murphy Commission proposed that the House Committee on International Relations be allowed to oversee reciprocal tariff negotiations. Murphy also proposed, modestly enough, that International Relations be allowed to share with the Banking and Currency Committee, supervision of U.S. policy toward international financial institutions. It said, with irrefutable logic, that "economic relations seem certain to constitute a growing proportion of future foreign policy."[78] The recommendation had no effect.[79]

Earlier, the Legislative Reorganization Act of 1946[80] and the Legislative Reorganization Act of 1970[81] consolidated numerous committees but failed to rationalize foreign policy jurisdiction, which remained as diffused as ever. In the House, the Bolling Committee was set up to conduct a "thorough and complete" study of the House rules giving jurisdiction to the various standing committees.[82] It made by far its most radical recommendations in relation to foreign affairs, where it proposed a top-to-bottom jurisdictional realignment to concentrate authority in the House Committee on Foreign Affairs (as it was then called). Most significantly—and logically—the committee recommended that "foreign trade be added to the Foreign Affairs Committee."[83] It argued that trade policy "is directly tied to international politics. For example, trade is increasingly replacing bilateral aid as a key factor in our relations with less-developed countries. . . ."[84] It also urged that the House Foreign Affairs Committee be made responsible for agricultural commodity export programs and for overseeing U.S. relations with international financial institutions.[85] Also in vain. The existing satrapies were all too effective in defending their marches.[86] By the time the Bolling plan had been mauled by the Democratic caucus and sidetracked to the Democratic Committee on Organization, Study and Review (the Hansen Committee), Foreign Affairs had gained very little.

An amendment to Rule X, passed by the House in 1974, does give the international relations committee jurisdiction over "measures relating to international economic policy" as well as over "export controls" and most "international commodity agreements."[87] But foreign trade remains firmly lodged with Ways and Means. The House has never adopted the Bolling Report's objective of enabling the international relations committee to become "the House's spokesman on international economic and political affairs."[88] It had also been one of Bolling's objectives to have the Armed Services Committee share its foreign intelligence jurisdiction with Foreign Affairs. According to a committee staff member, the fight was tough and dirty, with Armed Services Chairman Hébert passing the word that certain member (or members) of Foreign Affairs posed a "security risk."[89] In the end, Representative Clement Zablocki, then the second ranking Democrat on the Foreign Affairs Committee and its intelligence specialist, reluctantly agreed to a compromise by which his committee was given "special oversight functions . . . with respect to . . . intelligence activities relating to foreign policy" but no legislative jurisdiction.[90]

There matters stand today. Democratized, reorganized, heavily staffed, the committee on international relations still does not have responsibility for many subjects of fundamental foreign policy importance. It has no jurisdiction over "common defense" which is allotted to the Committee on Armed Services. "Valuation and revaluation of the dollar" falls in the domain of the Committee on Banking, Currency and Housing; the "prevention of importation of foreign labors" is within the purview of Committee on Education and Labor; "intergovernmental relationships between the United States . . . and international organizations of which the United States is a member" is a function of the Committee on Government Operations; "measures relating generally to the insular possessions of the United States" are handled by the Committee on Interior and Insular Affairs; "foreign commerce generally" belongs to the Committee on Interstate and Foreign Commerce; matters pertaining to the Panama Canal and the Canal Zone are within the purview of the Committee on Merchant Marine and Fisheries, as are measures relating to the regulation of ships and the management of the U.S. fisheries zone, both matters of intense international negotiation. "Oil and other pollution of navigable waters," another subject of international negotiation, falls to the Committee on Public Works and Transportation; supervision of the National Aeronautics and Space Administration is within the jurisdiction of the Committee on Science and Technology; CIA covert operations are now primarily watched over by the Permanent Select Committee on Intelligence.[91]

In the Senate, fragmentation of foreign affairs responsibility has proven an equally irreversible historical process. The overlapping is, if anything, greater and the fragmentation of responsibility for foreign relations gives a piece of the action to an even odder assortment of committees. Thus, for example, the Committee on the Judiciary has a Subcommittee on Refugees and Escapees headed by Senator Edward M. Kennedy.

Too often, Senate jurisdictional lines have been drawn with reference not to good managerial policy but more often to a committee chairman's sense of personal territoriality. The Foreign Relations Committee gained jurisdiction over "international financial and monetary organizations," by the Legislative Reorganization Act of 1946. Then its chairman, Senator Arthur Vandenberg, relinquished it to the Senate Banking and Currency Committee, where it remained until Senator Fulbright brought the jurisdiction back to Foreign Relations as part of his dowry on transferring from the chairmanship of Banking to that of Foreign Relations.[92] Banking has been trying to recover it, ever since.

By Resolution 109 of the 94th Congress, the Senate set up a Temporary Select Committee To Study the Senate Committee System. It was headed by Senator Adlai E. Stevenson III, and its object was to make recommendations on "optimum utilization of Senators' time [and] optimum effectiveness of committees in the creation and oversight of Federal programs."[93] It did briefly consider consolidating the Foreign Relations and Armed Services committees—at the urging, surprisingly, of Senator Barry Goldwater—but decided otherwise. It actually assigned Foreign Relations new "comprehensive policy oversight"—but no legislative responsibility—for "national security."[94] Consideration was also given to the consolidation of international economic policy but "comprehensive policy oversight" was assigned to Banking, Housing and Urban Affairs—where Stevenson heads the relevant subcommittee on international finance—rather than to the Foreign Relations Committee.[95] After a hard-fought turf war, the Foreign Relations Committee emerged with "primary control over international economic policy" including the international financial institutions.[96] "Economic policy" does not, however, include trade or tariffs. The most that can be said is that the result[97] did no harm to the Foreign Relations Committee, even adding a new category of jurisdiction—"national security"—which has been interpreted in practice to allow it to look into such matters as the activities of foreign intelligence services in the United States.

These reforms passed the Senate on February 4, 1977, as S.Res. 4: the first major Senate restructuring of its committees' jurisdiction in thirty years. It does not give the Committee on Foreign Relations jurisdiction over global distribution of U.S. food surpluses, international financial institutions, trade and tariff laws, immigration and refugees, or U.S. participation in international organizations.[98] Recently Senator Henry Jackson's Subcommittee on Arms Control of the Committee on Armed Services visibly outmaneuvered the Foreign Relations Committee in covering—and freely intervening in—the Strategic Arms Limitation Treaty negotiations. Chairman Ribicoff and subcommittee Chairman John Glenn, on the Government Affairs Committee, have taken possession of nuclear non-proliferation.[99]

THE INAPPROPRIATE APPROPRIATIONS POWER

By far the most significant obstacle to any genuine rationalization of foreign relations jurisdiction, in both chambers, is the multiple layering of financial responsibility for programs. For a program like U.S. foreign economic assistance, the Budget Committees of House and Senate establish a ceiling, the Senate Foreign Relations and House International Relations Committees authorize amounts to be spent and set program standards and priorities, and, finally, subcommittees of the Appropriations Committees decide the actual amounts to be made available.

The amounts appropriated often differ markedly from those authorized, reflecting radical differences in values and priorities of the authorizing and appropriating committees. In this fashion, responsibility tends to be diffused among the three different strata of foreign relations authority, thereby virtually ensuring conflict and creating a formidable course of obstacles for proponents of a coherent program.

Many members privately support a merger of authorizing and appropriating authority, particularly now that a third layer of jurisdiction—Budget Committees—has been added to the top. But few believe it possible. The last advocacy of such reform came from the Bolling Commission, in 1973. It called for the abolition of the House Appropriations Committee, recommending that the authorizing committees should also make appropriations. That proposal soon foundered when it was realized that its implementation would eliminate the jurisdictional empire of fifty-five House members.

Of the various House and Senate committees and subcommittees concerned with foreign policy oversight, it is the Appropriations Committees which have generally been identified in the literature as wielding the most influence over policy and programs.

Up to the time of the Civil War, appropriations and taxation were handled by the same committees in the two Houses. In 1865, the House Ways and Means Committee was stripped of responsibility for appropriations and this was transferred to a new, specializing committee. The Senate did the same in 1867. A little more than a decade later, in 1877, the House reversed gears, stripping the Appropriations Committee of jurisdiction over foreign affairs, the army, Indian affairs, the military academies, the navy, and the post office. The appropriations power for each of these areas of jurisdiction was given to the committees with substantive legislative, or authorizing, responsibility.

This attempt to unite rationally the functions of oversight, authorization, and appropriation in a single committee specializing in an issue cluster was criticized for creating too easy a target for bureaucratic co-option. It was also said to make it difficult to maintain overall budget priorities.[100] Once a central budgetary process was set up within the executive branch, in 1921, Congress reversed the reforms of 1865 and 1867. It decided that federal budgets should again be transmitted to one Appropriations Committee in each chamber, rather than to the authorizing committees. Ever since, the Appropriations Committees have been central to the funding of foreign relations programs and, increasingly, to the making of foreign policy.

There is thus in effect a separation of powers between the committee with legislative responsibility for foreign affairs and the several subcommittees of the Appropriations Committees which are responsible for funding the conduct of foreign policy and the implementing of foreign relations laws. In theory, Professor Richard E. Fenno observes,

> legislative committees expect the Appropriations Committee to support agency programs with sufficient funds, but *not* to engage in extensive program review and analysis. The Committee's main task, as they see it, is to inquire into waste and inefficiency and to implement the goal of economy where poor management is discovered. Yet the emphasis on

waste leads to the very kind of inquiry into nonprogrammatic detail to which executive agencies object.[101]

Even more emphatic objections are coming from the international affairs committees as they annually see the legislation they have labored to conceive shredded by the Appropriations Committees. They object also to laboring under the resultant psychological disadvantage. In purporting to speak for Congress to the Executive, the foreign affairs committees and their newly augmented staffs are all too aware that, to the State Department, the real "pressure point" in Congress is not Chairman Zablocki of International Affairs but Chairman Clarence Long of the Foreign Operations Subcommittee of Appropriations, or John M. Slack of West Virginia of the State Department Subcommittee. And the key staffers, from the downtown perspective, are William Jordan as well as Donald E. Richbourg and Donald L. Denton of the Senate and House Appropriations subcommittees, not Jack Brady and William Bader, the staff directors of the House and Senate committees on foreign affairs. What makes this intolerable is that Brady and Bader preside over a staff of more than eighty highly trained specialists in all areas of foreign policy, while the appropriations subcommittees are making the real decisions with a professional staff of one or two.

One scholar concludes that "the money committees of the House and Senate constitute a third house of Congress."[102] Moreover, any theoretical distinctions between the roles of the substantive committees and the appropriations committees tend to dissolve in practice, as the latter have increasingly absorbed the functions of the former. Control over the purse has been parlayed by Appropriations into an annual review of the departments' activities and future plans.

The Agencies, knowing who holds the purse strings, tend to yield to Appropriations chairmen's—and even staffers'—continuous interventions in the direction and supervision of day-to-day policies and administration. One observer notes that the appropriations subcommittees of the two Houses, through hearings, investigations, and reports as well as through the line-by-line budget itemization in the appropriations bill, are actively involved in "policy decisions and directives." He reports that, although

> policy decisions are often written into the appropriations acts, it is usually not necessary to do so, since the subcommittees can issue verbal instructions to department officers, secure commitments from them as to future actions, or write policy directives in the reports, all of which actions have about the same effect as law. The questions asked of department witnesses during a hearing are strong indications of the subcommittee's wishes about policies and thus have an important effect on department administration and future plans. The determination of the

amount of funds allocated to each program is in itself an important policy decision.[103]

A senior AID official has reported that when Otto Passman was chairman of the House Foreign Operations Subcommittee (until 1976), "he used to be on the telephone to [AID Administrator] John Hannah almost daily. The present chairman is more formal and tends to communicate with the Administrator by letter. But both are very active in keeping on top of what goes on over here." Each subcommittee member receives regular project sheets from AID, listing proposed undertakings before final commitments are made. By flagging any project, the member can, in effect, hold it up until it has been explained, or modified, to his satisfaction.

The present chairman, Dr. Clarence Long, is a former economic professor with very strong views on such diverse subjects as India—which he feels has wasted billions of U.S. taxpayers' dollars—and the need to reduce and reorient U.S. foreign aid in the direction of what he calls "light capital technology."[104] In demanding labor intensive, small projects that cost no more than $100 per worker, Long has excoriated the international financial institutions because "they do not seem to understand what [light capital technology] . . . means."[105] He has favored sharp cuts in funding for the World Bank even when, as in 1978, that has meant opposing his own subcommittee's majority on the floor. His subcommittee's bills bristle with ostensible money allocations that usurp substantive lawmaking functions of the foreign affairs committees with such ill-disguised law-making riders as: "None of the funds appropriated under this heading may be available to provide a United States contribution to the United Nations University."[106] The 1977 prohibition on military aid to Uruguay, typically, came not from the foreign relations committees but from the House Appropriations Committee.[107] The 1978 Foreign Aid Appropriations law directs the President to open negotiations with other aid-giving nations of the West in the Organization for Economic Cooperation and Development to develop a common policy against helping the developing nations produce "commodities which are in surplus in the world market and if produced for export would cause substantial harm to producers of the same, similar or competing products."[108] The President is to report back to the Appropriations Committees' chairmen within a year "on the progress made in carrying out this section."[109] It would be difficult to imagine a provision less relevant to funding, or more substantively law-making in intent.

In recent years, the most serious problem about the appropriations process has been the floor action these bills attract. Since the sponsoring committees cannot assert any particular foreign relations expertise, appropriations bills extend an open invitation to every member to write foreign policy. Even the Staff Director of the House Appropriations Committee, Keith Mainland, has objected to "the attempt by Congressmen, on the floor, to use Appropriations to take over direction of substantive policy."[110]

Chairman Zablocki, joined by several other chairmen, has written the chairman of the Rules Committee—with a copy to the Speaker—complaining that Rules has been far too soft in failing to crack down on substantive legislation masquerading as money bills. Supported by thirteen other chairmen of authorizing committees, Zablocki wrote: "We believe that the practice" of including substantive measures in money bills "constitutes a serious infringement on the jurisdictional responsibilities of the authorizing committees and on the integrity of the authorization/appropriation process. Policy decisions," he added, "should be made independently of decisions to fund those policies."[111] Zablocki has thus launched a major campaign against these "mischievous amendments" that perpetrate "violence" on the legislative process.[112] Even Chairman Mahon of the full Appropriations Committee has said wistfully, "I wish we could just go about our business of voting money and setting fiscal priorities without Members' pushing us into substantive lawmaking through issues like human rights and abortion."[113]

He is right. The ability of Congress to act responsibly and efficaciously in exercising its new powers of codetermination over foreign policy depends on focusing control in the appropriate—not, certainly, the appropriations—committees of specialist members and staff.

THE IMPACT OF THE NEW BUDGET PROCEDURES ON THE FOREIGN RELATIONS POWER IN CONGRESS

Legislation passed in 1974[114] added a third layer, in addition to the authorizing and appropriating process. Actually, the annual Congressional budget process is a first reading, coming before the authorizing and appropriating procedures.

The law, starting in 1977, established a new budget cycle which, while concerned only with targets of expenditure, has significant foreign policy implications. Since the principal justification for a separate appropriations process had been to bring unifying priorities and an integrating perspective to the many separate heads of Congressional expenditure, it was reasonable to assume that the creation of new Budget Committees in House and Senate, to do exactly that, would make the Appropriations Committees redundant. The assumption was reasonable, but not prescient. What has happened, in practice, is that a third layer of substantive jurisdiction has been added. Far from making Appropriations obsolete, the Budget and Appropriations Committees have tended to join forces to cut back still further the powers of the foreign affairs committees.

The new budget procedures have transformed the way Congress operates. On March 15 of each year the House International Relations and Senate Foreign Relations Committees, like all others, must submit proposed estimates of how much spending they plan to authorize for the next fiscal year, which begins October 1. One month later the Budget Committee presents Congress with a proposed first concurrent resolution, setting an overall spending ceiling as well as allocating target amounts for each budget "function." In the Senate, the first concurrent resolution is drafted in fifteen broad categories, of which international relations is one. In the House version, the functions are broken down into more specific "line items."

By May 15, the foreign relations committees have reported out to the floor all legislation which starts up, continues, or redefines programs costing money. By the same date the two chambers must complete action on the first budget resolution. Work on all authorization bills is completed by the seventh day after Labor Day, and by September 15 Congress "puts the fiscal year to bed" by passing its second concurrent budget resolution. This incorporates all actions of Congress in appropriating funds. Thereafter, no further expenditures may be approved during that fiscal year. The second resolution should not exceed the first, and the Budget Committee is entitled to intervene anywhere in the process—in committee as well as floor action—to see that it does not.

In response to the March 15 deadline, the foreign affairs committees prepare an item-by-item explanation of all programs for which legislative authority will be sought that year. These are examined by the Budget Committees of each House in preparing the first resolution. In this process staff plays a key role. But the Budget Committees are staffed with fiscal, not primarily foreign relations, specialists.

Do foreign policy considerations enter into the Budget Committee's considerations? Since the process is complex and sensitive, it may most effectively be illustrated without breach of confidence by citing an imaginary example. "Suppose," we asked a Budget Committee staffer, "the Foreign Relations Committee reports to you that it plans action on a bill authorizing a billion dollar bubble gum project for Lusitania."

"Well, I wouldn't go out to Lusitania, myself, to see whether the population's teeth were up to chewing that much bubble gum," the staffer explained.

I'd expect the Foreign Relations Committee would already have done that. I would talk to their Chief of Staff to get a feel for how serious the members were about the project. And I'd want him to help me understand it better, so I could explain to our committee members, during mark-up of the first resolution, when they ask me what it's all about.

It would also be my job to make an assessment of whether the proposal is likely to pass when it comes to the floor vote because, of course, its prospects affect our bottom line estimates. If it doesn't have a chance, we can disregard it in our totals for the year.

Clearly, policy considerations do enter into that assessment of the future of the project. An analysis of staff memos to the Budget Committee chairman, Senator Edmund Muskie of Maine, also suggests that other policy considerations, unrelated to fiscal concerns, play a considerable part in informing a decision whether to include or exclude the project in the budget total for the international relations function, even though such policy recommendations are usually put in strictly objective terms. Aid to poor countries or to international institutions, for example, have been considered by the Budget Committee in the light of evidence concerning the performance and failures of the recipients. It is at least very possible that the Budget Committee, in addition to all other considerations, will develop its own views on whether there *ought* to be a bubblegum project.

Examination of the Budget Committee's practice bursts whatever bubble of illusion there may have been that, in initiating the new budgeting system, Congress would phase out the appropriations process. "Actually, our committee has formed a very close alliance with the Appropriations Committees," a Budget staffer has said,

> much closer than with the authorizing committees. Much of what the substantive committees do, concerns legislative policy, which is of interest to the people on the Hill but not particularly to us. We are concerned primarily with levels of expenditure and, to the extent the authorizing committees get into that, it doesn't mean very much. The real action is with the Appropriations Committee. So, when it comes to the bubble gum bill, my first call would probably be to [Senate Appropriations staffer] Bill Jordan to get his views on what his Committee is likely to do. If Jordan tells me that his people are very unlikely to vote funds for the project, our committee would probably delete the item in setting the targets. That is, we would reduce the target figure for the foreign assistance function by a billion dollars and verbally notify the authorizing committee that we were doing it because we weren't convinced the bubble gum project would be funded.

Unexpectedly, it is the foreign affairs committees, not the Appropriations Committees, that are jurisdictionally threatened. The coalescing of Budget and Appropriations Committees continues at the next stage of the process. As a Foreign Relations Committee bill goes through the legislative mill, Budget staffers will flag items for the chairman which

appear to authorize expenditures above the amount permitted by the
first budget resolution. "But hold your fire," the staffers' memo may say,
"because we know from talks with Appropriations [staff] that they intend
to make a sharp reduction in the amount. So you can afford to be nice to
Foreign Relations. Support the bill on the floor. Appropriations will take
care of it for you, later."

The effect of this strategy is to lock the foreign relations committees
into a sort of legislative padded cell, protected on either side by two
fiscal watchdog committees. Nothing is better suited to produce irre-
sponsibility and irrelevance on the part of the very unit which has been
designated by Congress to manifest its seriousness and competence in
the foreign relations field.[115]

In the first important jurisdictional showdown between the Senate
Foreign Relations Committee and the Appropriations Committee since
passage of the 1974 Budget Act, the Budget Committee sided decisively
with Appropriations. In 1977 the Foreign Relations Committee wrote a
bill giving the President authority to commit the U.S. to a $2.4 billion
contribution to the International Development Association, to be made
over a three-year period. The effect of such a commitment, while actual
funding depends on annual appropriations, is to allow IDA to plan
longer-range projects. It also exerts some pressure on the Appropriations
Committees to vote the funds necessary for carrying out the moral commitment made by the President. The effect of such an authorization, in
other words, has been to permit the President to make a promise, which
puts the Appropriations Committees in the position, if they refuse funding, of causing the U.S. to default on its pledge.

Although this tactic had been commonly used in the past, in 1977,
after the new budget system began to operate, the Appropriations Committee insisted that the 1977 bill contain the nullifying words: "any
commitment to make such contributions [to IDA] shall be made subject
to obtaining the necessary appropriations." In other words, Congress
would no longer be able to authorize the President to make a real commitment, because he would be obliged to disavow any moral obligation
by Congress to follow through with funding.

Foreign Relations' counsel took the position that Appropriations'
demand, if met, "will have extremely important consequences not only
for the Foreign Relations Committee but for our nation's ability to make
multi-year international commitments under which the United States
incurs financial obligations."[116] The Budget Act, he argued, had not
been intended to take away the important power of the Foreign Relations Committee to authorize multi-year commitments.

The staff of the Budget Committee, however, weighed in solidly on
the side of Appropriations. Senator Muskie was advised by staff to sup-

port the Appropriations chairman's floor amendment to the Foreign Relations Committee's bill on the ground that there is no "mystical" exclusive jurisdictional relationship between Foreign Relations and the President's power to make commitments. Under section 401(a) of the Budget Act, it was argued, no committee any longer could authorize "back-door" multi-year commitments in the absence of an appropriation.

Foreign Relations argued, in vain, that section 401(a) has been presented to Congress as a way of dealing with the prevalent tendency to authorize the signing of multi-year contract obligations for the construction of public works, thereby irreversibly committing project funds for future years. There had been no discussion of its effect on the President's power to make long-range fiscal arrangements with other states and international organizations. In that context, it was urged, quite different considerations of national interest and world order must take precedence.

To the Budget Committees, however, as to the Appropriations Committees, world order had nothing to do with it. What was involved was a straightforward question of turf. During floor debate on Appropriations' amendment, Senator Muskie opposed vehemently the Foreign Relations Committee's position, arguing that "our Appropriations Committee must continue to have the last word on financial commitments if the integrity of our budget processes are to be maintained. . . . [I]t is virtually impossible for us to adopt special procedures for each function in the budget. . . ."[117]

This incident primarily reflects one aspect of jurisdictional disputes: that different committees locate the same subject-matters—IDA replenishments, for example—on quite different mental maps of reality. Different context dictates different attitudes. To the Budget Committee, any three-year fiscal commitment is an exception to hard-won budgetary integrity. To the Foreign Relations Committee, it is a necessity for effective global attack on poverty, despair, and violence.

The House and Senate international relations committees represent an aggregation of interest and expertise that emphasizes the global setting within which issues arise and forces operate. Trade, the World Bank, weapons development, covert operations, the U.N., food for poor countries, need not inevitably be considered in that context. But it is at least paradoxical, and also probably dangerous to the national interest, that at the very time Congress has taken to itself so large a share of responsibility for the conduct of foreign relations, it should be scattering substantial, even crucial, bits and pieces of that responsibility among committees established for quite different purposes and holding other perspectives.

IV

IN SEARCH
OF THE LOST CONSENSUS

11

STRENGTHENING
RELATIONS WITH AN
INCONGRUOUS CONGRESS

DECISIONS once effected by a few men are now made by many persons. The implication of this transformation is that much time once spent on doing things must now be devoted to consultations about what to do. This may be a good thing. Adlai Stevenson had the State Department in mind when he cautioned, "Don't just do something, sit there." Nevertheless, a superpower responsible still for the leadership, if not the very survival, of the free world cannot always afford to "sit there." To the extent that the Executive capacity to make and carry out policy has recently come to depend on effective and timely consultations and negotiations with Congress, the former has had to upgrade radically its capacity to operate in a pluralist milieu, to speak and listen to the latter. Liaison, diplomacy between the branches, has thus assumed unprecedented importance.

"REMEMBER THE LMO"

No one observing the growing role of Congress in the conduct of foreign relations can fail to be impressed with the importance of liaison. As the domestic counterpart to diplomacy, liaison is the professionally organized process by which the parts of government speak to each other. The equivalent of the striped pants brigade, in this process, are the LMO's (legislative management officers) of the Department of State, or their counterparts in the National Security Council, White House, Department of Defense, and, to a lesser extent, such departments as Commerce, Treasury, Labor, and Interior—each of which has some international responsibilities. It is their task to keep Congress informed, while informing themselves of Congressional mood and activity. Consultation, the most important—and, in some ways, most difficult—aspect of liaison, is increasingly part of their function, although some of the most serious consulting with Senators and Representatives must be conducted by more senior officials at the Departments and the White House.

Informing Congress is closely related to influencing it. In part, the liaison function is intended to win hearts and minds, or at least votes, on Capitol Hill; it is, frankly, executive branch lobbying. Such frankness, however, is prohibited by law. Section 1913 of Title 18 of the U.S. Code, enacted in 1919, prohibits use of public funds to pay for services "intended or designed to influence in any manner a member of Congress, to favor or oppose by vote or otherwise, any legislation or appropriation by Congress." Since enforcement depends on the Justice Department, few laws have been so easily circumvented. The word "lobbying," however, is eschewed.

Much of the discussion of Executive liaison inevitably has taken the form of discourse in public administration: how best to organize the institutional network along which communications flow from the Executive to members of Congress and back. But the issue is less studded with instrumental "how's" than policy "ought's." To what extent *should* the executive branch communicate with another, constitutionally separated branch, sharing its secrets, divulging its plans, and admitting Congress into the inner precincts of Presidential policy-making?

From the very beginning, Congress and the President have searched for a more perfect liaison. Washington thought that personal "oral communications" were "indispensably necessary."[1] It soon became clear that while the Chief Executive could not ordinarily negotiate foreign policy issues with the whole Senate,[2] he could perhaps negotiate with a representative committee of interested members. President Madison, asked to meet with such a committee to discuss the impending appointment of a Minister to Sweden, refused—taking the position that his Constitutional obligations were exclusively to the Senate as a whole and that he could not negotiate with a committee.[3] On August 19, 1919, President Wilson requested a meeting with the Senate Foreign Relations Committee to explain the case for the Treaty of Versailles. This time, however, it was the committee's chairman, Senator Lodge, who was opposed. The "ground which Madison took, that he could not receive officially a committee of the Senate," he said, "has always seemed to me the absolutely correct ground."[4]

After the beginning of World War II, chairmen of the Senate and House committees have tended to become what Senator Fulbright has contemptuously called "the President's lapdogs,"[5] faithfully trotting over to the White House to receive instructions, rewards, or chastisement. All that changed again, however, with the Congressional revolution of the mid-'70's. With the advent of the "new oversight" and policy code-termination, liaison has now become equally more difficult and more necessary, both by reason of the Congressional leadership's rediscovered independence and because power within Congress, not least in matters of foreign relations, has proliferated. The numerous *ad hoc* and single-issue caucuses as well as the newly assertive rank and file make the process of liaison far more difficult than before. So does the proliferation of staff. There are, in the language of the Hill, so many bases to touch that liaison currently resembles not so much baseball as 36-hole golf.

Also of growing complexity is the foreign relations constituency *within* recent Administrations. Its dispersion makes effective liaison more difficult to manage. Even relatively simple Presidential initiatives such as are envisaged by the Food for Peace program (PL 480) affect such diverse government agencies and interests in AID, the Departments of Defense, Agriculture, State, and Commerce. It is by now a cliché that all foreign policy decisions have important effects on domestic options, but the truth of that has only recently been widely recognized. As a consequence the Executive now has a very difficult *internal* liaison problem, seeing to it that its "ducks are in order," that it speaks to Congress with a single voice. In most instances, the President is glad to settle for muted dissonance. To achieve even that much, a *liaison* bureau has had to be located in the White House to compel better *liaison* between the Departmental *liaison* bureaus.

First, however, came departmental liaison. In most Departments this was traditionally part of the task of its solicitor or general counsel. He drafted the bills, so it was his job to see them safely home on the Hill. It took a long time for the Executive to realize that this system was inadequate. Individual departments gradually concluded that a professional staff was necessary to serve two functions: as a communications link with Congress and to serve as gatekeeper controlling, or at least monitoring, traffic between all parts of the Department and legislators.

THE "H" FUNCTION: LIAISONS DANGEREUSES

"If the checks and balances written into the Constitution by the founding fathers are an open invitation for conflict between our executive and legislative branches of government," an informed observer of the Congress has written, "the role of the legislative liaison staff in the Congressional Relations Area of the Department of State is—at very least—to civilize the struggle by fostering accommodation between contending parties on matters affecting foreign policy."[6]

Excellent as is this general conceptualization of liaison's function, it does not do justice to the complexity of its roles, the numerous, often cross-purposive missions it is called upon to perform. In the State Department, the liaison or "H" bureau speaks and listens to Congress, tries to get the Department's policies aligned with those of the White House and with other Departments, and monitors the flow from the bureaus to Capitol Hill. It provides a sort of information, service, and travel bureau for legislators. In addition, liaison is cast in the role of "double agent" in that its officers must speak for Congress, or at least interpret the Congressional mood, within the policy-making councils of the Department. Finally, "H" must see to it that the consultation requirements of the new oversight, mandated by law, are duly carried out by the Department with the promptness and candor necessary to achieve a modicum of harmony between the branches.

This is not work for amateurs. When the Department of State was first organized, in 1790, with a staff of eight persons, Secretary Thomas Jefferson personally conducted all relations with Congress. Gradually, as the Department and its workload grew, Secretaries began to use personnel, on a part-time basis, to supplement their personal relations with Congressional committees and key members. Assistant Secretary A. A. Adee, for example, combined the coordination of Department policy with Congressional liaison.[7] Only fairly recently have Departmental officers come to be selected for liaison duty on the basis of their familiarity with problems of particular current concern to Congress[8] or because of their closeness to members. Franklin D. Roosevelt's Secretary of State, Cordell Hull, himself a former Congressman and Senator, shrewdly chose R. Walton Moore, another ex-member, to run his Congressional relations.[9] But the idea that liaison required sole and undivided attention was a long time winning acceptance, perhaps because Congressional liaison was not considered by the Foreign Service to be much of a job.[10]

Secretary of State Jimmy Byrnes believed that the word "liaison" could "destroy even a good man," and that "Members of Congress may well prefer to deal with policy-makers rather than policy-reporters."[11] It long continued to be a vestigial article of faith that a liaison officer would carry clout with Congress only if he were also substantively involved in handling the issues of greatest concern to Congress. In 1949, however, this argument in favor of part-time liaison was decisively rejected by the Hoover Commission, which concluded that part-time liaison was no longer adequate to the task.[12] Most members,[13] and those experts who testified at subsequent committee hearings,[14] agreed.

Former Secretary of State Henry O. Stimson, who headed the foreign affairs task force of the Hoover Commission, warned that Congressional relations were the number one foreign policy issue confronting the United States.[15] He urged consolidation of the liaison function under full-time professional direction by someone with direct access to leadership in Congress and the Department. But, he added, what is communicated, and when, is at least as important as how the communication is organized.[16] "Congress resents being told too little and too late," and

wants time to think, to hold hearings, and to get reactions from home. The objection often heard on the executive side that there is always danger of an advance legislative veto which will thwart executive leadership may be countered by the consideration that it is often better to learn of legislative objections early rather than late in order to attempt to meet or alter them. . . . In case of doubt, it is far better, national security permitting, to give too much information too soon rather than too little too late.[17]

This advice still has the ring of the visionary.

Since receiving its mandate from the Hoover Report, the "H" bureau has grown apace. In 1978, there were thirty-seven permanent positions assigned to it, compared to twenty-five only four years earlier. Its "front office," on the seventh floor at Foggy Bottom, consists of an Assistant Secretary, four Deputy Assistant Secretaries, a Special Assistant, and one staff assistant. One floor below, roughly eleven LMO's bear the day-to-day brunt of diplomatic relations with the Hill. They tend to be career foreign service officers at upper-middle professional echelons (FSO-3's and 4's) who specialize by geographical areas (e.g. the Middle East) and functional subjects (e.g. arms control).

One LMO recently characterized his role thus: "If you believe in representative democracy, then you must believe that the elected representatives have a role to play. That's where I come in. Congress tells the Department what's on the minds of the people, and we at State communicate to the Congressmen something about the international environment in which we're living. In that process, it's my function to assist the communicating both ways."[18]

While this open, cooperative attitude undoubtedly helps smooth the treacherous liaison route, it only fills in a few of the pot-holes. "Consultation" is the name of the game in Executive-Congressional relations. Thus, as Stimson foresaw, by far the largest factor in the success or failure of liaison in any particular instance will be the timing of consultations. In this there has been some significant improvement. For example, a key area of shared responsibility is that of treaties and executive agreements; in respect of these, the State Department has recently established liaison "criteria for consultation" with Congressional committees that set out "the desirability of timely consultation between the executive and legislative branches with respect to the making of important treaties and executive agreements." State's memorandum continues:

> It is our policy to initiate such consultation in each case as early as possible so as to ensure that negotiations with other governments may be pursued along lines that will, to the extent possible, reflect both executive and legislative views. The timing and extent of consultation is necessarily a matter of determination on a case-by-case basis. It depends on such factors as the kind and degree of commitment intended, the political sensitivity of the area involved, the effect on rights of individuals, the possible effect on domestic law, and in some cases the concerns of other governments. While retaining such freedom as appears essential for executive operations in the foreign affairs field, the Department will continue to make every effort to consult in a timely manner with the Senate Foreign Relations Committee and other interested Congressional committees whenever the importance of a negotiation warrants.[19]

There is still a vast, but nevertheless shrinking, gulf between this commendable aspiration and performance.

Although "H" has many varied responsibilities under the rubric of liaison—shadowing bills,[20] arranging testimony by senior officials, attending committee mark-ups, preparing summaries of events in Congress for circulation to key officials, giving early warning of Congressional attitudes likely to affect the Department, and handling all members' and staffers' requests for information[21] or travel assistance—the effectiveness of liaison is ultimately determined by its success in initiating consultation before Department policy has "hardened" or a commitment is made. This, in turn, depends, at least in part, on whether the Assistant Secretary in charge of "H" is able to get through to the Secretary of State regularly and frequently, as well as to other key Departmental officials, to convey the sense of what is happening in Congress, impending developments, reactions to proposed initiatives, danger signals, and whether these prognoses and messages are taken seriously. Ever since "H" was established as a separate unit, it has been urging the rest of the Department to involve the Congressional leadership and foreign affairs committees "long before executive decisions are finalized. . . ."[22]

This priority is reflected in work distribution. Studies show that liaison officers devote "a disproportionate effort . . . to educating State's own bureaucracy." Senior liaison personnel still feel "that their department's congressional relations suffered from the negative attitudes and inadequacies of the program-oriented career people."[23] This problem seems to have been more severe in State than in the other Departments, where the bureaucrats are more naturally attuned to domestic politics. A political appointee to the State Department headed by Dean Rusk has observed: "Most of the Foreign Service officers are extremely insensitive to domestic American politics; they have no interest or feeling for it."[24] Frederick G. Dutton, a former Assistant Secretary for liaison, complained that he was regarded as a double agent, making it difficult to overcome the entrenched departmental point of view,[25] which was that legislators are uninformed, opportunistic, controlled by special interests, and altogether unsuitable to the prudent management of the national interest. The "double agent" problem is virtually unavoidable. The best liaison chiefs are those, like the present Assistant Secretary, Douglas Bennet, and his Deputy, Brian Atwood, who are experienced former Congressional staffers. Yet they have difficulty being accepted by the senior career service at State as "one of us," precisely because they have kept intact their personal connections with the Hill.

The problem of initiating early consultation was aggravated by the general antagonism toward the Department of State on the part of members of Congress in general, which far exceeded the animus toward most other Departments. Diplomats were regarded as elitist snobs who spent all their time consorting with foreigners, imitating their ways, and adopting their attitudes: "cookie pushers" in the words of Representative John Rooney of New York, who, until 1974, was the Department's scourge on the Appropriations Committee. The worst scorn used to be reserved for the liaison staff. Sneering at "these silly, newfangled ideas you get that get you into continuous trouble,"[26] Rooney told the head of the Congressional Relations Bureau: "If I were Secretary of State I could save 10 jobs right there . . . they are about as much use to the Government as the interns or the diplomats in residence."[27]

In the words of a study of these attitudes by Professor Abraham Holtzman, "Foreign Service officers considered politics contemptible; legislators considered State to be unrealistic."[28] While these attitudes have been modified on both sides in the years since 1976, they have not been eradicated. During the thirteen years the State Department negotiated a new canal treaty with Panama, the Congress—even the committees with most direct responsibility—were kept almost entirely in the dark so they would not interfere with on-going diplomacy. Little effort was made to inform, let alone consult. Only in April 1977, after 95 percent of the terms of the treaty had been agreed, did the negotiators brief the Senate Foreign Relations Committee.

At that, the Foreign Relations Committee was touchingly grateful for even these crumbs of consultation. "You did much more than anybody I have ever known has done," Republican Senator Baker told Ambassador Linowitz at hearings in September,[29] and, indeed, he had. "I believe you were in my office on two separate occasions to advise me on your progress," marveled Baker.

Also about this time, Linowitz began to hold question-and-answer sessions with some seventy Senators to familiarize them with the general outlines of the agreed parts of the treaties, and to indicate what issues still remained unresolved. But, at most, he was informing, not consulting; and Senators got to see the text of the signed agreement when the media and public did.[30]

During Senate hearings on the treaty, it soon developed that there were important contradictions in U.S. and Panamanian interpretations[31] of key clauses of the agreement, particularly those concerning whether we had the right to make a unilateral decision that the Canal's neutrality needed defending, and whether our warships, in wartime, had the right to go to the head of any line of vessels awaiting transit.[32] In response to these revelations, the Carter Administration decided on a clarifying statement to be issued by Presidents Carter and Torrijos. But once more, although Ambassador Linowitz "consulted" the Foreign Relations Committee on the draft terms of such a statement, the White House Liaison Office later called to tell the members that, unfortunately, it was too late in the negotiations for the Senators' suggestions to be taken into account. As usual, consulting turned out to be a euphemism for informing.

The game, it seems, is still essentially adversarial. With the replacement of Senator Sparkman as chairman of the Senate Foreign Relations Committee by Senator Church, whose hero and role-model is the obstreperous Senator Borah, there is the prospect of an even more prickly relationship than usual. By trial and error the Department has learned that taking a member to lunch, whether on the seventh floor of the State Department or in the White House, does little to assuage this. Neither did Secretary Dean Rusk's weekly evening cruises for members on the President's yacht.[33]

These sorts of occasions, whether primarily social or informational, do have a role to play. The Department continues to arrange weekly briefing sessions on the Hill and seeks to attract members to Wednesday afternoon meetings with one or another Assistant Secretary discussing problems in his or her geographic area. Turnouts, however, tend to be small, drawing few staffers and fewer members.[34] Everyone wants to be consulted, few feel a pressing need simply to be informed.

Even informational, travel, and constituent services provided for members are not readily fungible as affirmative votes for Executive policies. The rendering of these services does not substantially gain Congressional converts to any specific policy or bill favored by the Department.[35] They are of marginal political value to the member, certainly compared to the ability of, say, the Department of Defense to arrange for the member to take credit for the awarding of a production contract to his or her district.[36]

The one kind of political patronage with high pay-off which is at the command of the Department of State is the planned, visible involvement of leading members in the foreign policy–making process. If members are consulted at a meaningful stage of the process, the liaison bureau can arrange to make that widely known, staging meetings with the President or Secretary in such a way as to make national news. Beyond that, if favors, or the withholding of favors, are a necessary part of a strategy, the Department must depend on the White House or special interest groups to help them augment a bare cupboard.

Favor-doing is not the State Department's strong suit; consulting could be and network-building is. Perhaps as networks are built, consultation will become an almost involuntary habit: that, in any event, is the hope. The Department, after all, is the home of the old boy circuit; and while this has previously been thought of as a tool in international conflict resolution, there is evidence that it can be as effective on the home front. In recent years, Congress has attracted a younger, better-educated membership even as State has recruited from a more representative cross-section of racial, economic, and social strata. The socio-intellectual gap has narrowed dramatically, between Hill and Foggy Bottom. Also, as previously noted, a new network already connects legislative aides with young Foreign Service Officers, mainly through job-hopping.

In the view of one key member of the "network," Assistant Secretary for Africa Richard Moose, its members ought to be able to call each other on the telephone to find out how the other branch is likely to react to a contemplated initiative, long before their chiefs make a decision on whether to proceed. These lines of communication, he believes, should be completely informal. "While we don't have to take each other's advice, we ought to be able to provide completely confidential but reliable readings that would help circumvent the suspicions and insularity of those higher up."[37]

It is a good sign that the Department is now aware of the need to build bridges. The prestigious Murphy Commission,[38] studying the Department in the mid-'70's, did not indicate any awareness of the problem. Now there are opportunities to effect change. One recent proposal would create a new LMO service, staffed primarily by regular career officers who would serve a term "in Congress" as they would in any foreign country, as part of their professional development. In time, most top career officials would have been sensitized to the Congressional perspective. LMO's would also be posted throughout the Department, not concentrated exclusively in "H." Thus, direct contacts between substantive bureaus—previously strenuously discouraged by the "gate-keepers"—would be facilitated. Network-building and sensitizing would also be advanced by rotating a Foreign Service Officer through a tour of staff duty with a member or committee on the Hill, for which career credit would be given, and by bringing more Congressional staffers into the Department for short-term assignments.

THE WHITE HOUSE

One of the Presidency's principal inherent powers under the Constitution is as Commander in Chief and chief spokesman in relations with foreign states. It is therefore not surprising, in this era of Congressional assertiveness, that a substantial portion of his communications with the Hill have to do with foreign policy. To this end, the President may use his liaison staff or, as has happened since Washington's time, he may communicate in person with key members.

Today, the White House becomes involved with Congressional relations primarily under three circumstances: first, when the subject of the communications is a Presidential initiative, such as the Camp David negotiations between Israeli and Egyptian leaders; second, when "heavy guns" are needed to prevent a costly defeat on the Hill; third, when the issue involves a multiplicity of Executive agencies with diverse interests and only the White House can keep the "ducks in order."

Otherwise, however, the brunt of liaison responsibility in the field of foreign affairs is usually carried by the Department of State on behalf of the executive branch. The extent to which primary responsibility for a piece of legislation bearing on foreign relations is assigned to the Department of State—rather than, say, the Departments of Defense, Commerce, Treasury, or Labor—is determined in cases of competing interests, by the White House Congressional Relations Office.

In recent years, however, the White House has increasingly taken over the direction of campaigns to win Congressional support for important foreign relations initiatives. This reflects both the increasing Presidential role in the conduct of foreign policy and the disarray in the way that policy has been presented on the Hill, with rival bureaus within the same department, and rival departments, undercutting each other and the White House. What Professor Roger Hilsman, a former State Department official, has called "the endless leaks of secret information"[39] has also mobilized the White House to act.

Instances of this disarray abound. During the crisis in Executive-Congressional relations over the 1975 CIA operation in Angola, the Administration sent CIA officials, including the Agency's Chief of Legislative Relations, to brief Senator Tunney, the leader of Congressional opposition. According to a participant in that briefing, the Agency's people debunked the Administration's position that Angola was a Soviet testing of America's will in the post-Vietnam era, arguing, instead, that there was basically little difference between the sides in the civil war. One CIA spokesman thought the MPLA [the side the CIA was supposed to be fighting] was "the only force capable of running the country." At that point, Tunney said, "Then I don't understand our policy," to which the CIA's man replied, "Senator, neither do I."[40]

According to a member of Tunney's staff, much of his information used in arguing for the termination of the operation came from the CIA. The Agency had assigned the operation to persons who thought it was a mistake, and did not fail to make their views known. Several CIA officers told Tunney that they were convinced the operation could not succeed and that the Agency was deeply split. They reported that the decision to go ahead had been made, not by the CIA's own top brass, but by Secretary Kissinger and the majority of the National Security Council.[41]

Opposition to the Angola operation also came from within the State Department's Africa bureau, where Assistant Secretary Nathaniel Davis resigned in protest, accepting a diplomatic posting to Switzerland, as we saw in Chapter 2. There he was visited by Mark Moran, Senator Tunney's legislative assistant, who found him "helpful."[42]

A little later, a Senate subcommittee was holding hearings on whether to make the ban on the CIA's operations in Angola permanent. Deputy Secretary of Defense Robert Ellsworth had come to testify for the Department. Senator Clark asked him whether, with additional funds, the forces being backed by the Administration in the Angolan civil war could have fought their Communist-backed opponents to a stalemate. In direct contradiction of what the State Department and President were vociferously arguing at that very time, Ellsworth replied, "No, I do not think so," and added: "I would be skeptical that that amount would have been sufficient given the level of Soviet-supplied military equipment—the kind of equipment, the number of Cuban forces there to handle it, and deploy it and use it in battle—it would have been sufficient to establish a conventional military balance at that time. That is off the top of my head."[43]

Kissinger must have felt like taking the top off Ellsworth's head. In testimony before the same committee, the Secretary of State had just said, "We believe our covert operation, by mid-December, had succeeded in causing a re-analysis on the part of the Kremlin and, despite the presence of 5,000–6,000 Cuban troops at that time, had succeeded in achieving a very favorable military alignment. That credibility was lost when the Soviets realized that Congress would not support the administration in a covert military program."[44] Conflicting testimony among Executive witnesses promoted Congressional doubts and led to a rejection of Presidential policy. This prompted the White House to conduct its own liaison with Congress and to attempt to ensure that all the departmental ducks would line up in order.

It was also during this revolutionary period that the White House perceived Departments increasingly making their own arrangements regardless of the interests of the President and the other Departments. According to a senior National Security Council liaison official, speaking in 1976, the "first instinct of the State Department's liaison staff is always to compromise with Congress. They know that, no matter who wins a Presidential election, they're going to continue to be in their jobs and have to work with Congress. The White House staff is far more political, less careerist. They don't necessarily want to compromise and might even prefer to fight. This difference in perspectives is responsible for many of the disagreements on strategy between State and White House. We always feel the State Department people are not quite on the same team."[45] He added: "Kissinger took with him from the White House to the State Department an unshakable conviction that the 'H' staff works primarily for Congress, not for us. And being in State didn't change his mind on that."[46]

Yet when Kissinger became Secretary of State he became a part of the same problem. During negotiations over the terms of the 1976 foreign assistance bill, Kissinger and Senator Humphrey, its floor manager, reached an agreement, only to have the bill vetoed by President Ford. The State Department's Assistant Secretary for Congressional Relations, Ambassador Robert McCloskey, explained: "We did, in the end, predict to Humphrey that the bill would be signed. But we only promised that if the negotiations got us the minimum of what we wanted, we, ourselves, would not recommend a veto. We didn't say we could speak for the White House. We couldn't even get the White House to focus on the problem."[47]

From the White House perspective, the State Department had made a separate peace with Congress which failed to alleviate several important intrusions on Presidential prerogatives in the bill. A liaison official said the Department had "failed to take account of the White House interests. They were unwilling to fight our battles. Both State and Defense tried to negotiate portions of the bill to make them satisfactory to themselves, offering promises, in return, in the name of the President. These exceeded their authority."[48]

President Carter's Administration has not escaped these sorts of problems. While the President was publicly charging Cuba with involvement in the invasion of Zaire by Katangan rebels in mid-summer 1978, "officials" at the State Department were telling the *Washington Post* that "President Carter had been misled," that Cuban Premier Fidel Castro "has played it straight" with the U.S., and his denials of involvement were "believable." They were quoted as being "opposed to current harsh administration censure of Cuba."[49] Inevitably, the effect was to make Carter's, more than Castro's, credibility the focus of debate in Washington.

White House professional liaison is an attempt to respond to these sorts of problems. Beginning with two Presidential aides in 1949,[50] each modern President has sought to organize this effort in somewhat different fashion, reflecting his personal operating style, but always with a view to protecting the paramount position of the White House in negotiating key issues with Congress.

When a President does get involved in liaison, he has at his disposal a wide range of weapons for rescuing a bill or treaty in trouble. Some are small caliber, such as the White House refusing to send congratulatory telegrams to an obstructionist member's constituents on their hundredth birthdays or golden wedding anniversaries. Others are more serious. In respect of every Administration since Franklin Roosevelt's, with the possible exception of Eisenhower's, it has been alleged that the White House engaged in patronage trading and arm-twisting. A study by Congressional staffer Dr. Rudolph Rousseau finds that Kennedy was a practitioner of "linkage": trading a member's support of an unpopular foreign policy for something that would produce direct benefits in the member's district.[51] Larry O'Brien, special assistant for Congressional relations to Presidents Kennedy and Johnson, has replied: "This suggestion that you trade the bridge or the dam or some project for a vote, and that sort of thing, well, it's just not the case."[52]

Perhaps so, but there are many reports to the contrary. It was Representative Gerald R. Ford who charged that the Kennedy Defense Department threatened to cancel military contracts in his district if he did not support a rise in the debt ceiling recommended by the President. "The Republicans in Michigan are not going to be blackmailed by this kind of an approach," he thundered.[53] On the other hand, according to Rousseau, when President Ford faced a close vote on the Foreign Assistance Act of 1974, "Republican legislators who had been defeated or were retiring and looking for federal appointments were informed that their vote on foreign assistance would be considered in making patronage appointments. Agency officials noted that some Republicans who had never voted for foreign assistance voted with the administration on the Foreign Assistance Act of 1974."[54]

Richard Nixon may not have liked calling up members to cajole or make deals, but during the later, difficult Vietnam years, there were many reports of legislators being threatened with the removal of their districts' HUD grants if they refused to support military appropriations for the war. A Nixon staffer has responded that, when he would call to explain the President's position on an upcoming vote and to offer information, "quite often the congressman comes right back and says, 'yes, it's a critical vote, and I don't know how I'm going to vote yet, but while I've got you on the phone could you tell me how the project is coming over at HUD for my district?' "[55]

The tactical use of small defense contracts, military base openings and closings, and public works can be perceived as "vote buying" but also, less direly, as fair effort to compensate a member for the down-home political costs of voting with the President for an initiative that is unpopular with his constituents. A new hospital may erase the voters' memory of their member's support for aid to Third World countries.

Whoever importuned whom in the Nixon years, the results were to reward with program grants and contracts those who were most cooperative, Republicans and the Southern Democrats. According to one informed estimate, there were about 100 Congressmen—in addition to 150 loyal conservative allies—who were willing to talk business over the pork-barrel with the Nixon White House, thereby neutralizing the Democrats' majority and putting together a coalition in support of the President's programs.[56]

The Carter Administration began with a professed determination to eliminate horse trading and return basic liaison work to the departments.[57] The White House capacity to trade votes for public works projects was also reduced when the Carter liaison team was reorganized by issue clusters rather than by regions of the U.S. Thus a White House liaison officer was less well positioned to discuss a sewage plant in the context of a foreign aid vote because the person handling foreign aid does not also handle environmental issues.[58]

The turning point in this self-effacing strategy came with the Panama Canal Treaties. As Rousseau has observed, Congress has been conditioned to expect the President to intervene when he really cares. "If the President does not become involved . . . word filters through the Senate that the President has not been calling and this information indicates a lower level of Presidential priority."[59] It became clear, early in 1978, that without active Presidential involvement—including traditional favor-doing and horse-trading—the Senate would not pass the Panama Canal Treaties.

PANAMA CANAL TREATY RATIFICATION:
THE NEAR-DISASTER

Agreement on the Canal Treaties came on August 10, 1977,[60] and the texts were signed on September 7. "Undue delay in ratification," President Carter warned the Senate, "could cause serious problems for our foreign relations. . . ."[61] Yet no steps had been taken to avoid delay: there had been little informing, no real consultation, no credit-sharing with Senators who now had to carry the burden of voting for a treaty the polls and mails showed to be far from popular with the public.[62]

This made it inevitable that there would be delays and grandstanding. Throughout January, hordes of Senators—the *Washington Post* counted forty-two of them—trekked to Panama to see Torrijos and try their hand at renegotiating various provisions. One such hegira, at least, was important. Foreign Relations Committee Chairman Sparkman reported after such a meeting that the General "would have no objection if the substance of [the Carter-Torrijos joint communique of October 14] were added to the treaty in any form the Senate decided."[63] Thus was born the "leadership amendment" which was later added to the Treaty by the Senate. Majority Leader Byrd also held frank discussions with General Torrijos leading to the repeal of certain repressive statutes, amnesty for some exiles, removal of some restrictions on political parties and the press[64] and abolition of special political crimes and trials.[65]

Not all visits were so productive. Senator Barry Goldwater announced on arrival at Panama's airport that what the country needed "was not the canal but a more substantial middle class."[66] A local newspaper complained that the stream of Senate visitors was making the Panamanians "feel like inhabitants of a zoo."[67]

Even Senators who privately supported the treaties as written, felt the need to be seen to be "improving" (i.e. strengthening) them before casting an affirmative vote. Given the thirteen years of exquisitely detailed haggling over the wording and balance of the agreements, this was bound to cause difficulties. Yet the Administration's tactics had made senatorial nit-picking inevitable. It altogether failed to heed the sage advice attributed to Secretary of State George Marshall: There is no limit to what you can accomplish in Washington provided you're willing to let someone else take the credit. Among those seeking a share of credit was the freshman Senator from Arizona. Dennis DeConcini had at first drafted an amendment stipulating that, on the expiration of the U.S. base leases in Panama, either party could request negotiations for an extension.[68] Since neither side would be obliged to do anything but talk, the proposal was both harmless and vapid. But DeConcini wanted it added to the treaty as an *amendment*, which, by Panamanian Constitutional law, would have had to be subjected to approval by plebiscite. For weeks, the State Department seemed mesmerized by this danger, fearing that a new vote would see the treaty defeated. The need to prevent this took up almost the entire liaison effort.

The Foreign Relations Committee staff, in a memorandum to Senators, tried to point out that amendments, reservations, understandings, interpretations, declarations, and statements all had the same binding force in international law.[69] At first, DeConcini and his staffer, Romano Romani, stuck to their guns in meeting after meeting with Deputy Secretary of State Warren Christopher. The Senator's staff even polled international law professors all over the country. Eventually, at an intense meeting with Senators Sarbanes, Cranston, and Church, the Arizonan agreed to go with a reservation instead of an amendment.[70]

This was the Administration's first victory, and it came primarily as a result of senatorial peer pressure. It had also been won, as it soon turned out, at an unexpectedly high cost.

"When we backed off," Dr. Romani said later, "we figured we'd been made to look pretty weak-kneed. So we decided that if we were going to be limited to a reservation, we'd make it a good one. We gave our original idea to Senator Nunn, who was looking for something he could add that wouldn't rock the boat, and we came up with a completely new idea."[71]

This, the DeConcini reservation, provided that if a labor dispute or other domestic problems were to cause the closing of the canal or interfered with its operation, the U.S. could use force "in Panama" to reopen it and restore operations. The text was a mine field. Back in 1936, President Roosevelt had renounced any implied U.S. right to protect the canal's operations by the use of force in Panama.[72] To Panama it looked as if DeConcini was trying to undo the 1936 reform. But the State Department, Deputy Secretary Christopher has conceded, was still so relieved that DeConcini was proceeding by a reservation attached to the Senate's advice and consent resolution, rather than by amending the treaty, that it failed to appreciate the explosive content of DeConcini's new initiative.[73]

DeConcini showed Christopher a draft of his new motion on Thursday, March 9. The Deputy Secretary asked if he might have the weekend to study it. Returning to the Hill on Monday, he met the Senator on his way to the floor. Handing it back, Christopher said he had made a few modifications. DeConcini looked at it, said it seemed fine, and went straight to the floor where he introduced it.[74] The redraft had deleted the offensive reference to the use of U.S. force "in Panama."[75] When Romani saw it, an hour later, he convinced DeConcini that his motion had been "gutted." The two men then drew up yet another, much tougher, version in which the use of force "in Panama" was once more prominently featured. DeConcini then went back to the floor to withdraw the one and substitute the other. A showdown seemed inevitable.

At first, it was thought that getting the canal treaties past the Senate would be an ordinary State Department exercise in Congressional relations, except that its importance and delicacy was recognized by taking responsibility from "H" and giving it to a higher level liaison team headed by Deputy Secretary Warren Christopher. Only Secretary Vance, Deputy Christopher, and Herbert J. Hansell, the legal adviser, were authorized to speak for the Department on Panama.

Once the treaties began to run into heavy fire on the Hill, however, the game plan had to be revised. Christopher was still to play a key role, but command control moved to the White House, where a public relations specialist, Robert Beckel, took over. In his words, "the President had no choice but to get involved once it became apparent that the treaties were affecting his national standing."[76] Under Beckel, a new foreign relations section of the Congressional Relations Office was mobilized, just two or three people, but with nothing except Panama on their minds. They worked alongside the smooth grass-roots campaign being put together by Hamilton Jordan and his staff.

Jordan's task was to focus on "opinion makers" in the fifty states. General William Westmoreland and John Wayne—the latter a friend of Omar Torrijos—were sent out to address the kind of groups that would not ordinarily listen to a speaker urging a U.S. pullout from anywhere. Leading citizens by the planeload were flown to Washington for meetings with the President, the National Security Adviser, and the Secretary of State. The Catholic Archbishop of Omaha was called to see what he could do about Nebraska's new Democratic Senator, Ed Zorinsky, who indicated that he would be bound by polls showing a vast majority in his state opposed to the treaties. Every cabinet member was told to draw up a "friends list" of Senators they could call.

Zorinsky, alone, got 250 Nebraskans invited to the White House. Every one of them accepted. Carter talked to the Senator on several occasions. Rosalynn Carter called Mrs. Zorinsky to hope she would urge her husband to do the right thing. Ambassador Sol Linowitz, one of the two top negotiators with Panama, played tennis with Zorinsky and, it is said, let him win. On the Hill, the Senator was visited by Vice President Mondale, Zbigniew Brzezinski, Cyrus Vance, Defense Secretary Harold Brown, Treasury Secretary Michael Blumenthal, even Henry Kissinger. In the end he still voted "no" although, if his vote had been needed to pass the treaties, he might have stepped forward.

The White House did more than simple ego-massaging. Frank Moore, its Chief of Congressional Liaison, was reported to have told uncommitted Senators that, despite the President's previous reluctance to swap favors for votes, he was now interested in learning "how he can be helpful."[77] The responses were not long in coming. Georgia's Herman E. Talmadge wanted a federal program that would pay cotton and grain farmers $2.3 billion in its first year not to plant part of their land. Carter, having previously denounced the plan as inflationary, now sent word to the Agriculture Committee that he would no longer oppose it. Talmadge voted for the treaties.[78] Senator Dole, a firm opponent, went around the Capitol joking that he was holding out for a naval base in Kansas. New York's Senator Daniel Patrick Moynihan told friends he regretted his early support of the President. Had he wavered, he said, New York City's financial problems would be over. One high Administration official sighed, "I just hope the Panamanians get as much out of this thing as some U.S. Senators."[79]

By the start of the second week in March, with the vote on the first treaty only a week away, Beckel still thought he was seven votes short of the required sixty-seven. At this point, Carter was told that it would be necessary to deal with DeConcini. In the face of a world-wide glut and falling prices, the White House had already announced it would buy $250 million of surplus copper production, much of it from Arizona, for the nation's strategic stockpile—something for which that state's junior Senator had long lobbied in vain. DeConcini, who had pushed for a half-billion dollar purchase, professed himself less than satisfied. In any event, he said, it would not change his stand on Panama.

DeConcini's motivation was fairly straightforward. He was convinced, probably correctly, that his state's voters were overwhelmingly opposed to the treaties. His own inclination was to vote for them, but only if, along the way, he could demonstrate a canny talent for driving a tough bargain. His leverage was increased by an informal alliance with two colleagues and friends. Senate Majority Leader Byrd, the best nose counter in Congress, told the White House that if Dennis were to vote "no," so would Senators Paul Hatfield of Montana and Kaneaster Hodges of Arkansas. In senatorial mathematics, that block of three votes meant a six-vote spread.

A lunch was arranged at the White House's request in Byrd's office, for March 9. Mondale and Christopher joined the pro-treaty senatorial leadership—Byrd, Cranston, and Church—in confronting five Democratic undecideds: DeConcini, Wendell Ford of Kentucky, Long, Nunn, and Talmadge. It was at this meeting that DeConcini agreed to allow Christopher to have a try at softening his proposed language, the effort that failed on the following Monday.

Immediately after that, on Tuesday, Christopher went back to see DeConcini. For this meeting, the Senator's staff had prepared a list of possible fall-back concessions. For example, he was ready to restrict the area in which U.S. force could be used to the original ten-mile wide canal zone strip. Four other alternatives were prepared. "But," says a DeConcini aide, "Christopher didn't even try to draw us into any real negotiations. He made a few more half-hearted efforts to get us to drop the 'in Panama' language, but basically, he just caved. We were really surprised."[80]

"I may well have been too soft in bargaining with DeConcini," Christopher later reflected, "but, then, you have to remember that we considered him very negative on the treaty. He seemed to be just looking for a reason to vote against it."[81]

"We were just looking for a reason to vote for it," recalls Romani.[82] Those were not the only mutual misperceptions. According to Senator Byrd, "Christopher told me at the March 9 lunch in my office that the Administration could live with Dennis' reservation. Otherwise," he adds, "I would have taken care of it."[83]

At the Tuesday meeting with Christopher, DeConcini asked to see President Carter, personally, to seal the Administration's approval of his reservation. It was an obvious attention-getting gambit, but it was part of his price. Christopher agreed to try to set it up. That meeting took place at the White House the next morning, March 15, one day before the scheduled floor vote. Just before it, Hatfield wired from Montana that if the President did not accept the DeConcini reservation, he was going to vote "no." Russell Long of Louisiana told the White House not to count on him to be a martyr, that he would only vote for the treaty after it was clear there were 66 others firmly pledged. "By Tuesday," Beckel said, "we were still losing."[84]

"Our advice to the President," Beckel reports, "was based on that calculation. We told him he had a clean choice between going with DeConcini or losing the treaty. We knew the reservation was offensive as hell to the Panamanians. But a defeated treaty would have been offensive, too."[85]

There are some differences in the reports of how well Carter understood the intensity of Panamanian opposition to the reservation. At his meeting with DeConcini, Carter asked Christopher how the language would be received in Panama. The Deputy Secretary reported that the Panamanians wouldn't be too happy, but they'd probably learn to live with it. Read reasonably, he said, the reservation, despite its unfortunate choice of words, really established no new infringements on Panamanian sovereignty. Later that morning, Deputy White House Press Secretary

Rex Granum was authorized to say, "When the Panamanians examine the work of the Senate as a whole, they will find that the basic spirit of the treaties has been maintained."[86]

This was not what was being heard out of Panama. From Panama City, the State Department's Ambler Moss, who had been sent to explain the reservation to Torrijos, cabled the White House that the Panamanian President might denounce the treaty rather than accept DeConcini's language. These soundings reached Washington on Tuesday, *before* the Carter-DeConcini meeting. There is conflicting evidence on whether Carter or even Christopher was unaware of them, or merely decided to discount them. By Wednesday afternoon, however, Panamanian Ambassador Gabriel Lewis Galindo, having heard the results of the morning meeting between the President and DeConcini, called Christopher with an ultimatum: get the reservation modified or the deal is off. A short time later, Torrijos called Carter with a similar message.

With that, on the very evening before the vote, Christopher went back to the Hill. He dropped in to see Senator Byrd at his suite in the Capitol. The Majority Leader was dressing for a Senate dinner while rehearsing his string band. Christopher said, "We really ought to make one more try at getting DeConcini to reconsider."

"Well, why don't you just go talk to him," Byrd advised. "He's in his office getting dressed." When Christopher came in, DeConcini was just putting on his tuxedo. The Senator listened while Christopher told him of Ambassador Lewis's call and Torrijos's stormy talk with Carter. He promised to think about it.

In the morning, DeConcini called Christopher to say he had had a sleepless night. Christopher replied that he was sorry, that he had not slept either. The Senator said he had decided to stand fast. Christopher said he was sorry to hear that, too. Then he called the President to report failure. Carter telephoned the Junior Senator to say that was all right, the deal was still on, to go ahead just as long as he voted for the treaty. This was exactly what DeConcini did. He prefaced his motion by reporting: "the President assured me yesterday in a meeting we had at the White House that he would accept and support my amendment. To the best of my knowledge, that is how things stand as of this moment."[87]

Meanwhile, Ambassador Lewis was back to the State Department. A rupture might still be prevented, he argued, if some language could be added to make it clear that the DeConcini motion did not intend to legitimate the use of force to intervene in Panamanian domestic affairs. Christopher jotted down a "rough draft" and called Byrd, reaching him forty-five minutes before the vote.

Byrd, startled at how wrong the Administration had been in its prediction of Panamanian reaction, had also just heard from Mondale about a similar proposal for a last-minute end run. "I told them," Byrd recalls, "that it was just too late to do anything about it. When the attic and first floor are on fire, I'm not going to run in to rescue the safe they left in the basement."[88]

Christopher called Lewis back to say that it was too late. To try for an amendment to DeConcini's reservation at this stage would mean losing everything. What about putting some assurance of non-intervention into the second treaty, which would only come to a vote in April? Lewis said he would see whether his government was interested.

That afternoon, the Neutrality Treaty passed with 68 votes. It was a joyless occasion. Senator Byrd waited to cast the deciding vote, number 67, "so that if anyone had to take the blame, I would."[89] Senator Howard Cannon of Nevada provided an unexpected extra vote so no one of his colleagues could be singled out as responsible for the Treaty's ratification. The club, after all, has its code.

But the treaty was a shambles. "If we were doing the whole thing over," Beckel later reflected, "we'd probably not try to negotiate with DeConcini directly but have the Senate leadership take him on. We now realize there's no ticket to publicity quite like saying 'no' to the President. We just wouldn't stick the President's head in the noose again."[90] Byrd concurs:

> The Department of State and White House should have known much earlier what needed to be done, and then come to me. They can't expect to achieve much when they negotiate with a single Senator. On the other hand, I can. I know a lot of things they don't know and can pull a whole lot of levers that aren't available to them. I know who is close to whom, who owes whom, all that sort of thing, and I can work on individuals indirectly. For example, I know that Senator Leahy was for a long time a fellow official of the national association of county attorneys and a friend of DeConcini's. So you persuade Leahy, and then you persaude him to work on Dennis.[91]

"I agree," Christopher said later, "we should have brought the Senate leadership in much sooner."[92]

THE SECOND ROUND

The Administration had now got the Neutrality Treaty past the Senate, subject to DeConcini's condition, which, by the terms of the resolution of consent, had to be "included in the instrument of ratification of the treaty to be exchanged with the Republic of Panama." It provided that,

> notwithstanding the provisions of Article V or any other provision of the treaty, if the canal is closed, or its operations are interfered with, the

United States of America and the Republic of Panama shall each independently have the right to take such steps as it deems necessary, in accordance with its constitutional processes, including the use of military force in Panama, to reopen the canal or restore the operation of the canal as the case may be.

Panamanian reaction to the DeConcini amendment was public and bitter. General Torrijos told an American interviewer, "I still don't believe that the American sense of justice is such that they would ask us to pay that price—the price of our sovereignty—to get new treaties" and he added that he doubted Panamanians would accept the reservation if it were subjected to a plebiscite.[93] Nevertheless, Ambassador Lewis was instructed to see whether something could be done in connection with the second treaty to undo some of the damage from the first. This effort began in late March. In an inspired move, the Panamanians invited former Under Secretary of State William Rogers to mediate. Rogers, who had been advising Senator Baker, accepted, after clearing his assignment with Torrijos, Byrd, Baker, and Christopher. He imposed one condition: that the White House be kept out of it. He wanted to work only with Lewis, the Senate leadership, and Christopher.

By April 7, the White House agreed. With the Senate set to vote ten days later, Rogers began to negotiate the wording of a new reservation, seeking a formula for a "neutralizing" reservation that would mollify Panama, yet which the Democratic and Republican leadership believed they could get past the Senate. For the most part, the White House kept its promise to stay out of the way, although, at one point, a spokesman mindlessly warned the Panamanians that "in no way should they become involved in proposing language for our amendments"[94]—this just when Ambassador Lewis and the Senate leadership were deep into direct negotiations, with Rogers as go-between.

On April 11, Senator DeConcini announced that he would do an encore. He had ready a reservation to the second treaty giving the United States an immediate right to send troops anywhere in Panama to keep the canal open.[95] The Senator also had a second reservation which would ensure that, if canal profits did not reach anticipated levels, the United States would not have to make up the short-fall in the year 2000. Announcing that he would be seeing President Carter the next day, DeConcini said the purpose of the meeting was simple: "If he'll accept these two amendments of mine, I'll vote for the second treaty."[96]

A meeting of the Senate Democratic leadership was called for the afternoon of April 12 to decide how to deal with the Arizona Senator. They agreed on an isolation strategy. There would be no negotiations. After the final wording of the neutralizing reservation had been worked out with Rogers and Lewis, they would collectively face DeConcini, telling him to take it or leave it. They also advised Christopher to hang tough.

That, in fact, is precisely what the Deputy Secretary had done. On the morning of the 12th, after a stormy session with Christopher, De-Concini publicly cancelled his scheduled meeting with the President. This calculated rebuff was extensively reported in the press, further promoting the tough-guy image being cultivated by the Senator's staff. But it was the last drop of publicity he could squeeze out of the ratification process, and some of it was not favorable. The *New York Times* harrumphed: "It must be fun being Dennis DeConcini these days. . . . Heady stuff for a freshman Senator from Arizona."[97] In the White House, the reaction was unprintable. After that, DeConcini's office heard nothing further from either the White House or the State Department. All of a sudden, "all negotiations were with the Senate leadership" Romani reports.[98]

The next day, on April 13, after several meetings with Ambassador Lewis, Senator Byrd announced that he would be proposing a reservation to the second Panama Canal Treaty that would meet the Panamanian objection to the DeConcini reservation. It would definitively restate United States' commitment to non-intervention in that country's domestic affairs,[99] and would have the support of the Republican leader, Senator Howard Baker, Jr.

On Sunday, April 16, William Rogers, Lewis with an assistant, and Senators Byrd, Church, and Sarbanes met on the Hill to put the finishing touches on the text. Its core was a Panamanian-drafted clause stating that nothing in either treaty would be interpreted to give the U.S. "a right of intervention in the internal affairs of the Republic of Panama or interference with its political independence or sovereign integrity." According to Byrd, "Lewis wanted more, but I told him that this was all he could hope to get and all I could get for him."[100] That evening, Lewis called the Majority Leader back to relay Torrijos's agreement. Panama, he said, regarded it as "a dignified solution to a difficult problem."[101]

The next morning—Monday, April 17—the Democratic leadership showed its *fait accompli* to DeConcini. It deliberately borrowed some DeConcini language, but rendered it harmless. While reiterating that the U.S. had the right "to assure that the Panama Canal shall remain open, neutral, secure, and accessible" the leadership reservation conspicuously failed to reiterate the key DeConcini phrase guaranteeing the right to employ "military force in the Republic of Panama. . . ." In its place was the non-intervention clause designed by Rogers and Lewis. Listening impassively to DeConcini's objections and proposed revisions, Byrd told him, "it has to be like this, Dennis. I will not accept any changes."[102] All eyes turned coldly to the Arizonan. DeConcini, the freshman who had sent ultimata to the President, crumbled. Later that evening Senator Baker came out with a full endorsement.[103]

On April 18, after adding several other peripheral reservations or understandings meant mainly to boost the profile of their sponsors,[104] the Senate passed the Panama Canal Treaty. The Panamanian Government responded with evident satisfaction[105] that the "DeConcini reservation has been rid of its imperialistic and interventionist claws, and the enforcement of the principle of nonintervention has been reestablished."[106]

LESSONS OF THE PANAMA CAMPAIGN

The experience of Panama Canal ratification teaches three lessons: (1) when the issue is of major importance and the outcome in doubt, the White House liaison team and the President must work with and, in most instances, *through* the leadership of both parties in Congress and the Foreign Relations Committee; (2) liaison is too important to be left wholly or principally to specialists in legislative liaison—as distinguished from the specialists in foreign policy; and (3) liaison, emphasizing consultation and credit-sharing, must begin when negotiations start, not after they have been concluded.

The first of these lessons was learned by the White House when it agreed to stay out of the negotiations between Panama and the Senate leadership that preceded passage of the second treaty. That experience convinced the President's own liaison team that a Senator DeConcini can be brought to heel by powerful peer-group pressure, whereas efforts expended by the White House merely increase the publicity the Senator can wring from a confrontation.

A different situation would arise if opposition to a Presidential policy were being led by the chairman of a key committee. In that case the White House would have to negotiate. But in dealing with the rank and file, the Senate and committee leadership have a better chance of success than a Deputy Secretary or even a President. The leadership has a highly developed intuitive feeling for how, when, and how hard to push a fellow member. And they have clout because they can affect his institutional prerogatives: from the committees on which he serves to the place he parks his car. The leadership, diminished as its control has been in the past few years, can still subtlely affect a Senator's ability to function effectively. Moreover, most members care every bit as deeply about their image and institutional effectiveness, the way they are perceived by colleagues, as about their standing with the electorate. All this is fungible when it comes to a showdown. In this revolutionary era of Congressional self-assertion, the Congressional and committee leadership may not always be able to deliver, but they remain the Presidency's best ally.

Then, too, by utilizing the floor and committee leaders, the Executive reinforces and helps rebuild the Congressional delivery system. In many ways this was the most important Panama campaign payoff, and it became evident later that year, when the leadership were able to rally Congress to resume military exports to Turkey and for the jet sale to Saudi Arabia.

The second lesson is that while liaison specialists, particularly those in the White House, have a role to play, it is dangerous to let them get too far out in front. "Neither Bob Beckel nor, for that matter, Warren Christopher, knows Latin America," said an NSC staffer who does. He was echoing a widely shared observation inside the government's policy establishment: "They may know Congress, but neither of them knew how to read, let alone transmit, the signals we were getting from Panama. We almost ended up with a treaty between the President and Congress, instead of between Panama and the United States."

These concerns are important because the concentration of the liaison function in the White House during the ratification campaign has proven a watershed event. "It became the model for future operations," according to the White House's Bob Beckel.[107] That has meant important changes. For example, National Security Council, which, under Nixon and Ford, carried the Congressional liaison ball for the White House, no longer plays that role. In the most important foreign policy initiatives, the State Department's Congressional Relations Bureau has also been downgraded or subsumed in White House–commanded Administration-wide liaison task forces.

One advantage of this new command structure is that it leaves the liaison staff at State and other agencies free to focus on the important but less dramatic issues, such as the annual authorization bills. A second benefit of White House direction is that it does tend to keep the ducks in line. Gerald Rafshoon has been added to the staff primarily with that responsibility—to make public dissent more costly to Administration dissidents. Third, it means that Presidential clout is likely to be used in support of foreign policy causes.

By the end of 1978, the White House had accumulated a front-line liaison operation of seven persons backed by a larger support staff and added a new grass-roots lobbying group under the direction of Anne Wexler.[108] The more effective this team becomes, the more crucial it will be to restrain it, to see that the messenger is not allowed to determine the message.

The third lesson of the Panama campaign is that the Senate was involved at too late a stage. Its "advice and consent" was sought *after* negotiations with Panama were nearly over. To the extent the Senate tried to play its Constitutional role, it succeeded in opening what amounted to a new trilateral round involving Panama, the Executive, and various Senators.

As is readily apparent, this is not a satisfactory pattern for the conduct of diplomacy. Foreign diplomats, having concluded a bargain with the delegates of the United States, will inevitably feel cheated if they then come under pressure to make new concessions to a different set of envoys. It would be unfortunate if one lesson of the Panama campaign were to be that U.S. negotiators should no longer be taken seriously by foreign governments.

While this has become a problem, the Constitution's involvement of the Senate in the "advice and consent" function also provides an opportunity. It creates a process for public consultation, consensus-building, credit-sharing. A treaty passed by two-thirds of the people's elected representatives, after searching debate, is as legitimate an instrument of national commitment as a free society can draft.

The role of Congress, and of the Senate in particular, thus has its risks and potential benefits. But timing is everything. If the benefits of the "advice and consent" function are to be maximized and the costs minimized, the Senate, or at least its foreign policy specialists, must be involved in the process before negotiations begin, not after they end.

THE LIMITS OF LIAISON

Not only are there limits to the White House role in liaison, but also to liaison in general. There is perhaps a tendency to expect too much of it. Recurrent criticism of the existing system and evidence that it has not closed the gulf, prompts, as already mentioned, tinkering with the institutional framework within which consultation occurs. Various writers have suggested a joint Executive-Legislative Council.[109] Senator Alexander Wiley of Wisconsin introduced a resolution during World War II inviting the President to join the Senate in creating a joint Foreign Relations Advisory Council of senior House and Senate members and key cabinet officers. Cordell Hull rejected this design, preferring less formal ways of communicating.[110] It would probably do more harm than good to seek better communication at the cost of blurring the separation of powers, a concept of unique genius about which Americans have always been of two minds, seeking its benefits without paying its considerable costs.

If one accepts that concept, then even a high level of dissonance between the branches is not necessarily a systemic dysfunction to be treated and, if possible, eradicated. The individual member of Congress interprets events by a different conceptual framework because, to borrow a favorite phrase of Walter Lippmann's, he carries different pictures in his head than does an official of the State Department. Members represent different interests, and come from different backgrounds. This difference in perspective provides the system with a three-dimensional reality which more "efficient" systems lack.

Nevertheless, the effective conduct of U.S. foreign relations does require a carefully constructed substratum of consensus, which effective liaison can help to create. The trouble with executive branch liaison is that it tends to enter the process at the wrong stages, at the lowest and highest levels of criticality. On the one hand, LMO's spend untold hours on trivia as a service to legislators. On the other, they tend not to get to the Hill until after a policy is set in concrete. The vast middle ground of consultation on important policy issues, *before* a bill is drafted or a treaty signed, is still largely untraveled. The object of liaison thus tends to be crisis management, when it ought to be crisis avoidance. Input and output are not yet seen as a systemic whole.

In the words of a recent Senate study, the Executive does not approach the Hill with a foreign policy initiative until it has chosen the course the nation is to follow. "It then musters its forces and goes to Congress— if it goes at all—with a firm decision in hand to ask that body for endorsement, funds, and the authority necessary to pursue the selected policy. At this point it approaches Congress in the manner of a *salesman* with a product to sell."[111] The result is often a sharply defined confrontational crisis, precisely because the Executive, as a deliberate strategy, has chosen to give the Congress only a stark choice between going along or taking responsibility for stopping an initiative to which the country has already been committed. An excellent example of this is the way the President, on December 15, 1978, announced the unprecedented decision to terminate the 1955 U.S.–Taiwan mutual defense pact without an iota of consultation with Congress,[112] this despite the fact that the 1978 foreign aid bill had specifically directed such prior consultation and that Article VI, Section 2, of the Constitution declares treaties to be "the supreme law of the land." In the Federal District Court, Judge Oliver Gasch subsequently opined, "the power to terminate treaties is a power shared by the political branches of this government, namely, the President and the Congress," although he stopped just short—on technical grounds—of giving Senator Goldwater the decision he sought invalidating the Presidential action. Encouraged, the Senate voted 59–35 to re-

buke the President by a resolution determining that "approval of the
United States Senate is required to terminate any mutual defense treaty
between the United States and another nation."[113] Yet, had the President
gone to Congress to get a resolution approving his decision on Taiwan,
he would have received it.[114] This was merely a case of short-cut taking.
Another instance is the by-passing of Congress in the Presidential decision
of March 7, 1979, to sell $390 million worth of arms to North Yemen, a
circumvention accomplished by exercising an emergency waiver clause in
Article 36b of the Arms Export Control law. In the words of Arthur
Schlesinger, this too was "a dangerous precedent."[115] No effort was made
to use the painstakingly constructed machinery for informal consultation, the "new boy network," to sound out the House and Senate specialists before jumping in.

These are exceptions. There are better ways of managing Congressional-Executive relations. An astute President will embrace the lessons
of our recent history and seek out Congressional codetermination.
Slowly, painfully, with many missteps, each side appears to be learning,
discovering the most felicitous ways to respond to the other's needs.

The revolution has not been perfected, but it has proven its viability
and, at times, its capacity for effectiveness. It may even have induced the
branches to rediscover the tree.

SALT II: TEST OF THE
POST-REVOLUTIONARY SYSTEM

The extent of that rediscovery, as well as the recurrent problems, are
neatly illustrated by the debate over ratification of SALT II. Rebuilding
a ruined consensus system: no one said it would be easy. But the Administration did apply the three lessons learned during the battle for
ratification of the Panama Canal treaties. It began consulting legislators
earlier—listening, as well as speaking. It augmented its liaison specialists
with a team of substantive experts. Finally, it sent a clear message that
the President would negotiate with the Senate's leadership, but not with
its rank and file.

Inevitably, the effectiveness of consultations is perceived differently in
the White House and the Senate. "We consulted them to death," a key
Presidential aide insists. "It was a triumph of quantity over quality,"
rejoins a staff member of the Senate Armed Services Committee, while
admitting that the Administration probably tried harder to keep members informed than during any comparable diplomatic exercise of the
past thirty years.

Of course, there are always new mistakes to be made and new lessons to learn. Consultation is no panacea and may even add to the Administration's troubles, if it is unable or unwilling to take the advice given by those consulted. The courting of Senator Henry Jackson is a case in point. As chairman of the Arms Control Subcommittee of the Armed Services Committee, the Washington Democrat was early targeted for very special care and feeding by the disarmament negotiators. Jackson shared this appreciation of his role. Although he had failed in an audacious effort to lure Majority Leader Byrd and Minority Leader Baker onto his subcommittee, he nevertheless set about establishing it as the center stage for the upcoming SALT debate. Throughout 1977, it was widely noted that Jackson and his subcommittee were receiving far more attention from the White House than was the "safe" Foreign Relations Committee and its somnolent chairman, John Sparkman.

At first, Jackson's vociferousness got results. The Defense Department was encouraged to hold out against Soviet efforts to limit the range of our new air- and sea-launched cruise missiles. Jackson stiffened the resolve of our negotiators to insist on strict limits to "fractionation"—the proliferation of independently targeted warheads carried by each long-range missile. Noting the Administration's homage to a subcommittee that included not only Jackson but Jake Garn and Jesse Helms, two committed opponents of SALT, Senator Gary Hart complained to the State Department that "the only guys around here who seem to know what's happening in the negotiations are the ones who're out to kill the treaty."

Then, after a year, the Administration became convinced that the courtship was not paying off. Senator Jackson continued to attack the negotiations in public and to demand changes—such as parity of "throw-weight," as opposed to the draft's provision for parity of delivery vehicles—that the negotiators considered unattainable. But the affair ended in an oddly unprofessional fashion. During October 1977, the *New York Times'* Richard Burt gave his readers an account of the secret draft terms of SALT II that contained much information even Jackson did not have.[116] The chairman justifiably concluded that Administration leakers were more interested in cultivating the press than in working with him. From that time on, the Administration and Jackson appear to have written each other off. But the leak to Burt also antagonized many other Senators who resented reading in the press what had been denied them, on national security grounds, in briefings. It was the Administration's most serious misstep.

To compensate, the Executive widened and intensified its consultations on the Hill. With its blessing, a 23-member SALT Group was organized under the aegis of the Majority Whip, Senator Alan Cranston.[117] It received extensive briefings from Admiral Stansfield Turner,

Ambassador Ralph Earle, CIA verification expert Ray McCrory, the chairman of the Joint Chiefs of Staff, Disarmament Agency Director Paul Warnke, National Security Adviser Zbigniew Brzezinski, and Hamilton Jordan.

The negotiators also began to respond actively to the concerns of the approximately ten Senators whose positions on key committees and substantive expertise marked them for special attention. At the urging of Democratic Senator Sam Nunn of Georgia, a treaty provision was renegotiated to permit cruise-missile technology-sharing with our Western European allies.[118] When the Soviets began to use code in radio transmissions from flight-tested missiles, Senator John Glenn of Ohio insisted on getting a prohibition on telemetry encryption added to the draft.[119] Republican Senator Charles Mathias of Maryland, in discussions with the Russians as well as U.S. SALT negotiators, held out for agreement on a "data base" to which parties must provide figures on their own strategic offensive forces.[120] Senators Thomas McIntyre of New Hampshire, John C. Culver of Iowa, and Dale Bumpers of Arkansas, all members of the Armed Services Committee's Subcommittee on Research and Development, prevailed on the negotiators to alter the expiration date of a key protocol. They wanted to make sure that the Soviets' obligation to reduce their missile armory, in 1982, would be carried out before the United States had to decide whether to renew its three-year pledge restricting the range of sea- and air-launched cruise missiles. Senator DeConcini was also able to extract from the White House a commitment that this three-year ban would not constitute a "precedent" for extending it.[121] Senator Gary Hart won quiet Presidential backing for an "understanding" requiring Senate consent before the cruise moratorium could be extended. He also held out for a change that exempts certain gyroscopic guidance technology, in which the U.S. has a lead, from treaty provisions restricting the upgrading of missiles systems. On the other hand, he and several other Senators prevailed on the Administration to narrow the definition of the treaty's "new type rule" which limits variations in systems' characteristics.

Perhaps the most important senatorial input had to do not with the terms of the treaty but with a collateral matter. In October 1977, the Soviets had tested their new SS-19, proving that it could deliver warheads with such precision as to be able to destroy our concrete Minuteman silos. Enemies of SALT had been quick to point out that the agreement will permit the Soviets to deploy up to ten independently targeted warheads on as many as 820 intercontinental missiles, thereby theoretically authorizing enough Soviet fire power to take out the entire U.S. land-based missile system in a single "first strike."[122] Senators Robert Byrd, John Stennis, and Sam Nunn—all three considered "crucial" by White House SALT strategists—told President Carter that if the treaty was to have a chance in the Senate, there must be a public commitment to a new U.S. weapons system able to match or exceed the new Russian capability. On June 8, 1979, Carter responded by announcing a decision to build the new MX missile with three times the throw-weight of Minuteman and capacity for ten independently targeted warheads.[123]

These and other examples illustrate the remarkable revival of a senatorial role in advising on the substance and tactics of treaty negotiations. It remains to be seen whether the revival of the "advice" function will succeed in dissipating the Senate's taste for tampering with the text at the "consent" stage of treaty ratification. If the agreement passes without attracting "killer amendments," that will be a clear sign that the new system of codetermination and better liaison are having their intended effect.

The Administration's overall liaison strategy hewed closely to the model developed during the Panama campaign. All relations with Congress concerning SALT began to be concentrated in the White House at the beginning of 1979. The need for centralized gate-keeping became all too apparent when the CIA's Director Turner testified, on the Hill, in a way that cast doubt on the Administration's crucial assertion that SALT's essential terms were verifiable. Among the ofttimes warring Departments, the leading position was assigned to Defense, partly because of its superior concentration of technical expertise, but also to emphasize the national security perspective, as opposed to the Department of State's "world order" and international relations bias. Hamilton Jordan again was drafted to head the White House operation, with Bob Beckel, aided by the NSC's Madeleine Albright, responsible for relations with Senators, committees, and Congressional staffs. Anne Wexler organized "public outreach" and Gerald Rafshoon and Jody Powell the media campaign. Ultimate responsibility was assigned by President Carter to Vice President Walter Mondale, in part because he could best deal with potential defections from the left—for example, over Carter's decision to proceed with development of the MX.

If all this followed closely the "game plan" used in securing Senate ratification of the Panama Canal treaty, there were also important differences. This time, the White House was at pains to reinforce its liaison operation with a seasoned contingent of technical experts headed by Roger Molander. Molander had been part of every SALT negotiating team since the Nixon era, and his inter-agency Working Group included specialists on every item covered by the treaty as well as on the negotiating behavior of Soviet leaders. The liaison staff were tied securely to the substantive specialists to avoid the most serious mistake made during the previous campaign, when the negotiators with Congress got separated from the negotiators with Panama. President Carter early ordained that all communications with Congress from any part of the executive branch must be cleared with Molander's Group.

As the SALT crunch approached, such communications focused increasingly on the Senate leadership. White House strategists believe they must have the support of at least four of five key leaders: Byrd, Baker, Stennis, Nunn, and Jackson. They also predicted that an important role would be played by Senator Edmund Muskie of Maine, the chairman of the Budget Committee, in convincing an economy-minded Senate that the defeat of SALT could start a ruinously expensive arms race. The White House game plan aimed to build up the role of these "honest brokers" by giving them ample public credit for the impact they had already had on the treaty negotiations, and by making them central to the working out of any other proposals for changes that would come from the rank and file.

"We have accepted that there will be understandings and reservations added to the text," a White House official had admitted. "The Senate has to put its imprimatur on the document. But we expect Baker and Byrd to lead the rank and file away from killer amendments—those that would cause the Russians to reject the treaty or require us to make compensating concessions—and, where necessary, toward constructive or at least harmless clarifications."

Administration strategists this time also understood that Senators, too, have strategies which the Administration should try to accommodate. From the Panama experience, members learned that they will appear to be more effective, and get more media coverage, if they do not commit themselves too early. Consequently, there has been no effort to force key legislators to come out for the treaty until after they have subjected the final text to a show of thorough examination and evaluation. "Last time, those who committed themselves early got nothing," the White House aide explained. "So they're not going to put themselves in that box again. We understand, and we're willing to wait and help them look as good as possible."

All this betokens notable progress in the White House's management of Congressional relations.

In the Senate, preparations were also made to give thorough and responsible consideration to the treaty. Primary responsibility for treaties rests with the Senate Foreign Relations Committee which conducts hearings, writes the report that accompanies the treaty to the floor, and proposes the resolution of consent—with or without modifications. The Armed Services Committee and the Select Committee on Intelligence announced that they, too, would hold hearings. To prepare itself, the

Senate Foreign Relations Committee added two arms specialists to its permanent staff and hired four SALT experts as temporary consultants. The committee has a new Staff Director who previously worked on verification problems while in the Defense Department. The recent addition of three conservative Senators has also made the committee more representative, and less easy to dismiss as a liberal-internationalist enclave.

Even so, the Foreign Relations Committee has problems converting its technical expertise into political currency. Its capacity for leadership was drained during several years of benign neglect by an aging Chairman Sparkman, and now that he has retired, his successor, Frank Church, is faced with an uphill battle for re-election in Idaho that has diverted his energies. Senatorial SALT supporters and the Majority leadership have worried privately about whether he will be able to floor-manage the treaty effectively.

Nevertheless, even White House managers have been impressed with the new capacity of Senators and staff to inform themselves on the complex issues of SALT—often securing expert services to augment those offered by the Administration—and to make a useful, independent contribution to the negotiations. That contribution has extended beyond the traditional (and still serviceable) "good cop/bad cop" routine to add significantly to the nation's reservoir of national security expertise.

The revived senatorial role has other potential benefits. The open debate on SALT can help educate the public, legitimate our international commitment, and provide an opportunity to set the outlines for negotiating SALT III. Of course, an open process has risks: not least, that it can generate unwisdom. Yet, is it really any longer open to Americans to question whether that risk is worth taking?

NOTES

INTRODUCTION

1. J. William Fulbright, "American Foreign Policy in the 20th Century under an 18th-Century Constitution," 47 *Cornell Law Quarterly*, No. 1 (Fall 1961), pp. 1–13 at pp. 1–6.

2. Senator J. W. Fulbright, "Congress and Foreign Policy," United States, Commission on the Organization of the Government for the Conduct of Foreign Policy, *Congress and Executive-Legislative Relations*, Vol. 5, Appendix L (June 1975); henceforth The Murphy Commission, Appendix L; pp. 58–59.

3. Arthur M. Schlesinger, Jr., *The Imperial Presidency*, Boston: Houghton Mifflin, 1973, pp. 76–99.

4. Abraham D. Sofaer, "The Presidency, War, and Foreign Affairs: Practice under the Framers," *Law and Contemporary Problems* (Spring 1976), 12–38.

5. Louis Henkin, "'A More Effective System' for Foreign Relations: The Constitutional Framework," The Murphy Commission, Appendix L, p. 15.

CHAPTER 1

1. U.S. Senate, *Congressional Record*, Jan. 26, 1973, S. 2204; Senator Church introduced S. 578 for himself and Senator Case on Jan. 26, 1973, "a bill requiring congressional authorization for the reinstatement of American Forces in further hostilities in Indochina."

2. Sen. Mansfield, U.S. Senate, *Congressional Record*, April 12, 1973, S. 12004.

3. Sen. Cotton, *New York Times*, May 16, 1973, p. 5.

4. *New York Times*, April 24, 1973, p. 5.

5. *Ibid.*, April 25, 1973, p. 10.

6. U.S. House of Representatives, Committee on Foreign Affairs Subcommittee on Asian and Pacific Affairs, *Hearings*, May, June 1973, 93rd Cong., 1st Sess., U.S. Policy and Programs in Cambodia, p. 8.

7. Statement of Secretary of State William P. Rogers before Senate Appropriations Committee, May 8, 1973, *ibid.*, pp. 20–24.

8. Abraham D. Sofaer, "The Presidency, War, and Foreign Affairs: Practice under the Framers," *Law and Contemporary Problems* (Spring 1976), 12 at 16, and cites therein.

9. U.S. House of Representatives, 6 *Annals of Congress* (1797), 2336–42, 2349, 2358.

10. Louis Fisher, *Presidential Spending Power*, Princeton, N.J.: Princeton University Press, 1975, pp. 111–12; the statutory reference is to PL 92-570, 86 Stat. 1198, sec. 713(d) (1972).

11. In addition, the President permitted the armed forces to spend at a deficiency rate–i.e. at a monthly rate higher than month-by-month apportionment of the annual appropriation would warrant–even though legislation in 1972 required the Secretary of Defense to "immediately advise" Congress whenever such deficiency rate was reached. Fisher, *op. cit.*, pp. 111–12.

12. *Ibid.*

13. *New York Times*, July 30, 1976, p. 1.

14. U.S. House of Representatives, Committee on Appropriations, *Hearings*, second supplemental appropriations bill, 1973 (Part 3), 93rd Cong., 1st Sess., p. 594.

15. *Ibid.*

16. Fisher, *op. cit.*, p. 114; see H.Doc. 66 (1973), 93rd Cong., 1st Sess.

17. Votes To Amend H.R. 7447, U.S. House of Representatives, *Congressional Record*, Addabbo Amendment, May 10, 1973, H. 3566, H. 3592–93; Long Amendment, H. 3593, H. 3598.

18. U.S. Senate, Committee on Foreign Relations, *Hearings*, Foreign Military Assistance and Sales Act, S. 1443, Testimony of Hon. Elliot Richardson, May 8, 1973, p. 348.

19. U.S. Senate, Committee on Appropriations, *Report*, second supplemental appropriations bill, 1973, H.R. 7447, and Additional Views, No. 93–160, May 18, 1973, p. 21.

20. U.S. Senate, *Congressional Record*, May 29, 1973, S. 9843; *ibid.*, May 31, 1973, S. 10128.

21. *Ibid.*, May 31, 1973, S. 17131.

22. Sen. Young, *New York Times*, May 16, 1973, p. 5.

23. Sen. McClellan, *Washington Post*, May 16, 1973, p. A13.

24. For Rep. Long's remarks, see U.S. House of Representatives, *Congressional Record*, June 25, 1973, H. 21171.

25. *Ibid.*, vote regarding Giaimo motion, see H. 21173.

26. *Ibid.*, for vote regarding Mahon motion, see H. 21179.

27. *Weekly Compilation of Presidential Documents*, IX, 861–62.

28. U.S. House of Representatives, *Congressional Record*, June 27, 1973, H. 5487–88.

29. See U.S. Senate, Committee on Foreign Relations, *Report on Department of State Authorization Act of 1973*, S. 1248, May 23, 1973, 93rd Cong., 1st Sess., p. 39.

30. Continuing Appropriations, 1974, PL 93–52; 87 Stat. 130, H.J.Res. 636.

31. *Congressional Record*, June 27, 1973, S. 21659 and June 29, 1973, S. 22389.

32. U.S. House of Representatives, *Congressional Record*, Statement by Hon. Gerald R. Ford, June 29, 1973, H. 22340–41.

33. Second Supplemental Appropriations Act, 1973, PL 93–50; 87 Stat. 99.

34. U.S. Senate, *Congressional Record*, Statement by Sen. McGovern, June 29, 1973, S. 22315.

35. U.S. Senate, *Congressional Record*, June 29, 1973, S. 22326.

36. Letter from President Richard M. Nixon to Speaker of the House Carl Albert, *Congressional Record*, Aug. 3, 1973, H. 28088.

37. White House Statement, Aug. 15, 1973, *Congressional Quarterly*, Aug. 18, 1973, p. 229.

38. Richard M. Nixon, *RN: The Memoirs of Richard Nixon*, in *New York Times*, May 3, 1978, p. 10.

39. *New York Times*, April 22, 1975, p. 15.

40. Continuing Appropriations, 1974, PL 93–52; 87 Stat. 130 (H.J.Res. 636).

41. Department of State Appropriations Authorization Act of 1973, PL 93–126; 87 Stat. 451 (HR 7645); sec. 13.

42. Department of Defense Appropriations Authorization Act for Fiscal Year 1974, PL 93–155, §806, 87 Stat. 615 (1973). *See also* Department of Defense Appropriations Act for Fiscal Year 1974, PL 93–238, §741, 87 Stat. 1026, and Department of Defense Appropriations Act for 1975, PL 93–437, §839, 88 Stat. 1212 (1974).

43. Foreign Assistance Act of 1973, PL 93–189; 87 Stat. 714. Sec. 30.

44. U.S. House of Representatives, *Conference Rept. No. 93–742*, Foreign Assistance Appropriations, Fiscal Year 1974, Dec. 19, 1974, 93rd Cong., 1st Sess., p. 8.

45. U.S. House of Representatives, Committee on Appropriations, *Rept. No. 93–694*, foreign assistance and related programs appropriation bill, 1974, 93rd Cong., 1st Sess., Dec. 4, 1973, p. 59. U.S. Senate, Committee on Appropriations, *Rept. No. 93–620*, foreign assistance and related programs appropriation bill, 1974, 93rd Cong., 1st Sess., Dec. 13, 1973, p. 124; also, U.S. House of Representatives, *Conference Rept. No. 93–742*, Foreign Assistance Appropriations, Fiscal Year 1974, Dec. 19, 1974, 93rd Cong., 1st Sess., p. 11.

46. Department of Defense Appropriation Act, 1974, PL 93–238, 87 Stat. 1026 (H.R. 11575), Sec. 737.

47. U.S. Senate, Committee on Appropriations, *Rept. No. 93–617*, Department of Defense appropriation bill, 1974, 93rd Cong., 1st Sess., Dec. 12, 1973, p. 18.

48. U.S. House of Representatives, Committee on Armed Services, *Rept. No. H.R. 12565* (1974).

49. For vote defeating Rep. Hébert's compromise motion to raise the authorization ceiling to $1.4 billion, U.S. House of Representatives, *Congressional Record*, April 4, 1974, H. 9819.

50. Sen. Kennedy, U.S. Senate, *Congressional Record*, May 6, 1974, S. 13237.

51. *Ibid.*

52. U.S. House of Representatives, Committee on Foreign Assistance, *Hearings*, Fiscal Year 1975 Foreign Assistance Request, 93rd Cong., 2d Sess., June, July 1974, p. 44.

53. *Ibid.*, p. 27.

54. *Ibid.*, p. 55.

55. *Ibid.*

56. U.S. House of Representatives, *Rept. No. 93–1610*, Conference Report on Foreign Assistance Act of 1974, S. 3394, 93rd Cong., 2d Sess., Dec. 17, 1974. *Ibid.*, p. 46.

57. *Ibid.*, pp. 13–14.

58. U.S. House of Representatives, *Rept. No. 93–1212*, Conference Report To Accompany H.R. 14592, 93rd Cong., 2d Sess., pp. 13, 43.

59. U.S. House of Representatives, Committee on Appropriations, *Rept. No. 93–*

1255, Department of Defense authorization bill, 1975, to accompany H.R. 16243, 93rd Cong., 2d Sess., Aug. 1, 1974, p. 146.

60. For Kissinger's letter regarding Flynt Amendment, see *ibid.*, H. 26975; the letter was addressed to Hon. William E. Minshall, dated July 31, 1974.

61. U.S. House of Representatives, *Congressional Record*, Aug. 6, 1974, H. 27020, for vote on Flynt Amendment.

62. For Bingham Amendment and vote *see* U.S. House of Representatives, *Congressional Record*, Aug. 6, 1974, H. 27020–21.

63. Arthur M. Schlesinger, Jr., *The Imperial Presidency*, Boston: Houghton Mifflin, 1973, p. 76.

64. Senator William Proxmire narrowly failed to lop off another $150 million. For Proxmire Amendment and debate, *see* U.S. Senate, *Congressional Record*, Aug. 20, 1974, S. 29174ff.

65. For Senator Kennedy's Amendment, see *ibid.*, Aug. 21, 1974, S. 29611, S. 29615. For the final appropriations sum of 700 million dollars and conference report, *see* U.S. House of Representatives, *Rept. No. 93–1363*, Conference Report To Accompany H.R. 16243, Making Appropriations for the Department of Defense, Fiscal Year 1975, 93rd Cong., 2d Sess., Sept. 18, 1974, p. 31.

66. President Ford's news conference, Jan. 21, 1975, *New York Times*, Jan. 22, 1975, p. 20.

67. Message to the Congress of the United States, President Ford, dated Jan. 23, 1975, U.S. Senate, *Congressional Record*, Jan. 28, 1975, S. 1505–06.

68. *New York Times*, January 22, 1975, p. 20.

69. U.S. Senate, Subcommittee on Foreign Assistance and Economic Policy of the Committee on Foreign Relations, *Hearings*, Supplemental Assistance for Cambodia, S. 663, 94th Cong., 1st Sess., February and March 1975, p. 4.

70. Senator Mansfield, *Congressional Quarterly*, Feb. 15, 1975, p. 343.

71. U.S. Senate, Subcommittee on Foreign Assistance and Economic Policy of the Committee on Foreign Relations, *Hearings*, Supplemental Assistance to Cambodia, S. 663, 94th Cong., 1st Sess., February and March 1975, p. 39.

72. U.S. House of Representatives, Special Subcommittee on Investigations of the Committee on International Relations, *Hearings*, "The Vietnam-Cambodian Emergency, 1975" (Part II—The Cambodian-Vietnam Debate), March and April 1975, p. 245.

73. U.S. House of Representatives, Rep. Waxman, *Congressional Record*, Feb. 3, 1975, H. 2162.

74. U.S. House of Representatives, Special Subcommittee on Investigations of the Committee on International Relations, *Hearings*, "The Vietnam-Cambodian Emergency, 1975" (Part II—The Cambodian-Vietnam Debate), March, April, 1975, pp. 244–45.

75. Letter from President Ford to Speaker Carl Albert, dated Feb. 25, 1975, in U.S. House of Representatives, *Congressional Record*, Feb. 25, 1975, H. 4151.

76. Rep. Mahon, U.S. House of Representatives, Subcommittee on Defense Appropriations, *Hearings*, February 26, 1975, p. 6.

77. McCloskey's statement, *New York Times*, March 5, 1975, p. 8.

78. U.S. House of Representatives, Special Subcommittee on Investigations of the Committee on International Relations, *Hearings*, "The Vietnam-Cambodian Emergency, 1975" (Part II—The Cambodian-Vietnam Debate), March and April 1975, p. 315.

79. *New York Times*, March 14, 1975, p. 1.

80. *Ibid.*, March 12, 1975, pp. 1 and 12.

81. U.S. Senate, *Rept. No. 94–54*, Supplemental Assistance for Cambodia To Accompany S. 663, 94th Cong., 1st Sess., March 21, 1975, pp. 1–2.

82. *Ibid.*, p. 2.

83. *New York Times*, April 3, 1975, p. 16.

84. *Ibid.*, April 4, 1975, p. 12.

85. *Ibid.*, April 11, 1975, p. 10.

86. *Ibid.*

87. *Ibid.*

88. *Ibid.*, April 18, 1975, p. 1.

89. U.S. House of Representatives, Committee on International Relations, *Hearings*, on H.R. 5960 and H.R. 5961, "The Vietnam-Cambodian Emergency, 1975," April and May, 1975, pp. 78–79.

90. U.S. Senate, *Congressional Record*, April 23, 1975, S. 6611.

91. *Ibid.*, S. 6610.

92. *Ibid.*, S. 6625.

93. *Ibid.*, S. 6626.

94. *Ibid.*, S. 6640.

95. U.S. House of Representatives, *Congressional Record*, April 22, 1975, H. 3083.

96. *Ibid.*, April 23, 1975, H. 3143–44.

97. U.S. Senate, *Congressional Record*, April 25, 1975, S. 6873.

98. U.S. House of Representatives, President Ford to Speaker Albert, letter dated April 30, 1975. *Ibid.*, May 1, 1975, H. 3540.

99. *Ibid.*, H. 3550.

100. Interview with Hon. Donald Fraser (D–Minn.), Washington, D.C., June 19, 1978.

CHAPTER 2

1. *See* Tad Szulc, *The Illusion of Peace*, New York: Viking Press, 1978, pp. 794–97. According to a *Los Angeles Times–Washington Post* account, datelined Athens and apparently leaked by U.S. embassy sources, Secretary Kissinger had learned in advance of Turkish plans to invade Cyprus, as early as July, but had rejected appeals from U.S. Ambassador to Athens Henry Tasca to interpose the U.S. Mediterranean-based 6th Fleet to prevent a Turkish landing. *Washington Post*, Nov. 22, 1974, p. A1. The State Department asserted that the *Washington Post* story contained inaccuracies, but declined to specify them. *Crisis on Cyprus. 1976: Crucial Year for Peace.* Staff Report by Subcommittee To Investigate Problems Connected with Refugees and Escapees of the Committee on the Judiciary. U.S. Senate, 94th Cong., 2d Sess., Jan. 19, 1976, p. 40. Henceforth *Crisis on Cyprus.*

2. *Ibid.*, p. 38.

3. *Ibid.*, p. 7.

4. *New York Times*, August 19, 1974, pp. 1, 5.

5. *Crisis on Cyprus*, p. 38.

6. *Ibid.*

7. Rep. Biaggi, U.S. House of Representatives, *Congressional Record*, Aug. 8, 1974, H. 27537.

8. Rep. Brademas, *ibid.*, Aug. 14, 1974, H. 28297.

9. Sen. Tunney, *Congressional Record*, Aug. 19, 1974, S. 28820–22.

10. Executive Branch Consultations with Congress on Military Assistance to Turkey. White House Memo. Unpub. March 1975.

11. The comparison is to the equivalent quarter of the preceding year. *New York Times*, Dec. 2, 1974, p. 7.

12. U.S. House of Representatives, *Congressional Record*, Sept. 24, 1974, H. 9481.

13. *Ibid.*, H. 9482.

14. *New York Times*, Sept. 27, 1974, p. 1.

15. *Ibid.*

16. *Ibid.*, Oct. 1, 1974, pp. 1, 3.

17. Sen. Scott, U.S. Senate, *Congressional Record*, Oct. 1, 1974, S. 17936.

18. Sen. Eagleton, *ibid.*, S. 17937 at S. 17938.

19. U.S. House of Representatives, *Congressional Record*, Oct. 7, 1974, H. 9989.

20. *Ibid.*, H. 9996.

21. *Ibid.*, H. 9997–98.

22. *New York Times*, Oct. 12, 1974, p. 1.

23. U.S. House of Representatives, *Congressional Record*, Oct. 17, 1974, H. 10673.

24. *Ibid.*, H. 10675–76; H.R.J.Res. 1167; PL 93–448.

25. U.S. House of Representatives, *Congressional Record*, Dec. 11, 1974, H. 11599 and H. 11604. See also *New York Times*, Dec. 11, 1974, p. 6.

26. *New York Times*, Dec. 18, 1974, p. 3.

27. *Ibid.*, Jan. 25, 1975, p. 6.

28. *Ibid.*

29. *Ibid.*, Feb. 5, 1975, p. 5.

30. U.S. Senate, *Congressional Record*, May 19, 1975, S. 8623–51; Senator Eagleton did, however, have the support of Senator Church, the third ranking member of the committee.

31. *New York Times*, July 10, 1975, p. 1.

32. *Ibid.*, July 21, 1975, p. 3.

33. *Ibid.*, July 23, 1975, p. 11.

34. *Ibid.*, July 25, 1975, p. 1.

35. *Ibid.*, July 25, 1975, p. 2. The Incinlik airbase was permitted to remain open because it was the major NATO installation in Turkey.

36. *New York Times*, July 26, 1975, p. 1; *ibid.*, p. 7.

37. *Ibid.*, July 30, 1975, p. 3.

38. John Stockwell, *In Search of Enemies*, New York: W. W. Norton, 1978, p. 232.

39. *New York Times*, Feb. 11, 1976, p. 1.

40. Stockwell, *op. cit.*, p. 43.

41. *New York Times*, Sept. 25, 1975, pp. 1, 22.

42. Stockwell, *op. cit.*, p. 258.

43. *New York Times*, Dec. 12, 1975, p. 1.

44. Stockwell, *op. cit.*, pp. 164–65.

45. *Ibid.*, p. 185.

46. *Ibid.*, p. 259.

47. *New York Times*, Dec. 12, 1975, p. 1.

48. Stockwell, *op. cit.*, p. 135.

49. *Ibid.*, p. 158.

50. *Ibid.*, p. 186.

51. *New York Times*, Sept. 25, 1975, pp. 1, 22.

52. Stockwell, *op. cit.*, p. 93.

53. U.S. Senate, Subcommittee on African Affairs of the Committee on Foreign Relations, *Hearings*, 94th Cong., 2d Sess., "U.S. Involvement in Civil War in

Angola," Jan. 29, Feb. 3, 4, and 6, 1976, Prepared Statement of Hon. Henry A. Kissinger, pp. 14–23 at p. 20.

54. Stockwell, *op. cit.*, pp. 178–79.

55. *Ibid.*, p. 179.

56. *Ibid.*, p. 189.

57. *Ibid.*, p. 230.

58. Interview with Mr. Mark Moran, legislative assistant to Sen. Tunney, Washington, D.C., June 22, 1976.

59. *Ibid.*

60. *Ibid.*

61. *Ibid.*

62. *Ibid.*

63. *New York Times,* Dec. 20, 1975, p. 1.

64. *Ibid.*, Dec. 24, 1975, p. 7.

65. U.S. Senate, Subcommittee on African Affairs of the Committee on Foreign Relations, *Hearings,* 94th Cong., 2d Sess., "U.S. Involvement in Civil War in Angola," Feb. 3, 1976, Statement of Hon. Robert Ellsworth, pp. 59–87 at p. 83.

66. Interview with Mr. Steven D. Bryen, legislative assistant to Sen. Clifford P. Case, Washington, D.C., July 22, 1976.

67. *Ibid.*

68. U.S. Senate, Subcommittee on African Affairs of the Committee on Foreign Relations, *Hearings,* 94th Cong., 2d Sess., "U.S. Involvement in Civil War in Angola," Statement of Hon. Henry A. Kissinger, Jan. 29, 1976, pp. 6–55 at p. 18. Interview with Mr. Les Janka, Senior Staff Member for Congressional Relations and Public Affairs, National Security Council, Washington, D.C., June 25, 1976.

69. U.S. Senate, Subcommittee on African Affairs of the Committee on Foreign Relations, *Hearings,* 94th Cong., 2d Sess., "U.S. Involvement in Civil War in Angola," pp. 18–22.

70. *Ibid.*

CHAPTER 3

1. Resolution To Establish a Standing Committee of the Senate on Intelligence, and for Other Purposes, S.Res. 400, 94th Cong., 2d Sess., *Congressional Record* 253 (1976).

2. International Security Assistance and Arms Export Control Act of 1976, PL 94–329, 90 Stat. 729 (1976).

3. 1 U.S.C. §112(b) (Supp. V 1975).

4. Foreign Assistance Act of 1961, 22 U.S.C. §2151 (Supp. V 1975). Section 116, 22 U.S.C. §2151n, dealing with Congressional supervision over the application of human rights standards, was added by Act of Dec. 20, 1975, PL 94–161, §130, 89 Stat. 849.

5. 50 U.S.C. §1451 (Supp. V 1975).

6. Abraham D. Sofaer, *War, Foreign Affairs and Constitutional Power: The Origins,* Cambridge, Mass.: Ballinger Publishing Co., 1976, p. 4.

7. 30 Fitzpatrick 431–32, in J. Fitzpatrick, ed., *The Writings of George Washington* (39 vols.), Washington, D.C.: U.S.G.P.O. (1931–44).

8. Abraham D. Sofaer, "The Presidency, War, and Foreign Affairs: Practice under the Framers," *Law and Contemporary Problems* (Spring 1976), 12–38 at p. 18ff and cites therein.

9. 4 U.S. (4 Dall.) 37 (1800).

10. Sofaer, *op. cit.* note 8, pp. 25–27.

11. *Ibid.*, pp. 30–36.

12. Lincoln to Herndon, February 15, 1848, Abraham Lincoln, *Collected Works*, Vol. 1, R. P. Basler, ed., New Brunswick: Rutgers Univ. Press, 1953–55, pp. 451–52.

13. "Totally missing was any debate that would have accompanied an understanding of the comander-in-chief clause as creating an undefined reservoir of power to use the military in situations unauthorized by Congress." Sofaer, *op. cit.* note 6, p. 36.

14. 1 Farrand 318–19, in M. Farrand, ed., *Records of the Federal Convention of 1787* (1911–37) (4 Vols.), New Haven: Yale Univ. Press, 1967.

15. Louis Henkin, *Foreign Affairs and the Constitution*, Mineola, N.Y.: The Foundation Press, 1972, p. 52.

16. Statement of Prof. Abram Chayes in U.S. House of Representatives, Subcommittee on National Security Policy and Scientific Developments of the Committee on Foreign Affairs, *Hearings*, "Congress, the President, and the War Powers," 91st Cong., 2d Sess., 1970, pp. 135–67 at p. 137.

17. Sofaer, *op. cit.* note 6, p. 56. Cited for this proposition are J. Maurice, *Hostilities Without Declarations of War*, London: H. M. Stationery Office, 1883; C. Ver Steeg, *The Formative Years*, 288–300 (1964); R. Ward, *An Enquiry into the Manner in Which the Different Wars in Europe Have Commenced* (1805).

18. Emerson, J. T., "War Powers Legislation," 74 *W. Va. L. Rev.* (1972), 53, 88–119.

19. In the judgment of diplomatic historian Richard W. Leopold, "Polk . . . remains the sole president in history who, by needlessly deploying the armed forces, provoked an attack by a potential enemy. War with Mexico may have been justified, it may have even been inevitable. . . . But there can be no dissent from the judgment that its commencement is on constitutional grounds to be deplored"; Richard W. Leopold, *The Growth of American Foreign Policy*, New York: Alfred A. Knopf, 1964, pp. 101–2.

20. Sofaer, *op. cit.* note 6, p. 57.

21. U.S. Senate, Committee on Foreign Relations, *Documents Relating to the War Power of Congress, the President's Authority as Commander-in-Chief and the War in Indochina*, 91st Cong., 2d Sess., 1970, esp. 13–14. Hereafter, *Documents Relating to the War Power.*

22. Arthur M. Schlesinger, Jr., *The Imperial Presidency*, Boston: Houghton Mifflin, 1973, pp. 88–89.

23. *Documents Relating to the War Power*, pp. 14–15.

24. Resolution of the Security Council, 27 June 1950, S/1511; SCOR, V, No. 16, pp. 4, 16.

25. Eventually, the Organization of American States provided a vestige of legitimation by agreeing to participate in an Inter-American Peace Force. Text in 52 *U.S. Department of State Bulletin* (1965), pp. 862–63. This resolution establishing the Inter-American Force was passed by the Tenth Meeting of Consultation of Ministers of Foreign Affairs of the Organization of American States on May 6, 1965, by a vote of 15–5 with one abstention.

26. John J. Sparkman, "The Role of the Senate in Determining Foreign Policy," in Nathaniel Stone Preston, ed., *The Senate Institution*, New York: Van Nostrand Reinhold, 1969, p. 31 at 34.

27. PL 88–408, 78 Stat. 384 (1964).

28. Note, however, *Mitchell v. Laird*, 488 F. 2d 611 at 615, slip op. (D.C. Cir. 1973), where the Court said, "This Court cannot be unmindful of what every schoolboy knows: that in voting to appropriate money or to draft men a Congress-

man is not necessarily approving of the continuation of a war no matter how specifically the appropriation or draft act refers to that war."

29. S.Res. 85, 91st Cong., 1st Sess., *Congressional Record*, S. 17245 (1969).

30. H. *Rept. No.* 547, 93d Cong., 1st Sess. (1973).

31. The operative parts of the law "are not dependent upon the language" of the statement of purposes and policy. U.S. House of Representatives, Subcommittee on International Security and Scientific Affairs of the Committee on International Relations, *The War Powers Resolution: Relevant Documents, Correspondence, Reports*, 94th Cong., 1st Sess., 1975, p. 13 at p. 14.

32. Statement of Hon. Clement J. Zablocki, unpublished.

33. Thomas F. Eagleton, *War and Presidential Power: A Chronicle of Congressional Surrender*, New York: Liveright, 1974, p. 220.

34. Interview with Mr. J. Brian Atwood, formerly legislative assistant to Sen. Eagleton, currently Deputy Assistant Secretary of State for Congressional Relations, Washington, D.C., July 22, 1976.

35. Interview with Hon. Clement Zablocki (D–Wis.), chairman of the House International Relations Committee, Washington, D.C., July 22, 1976.

36. U.S. Senate Foreign Relations Committee Hearing on Proposed Amendments to the War Powers Resolution, July 14, 1977.

37. War Powers Resolution, PL 93–148 [H.J.Res. 542], 87 Stat. 555, s. 4, passed over President's veto, November 7, 1973. 50 U.S.C. 1542, 1543 (Supp. V 1975).

38. *Ibid.*, §1643(a) (A), (B), and (C).

39. U.S. House of Representatives, Subcommittee on International Security and Scientific Affairs of the Committee on International Relations, *The War Powers Resolution: Relevant Documents, Correspondence, Reports*, 94th Cong., 1st Sess., 1975, pp. 40–41; excerpted from "Report Dated April 4, 1975, From President Gerald R. Ford to Hon. Carl Albert, Speaker of the House of Representatives, in Compliance with Section 4(a) (2) of the War Powers Resolution."

40. Letters to Carl Albert of April 4, April 12, April 30, and May 15, 1975, in U.S. House of Representatives, Subcommittee on International Security and Scientific Affairs of the Committee on International Relations, *War Powers: A Test of Compliance Relative to the Danang Sealift, The Evacuation of Phnom Penh, The Evacuation of Saigon and The Mayaguez Incident, Hearings*, 94th Cong., 1st Sess., 1975, pp. 4, 5, 7, 76; henceforth *Hearings, War Powers: A Test of Compliance*.

41. A Memorandum of the Legal Adviser, Department of State, June 16, 1978 (unpub.).

42. *Ibid.*

43. *International Herald Tribune*, August 12–13, 1978, p. 3.

44. War Powers Resolution, §3, 50 U.S.C. §1542 (Supp. V 1975), passed over President's veto, November 7, 1973.

45. "Ford Scores Limit on War Power," *New York Times*, April 12, 1977, p. 14.

46. *Hearings, War Powers: A Test of Compliance*, p. 72; according to the legal adviser, " 'Hostilities' was used to mean a situation in which units of the Armed Forces are actively engaged in an exchange of fire with opposing units of hostile forces, and 'imminent hostilities' was considered to mean a situation in which there is a serious risk from hostile fire to the safety of U.S. forces."

47. *Ibid.*, p. 6; excerpted from "Report Dated April 12, 1975, from President Gerald R. Ford to Hon. Carl Albert, Speaker of the House of Representatives, in Compliance with Section 4(a)(2) of the War Powers Resolution."

48. Report Dated April 30, 1975, From President Gerald R. Ford to Hon. Carl Albert, Speaker of the House of Representatives, in Compliance with Section 4 of War Powers Resolution. *Ibid.*, p. 7.

49. *Ibid.*, p. 6.

50. *New York Times*, May 16, 1975, p. 15.

51. *Ibid.*

52. *Ibid.*

53. *Ibid.*, May 15, 1975, p. 18.

54. *Ibid.*

55. *Hearings, War Powers: A Test of Compliance*, p. 81.

56. *Ibid.*, p. 7.

57. A Letter from Hon. James P. Johnson and Others to Hon. John Sparkman, June 13, 1978 (unpub.).

58. *Ibid.*

59. S. 1790, 94th Cong., 1st Sess., *Congressional Record* S. 8829 (1975).

60. Sofaer, *op. cit.* n. 6, p. 58.

61. War Powers Resolution, *op. cit.*, Sec. 1544(c).

62. Legislative Appropriation Act, PL 72–212, 47 Stat. 414 (1932), sec. 407.

63. H.R.Res. 334, 72d Cong., 2d Sess. (1932).

64. U.S. Library of Congress, Congressional Research Service, Clark F. Norton, *Congressional Review, Deferral and Disapproval of Executive Actions: A Summary and an Inventory of Statutory Authority* (mimeo.), April 30, 1976.

65. Opinions of the Attorney General, 56, 58 (1933).

66. Letter from Attorney General Griffin B. Bell to President Carter, January 31, 1977.

67. *Ibid.*

68. U.S. Library of Congress, Congressional Research Service, Clark F. Norton, *Congressional Review, Deferral and Disapproval of Executive Actions: A Summary and an Inventory of Statutory Authority* (mimeo), April 30, 1976.

69. U.S. Senate, *Congressional Record*, November 7, 1919, S. 8074.

70. For debate of the Constitutional issue, *ibid.*, S. 8074–S. 8080; *see also* Robert W. Ginnane, "The Control of Federal Administration by Congressional Resolutions and Committees," 66 *Harvard Law Review*, No. 4 (February 1953), 569–611, at 575.

71. 55 Stat. 32 (1941).

72. Letter to the Attorney General from President Franklin D. Roosevelt, dated April 7, 1941, reprinted in Robert H. Jackson, "A Presidential Legal Opinion," 66 *Harvard Law Review*, No. 8 (June 1953), 1359.

73. *Ibid.*, 1357–58.

74. *Springer et al. v. Government of the Philippine Islands*, 277 U.S. 189 (1928).

75. *Ibid.*, at 202.

76. *Ibid.*, at 201–2.

77. Act of May 22, 1947, PL 80–75, ch. 81, §2153(d), 61 Stat. 103.

78. 69 Stat. 301, 321 (1955).

79. Joseph P. Harris, *Congressional Control of Administration*, Washington, D.C.: Brookings Institution, 1964, p. 229.

80. 41 *Opinions of the Attorney General*, 230 (1955).

81. *Public Papers of the Presidents: Dwight D. Eisenhower*, 1955, "Special Message to the Congress upon Signing the Department of Defense Appropriation," July 13, 1955, p. 688.

82. Harris, *op. cit.*, p. 229.

83. *Ibid.*, p. 230.

84. 42 U.S.C. (1970), as amended by Act of July 2, 1958, PL 85–479, §4, 72 Stat. 276.

85. *Public Papers of the Presidents: John F. Kennedy*, 1963, "Memorandum on

Informing Congressional Committee of Changes Involving Foreign Economic Assistance Funds," January 8, 1963, p. 6.

86. 22 U.S.C. §2367 (1970), as amended by the Foreign Assistance Act of 1961, PL 87–195, §617, 75 Stat. 424.

87. 42 U.S.C. §2074 (Supp. V 1975), as amended by Atomic Energy Act Amendments of 1974, PL 93–377, §2, 88 Stat. 472; also, 42 U.S.C. §2153(d) (Supp. V 1975), as amended by Atomic Energy Act Amendments of 1974, PL 93–377, §55, 88 Stat. 475, and Act of October 26, 1974, PL 93–485, §1, 88 Stat. 1460.

88. PL 93–618, tit. II, III, IV, 88 Stat. 1978 (1975) (codified in scattered sections of 19 U.S.C.).

89. PL 93–552, §613, 88 Stat. 1745 (1974).

90. The Arms Export Control Act, PL 90–629, 82 Stat. 1320, October 22, 1968, as amended, Sec. 36(b). 22 U.S.C. §2776 (Supp. V 1975), as amended by International Security Assistance and Arms Export Control Act of 1976, §211(a).

91. Resolution To Implement the United States Proposal for the Early Warning System in Sinai, PL 94–110, §1, 89 Stat. 572 (1975).

92. 7 U.S.C. §1711 (Supp. V 1975), as amended by the International Development and Food Assistance Act of 1975, PL 94–161, §207, 89 Stat. 853.

93. Foreign Assistance Act of 1961, 22 U.S.C. §2151n (Supp. V 1975), as amended by International Development and Food Assistance Act, PL 94–161, §310, 89 Stat. 860 (1975).

94. Library of Congress, Congressional Research Service, Memorandum: "Constitutionality of the Legislative Veto Amendment to the Foreign Military Sales and Assistance Act," for Hon. Gaylord Nelson, September 4, 1973, p. 13.

95. This argument is made in H.R. Rept. No. 120, 76th Cong., 1st Sess., 4–6 (1939).

96. A similar distinction appears to have been implied by the Attorney General in 1949, in arguing in favor of the constitutionality of the Congressional veto in the Reorganization Acts of 1939 and 1945. The opinion speaks of "consultation" as a required prerequisite for the exercise of authority delegated by Congress but notes that the President frequently consults also "on matters which may be considered to be strictly within the purview of the Executive, such as those relating to foreign policy." Memorandum Re: Constitutionality of Provisions in Proposed Reorganization Bills Now Pending in Congress, reprinted in S. Rept. No. 232, 81st Cong., 1st Sess., 18–20 (1949).

97. Allen Schick, "Congress and the 'Details' of Administration," 36 Public Administration Rev., No. 5 (Sept./Oct. 1976), 516, 523.

98. Ibid.

99. The concurrent resolutions in respect of the Hawk sale were introduced under the terms of the 1974 Nelson-Bingham Amendment to the 1961 Foreign Assistance Act, PL 90–629, §36(b), 82 Stat. 1320.

100. Both cases arose in the context not of a law pertaining to the foreign relations power but of the Federal Election Campaign Act. (Federal Election Campaign Act Amendments of 1974, PL 93–443, 88 Stat. 1263 [codified in scattered sections of 2, 5, 18, 20, 47 U.S.C. (Supp. V 1975)], as amended by Federal Election Campaign Act Amendments of 1976, PL 94–283, 90 Stat. 475.) In Buckley v. Valeo (Buckley v. Valeo, 424 U.S. 1 [1976]) the Supreme Court was able to avoid a decision on the constitutionality of one-House vetoes twice invoked against regulations made by the Federal Electoral Commission by instead holding unconstitutional the legislative scheme by which the Commission was appointed. (Ibid., at p. 140, n. 176). One year later, in Clark v. Valeo (No. 76–1825 [D.C. Cir. Jan. 21, 1977] [per curiam]) the Court of Appeals of the District of Columbia said: "whether

legislative review of regulations constitutes legislation to which the presidential veto necessarily applies . . . need not be reached in these proceedings because of the unripeness of a challenge based upon the veto power." (*Ibid.*, slip op. at p. 12.) The adoption of a veto resolution had not yet occurred under the revised legislation. (*Ibid.*, slip op. at p. 15.) Although it was argued that the "one-house veto is so patently unconstitutional that nothing more is needed to inform the judgement of the court," the Court refused to decide. (*Ibid.*, slip op. at p. 15, n. 8.) In so doing, Judge Tamm noted that Justice White, in a concurring opinion in *Buckley v. Valeo*, "had found the provision *constitutional* on its face." (*Ibid.*, citing *Buckley v. Valeo*, slip op. at 284–86, n. 81.) The majority did not adopt this view, but neither did they reject it ("Be that as it may," Judge Tamm said of Mr. Justice White's view. *Clark v. Valeo*, slip op. at p. 15, n. 8.), maintaining that a court, before making a ruling on an issue which has been the subject of controversy for forty years, should know a great deal more about what a specific Congressional veto means in practice and how it affects the operation of that part of the government at which it is aimed. Only on a fuller record, they said, can a court make the "landmark" determination whether the device "is really a violation of, or perhaps might be a furtherance of, the objective of pragmatic government that combines checks and balances with the principle of coordination between branches." (*Ibid.*, at p. 17.)

It is significant that the test arose in an area of domestic legislative jurisdiction. The Court hinted at the importance of this in distinguishing the government's claim of standing based on *New York Times Co. v. United States*. (403 U.S. 713 [1971].) It said: "The Constitution does not give the President any duty to protect the Constitution from allegedly unconstitutional legislation *comparable to his self-executing mandate to conduct foreign affairs*." (Italics added) (*Clark v. Valeo*, slip op. at 3, concurring opinion of Tamm, J., Bazelon, C. J., and Wright, J.) It should be noted, however, that these perhaps rather unwittingly expansive echoes of *Curtiss-Wright* (*United States v. Curtiss-Wright Export Corp.*, 299 U.S. 304 [1936]) besides being *dicta*, were not addressed to the exercise of the Congressional veto but to the question of standing.

101. *Clark v. Valeo, slip op.* at p. 4, concurring opinion of Leventhal, J.

102. The case also generated one dissent, by MacKinnon, J., which addresses itself specifically to the unconstitutionality of the one-House veto, asserting that it "greatly increases the authority of a small *minority* of the entire Congress to achieve a legislative result, when compared with the constitutionally prescribed legislative procedure." (*Ibid.*, at p. 7, dissenting opinion of MacKinnon, J.) Thus a small number of members of Congress, a bare majority of the quorum, can unmake regulations made by the executive branch without recourse to legislative enactment. "That naked intrusion violates the basic three branch constitutional scheme for our Government and the legislative scheme provided by art. I, sections 1, 7 of the Constitution." (*Ibid.* at p. 9.) For a discussion of this subject, *see* Thomas M. Franck, "After the Fall: The New Procedural Framework for Congressional Control over the War Power," 71 *The American Journal of International Law*, No. 4 (October 1977), pp. 605–41.

103. U.S. Senate, Committee on Foreign Relations, *Hearings*, "Vance Nomination," 95th Cong., 1st Sess. (Jan. 1977), p. 38.

104. *New York Times*, March 6, 1977, p. 33.

105. Letter from Griffin B. Bell, Attorney General, to President Carter, January 31, 1977.

106. U.S. Senate, The "Legislative Veto" Message from the President, *Congressional Record*, June 22, 1978, S. 9443–S. 9444.

107. *Hearings, War Powers: A Test of Compliance*, pp. 90–91.

108. James L. Sundquist, "Congress and the President: Enemies or Partners?" in Henry Owen and Charles L. Schultze, eds., *Setting National Priorities: The Next Ten Years*, Washington, D.C.: The Brookings Institution, 1976, pp. 583–618 at p. 597.

CHAPTER 4

1. *Annals of Congress* (1790), 1168. For an account of this incident, *see* Abraham D. Sofaer, *War, Foreign Affairs and Constitutional Power: The Origins*, Cambridge, Mass.: Ballinger Publishing Co., 1976, p. 79.

2. Richard W. Leopold, *The Growth of American Foreign Policy: A History*, New York: Alfred A. Knopf, 1964, p. 75.

3. Telford Taylor, *Grand Inquest: The Story of Congressional Investigations*, New York: Simon and Schuster, 1955, pp. 19–22; 3 *Annals*, 490–93.

4. 2 *The Works of Thomas Jefferson* (Fed. ed.), 1904, pp. 213–14.

5. On February 2, 1843, for example, the House began an inquiry into the seizure of Monterey in Mexican California in October of 1842. This investigation began with a request to the President for all relevant correspondence from or to Commodore Thomas Jones, who had led the expedition. The request omitted the customary qualification that documents should be submitted only when it was "compatible with the public interest." President Tyler complied. But he noted disapprovingly that the House request had not allowed for his exercise of judgment to withhold papers "in the public interest." He added that, even though the release of these papers posed no danger, there might be cases in which the publication of instructions to military officers "would be highly injudicious" and underscored the Presidential position that "the discretion of the Executive can not be controlled by the request of either House of Congress for the communication of papers"; *see* Leopold, *op. cit.*, p. 74.

6. After John Jay negotiated his famous treaty with Britain, members of Congress came to believe that Jay had agreed to restrictions on American commerce that were contrary to his instructions. When Washington sent the Senate the treaty for ratification, to meet these objections he also included his instructions to Jay, follow-up instructions—some of which had not reached Jay in time—and letters from Jay to Secretary of State Edmund Randolph, criticizing his instructions and answering Randolph's objections to the way Jay was proceeding. Washington transmitted this complete docket to the Senate despite misgivings by the Secretary of State. The Senate approved the treaty on June 24, after deleting one article. See 4 *Annals of Congress*, 863; *ibid.*, pp. 85–86.

7. The Senate Foreign Relations Subcommittee on United States Security Agreements and Commitments Abroad, established on February 3, 1969, under the chairmanship of Sen. Stuart Symington, engaged in a two-year investigation of the Nixon Administration's conduct of war in Indochina and Cambodia. It produced telling evidence of Administration lies about its conduct of the war that profoundly affected public and Congressional opinion, contributing much to the decision to prohibit U.S. ground operations in Laos. For a full discussion *see* John Lehman, *The Executive, Congress, and Foreign Policy: Studies of the Nixon Administration*, New York: Praeger Publishers, 1974; *see* p. 146 and chap. 5, pp. 108–69.

Similarly, a study by a special subcommittee of the Senate Foreign Relations Committee of the role of multinational corporations—in destabilizing the Marxist Allende regime in Chile, for example—led to legislation prohibiting bribery and intervening in the political affairs of foreign countries. *See* U.S. Senate, Committee on Foreign Relations, "Background Information on the Committee on Foreign Relations," 3rd rev. ed., 94th Cong., 1st Sess., May 1975, pp. 36–37; hereinafter "Background Information on the Committee on Foreign Relations."

Most recently, after newspaper revelations of unauthorized CIA activities, the Senate established a special investigatory committee under Senator Church which documented misdeeds and made extensive proposals for reform. Some of these have since been implemented by legislation and a new Executive order.

While the investigatory committee thus continues to be of importance, the major Congressional effort to take hold of foreign relations is now concentrated on a different kind of oversight, featuring statutory requirements for Congressional codetermination. The instruments for ensuring codetermination are the Congressional veto, reporting requirements, "lie-in-wait" and "come-into-agreement" provisions. These all have the effect of requiring the President to involve Congress before taking an important action; and there has been no shortage of outrage on the part of successive occupants of the White House when such prior constraints have been imposed on the exercise of his discretion.

8. In 1874 a joint House-Senate investigating committee was established to investigate the governance of the District of Columbia; and in 1878 still another examined the operations of the Indian Bureau; see Taylor, *op. cit.*, p. 45. Sometimes, however, investigatory oversight does go in search of bigger game, responding to a major scandal or palpable disaster in the conduct of foreign policy. For example, the Truman Committee, the Senate Special Committee To Investigate the National Defense Program, from March 1, 1941, to April 28, 1948, worked effectively to keep the national mobilization effort honest. "I want the best investigator you've got," Senator Truman had told the Attorney General, and he put together a staff and machine that continues to be a model of investigative diligence and discretion. For an analysis of the Truman Committee *see* Donald H. Riddle, *The Truman Committee*, New Brunswick, N.J.: Rutgers University Press, 1964; citation is located, p. 22.

In 1951, President Truman, in turn, became the target of a highly sensitive Senate investigation of his conduct as President. His precipitous dismissal of Douglas MacArthur as Far Eastern commander prompted the Senate to organize hearings before a special joint committee consisting of the Armed Services and Foreign Relations Committees. The inquest lasted for forty-three days. General MacArthur was on the stand for three days, Secretary of State Dean Acheson for eight, while the four Joint Chiefs of Staff testified for thirteen days. The focus gradually grew to include all aspects of military and political policy toward Asia and the Far East. The final report of the committee was a strident diatribe against those policies. *See* David N. Farnsworth, *The Senate Committee on Foreign Relations*, Urbana: University of Illinois Press, 1961, pp. 128–30.

9. The Supreme Court wrote a landmark decision limiting the scope of Congressional inquest in the case of *Kilbourn v. Thompson*. See *Kilbourn v. Thompson*, 103 U.S. 168 (1881); *U.S. v. Rumely*, 345 U.S. 41 (1953); *Watkins v. United States*, 354 U.S. 178 (1957). The Court conceded the right of Congress to conduct investigations and punish for contempt, but ruled that these powers are limited by the Constitution. They found that Kilbourn had been the subject of "a fruitless investigation" and that the Congressional inquest had overstepped its jurisdictional bounds because it "could result in no valid legislation" and was too "indefinite" in its objective. 103 U.S. at 195.

Legislative relevance and sharpness of focus have ever since remained tests of investigative legality. Congress may not investigate matters outside its law-making jurisdiction, nor may it go on "fishing expeditions." In 1927, in *McGrain v. Daugherty*, the Supreme Court again affirmed that "the power of inquiry—with process to enforce it—is an essential and appropriate auxiliary to the legislative function." They added that the "power to legislate carries with it by implication ample authority to obtain information needed in the rightful exercise of that power and to employ compulsory process for the purpose." 273 U.S. 135 at 174 (1927).

Nevertheless, there continues a lively tension between the Congress's "right to know" and the need for administrative integrity and official secrecy in the executive branch. See Thomas M. Franck and Edward Weisband, eds., *Secrecy and Foreign Policy*, New York: Oxford University Press, 1974, and Edward Weisband and Thomas M. Franck, *Resignation in Protest: Ethical Choices Between Loyalty to Conscience and Loyalty to Team in American Public Life*, New York: Grossman Publishers/Penguin, 1975.

During the Watergate crisis, the Supreme Court held that it could compel the President to produce the White House tapes "(a)bsent a claim of need to protect military, diplomatic, or delicate national security secrets" but also added that, while they were able to "conclude that the legitimate needs of the judicial process may outweigh Presidential privilege . . ." they were not passing on the balance "between the confidentiality interest and Congressional demands for information." *United States v. Nixon*, 418 U.S. 683 (1974).

When Senator Ervin's Senate Select Committee attempted to subpoena certain tapes (to which access had already been obtained in different, criminal litigation by Special Prosecutor Cox), Federal District Judge Gesell turned it down. He concluded that the Committee's need to know did not outweigh the interest in Executive confidentiality. *Senate Select Committee on Presidential Campaign Activities v. Nixon*, 370 F. Supp. 521 (D.D.C. 1974). That decision seems to be a setback to investigatory oversight. But it should be interpreted in the light of the fact that criminal proceedings were then underway which might have been prejudiced had evidence needed to prosecute been leaked from the Ervin Committee. See Gerald Gunther, *Constitutional Law: Cases and Materials* (ninth ed.), Mineola, N.Y.: The Foundation Press, 1975, p. 468.

10. The Foreign Assistance Act of 1973, as amended; PL 93–189, 87 Stat. 714, §32.

11. U.S. House of Representatives, Committee on International Relations, Subcommittee on International Organizations and Movements, "Human Rights in the World Community: A Call for U.S. Leadership," March 27, 1974.

12. *Ibid.*, p. 9.

13. *Ibid.*, p. 3.

14. Foreign Assistance Act, 1974. PL 93–559, 88 Stat. 1795, Sec. 25, Dec. 30, 1974.

15. *Ibid.*, Sec. 26.

16. The Foreign Assistance Act of 1961, as amended; 22 U.S.C. §2304; PL 87–195, 75 Stat. 424, Sec. 502B. The amendment was added by the Foreign Assistance Act of 1974, PL 93–559, 88 Stat. 1795, §46.

17. U.S. Department of State, Unclassified Telegram to All Diplomatic Posts, No. 012320; Jan. 17, 1975. See also U.S. Department of State, Unclassified Airgram to All Diplomatic Posts, No. A-1045; Feb. 14, 1975.

18. U.S. Agency for International Development AIDTO Circular A 687, unclassified, airgram, Dec. 9, 1975.

19. U.S. House of Representatives, Committee on International Relations, International Development and Food Assistance Act of 1975, *Hearings and Markup*, 94th Cong., 1st Sess., H.Doc. 94–158 and H.R. 9005, July 14–30, 1975, pp. 539ff.

20. Interview with Hon. Tom Harkin (D–Iowa), Washington, D.C., June 24, 1976.

21. *S.Rept. No. 94–406*, H.R. 9005, Oct. 1, 1975.

22. U.S. Senate, H.R. 9005, *Rept. No. 94–406*, 94th Cong., 1st Sess., Sept. 11, 1975, at 35.

23. Sen. Hubert Humphrey, opening statement, U.S. Senate, Committee on Foreign Relations, Subcommittee on Foreign Assistance, Foreign Assistance Authorization, *Hearings* on S. 1816 and H.R. 9005, 94th Cong., 1st Sess., July 23, 1975, p. 423.

24. PL 94–161, 89 Stat. 849 (December 20, 1975), Sec. 310 amending the Foreign Assistance Act of 1961 by including a new Sec. 116.

25. H.R. 11963. Tentatively approved by the Committee through December 18, 1975. Sec. 101 to amend Sec. 502B of the Foreign Assistance Act of 1961.

26. U.S. Senate, Committee on Foreign Relations, Subcommittee on Foreign Assistance, "Report to the Congress on the Human Rights Situation in Countries Receiving U.S. Security Assistance," *Foreign Assistance Authorization: Arms Sales Issues. Hearings*, 94th Cong., 1st Sess. between June 17 and Dec. 5, 1975, pp. 376–80.

27. *Ibid.*, p. 377.

28. *Ibid.*, pp. 377–78.

29. U.S. Senate, Sen. Cranston, *Congressional Record*, Nov. 20, 1975, S. 37602.

30. *Ibid.*, at S. 37603.

31. Interview with Mr. Les Janka, Senior Staff Member for Congressional Relations and Public Affairs, National Security Council, Washington, D.C., June 23, 1976; Interview with Ambassador Robert J. McCloskey, Assistant Secretary of State for Congressional Relations, Washington, D.C., June 24, 1976.

32. The second communication pertaining to the country reports was a prepared statement by James M. Wilson, Coordinator for Humanitarian Affairs in U.S. Senate Committee on Foreign Relations, Subcommittee on Foreign Assistance, *Foreign Assistance Authorization: Arms Sales Issues, Hearings*, 94th Cong., 1st Sess., between June 17, 1975, and December 5, 1975, "Prepared Statement by James M. Wilson, Coordinator for Humanitarian Affairs," U.S. Department of State, pp. 464–66.

33. The White House, Message of May 7, 1976.

34. House of Representatives, 94th Cong., 2d Sess., *Rept. No. 94–1272, Conference Report* on H.R. 13680, pp. 50–51.

35. Foreign Assistance Act of 1961 as amended, Sec. 116(c) and (d), *op. cit.*

36. *Ibid.*, Sec. 502B(3)(b).

37. *Ibid.*, Sec. 116(b).

38. *Ibid.*, Sec. 502B(c)(1).

39. *Ibid.*, Sec. 116(b).

40. *Ibid.*, Sec. 502B(c)(1)(C).

41. *Ibid.*, Sec. 116(a).

42. U.S. House of Representatives, *Reports* Submitted by the Department of State to the Committee on International Relations, "Human Rights and U.S. Policy: Argentina, Haiti, Indonesia, Iran, Peru, and the Philippines," 94th Cong., 2d Sess., December 31, 1976, Appendix: Correspondence with State Department Requesting Reports, pp. 35–36; document henceforth referred to as "Human Rights and U.S. Policy."

43. *New York Times*, January 2, 1977, p. 1.

44. The 1978 report ran to 426 pages.

45. U.S. Department of State, *Report* Submitted to the House Committee on International Relations and Senate Foreign Relations Committee, "Country Reports on Human Rights Practices," 95th Cong., 2d Sess., Joint Committee Report, February 3, 1978 (hereinafter "Country Reports on Human Rights Practices: 1978").

U.S. Department of State, *Report* Submitted to the House Committee on International Relations, "Human Rights Practices in Countries Receiving U.S. Security Assistance," 95th Cong., 1st Sess., April 25, 1977 (hereinafter "Human Rights Practices in Countries Receiving U.S. Security Assistance: 1977").

46. *New York Times*, March 1, 1977, p. 6.

47. *Ibid.*, April 6, 1977, p. 3.

48. *Ibid.*

49. *Ibid.*, March 6, 1977, p. 11.

50. *Ibid.*, March 12, 1977, pp. 1, 7.

51. *Ibid.*, March 18, 1977, p. 7.

52. *Ibid.*, April 25, 1977, pp. 3, 4.

53. *Ibid.*, March 13, 1977, p. 18; also, the "News in Review," p. 4.

54. *Ibid.*, April 6, 1977, p. 3.

55. "Human Rights Practices in Countries Receiving U.S. Security Assistance: 1977," pp. 12–13, 17–18.

56. *New York Times*, February 25, 1977, p. 1.

57. *Ibid.*, February 23, 1978, p. 8; also, interview with Mr. John Salzberg, Staff Consultant, House International Relations Committee, Subcommittee on International Organizations, Washington, D.C., June 2, 1978.

58. Interview with Hon. Donald Fraser (D–Minn.), Washington, D.C., June 19, 1978.

59. Foreign Assistance and Related Programs Appropriations Act, 1978, PL 95–148, 91 Stat. 1230 of October 31, 1977, Secs. 107, 114, 503A.

60. Foreign Assistance Act of 1961, *op. cit.* Sec. 620(f); *see also* Foreign Assistance and Related Programs Appropriations Act, 1979, PL 95–481, Oct. 18, 1978, Sec. 108. Prohibited is aid to Cambodia, Laos, and the Socialist Republic of Vietnam.

61. Not all these attacks were successful. Iran, Indonesia, and the Philippines emerged relatively unscathed. The aid prohibition on Argentina is contained in *ibid.*, Sec. 620B. The prohibition on Uruguay is found in Foreign Assistance and Related Programs Appropriations Act, 1978, PL 95–148, 91 Stat. 1230 of October 31, 1977, Sec. 503A. Limitations on Argentina, Brazil, El Salvador, and Guatemala are in *ibid.*, Sec. 503B. An additional prohibition on Chile is found in the International Security Assistance and Arms Export Control Act of 1976, PL 94–329, 90 Stat. 729 of June 30, 1976, Sec. 406. The mild prohibition on the Philippines is in Foreign Assistance and Related Programs Appropriations Act, 1978, *ibid.*, Sec. 503C.

62. Foreign Assistance and Related Programs Appropriations Act, 1978, *ibid.*, Sec. 107.

63. Foreign Assistance Act of 1961 as amended, *op. cit.*, Sec. 620(x)(1).

64. International Security Assistance Act of 1978, of Sept. 1978, PL 95–384, 92 Stat. 730, Sec. 13(a) revising 22 U.S.C. 2370, 22 U.S.C. 2751, 22 U.S.C. 2776.

65. Foreign Assistance Act of 1961 as amended, *op. cit.*, Sec. 620(f).

66. Foreign Assistance and Related Programs Appropriations Act of 1978, *op. cit.*, Sec. 503B.

67. *Ibid.*, Sec. 503A.

68. U.S. House of Representatives, Committee of Conference, *Conference Report*, "Making Appropriations, Foreign Assistance, Fiscal Year, 1979," *Rept.* No. 95–1754, 95th Cong., 2d Sess., October 10, 1978.

69. International Security Assistance Act of 1978, Sept. 26, 1978, PL 95–384, 92 Stat. 730, Sec. 10a, amending 22 U.S.C. 2346b.

70. *Ibid.*, pp. 10, 18.

71. International Security Assistance Act of 1978, Sept. 26, 1978, PL 95–384, 92 Stat. 730, Sec. 27, 22 U.S.C. 2346a.

72. PL 95–630, 92 Stat. 3641, November 10, 1978, Sec. 1915 amending 12 U.S.C. 635(b)

73. *New York Times*, July 17, 1977, p. 7.

74. Debate on H.R. 9721, U.S. House of Representatives, *Congressional Record*, December 9, 1975, H. 12053, H. 12060; *see also*, U.S. Senate, *Rept. No. 94–673* (1976). The law is 22 U.S.C. 283y; PL 94–302, May 31, 1976, 90 Stat. 591.

75. PL 95–118, 91 Stat. 1067 of October 3, 1977, Sec. 701(f).

76. *New York Times*, April 2, 1978, Part V, p. 3.

77. Amendment No. 300 to H.R. 5262, 95th Cong., 1st Sess., May 19, 1977.

78. *New York Times*, July 15, 1977, p. 20.

79. *Ibid.*, October 19, 1977, p. 10.

80. Letter to Hon. Clarence Long, Chairman, Committee on Appropriations, Subcommittee on Government Foreign Operations, from the President, The White House, unpub.

81. *International Herald Tribune*, August 5–6, 1978, p. 3; *Congressional Quarterly*, August 5, 1978, p. 2012.

82. U.S. House of Representatives, Committee of Conference, *Conference Report*, "Making Appropriations, Foreign Assistance, Fiscal Year, 1979," *Rept. No. 95–1754*, 95th Cong., 2d Sess., October 10, 1978, p. 17.

83. *Ibid.*, p. 18.

84. Memorandum to the Members of Senate Foreign Relations Committee, Subject: "Legislative Restrictions Regarding Assistance to Africa and Other Restrictions Compiled by the State Department," from Pauline Baker, Hans Binnendijk, and Michael Glennon (Staff Members), dated May 24, 1978, and attachments, unpub.

85. Since August 1977, the "food for peace program" administered by the agriculture department is required by law to apply human rights standards and to deny aid to violators except where it directly benefits needy people. International Development and Food Assistance Act of 1977, PL 95–88, 91 Stat. 533 at 545, of August 3, 1977, Sec. 2031 . This is now Sec. 112 of the Agricultural Trade Development and Assistance Act of 1954, PL 83–480, 68 Stat. 454 of July 10, 1954, as amended.

86. U.S. Department of State, Memorandum: "The Interagency Group on Human Rights and Foreign Assistance," March 9, 1978, p. 4, unpub.

87. Interview with Mr. Mark Schneider, Deputy Assistant Secretary of State for Human Rights, Washington, D.C., June 15, 1978.

88. *Ibid.*

89. U.S. Department of State, Memorandum: "The Interagency Group on Human Rights and Foreign Assistance," March 9, 1978, p. 8, unpub.

90. *Ibid.*

91. *Ibid.*, p. 9. Also, U.S. House of Representatives, Committee on International Relations, Subcommittee on International Organizations, *Hearings*, "Human Rights and United States Policy: A Review of the Administration's Record," 95th Cong., 1st Sess., October 25, 1977, p. 14.

92. Interview with Mr. Mark Schneider, Deputy Assistant Secretary of State for Human Rights, Washington, D.C., June 15, 1978.

93. *New York Times*, June 29, 1977, p. 3.

94. Interview with Mr. Mark Schneider, Deputy Assistant Secretary of State for Human Rights, Washington, D.C., June 15, 1978.

95. *New York Times*, May 5, 1978, p. 7.

96. *Washington Post*, May 29, 1978, p. A18; *New York Times*, January 31, 1978, p. 1; *ibid.*, February 28, 1978, p. 6.

97. *International Herald Tribune*, July 29–30, 1978, p. 5.

98. For evidence of this shock, *see* editorial, *International Herald Tribune*, August 4, 1978, p. 4, and *ibid.*, August 2, 1978, p. 5.

99. U.S. Department of State, Report of the Secretary of State to the Congress of the United States Regarding the Operations and Mandate of the Bureau of Human Rights and Humanitarian Affairs, February 5, 1975, released by the office of Sen. Edward M. Kennedy.

100. *New York Times*, August 12, 1977, p. 5.

101. *Ibid.*, April 8, 1978, p. 3.

102. Tom Wicker, "Rights in Americas: A Modest Success," *New York Times*, July 23, 1978, Sec. IV, p. E19.

103. *New York Times*, December 21, 1977, p. 9.

104. "The Diplomacy of Human Rights: The First Year," An Address by The Hon. Warren Christopher, Deputy Secretary of State, before the American Bar Association, New Orleans, February 13, 1978, unpub., p. 21.

105. *Ibid.*

106. *Ibid.*, p. 20.

107. *Ibid.*, p. 21.

108. 22 U.S.C. §2409. Foreign Assistance Act of 1961, PL 87–195, 75 Stat. 424, Sec. 650; this provision was enacted by the Foreign Assistance Act of 1967, 81 Stat. 445, s. 302(b).

109. The Foreign Military Sales Act of 1968 as amended, 22 U.S.C. §2776, PL 90–629, 82 Stat. 1320, Sec. 36.

110. Interview with Dr. Paula Stern, senior legislative assistant to Sen. G. Nelson, Washington, D.C., July 20, 1976.

111. U.S. Senate, Amendments to S. 3394, Amendment No. 1399, 93rd Cong., 2d Sess., June 6, 1974, pp. 2–3.

112. U.S. Senate, Amendments to S. 3394, Amendment No. 2002, 93rd Cong., 2d Sess., December 3, 1974, pp. 2–3.

113. The Foreign Military Sales Act of 1968 as amended, 22 U.S.C. §2776; PL 90–629, 82 Stat. 1320, Sec. 36(b), added by Sec. 45(a)(5) of the FAA of 1974, PL 93–559.

114. H.Res. 552, June 18, 1975.

115. Letter from Max L. Friedersdorff, Assistant to the President, to Rep. Thomas Morgan, Chairman, House International Relations Committee, June 25, 1975, White House Document, unpub.

116. William M. Constantine, "The 'Hawk' Controversy: The Proposed Sale of Air Defense Systems to Jordan," the National War College, April 1976, unpub., p. 5.

117. Letter from Friedersdorff to Chairman Morgan, June 25, 1975, *op. cit.*

118. U.S. House of Representatives, "Resolution of Inquiry—The Missing Facts Behind a Fundamental Change in Foreign Policy and Debate," *Congressional Record*, July 9, 1975, H. 6474.

119. *Ibid.*

120. *New York Times*, July 12, 1975, p. 1. The Bingham Resolution was H.R. Con.Res. 337.

121. Senator Case, U.S. Senate, *Congressional Record*, July 11, 1975, S 12389. The Case Resolution was S.Con.Res. 50.

122. *New York Times*, July 22, 1975, p. 4.

123. Constantine, *op. cit.*, pp. 22–23; *New York Times*, July 22, 1976, p. 4; *ibid.*, July 24, 1975, p. 3.

124. Interview with Mr. Stephen D. Bryen, legislative assistant to Sen. Clifford P. Case, Washington, D.C., July 28, 1976.

125. *New York Times*, Sept. 17, 1975, p. 3.

126. Constantine, *op. cit.*, p. 33.

127. *Ibid.*, also interview with Hon. Jonathan B. Bingham (D–N.Y.), Washington, D.C., June 13, 1978.

128. Interview with Mr. Michael Van Dusen, Staff Consultant, U.S. House of Representatives Committee on International Relations, Washington, D.C., July 25, 1976.

129. In October 1974, Foreign Minister Gromyko warned Secretary Kissinger that if the understanding on liberalized Soviet emigration were made public and tied to laws giving effect to the U.S.–Soviet Trade Agreement, the Soviet Government would repudiate the understanding. After the understanding, together with various objectionable limitations on credit, was incorporated into law and after a public exchange of correspondence between Senator Jackson and Secretary Kissinger, the Russians repudiated. *See* 19 U.S.C. §2101–2408; PL 93–618, 88 Stat. 1978; 12 U.S.C. §635e; PL 93–646, 88 Stat. 2333, sec. 8; "U.S.S.R.–U.S.: Exchange of Letters Concerning Emigration from the U.S.S.R., October 18–December 18, 1974," XIV *International Legal Materials*, No. 1 (January 1975), Washington, D.C.: for the American Society of International Law, pp. 248–50. *See also* Joseph Albright, "The Pact of Two Henrys," *New York Times Magazine* (January 5, 1975), p. 16ff; and Stanley J. Marcuss, "New Light on the Export-Import Bank," in Paul Marer (ed.), *U.S. Financing of East-West Trade: The Political Economy of Government Credits and the National Interest*, Bloomington: Indiana University Press, 1975, p. 255ff.

130. The Arms Export Control Act of 1968 as amended, 22 U.S.C. §2776; PL 90–629, 82 Stat. 1320; Sec. 36(b)(1). This provision was added by the International Security Assistance and Arms Export Control Act of 1976; H.R. 13680, 90 Stat. 729, approved June 30, 1976.

131. U.S. House of Representatives, "Joint Explanatory Statement of the Committee of Conference," Conference Report on International Security Assistance and Arms Export Control Act of 1976 (S. 2662), *Rept. No. 94–103*, 94th Cong., 2d Sess., April 6, 1976, p. 52.

132. The Arms Export Control Act of 1968 as amended, 22 U.S.C. §2776; PL 90–629, 82 Stat. 1320; Sec. 38(b)(3).

133. *Ibid.*, Sec. 36(b)(1) (A-M).

134. Interview with Mr. Robert M. Mantel, Staff Member of the Subcommittee on Foreign Assistance of the Committee on Foreign Relations, June 24, 1976.

135. International Security Assistance Act of 1978, Sept. 26, 1978, PL 95–384, 92 Stat. 730, Sec. 19 amending Sec. 26 of the Arms Export Control Act, 22 U.S.C. 2766 and 2776.

136. *Ibid.*

137. Interview with Mr. Hans Binnendijk, Professional Staff Member, Senate Foreign Relations Committee, Subcommittee on Foreign Assistance, Washington, D.C., June 9, 1978.

138. The increase was expected to be 30 percent in the first year. Interview with Lt. Col. Carl Lauenstein, Office of Public Affairs, Department of Defense, August 4, 1976.

139. *Congressional Quarterly, Weekly Report*, Sept. 11, 1976, p. 2463.

140. *New York Times*, Feb. 8, 1976, p. 1.

141. *Ibid.*, April 3, 1976, p. 2.

142. It is probable that foreign requests for military sales are now deliberately overstated to permit bargaining with Congress.

143. Foresight by several members was also correct, as they had predicted the fall

of the Shah, which soon occurred and which, in turn, endangered highly sensitive U.S. manufactured equipment sold to his regime.

144. *New York Times*, July 8, 1977, p. A2.

145. The Studds Resolution, H.Con.Res. 275, to disapprove the sale of AWACS is published as Appendix 9 in U.S. House of Representatives, Subcommittees on International Security and Scientific Affairs and on Europe and the Middle East, *Hearings*, "Prospective Sale of Airborne Warning and Control System (AWACS) to Iran," 95th Cong., 1st Sess., June 29 and July 19, 21, 1977, p. 119.

146. *New York Times*, July 16, 1977, p. 34. The Senators who joined Mr. Culver in the resolution to disapprove the sale were Henry L. Bellmon, Republican of Oklahoma; Alan Cranston, Democrat of California; Thomas P. Eagleton, Democrat of Missouri; Patrick J. Leahy, Democrat of Vermont; William Proxmire, Democrat of Wisconsin; Donald W. Riegle, Jr., Democrat of Michigan; and William W. Roth, Jr., Republican of Delaware. Culver is a Democrat from Iowa.

147. *Ibid.*, July 21, 1977, p. A5.

148. Interview with Mr. William Woodward, legislative assistant to Rep. Gerry E. Studds, Washington, D.C., June 21, 1978. See also, *Congressional Quarterly*, "Case Study: Carter and Congress on AWACS," Sept. 3, 1977, pp. 1857–63 at p. 1858.

149. Letter to the President from Senator Hubert H. Humphrey, Washington, D.C., July 27, 1977; unpub.; Letter to the Honorable Hubert H. Humphrey, from the President, Jimmy Carter, The White House, Washington, D.C., July 28, 1977, unpub.

150. *Hearings*, "Sale of AWACS to Iran," *op. cit.*, pp. 86–87.

151. *Ibid.*, pp. 107–8.

152. Statement of Richard W. Guttmann, Director, Procurement and Systems Acquisition Division, General Accounting Office, in *ibid.*, pp. 97–107, at p. 97.

153. *New York Times*, February 19, 1977, p. 4.

154. *Ibid.*, August 27, 1976, p. A10.

155. U.S. House of Representatives, Committee on International Relations, Transmittal No. 78–35, Notice of Proposed Letter of Offer Pursuant to Section 36(b) of the Arms Export Control Act, April 28, 1978, attaching U.S. Defense Security Assistance Agency materials, unpub.

156. *New York Times*, February 28, 1978, p. 2; from a news analysis, "The Mideast Plane Sales Package: How U.S. Decision Was Reached," by Richard Burt.

157. U.S. Department of State, Announcement by the Hon. Cyrus R. Vance, Secretary of State, on Sale of Aircraft to Middle East Countries, February 14, 1978, unpub.

158. *New York Times*, April 27, 1978, p. 3.

159. Interview with Mr. Gordon Kerr, legislative assistant to Rep. Jonathan Bingham, Washington, D.C., June 2, 1978.

160. *New York Times*, April 23, 1978, p. 7.

161. Interview with Sen. Robert C. Byrd (D–W.Va.), Senate Majority Leader, Washington, D.C., June 23, 1978.

162. *New York Times*, April 29, 1978, pp. 1, 11.

163. Interview with Sen. Robert C. Byrd (D–W.Va.), Senate Majority Leader, Washington, D.C., June 23, 1978.

164. Interview with Hon. Benjamin S. Rosenthal (D–N.Y.), Washington, D.C., May 30, 1978.

165. *New York Times*, March 23, 1978, p. 13.

166. U.S. House of Representatives, Committee on International Relations, Trans-

mittal No. 78–35, Notice of Proposed Issuance of Letter of Offer Pursuant to Section 36(b) of the Arms Export Control Act, April 28, 1978, attaching U.S. Defense Security Assistance Agency materials, unpub.

167. *New York Times*, April 25, 1978, p. 3.

168. H.Con.Res. 806, May 2, 1978.

169. Interview with Hon. Benjamin S. Rosenthal (D–N.Y.), Washington, D.C., May 30, 1978.

170. For testimony by the Secretaries of State and Defense before the House Committee *see* U.S. House of Representatives, Committee on International Relations, *Hearings*, "Proposed Aircraft Sales to Israel, Egypt, and Saudi Arabia," 95th Cong., 2d Sess., May 8, 9, 10, and 16, 1978, pp. 33ff. For the letter from Hon. Harold Brown, Secretary of Defense, to Sen. John J. Sparkman, Chairman, Senate Foreign Relations Committee, dated May 9, 1978, U.S. Senate, *Congressional Record*, May 15, 1978, S. 7376–S. 7377. The letter was also addressed to Hon. Clement J. Zablocki, Chairman, House International Relations Committee.

171. For the letter from the President to Sen. John J. Sparkman, Chairman, Senate Foreign Relations Committee, see *ibid*. The letter was also addressed to Hon. Clement J. Zablocki, Chairman, House International Relations Committee.

172. For the vote on S.Con.Res. 86, the resolution of disapproval on certain arms sales to the Middle East, *see* U.S. Senate, *Congressional Record*, May 15, 1978, S. 7446.

173. For Sen. Stevenson's statement, *ibid.*, S. 7418–S. 7419.

174. *New York Times*, August 6, 1977, p. 4.

175. Interview with Mr. Robert A. Flaten, legislative management officer, Department of State, Washington, D.C., June 7, 1978.

176. *New York Times*, February 3, 1978, p. 9.

177. Letter to the Democratic members of Congress, from Hon. Jonathan Bingham and others, November 26, 1976, unpub.

178. Interview with Mr. Gerald Warburg, legislative assistant to Rep. Bingham, Washington, D.C., June 13, 1978; News Release from Rep. Bingham, December 8, 1976, unpub.

179. *New York Times*, January 5, 1977, p. 1.

180. H.R. 6910, "Nuclear Non-Proliferation Policy Act of 1977" (The Administration bill), 95th Cong., 1st Sess., May 4, 1977.

181. H.R. 4409, "Nuclear Antiproliferation Act" (The Bingham bill), 95th Cong., 1st Sess., March 3, 1977; also, S. 897, "Nuclear Non-Proliferation Act of 1977" (The Glenn, Percy, Ribicoff bill), 95th Cong., 1st Sess., March 3, 1977.

182. Nuclear Non-Proliferation Act of 1978, PL 95–242, 22 U.S.C. 3201 of March 10, 1978, Sec. 304(a).

183. *Ibid.*, Sec. 305.

184. *Ibid.*, Sec. 304(a).

185. *Ibid.*

186. *Ibid.*, Sec. 306.

187. *Ibid.*

188. *Ibid.*

189. *Ibid.*, Sec. 401.

190. *See* Letter to Hon. Henry Jackson, Chairman, Senate Committee on Energy and Natural Resources, from Hon. Cyrus Vance, Secretary of State, dated September 12, 1977, and letter to Hon. John Sparkman, Chairman, Senate Committee on Foreign Relations, from Hon. Douglas J. Bennet, Jr., Assistant Secretary for Congressional Relations, dated September 19, 1977, in U.S. Senate, *Rept. No. 94–467,*

"Nuclear Non-Proliferation Act of 1977," 95th Cong., 1st Sess., October 3, 1977, pp. 41–42, pp. 59–60, respectively.

191. *New York Times*, September 20, 1977, p. 40.

192. *See* U.S. House of Representatives, *Congressional Record*, February 9, 1978, H. 908–H. 919 and *ibid.*, February 16, 1978, E 683.

193. *Presidential Papers*, The Administration of Jimmy Carter, 1978, March 10, 1978, pp. 500–502.

194. The White House, Executive Order: Export of Special Nuclear Material to India, April 27, 1978.

195. U.S. House of Representatives, Committee on International Relations, H. Doc. No. 95–327, "Message from the President of the United States: Export of Special Nuclear Material to India," April 27, 1978, p. 1.

196. U.S. House of Representatives, Committee on International Relations, *Rept. No. 95–1314. Adverse Report*, "Proposed Export of Low-Enriched Uranium to India," 95th Cong., 2d Sess., June 21, 1978, p. 2.

197. *Ibid.*, p. 2.

198. Statement of Hon. Joseph S. Nye, Senate Foreign Relations Committee, May 24, 1978.

199. Letter to the President, Jimmy Carter, from Sen. John Sparkman, Chairman, Senate Foreign Relations Committee, Washington, D.C., June 21, 1978, unpub.

200. U.S. Senate, Committee on Foreign Relations, Subcommittee on Arms Control, Oceans and International Environment, *Hearings*, "Proposed Export of Enriched Nuclear Fuel to India for Tarapur Reactor," May 24, 1978 (Stenographic Transcript), pp. 76–77.

201. Letter to the President, Jimmy Carter, from Sen. John Sparkman, Chairman, Senate Foreign Relations Committee, Washington, D.C., June 21, 1978, unpub. But for a negative Indian reaction, *see* T. T. Poulose, "Atomic Colonialism," *Bulletin of the Atomic Scientists* (October 1978), pp. 58–60.

202. David Calleo, "Of Atoms and Allies," in the *New York Times*, June 18, 1978, Part V, p. 19; Enrico Jacchia, "Bridging the Nuclear Rift," in *International Herald Tribune*, July 15–16, 1978, p. 4.

203. *Ibid.*, July 11, 1978, p. 1.

204. *New York Times*, June 29, 1978, p. 5.

CHAPTER 5

1. Lyman B. Kirkpatrick, Jr., *The U.S. Intelligence Community: Foreign Policy and Domestic Activities*, New York: Hill and Wang, 1973, pp. 59–60; U.S. Senate, Committee on Foreign Relations, "Background Information on the Committee on Foreign Relations," 3rd rev. ed., 94th Cong., 1st Sess., May 1975, p. 8; henceforth "Background Information on the Committee on Foreign Relations."

2. Kirkpatrick, *op. cit.*, p. 60.

3. 50 U.S.C. §§403a–403j (1970); for a fuller description of Congressional budgetary oversight of intelligence agencies, *see* Robin B. Schwartzman, "Fiscal Oversight of the Central Intelligence Agency: Can Accountability and Confidentiality Coexist?" 7 *New York University School of Law Journal of International Law and Politics* (1974), 493–544.

4. *Ibid.*, §403f.

5. Stanley Bach, "Congressional Oversight of Intelligence Activities," Preliminary Draft, June 24, 1976, mimeo., p. 4.

6. The National Security Act of 1947, 50 U.S.C. §430, and The Central Intelligence Agency Act of 1949, 50 U.S.C. §403.

7. Bach, *op. cit.*, p. 11.

8. *Ibid.*, pp. 11–12.

9. PL 86–36 (1959), 73 Stat. 63 §6, amending the Classification Act. 5 U.S.C. 1082 (1949), §202.

10. U.S. Senate, *Rept. No. 94–755, Foreign and Military Intelligence*, Select Committee To Study Governmental Operations (Intelligence Activities) (The Church Committee), 94th Cong., 2d Sess., April 26, 1976; henceforth referred to as *The Church Committee Report*.

11. 22 U.S.C. 2422; PL 93–559, 88 Stat. 1795, Sec. 32. The Foreign Assistance Act of 1961 as amended, §662.

12. The Foreign Assistance Act, as amended; PL 87–195, 75 Stat. 424, Sec. 662(a).

13. *Ibid.*, Sec. 662(b).

14. U.S. Senate, *Congressional Record*, December 3, 1974, S. 37822; U.S. House of Representatives, *Rept. No. 93–1610*, Conference Report on Foreign Assistance Act of 1974 (S. 3394), 93rd Cong., 2d Sess., December 17, 1974, pp. 42–43.

15. For the Abourezk Amendment, U.S. Senate, *Congressional Record*, October 2, 1974, S. 33477.

16. *The Church Committee Report*, pp. 425–26.

17. S.Res. 21, January 27, 1975, and H.Res. 138, February 19, 1975.

18. H.Res. 591, July 17, 1975.

19. Interview with Hon. Les Aspin (D–Wis.), Washington, D.C., August 6, 1976.

20. U.S. House of Representatives, *Congressional Record*, February 19, 1976, H. 1179.

21. *Ibid.*

22. *Ibid.*

23. R.C.A., I.T.T., W.U.I.

24. U.S. Senate, Select Committee To Study Governmental Operations with Respect to Intelligence Activities, "Intelligence Activities: Mail Opening," *Hearings*, Vol. 4, October 21, 22, and 24, 1975, 94th Cong., 1st Sess., Washington, D.C., 1976.

25. U.S. Senate, Select Committee To Study Governmental Operations with Respect to Intelligence Activities, "Alleged Assassination Plots Involving Foreign Leaders," November 20, 1975, *S. Rept. No. 94–465*, 94th Cong., 1st Sess., Washington, D.C.

26. U.S. Senate, Select Committee To Study Governmental Operations with Respect to Intelligence Activities, "Covert Action in Chile 1963–1973," *Staff Report*, 94th Cong., 1st Sess., Washington, D.C., 1975. For testimony and other documents related to covert action in Chile, *see* U.S. Senate, Select Committee To Study Governmental Operations with Respect to Intelligence Activities, "Covert Action," *Hearings*, Vol. 7, December 4 and 5, 1975, 94th Cong., 1st Sess., Washington, D.C., 1976.

27. U.S. Senate, Select Committee To Study Government Operations with Respect to Intelligence Activities, "Intelligence Activities: The National Security Agency and Fourth Amendment Rights," *Hearings*, Vol. 5, October 29 and November 6, 1975, 94th Cong., 1st Sess., Washington, D.C., 1976.

28. U.S. House, Select Committee on Intelligence, "U.S. Intelligence Agencies and Activities: The Performance of the Intelligence Community," *Hearings*, Part 2, September and October 1975, 94th Cong., 1st Sess., Washington, D.C., 1975.

29. *Ibid.* Also, U.S. Senate, Select Committee To Study Governmental Operations with Respect to Intelligence Activities, "Unauthorized Storage of Toxic Agents," *Hearings,* Vol. 1, September 16, 17, 18, 1975, Washington, D.C., 1976.

30. *The Church Committee Report,* pp. 425–26.

31. U.S. Senate, S. 2893, 94th Cong., 2d Sess., January 29, 1976.

32. U.S. Senate, Senate Resolution 400, 94th Cong., 2d Sess., March 1, 1976, Sec. 2.

33. Interview with F. A. O. Schwarz, Jr., formerly Chief Counsel, The Senate Select Committee To Study Governmental Operations (Intelligence Activities), New York City, July 29, 1976.

34. U.S. Senate, S. 2893, Sec. 13(c), *op. cit.* n. 31.

35. Interview with Mr. David Aaron, formerly Task Force Leader, Senate Select Committee To Study Governmental Operations (Intelligence Activities) and currently Deputy National Security Adviser, Washington, D.C., August 3, 1976.

36. U.S. Senate, Senate Resolution 400, Sec. 11(a), *op. cit.* n. 32.

37. U.S. Senate, *Congressional Record,* May 12, 1976, S. 7088.

38. *Ibid.,* May 13, S. 7261.

39. U.S. Senate, Committee on Governmental Operations, *Hearings,* "Oversight of U.S. Government Intelligence Function," 94th Cong., 2d Sess., 1976, p. 20.

40. *Ibid.,* p. 33.

41. *Ibid.,* p. 305.

42. U.S. Senate, Senate Resolution 400, Sec. 8, *op. cit.* n. 32.

43. *Ibid.,* Sec. 8(a).

44. *Gravel v. United States,* 408 U.S. 606 (1972).

45. *Hearings, op. cit.* n. 39, at p. 305.

46. U.S. Senate, Senate Resolution 400, Sec. 6, *op. cit.* n. 32.

47. Interview with Sen. Daniel K. Inouye (D–Hawaii), Washington, D.C., August 6, 1976.

48. *Ibid.*

49. *Ibid.*

50. *Ibid.*

51. *Ibid.*

52. *Ibid.*

53. *Ibid.*

54. H.Res. 1042, *ibid.,* H. 1178–79.

55. U.S. House of Representatives, Committee on Standards of Official Conduct, "Investigation of Publication of Select Committee on Intelligence Report," *Hearings,* 94th Cong., 2d Sess., July and September, 1976.

56. U.S. House of Representatives, Select Committee on Intelligence, Recommendations of the Final Report Pursuant to H.Res. 591, *Rept. No.* 94–833, 94th Cong., 2d Sess., February 11, 1976, p. 1.

57. H.Res. 1258, 94th Cong., 2d Sess., June 4, 1976.

58. H.Res. 335, 95th Cong., 1st Sess., February 24, 1977.

59. *New York Times,* July 15, 1977, p. 21.

60. *Washington Post,* July 15, 1977, p. A3.

61. H.Res. 658, 95th Cong., 1st Sess., July 14, 1977.

62. *Ibid.,* Sec. 2.

63. *Ibid.,* Sec. 1.

64. *Ibid.,* Sec. 2 amending House Rule XLVIII.

65. *Ibid.*

66. U.S. House of Representatives, Permanent Select Committee on Intelligence, *Rules of Procedure* (March 1978, rev.), p. 4.

67. For a critique of Executive Order 12036, *see* Center for National Security Studies, *Report*, "Comparison of Proposals for Reforming the Intelligence Agencies," August 1978, pp. 1ff.

68. S. 2525, A Bill To Improve the Intelligence System of the United States. . . . 95th Cong., 2d Sess., February 9, 1978.

69. *Washington Post*, June 16, 1978, p. A14.

70. *New York Times*, January 23, 1978, p. 21.

71. Foreign Intelligence Surveillance Act, S. 1566, passed by Congress, October 12, 1978.

72. Interview with Mr. Elliot Maxwell, Staff Member of the Senate Permanent Select Committee on Intelligence Oversight, Washington, D.C., August 5, 1976.

73. Interview with Mr. John Clarke, formerly Deputy Director, Central Intelligence Agency, and at the time of interview, Vice President for Planning, AMTRAK, Washington, D.C., August 5, 1976.

74. U.S. Senate, *Congressional Record*, May 12, 1976, S. 7097.

75. *Ibid.*, May 13, 1976, S. 7256.

76. *New York Times*, July 30, 1975, p. 3.

77. *International Herald Tribune*, July 12, 1978, p. 3; *New York Times*, February 25, 1977, p. 9.

78. U.S. House of Representatives, Permanent Select Committee on Intelligence, *Rules of Procedure* (March 1978, rev.), pp. 6–7.

79. *New York Times*, June 17, 1978, p. 10.

80. *Ibid.*, June 10, 1978, p. 1.

81. U.S. Senate, Temporary Select Committee To Study the Senate Committee Systems, *Second Report*, "Operation of the Senate Committee Systems . . . ," 1977, p. 13.

82. An Act To Amend the Federal Insecticide, Fungicide, and Rodenticide Act, PL 95–396, Sept. 30, 1978, 92 Stat. 819, Sec. 15, amending 7 U.S.C. 136a.

83. Interview with Mr. David Aaron, Deputy National Security Adviser, Washington, D.C., August 3, 1976.

84. *New York Times*, November 13, 1978, p. 3.

85. *Ibid.*, November 23, 1978, p. 23.

86. *Ibid.*, May 16, 1977, p. 1.

87. U.S. Senate, Permanent Select Committee on Intelligence, Press Release, May 3, 1977.

88. *Ibid.*

89. *Ibid.*

90. *New York Times*, February 26, 1977, p. 1.

91. U.S. Senate, Permanent Select Committee on Intelligence, Press Release, May 3, 1977.

92. *New York Times*, June 1, 1978, p. 2.

93. A Letter to the Editor from Hon. Birch Bayh, Chairman, U.S. Senate, Permanent Select Committee on Intelligence, June 5, 1978, in *ibid.*, June 9, 1978, p. 26.

94. A Letter to the Editor from Hon. Edward P. Boland, Chairman, U.S. House, Permanent Select Committee on Intelligence, June 1, 1978, in *ibid.*, June 8, 1978, p. 38.

95. *Ibid.*, April 1, 1977, p. 1.

96. *Ibid.*, April 28, 1977, p. 17.

97. *Ibid.*

98. *Ibid.*, November 23, 1978, p. 1.

99. *Ibid.*, p. 6.

100. *Ibid.*

CHAPTER 6

1. Article II, Sec. 2, of the U.S. Constitution.

2. Max Farrand, *The Records of the Federal Convention of 1787*, Vol. II, New Haven: Yale Univ. Press, 1967, p. 183.

3. John M. Mathews, *The Conduct of American Foreign Relations*, New York: The Century Co., 1922, p. 133.

4. *The Federalist*, Number 64. Alexander Hamilton et al., Benjamin C. Wright, ed., Cambridge, Mass.: Harvard Univ. Press, 1961.

5. C.F. Adams, ed., *John Adams, Works*, Vol. III, Boston: Little and Brown, 1851, p. 409.

6. Charles C. Tansill, "The Treaty-Making Powers of the Senate," 18 *American Journal of International Law* (1924), p. 459 at p. 464.

7. E. S. Maclay, ed., *Journal of William Maclay*, New York: D. Appleton, 1890, pp. 128–32.

8. Tansill, *op. cit.*, p. 466.

9. U.S. Senate, *Executive Journal*, Vol. I, pp. 36–37, 42.

10. Tansill, *op. cit.*, p. 468, citing Mss. Jefferson Papers, Vol. 73.

11. *Ibid.* Citing: *Writings of Thomas Jefferson* (Ford ed., N.Y. 1892–98), Vol. V, p. 442; *see also* U.S. Senate, *Executive Journal*, Vol. I, pp. 106, 115.

12. Tansill, *op. cit.*, p. 468, citing Mss. Jefferson Papers, Vol. 73.

13. *Ibid.*

14. U.S. Senate, *Executive Journal*, Vol. I, pp. 186–87.

15. Monroe to Madison, June 3 and October 3, 1804, in U.S., Department of State, American State Papers, *Foreign Relations*, Vol. III, pp. 92–94, pp. 98–99; cited in George H. Haynes, *The Senate of the United States*, Vol. II, Boston: Houghton Mifflin, 1938, pp. 611–12.

16. Allan Nevins, *Henry White*, New York: Harper & Brothers, 1931, pp. 150–51.

17. Henry Cabot Lodge, ed., Selections from the *Correspondence of Theodore Roosevelt and Henry Cabot Lodge*, 1925, Vol. II, p. 111.

18. W. R. Thayer, *Life and Letters of John Hay*, Boston: Houghton Mifflin Co., 1915, Vol. II, p. 393.

19. U.S. Senate Document, No. 476, 62d Cong., 2d Sess., August 3, 1911.

20. J. W. Garner, *American Foreign Policies*, New York: New York Univ. Press, 1928, p. 160.

21. U.S. Senate, *Executive Journal*, Vol. IV, pp. 97–99.

22. Richard W. Leopold, *The Growth of American Foreign Policy: A History*, New York: Alfred A. Knopf, 1964, p. 83.

23. U.S. Senate, *Executive Journal*, Vol. VII, pp. 84–85.

24. Appendix to the *Congressional Globe*, Vol. XV, 1846, 29th Cong., 1st Sess., 1168–69.

25. Olney to Henry White, May 14, 1897. Ms. Olney Papers. Quote in W. Stutt Holt, *Treaties Defeated by the Senate*, Baltimore: The Johns Hopkins University Press, 1933, p. 159.

26. C. H. McLaughlin, "The Scope of the Treaty Power in the United States," 43 *Minnesota Law Review* (1958–1959), p. 651; Elmer Plischke, *Conduct of American Diplomacy*, New York: Van Nostrand, 1950, p. 288; Royden J. Dangerfield, *In Defense of the Senate: A Study in Treaty Making*, Norman, Okla.: Univ. of Oklahoma Press, 1933, p. 152.

27. Holt, *op. cit.*, p. 180.

28. *New York Sun*, March 8, 1927, p. 23.

29. Haynes, *op. cit.*, p. 696.

30. *Ibid.*

31. Haynes, *op. cit.*, p. 180.

32. President Washington, on April 19, 1794, appointed Chief Justice John Jay to be envoy extraordinary to Great Britain and empowered him to negotiate the treaty that bears his name. He remained Chief Justice during the entire term of his special mission to London. The third federal Chief Justice, Oliver Ellsworth, was appointed envoy extraordinary to France by President John Adams on February 26, 1799, successfully negotiating the convention of peace, commerce, and navigation of September 30, 1800. Ellsworth, too, did not resign the office of Chief Justice until after the making of this treaty. Chief Justice John Marshall, the fourth chief justice of the United States, was confirmed in the chief justiceship on January 27, 1801, but continued to act as Secretary of State for the last month of the Adams Administration. President Jefferson continued the latter appointment "until a successor shall be appointed." U.S. Senate, *Congressional Record*, March 2, 1905, S. 3849.

33. American Historical Association, *Papers of J. A. Bayard* (1915), p. 221; James Hopkins, ed., *The Papers of Henry Clay*, Lexington: University of Kentucky Press, 1959, p. 856.

34. U.S. Senate, *Congressional Record*, March 2, 1905, S. 3850.

35. Haynes, *op. cit.*, p. 597.

36. U.S. Senate, *Congressional Record*, March 2, 1905, S. 3850.

37. *Ibid.*; also, James Ford Rhodes, *McKinley and Roosevelt Administrations*, New York: Macmillan, 1922, p. 259. The five members were Sen. Charles W. Fairbanks of Indiana, Sen. George Gray of Delaware, and Rep. Nelson Dingley of Maine; later, after vacancies occurred, Sen. Charles J. Faulkner of West Virginia and Rep. Sereno E. Payne of New York received appointments.

38. *Ibid.*, Sen. Shelby M. Cullom of Illinois, Sen. John J. Morgan of Alabama, and Rep. Robert R. Hitt of Illinois.

39. U.S. Senate, *Congressional Record*, February 26, 1903, S. 2695; *see also* Denna Frank Fleming, *The Treaty Veto of the American Senate*, New York: G. P. Putnam's Sons, 1930, p. 28.

40. George F. Hoar, *Autobiography of Seventy Years*, Vol. II. New York: Charles Scribner's Sons, 1903, pp. 49–50.

41. Haynes, *op. cit.*, p. 597.

42. *Ibid.*; U.S. Senate, *Congressional Record*, February 26, 1903, S. 2698.

43. *Ibid.*

44. Hoar, *op. cit.*, p. 50.

45. Peace Commissioners to Mr. Hay, Telegram, Paris, October 25, 1898, *ibid.*, pp. 313–14.

46. The sole exception appears to be Roosevelt's appointment of Senator Lodge, in 1903, to the tribunal to delimit the boundary between Alaska and Canada. U.S. Senate, *Congressional Record*, March 2, 1905, S. 3850.

47. Haynes, *op. cit.*, p. 704.

48. Denna Frank Fleming, *The United States and World Organization 1920–1933*, New York: Columbia University Press, 1938, p. 48.

49. *Ibid.*, pp. 87–88.

50. Thomas H. Buckley, *The United States and the Washington Conference, 1921–1922*, Knoxville: University of Tennessee Press, 1938, p. 176.

51. John Chalmers Vinson, *The Parchment Peace: The United States Senate and the Washington Conference, 1921–1922*, Athens: University of Georgia Press, 1937, p. 119.

52. U.S. Senate, *Congressional Record*, March 21, 1922, S. 4190. *Ibid.*, March 22, 1922, S. 4242.

53. PL 67–139, Appendix A, *ibid.*, April 11, 1922, S. 5260.

54. U.S. Senate, *Congressional Record*, February 22, 1922, S. 2893; *ibid.*, February 23, 1922, S. 2928; *ibid.*, February 24, 1922, S. 2991.

55. *Ibid.*, February 23, 1922, S. 2928.

56. *Ibid.*, April 11, 1922, S. 5257.

57. *Ibid.*

58. Haynes, *op. cit.*, p. 184.

59. Of the 200 instances of participation by members of Congress in regular sessions of assemblies and congresses of international organizations, the majority, 122, attended in the capacity of "Congressional Advisers" while 78 attended as delegates. Although these meetings, for the most part, are less important than the negotiating conferences intended to lead to the establishment of new organizaions and the writing of treaties, this is not always apparent from the seniority of the participants. The U.S. delegation to the first session of the General Assembly of the United Nations consisted of five Representatives, three of whom were members of Congress: Sens. Tom Connally and Arthur Vandenberg, respectively chairman and ranking minority member of the Senate Foreign Relations Committee, and Rep. Sol Bloom, chairman of the House Committee on Foreign Affairs. Two more Congressional members of the Foreign Affairs Committee, Reps. Charles A. Eaton and Helen Gahagan Douglas, were Alternate Representatives. The current practice is that two Senators are appointed U.S. representatives to the U.N. General Assembly during even-numbered years, with two members of the House named in odd-numbered ones.

60. Among these conferences were the General Disarmament Conference of 1932; the International Monetary and Economic Conference of 1933; the Bretton Woods Monetary and Financial Conference of 1944; the Conference To Establish an International Civil Aviation Organization of 1944; the Bermuda Meeting To Consider the Refugee Problem, 1943; the Inter-American Conference on Problems of War and Peace; the San Francisco Conference of 1945 (United Nations Conference on International Organization); the Paris Conference of 1946; the Rio Inter-American Conference for the Maintenance of Continental Peace and Security of 1947; the United Nations Conference on Trade and Employment held at Havana from November 1947 to March 1948 to create an International Trade Organization; the Conference on International High Frequency Broadcasting of 1949; the 1951 Peace Conference with Japan in San Francisco; the Conference on Migration (Brussels, 1951); the Diplomatic Conference on International Air Law held in Rome, 1952; the 1952 Geneva Conference on International Copyright; the Manila Conference of 1954; the International Conference on the Peaceful Uses of Atomic Energy of 1955; and the Conference on Antarctica held in Washington, D.C., in 1959.

61. Senators with important committee posts who attended as regular delegates include Key Pittman (International Monetary and Economic Conference); Charles Tobey and Robert Wagner, senior minority member and chairman, respectively, of the Committee on Banking and Currency, who attended the Bretton Woods Conference; Owen Brewster, member of the Committee on Commerce, who participated in the International Civil Aviation Conference that led to the creation of ICAO. Sens. Tom Connally and Arthur H. Vandenberg, together with Reps. Sol Bloom and Charles A. Eaton, chairman and ranking minority members of the respective international affairs committees of the two chambers, were leading delegates to the San Francisco Conference that established the U.N., while a delegation of six U.S. Senators attended the San Francisco Conference that concluded the peace treaty

with Japan in 1951 (Sens. Tom Connally, Alexander Wiley, John J. Sparkman, H. Alexander Smith, Walter F. George, Bourke B. Hickenlooper, together with Reps. James P. Richards and Robert B. Chipperfield). The Manila Conference of 1954 was attended by three full delegates of whom two were Senators: H. Alexander Smith and Mike J. Mansfield. The Conference on Peaceful Uses of Atomic Energy, the following year, was attended by four Senators and four Representatives as "Congressional Advisers." The negotiations for an Antarctica treaty (1959) were attended by Sens. Frank Carlson and Gale W. McGee, again as "Congressional Advisers."

62. Joint Resolution To Implement the United States Proposal for the Early Warning System in Sinai. PL 94–110, 94th Cong., H.J.Res. 683, Oct. 13, 1975. For the U.S. Proposal on an Early Warning System, an integral part of the Agreement between Egypt and Israel, see 14 *International Legal Materials* 1455. The Agreement between Egypt and Israel of Sept. 4, 1975, to which the United States is not a party, is published as U.N. Security Council Doc. S/11818/Add. 1 of Sept. 2, 1975, and reproduced in 14 *International Legal Materials*, at 1450.

63. U.S. Senate, *Congressional Record*, Oct. 9, 1975, S. 17957–65.

64. The Opinion of Senate Counsel is reproduced in 14 *International Legal Materials* 1585 (1975).

65. 3 U.S.T. 3947; T.I.A.S. 2529; 177 U.N.T.S. 133.

66. 3 U.S.T. 3420; T.I.A.S. 2493; 131 U.N.T.S. 83.

67. 5 U.S.T. 2368; T.I.A.S. 3097; 238 U.N.T.S. 199.

68. *New York Times*, October 1, 1975, p. 14.

69. H.J.Res. 683; PL 94–110, Oct. 13, 1975; *ibid*.

70. *Ibid*.

71. *Ibid*.

72. France: August 27 and September 3 and 9, 1784. Exchange of Notes Referring to Articles 2 and 3 of the Treaty of Amity and Commerce with France of February 6, 1778. 2 Miller, *Treaties and Other International Agreements of the United States of America*, 1936, p. 158, and W. McClure, *International Executive Agreements*, New York: Columbia University Press, 1941, pp. 37–38.

73. 1 Stat. 236.

74. Hon. Monroe Leigh in U.S. House of Representatives, Committee on International Relations, Subcommittee on International Security, *Hearings*, "Congressional Review of International Agreements," 94th Cong., 2d Sess., June, July 1976, pp. 164–65.

75. 3 Stat. 217, 218 (1815).

76. McClure, *op. cit.*, p. 49.

77. 2 *Annals of Congress: Debates and Proceedings*, 1488; Abraham D. Sofaer, *War, Foreign Affairs and Constitutional Power: The Origins*, Cambridge, Mass.: Ballinger Publishing Co., 1976, p. 35.

78. Leopold, *op. cit.*, p. 90.

79. *New York Times*, February 24, 1979, p. 4; *id*. February 25, 1979, p. 7.

80. Monroe Leigh, *op. cit.* n. 74, p. 165.

81. Spain: August 11, 1802. Convention for Indemnification, signed at Madrid, August 11, 1802. Submitted to the Senate January 11, 1803. Resolution of advice and consent January 9, 1804. Ratified by the United States, January 9, 1804. Ratified by Spain, July 9, 1818. Ratifications exchanged at Washington, December 21, 1818. Proclaimed December 22, 1818, 2 Miller, *op. cit.*, p. 492; *see also* France: April 30, 1803, Convention for the Payment of Sums Due by France to Citizens of the United States, *id.*, p. 516.

82. Great Britain: May 12, 1813. Cartel for the Exchange of Prisoners of War. *Ibid.*, pp. 557–73.

83. *United States v. Belmont*, 301 U.S. 324 (1937), *United States v. Pink*, 315 U.S. 203 (1942).

84. Leopold, *op. cit.*, p. 566.

85. Senator Sam Ervin in United States, Committee on the Judiciary, Subcommittee on Separation of Powers, *Hearings*, "Congressional Oversight of Executive Agreements" (S. 3475), 92d Cong., 2d Sess., April, May 1972, p. 3.

86. For a discussion of 20th Century Executive Agreement practice, *see* John Norton Moore, "Executive Agreements and Congressional Executive Relations," in U.S. House of Representatives, Committee on International Relations, Subcommittee on International Security, *Hearings*, "Congressional Review of International Agreements," 94th Cong., 2d Sess., June, July 1976, pp. 207–19.

87. "United States Memoranda on the Middle East Agreements" in XIV *International Legal Materials*, No. 6, Washington, D.C.: The American Society of International Law (November 1975), p. 1585 at p. 1586.

88. James A. Robinson, *Congress and Foreign Policy-Making*, rev. ed., Homewood, Ill.: Dorsey Press, 1967, p. 42.

89. Richard E. Neustadt, *Presidential Power: The Politics of Leadership*, New York: John Wiley and Sons, 1960, pp. 52–53.

90. Robinson, *op. cit.*, p. 43.

91. Heindel, Kalynari, and Wilcox, "The North Atlantic Treaty in the U.S. Senate," 43 *American Journal of International Law* (1949), p. 661.

92. *Congressional Record*, July 6, 1949, S. 9071.

93. Field Staff Report to the Temporary Select Committee To Study the Senate Committee System, July 1976, p. 27.

94. Trade Act of 1974, 19 U.S.C. §2211(a), Supp. V 1975.

95. Interview with Mr. Robert Cassidy, Staff Consultant, Senate Finance Committee, Washington, D.C., June 6, 1978.

96. Letter to Hon. Thomas P. O'Neill, Jr., Speaker of the House of Representatives, from Hon. Paul C. Warnke, Director, United States Arms Control and Disarmament Agency, May 9, 1977, unpub.

97. Interview with Hon. Thomas Downey (D–N.Y.), Washington, D.C., June 16, 1978.

98. *Ibid.*

99. PL 92–403; 86 Stat. 619, August 22, 1972; 1 U.S.C. 112 (Case-Zablocki Act).

100. U.S. House of Representatives, Foreign Affairs Committee, *H. Rept. No. 92–1301* to accompany S. 596, 92d Cong., 2d Sess., August 3, 1972, p. 3068.

101. *Ibid.*, p. 3069.

102. *Ibid.*, p. 3070.

103. United States, General Accounting Office, *Report* of the Comptroller General of the United States, "U.S. Agreements with the Republic of Korea," February 20, 1976.

104. 2 U.S.C. 112b.

105. A bill to provide for Congressional review of international executive agreements which create a national commitment. H.R. 4438, 94th Cong., 1st Sess., sec. 3(b); PL 92–404, 86 Stat. 619, approved August 22, 1972, "Transmittal of International Agreements."

106. *Ibid.*, sec. 6(a).

107. S.Res. 486, 94th Cong., 2d Sess., July 1, 1976, reprinted in U.S. Senate

Committee on Foreign Relations, *Hearings*, "S.Res. 486," 94th Cong., 2d Sess., July 1976, pp. 3–6, espec. secs. 4(a)(1), (b)(1), and (b)(2).

108. U.S. Senate, *Congressional Record*, July 2, 1976, S. 11588.

109. For the failure of the Clark resolution *see* S.Res. 24, 95th Congress incorporated in Foreign Relations Authorization Act, Fiscal Year 1979 (S. 3076) as Sec. 502; *see also* S.Res. 536, 95th Cong., 2d Sess., August 9, 1978, and U.S. Senate, "International Agreements Consultation Resolution," *S.Rept. No. 95–1171*, 95th Cong., 2d Sess., August 25, 1978, accompanying S.Res. 536. The resolution was deleted in conference, then reintroduced as a non-binding one-House resolution, but not passed.

110. Letter from Hon. John Sparkman, Chairman, Senate Foreign Relations Committee, to Hon. Douglas J. Bennet, Jr., Assistant Secretary for Congressional Relations, July 28, 1978, Washington, D.C., in *ibid.*, S. *Rept. No. 95–1171*, pp. 2–3.

111. Letter from Hon. Douglas J. Bennet, Jr., Assistant Secretary for Congressional Relations, to Hon. John Sparkman, Chairman, Senate Foreign Relations Committee, *ibid.*, p. 3.

112. *Op. cit.* n. 109.

113. *Op. cit.* n. 110.

114. Circular 175 Procedures, 11 *Foreign Affairs Manual*, Chapter 700 (October 25, 1974), as reprinted in U.S. House of Representatives, Committee on International Relations, *Hearings*, *op. cit.* n. 74, pp. 392–93.

115. Arms Control and Disarmament Act, as amended, PL 87–297, 75 Stat. 631, approved September 26, 1961, Sec. 33, 22 U.S.C. 2573.

116. U.S. Senate, "Concurrence of the Congress with Respect to Presidential Action Affecting the Limitation of Strategic Armaments," *S.Rept. No. 95–499*, 95th Cong., 1st Sess., October 17, 1977, Hon. John Sparkman to Hon Cyrus R. Vance, Washington, D.C., July 22, 1977, p. 4.

117. Hon. Cyrus R. Vance to Hon. John Sparkman, Washington, D.C., September 13, 1977, *ibid.*, S. *Rept. No. 95–499*, p. 5.

118. The Department of State statement of September 23, 1977, declared, "In order to maintain the status quo while SALT II negotiations are being completed, the United States declares it intention not to take any action inconsistent with the provisions of the Interim Agreement on Certain Measures with Respect to the Limitation of Strategic Offensive Arms which expires October 3, 1977, and with the goals of these on-going negotiations provided that the Soviet Union exercises similar restraint." *Ibid.*, S. *Rept. No. 95–499*, p. 1; the Soviet unilateral statement is printed, p. 8.

119. *New York Times*, September 23, 1977, p. 1.

120. *Ibid.*, September 27, 1977, p. 38.

121. U.S. Senate, *Congressional Record*, October 3, 1977, S. 16129.

122. *Ibid.*, S. 16129–S. 16130.

123. *Ibid.*, S. 16130.

124. Senator Sparkman indicated that the State Department had consulted the Senate Foreign Relations Committee; *op. cit.* n. 110. As to whether a unilateral declaration is binding in international law, *see* Nuclear Tests (*Australia v. France*), Judgment of December 20, 1974 [1974] ICJ 253; Nuclear Tests (*New Zealand v. France*), Judgment of December 20, 1974 [1974] ICJ 457; *see also* Thomas M. Franck, "Word Made Law: The Decision of the ICJ in the Nuclear Test Cases," 69 *The American Journal of International Law*, No. 3 (July 1975).

125. *New York Times*, September 27, 1977, p. 6.

126. S.Con.Res. 47, September 30, 1977, 95th Cong., 1st Sess.

127. U.S. Senate, *Congressional Record*, October 3, 1977, S. 16136.

128 *Ibid.*, S. 16139.

129. *Ibid.*

130. *Ibid.*

131. *Ibid.*, S. 16140.

132. *Ibid.*

133. *Ibid.*, S. 16141.

134. *Ibid.*, S. 16142. For subsequent failed efforts to pass a resolution on this subject *see* S.Con.Res. 56, October 20, 1977, 95th Cong., 1st Sess.

CHAPTER 7

1. *United States v. Curtiss-Wright Export Corp.*, 299 U.S. 304 (1936).

2. For an outline of Sutherland's views written prior to his tenure on the Court, see his statement published in U.S. Senate, S. Doc. 417, 61st Cong., 2d Sess. (1910).

3. Elliot Richardson, Statement, April 3, 1973, United States, House of Representatives, Committee on Appropriations, Subcommittee on Department of Defense, *Hearings*, 93rd Cong., 1st Sess., p. 153. Statement by Rep. Donald W. Riegle, Jr. (D–Mich.), before the Senate Appropriations Committee, May 8, 1973; in U.S. House of Representatives, Committee on Foreign Affairs Subcommittee on Asian and Pacific Affairs, *Hearings*, May, June 1973, 93rd Cong., 1st Sess., U.S. Policy and Programs in Cambodia, p. 36.

4. International Security Assistance Act of 1978, PL 95–348, Sept. 26, 1978, §26(a) and (b).

5. U.S. Senate, *Congressional Record*, May 29, 1973, S. 17131.

CHAPTER 8

1. Interview with Hon. Clement J. Zablocki (D–Wis.), Washington, D.C., July 22, 1976. The authors wish to acknowledge the kind assistance of Mr. Paul Bernstein and Mr. Bruce Lerner, formerly of Harpur College, in the preparation of this chapter.

2. *New York Times*, October 9, 1977, Part V, p. 15.

3. Lester W. Milbrath, *The Washington Lobbyist*, Chicago: Rand McNally, 1963, pp. 266–70.

4. *New York Times*, February 5, 1977, p. 16.

5. *Ibid.*, April 5, 1977, p. 12.

6. *Ibid.*

7. *Ibid.*, July 11, 1977, p. 1.

8. *Ibid.*, December 2, 1976, p. 21.

9. *Ibid.*, December 6, 1976, p. 15.

10. *Ibid.*

11. *Ibid.*

12. *Ibid.*

13. *Ibid.*

14. *Ibid.*

15. *Ibid.*

16. *Ibid.*, April 27, 1977, p. A1.

17. *Ibid.*, October 15, 1976, p. A1.

18. *Ibid.*, November 7, 1976, p. 3.

19. *Washington Post,* June 8, 1976, p. A4.

20. *Ibid.,* November 13, 1976, p. A1.

21. *Ibid.,* p. A6.

22. *Ibid.,* August 23, 1976, p. A1.

23. *Ibid.,* p. A10.

24. *Ibid.*

25. *New York Times,* December 9, 1977, p. 13.

26. *Ibid.*

27. U.S. Criminal Code, Title 18, §613.

28. U.S. Constitution, Article I, Section 9.

29. *Washington Post,* January 28, 1976, p. A1.

30. *Ibid.,* October 15, 1976, p. A6.

31. *Ibid.,* February 19, 1976, p. A1.

32. *Ibid.,* February 29, 1976, p. A2.

33. *Ibid.,* October 26, 1976, p. A4.

34. *New York Times,* November 9, 1976, p. 1; *Washington Post,* November 27, 1976, p. A1.

35. *Washington Post,* November 28, 1976, p. A1.

36. *Ibid.*

37. *New York Times,* December 12, 1976, p. 38.

38. *Ibid.,* July 11, 1977, p. 1.

39. *Ibid.,* November 3, 1976, p. 4.

40. 2 U.S.C. §441(e).

41. *New York Times,* November 30, 1977, pp. 1, 23.

42. *Washington Star,* May 24, 1978, p. A1.

43. *Washington Post,* June 23, 1978, pp. A1, A4; *New York Times,* June 1, 1978, p. 16.

44. The other three were Reps. Charles H. Wilson (D–Cal.), Edward R. Roybal (D–Cal.), and Edward J. Patten (D–N.J.).

45. *New York Times,* April 4, 1978, p. C8.

46. *Ibid.,* April 9, 1978, pp. 1, 23.

47. *International Herald Tribune,* July 29–30, 1978, p. 3.

48. John Stuart Mill, *Utilitarianism, On Liberty, and Considerations on Representative Government,* H.B. Action, ed., London: J.M. Dent and Sons Ltd., 1976, pp. 239–40.

49. Hope Eastman, *Lobbying: A Constitutionally Protected Right,* Washington, D.C.: American Enterprise Institute for Public Policy Research, 1977, p. 5.

50. Public Utility Holding Company Act of 1935, 49 Stat. 838, U.S.C. 15 Sec. 79 et seq., Aug. 26, 1935, C687 Title 1, sec. 33.

51. Merchant Marine Acts, 21 Stat. 1008, U.S.C. 46, Sec. 861, et seq.

52. PL 75–583, 52 Stat. 631, of June 8, 1938, as amended, 22 U.S.C. 611–621.

53. PL 79–601 of 1946, 2 U.S.C. §261 et seq.

54. *U.S. v. Rumely,* 345 U.S. 41 (1953).

55. *Ibid.,* p. 47. "Surely it cannot be denied that giving the scope to the resolution for which the Government contends, that is, deriving from it the power to inquire into all efforts of private individuals to influence public opinion through books and periodicals, however remote the radiations of influence which they may exert upon the ultimate legislative process, raises doubts of constitutionality in view of the prohibition of the First Amendment." *Id.* at 46.

56. *U.S. v. Harriss,* 347 U.S. 612 at 623–25 (1953).

57. *Id.* at 625.

58. *Id.* at 620.
59. *Ibid.*
60. H.R. 1180, later H.R. 8494, was written by the Subcommittee on Administrative Law and Governmental Relations, chaired by Rep. George Danielson.
61. *New York Times*, April 27, 1978, p. 1.
62. *Congressional Quarterly*, July 29, 1978, p. 1918. *Ibid.*, October 21, 1978, p. 2998. For a Library of Congress study of "Constitutional Disclosures under Proposed Lobbying Act Reforms" see *Congressional Record*, Sept. 7, 1977, S. 14281–84.
63. The Foreign Agents Registration Act of 1938, *op. cit.* n. 52.
64. Russell Warren Howe and Sarah Hays Trott, *The Power Peddlers*, Garden City, N.Y.: Doubleday, 1977, p. 17.
65. U.S. Senate, Committee on Foreign Relations, *The Foreign Agents Registration Act*, 95th Cong., 1st Sess., August 1977, p. 15.
66. Howe and Trott, *op. cit.*, p. 26.
67. An agent is defined as any person or group engaged in political activity, public relations, financial dealings, or government lobbying as agent or representative, in the employ of, or subsidized by, a foreign government. The Foreign Agents Registration Act of 1938, as amended, *op. cit.* n. 52, Sec. 1(c).
68. *Ibid.*, Sec. 1(b). A foreign principal is defined as a foreign government, foreign political party, a non-American outside the United States, an American domiciled outside the U.S., or a group based mainly in another country.
69. *Ibid.*, Sec. 3(a), (b), (c), (d), (e).
70. *Ibid.*, Sec. 3(f).
71. *Ibid.*, Sec. 2.
72. *Washington Post*, April 17, 1977, p. A10.
73. U.S. General Accounting Office, *Report to the Committee on Foreign Relations Effectiveness of the Foreign Agents Registration Act of 1938, as amended, and Its Administration by the Department of Justice*, Washington, D.C., 1974.
74. *Ibid.*, p. 2.
75. 18 U.S.C., §613.
76. The Federal Election Campaign Act of 1971, 2 U.S.C., §441(e).
77. Foreign Agents Registration Act, *Attorney General of the U.S. v. Covington and Burling*, 411 F. Supp. 371 (1976).
78. Federal Election Campaign Act of 1971, 2 U.S.C. §431ff, espec. §434.
79. *Buckley v. Valeo*, 424 U.S. 1 at 64.
80. *Id.* at 68.
81. *Buckley v. Valeo*, 519 F.2d 817 at 870 (D.C. Cir. 1975).
82. *Ibid.*, at 873.
83. 2 U.S.C. §441a(a)(1)(A), (3).
84. 2 U.S.C. §441a(a)(2)(A).
85. 2 U.S.C. §441a(a)(1)(B), (C).
86. *New York Times*, November 7, 1978, p. 27.
87. *Ibid.*, March 13, 1977, Part IV, p. 2.
88. Democrats received 63 percent of PAC contributions in the 1978 Congressional campaign and all but $400,000 of the $6 million contributed by the larger donors, the labor unions. Business PAC's split their support almost equally between the two parties, tending to favor incumbents.
89. *New York Times*, March 13, 1977, Part IV, p. 2.
90. *Ibid.*
91. See the article entitled, "Rep. Flood Had Secret Ties to Haiti While Pushing U.S. Aid to Duvalier," in *New York Times*, February 5, 1978, p. 1; the story alleges

that Rep. Daniel Flood (D–Pa.) "was acting as an agent of the Haitian Government" in violation of FARA.

92. *Congressional Quarterly*, April 16, 1977, pp. 695–705 at p. 700.

93. "After 30 Years, Arab Cause Gets a Hearing," *U.S. News & World Report*, March 27, 1978, p. 26.

94. *New York Times*, March 31, 1978, p. 4, and May 12, 1978.

95. *Ibid.*, April 30, 1978, Part V, p. 4.

96. See *The Washington Lobby*, Washington, D.C.: Congressional Quarterly Inc., 1974, p. 94, and *Washington Post*, July 18, 1976, p. L3.

97. *New York Times*, April 30, 1978, Part V, p. 4.

98. *Washington Post*, May 7, 1978, p. A14.

99. *International Herald Tribune*, August 26–27, 1978, p. 3.

100. *New York Times*, April 30, 1978, Part V, p. 4.

101. 4 *Annals of Congress*, Senate, April, 1794, 88, and 6 *Annals of Congress*, Senate, January 1796, 32–36.

102. *Ibid.*, p. 32.

103. King Hussein's letter is reprinted in U.S. Senate, *Congressional Record*, September 9, 1975, S. 15593.

104. Interview with Mr. Michael Van Dusen, Staff Director, House International Relations Committee, Subcommittee on Europe and the Middle East, Washington, D.C., July 25, 1976.

105. U.S. House of Representatives, *Congressional Record*, September 1, 1975, H. 8344.

106. Interview with Mr. John J. Brady, Chief of Staff, House International Relations Committee, Washington, D.C., June 15, 1978.

107. Interview with Ms. Elizabeth Mary Daoust, Staff Coordinator for Protocol, House International Relations, Washington, D.C., June 12, 1978.

108. Quoted in the *New York Times*, March 16, 1978, p. 16.

109. *Ibid.*, April 28, 1978, p. 27. The observer was James Reston.

110. Interview with Ms. Pauline Baker, Senate Foreign Relations Committee Staff, November 8, 1978.

111. *International Herald Tribune*, July 12, 1978, p. 3.

112. *New York Times*, June 21, 1978, p. 11.

113. *Ibid.*, February 12, 1978, p. 1.

114. *Ibid.*, June 27, 1977, p. 10.

115. Interview with Mr. Stephen D. Bryen, legislative assistant to Sen. Clifford P. Case, Washington, D.C., July 28, 1976.

116. Robert H. Trice, *Interest Groups and the Foreign Policy Process: U.S. Policy in the Middle East*, Sage Professional Papers in International Studies, Beverly Hills, Cal.: Sage Publications, 1976, p. 54.

117. *New York Times*, August 8, 1975, p. 2.

118. Interview with Mr. Morris Amitay, Director, American-Israeli Public Affairs Committee, Washington, D.C., July 7, 1976.

119. William M. Constantine, "The Hawk Controversy: The Proposed Sales of Air Defense Systems to Jordan," The National War College, April 1976, unpub., pp. 1–2.

120. Interview with Mr. Stephen D. Bryen, legislative assistant to Sen. Clifford P. Case, Washington, D.C., July 28, 1976.

121. Interview with Mr. Michael Van Dusen, Staff Director, House International Relations Committee, Subcommittee on Europe and the Middle East, Washington, D.C., July 25, 1976.

122. Joseph Albright, "The Pact of Two Henrys," *New York Times*, January 5, 1975, Sec. V, p. 16 at p. 17.

123. *Ibid.*, p. 30.

124. *Ibid.*, p. 31.

125. Statement of Sen. Gravel, U.S. Senate, *Congressional Record*, May 15, 1978, S. 7396–S. 7397.

126. Elizabeth Drew, "A Reporter at Large," *The New Yorker*, September 18, 1978, p. 119.

127. Interview with Mr. Les Janka, Senior Staff Member for Congressional Relations and Public Affairs, National Security Council, Washington, D.C., June 10, 1976.

128. *Ibid.*

129. Jacob M. Landau, "Johnson's 1964 Letter to Inonu and The Greek Lobbying at the White House," *Ankara: The Turkish Yearbook of International Relations*, 1974, p. 45 at p. 50; *see also* B. C. Rosen, "Race, Ethnicity and the Achievement Syndrome," XXIV *American Sociological Review*, No. 1 (February 1959), pp. 47–60; James W. Vander Zanden, *American Minority Relations: The Sociology of Race and Ethnic Groups* (2d ed.), N.Y.: The Ronald Press, 1966, pp. 292–93.

130. Landau, *op. cit.*, p. 51.

131. *Ibid.*, p. 46.

132. U.S. Senate, *Congressional Record*, September 30, 1974, S. 17760.

133. U.S. House of Representatives, *Congressional Record*, July 24, 1975, H. 7410–11.

134. Howe and Trott, *op. cit.*, pp. 452–59.

135. Interview with Hon. Benjamin Rosenthal (D–N.Y.), Washington, D.C., July 21, 1976.

136. Interview with Hon. Carlyle Maw, former Undersecretary of State for International Security Assistance, Washington, D.C., July 21, 1976.

137. "The gang of four" consists of Sens. Eagleton and Sarbanes, Reps. Brademas and Rosenthal. See the *Washington Post*, June 20, 1978, p. A7.

138. U.S. House of Representatives, Committee on International Relations, *Hearings*, Authorization of Appropriations for the Board of International Broadcasting and Partial Lifting of the Turkish Arms Embargo, 94th Cong., 1st Sess., September 17, 1975, pp. 4–6.

139. *Washington Post*, June 2, 1978, p. A9.

140. *Time*, Vol. 112, No. 6, August 7, 1978, p. 19.

141. *New York Times*, December 13, 1977, p. 16.

142. *Op. cit.* n. 140, p. 21; for slightly different estimations of these figures *see* Howe and Trott, *op. cit.*, p. 527.

143. *Ibid.*

144. Howe and Trott, *op. cit.*, p. 231.

145. *New York Times*, January 15, 1978, Part III, pp. 1, 5; from an article entitled, "Steel Industry Wins Friends and Influences People."

146. U.S. House of Representatives, Committee on Merchant Marine and Fisheries, Subcommittee on Fisheries and Wildlife Conservation and the Environment, *Hearings*, "Fisheries Jurisdiction," 94th Cong., 1st Sess., March 1975, *passim*.

147. H.R. 200, 94th Cong., 2d Sess.

148. H.R. 1270, H.R. 6017, 94th Cong., 1st Sess., H.R. 11879, 94th Cong., 2d Sess.

149. The growers demanded a 17-cent-a-pound minimum domestic price, well above the support floor provided under the international agreement.

150. *Washington Post*, June 23, 1978, p. A8.

151. *New York Times*, October 10, 1977, p. 19.

152. *Ibid.*, October 20, 1975, p. 52; from an article entitled, "Arms Lobby Allies on Varied Sources, Including Liberals Seeking To Protect Workers Jobs."

153. *Ibid.*, November 11, 1977, p. 1; December 7, 1977, p. 17. See also *The Washington Monthly*, October, 1978, p. 9.

154. Interview with Hon. Thomas Downey (D–N.Y.), Washington, D.C., June 16, 1978.

155. Statement of Mr. Richard A. Frank, U.S. House of Representatives, Committee on Merchant Marine and Fisheries, Subcommittee on Oceanography, *Hearings*, "Deep Seabed Mining," 94th Cong., Serial No. 94–27, May 1975, February and March 1976, p. 535.

156. William Languette, "The Panama Canal Treaties: Playing in Peoria and in the Senate," *National Journal*, October 8, 1977, p. 1560.

157. Don Campbell, "Canal Treaty Foes Trust in Mail," *The Sunday Press and Bulletin*, September 11, 1977, p. 2D.

158. Terry Smith, "Reagan, Connally and Baker Open a Broad Attack on Administration," *New York Times*, November 19, 1977, p. 10.

159. Warren Brown, "Drawing Battle Lines on the Canal Issue," *Washington Post*, August 22, 1977, p. A5.

160. Languette, *op. cit.*, p. 1560.

161. U.S. House of Representatives, Committee on Merchant Marine and Fisheries, Subcommittee on the Panama Canal, *Hearings*, "Panama Canal Finances," 94th Cong., 2d Sess., April 1976, p. 278.

162. *New York Times*, October 25, 1977, p. 3; *see also* Jack Anderson, *Washington Post*, November 2, 1977, p. A17.

163. *Washington Post*, December 12, 1976, p. B1; from an article entitled, "The Growing Lobby for Human Rights."

164. "A Time for New Directions," from unpublished materials printed by and for New Directions, Washington, D.C.

165. Interview with Hon. Charles W. Whalen, Jr. (R–Ohio), Washington, D.C., June 26, 1978.

166. Nancy Turk, "The Arab Boycott of Israel," Vol. 55, *Foreign Affairs*, No. 3 (April 1977), pp. 484–85; see also *National Journal*, January 29, 1977, p. 164; *Congressional Quarterly*, March 12, 1977, p. 435; Robert J. Samuelson, "As the Oil Flows So Flows the Trade," *National Journal*, January 29, 1977, p. 161.

167. Interview with Mr. David Morrison, Office of Assistant Secretary of State for Economic Affairs, Washington, D.C., October 14, 1977.

168. Interview with Mr. Julien Spirer, legislative assistant to Rep. B. Rosenthal, Washington, D.C., October 18, 1977.

169. Interview with Mr. Ira Silverman, American Jewish Committee, Washington, D.C., October 21, 1977.

170. Interview with Mr. Roger Majak, Staff Consultant, House International Relations Committee, October 17, 1977; also, interview with Mr. Kent Nolls, Department of Commerce, October 17, 1977.

171. President Carter, Ford-Carter Debate, October 6, 1976, quoted in U.S. Senate, *Congressional Record*, May 5, 1977, S. 7156.

172. Interview with Mr. Julien Spirer, legislative assistant to Rep. B. Rosenthal, Washington, D.C., October 18, 1977.

173. S. 69 and S. 92 can be found in U.S. Senate, Subcommittee on International Finance of the Committee on Banking, Housing, and Urban Affairs, *Hearings*,

"Arab Boycott," 95th Cong., 1st Sess., February and March 1977, pp. 5–75; henceforth *Hearings: Arab Boycott*. H.R. 1561 was introduced on January 10, 1977, 95th Cong., 1st Sess., and was referred to as the "Export Administration Amendments of 1977."

174. Alfred H. Moses, "Battling the Boycott: The Achievement of Federal Legislation, 1977," for the American Jewish Committee, September 1977, unpub., p. 3.

175. *New York Times*, August 21, 1977, Sec. III, p. 1.

176. *Ibid.*

177. *Ibid.*

178. Moses, *op. cit.*, p. 4.

179. Joint Statement of Principles Regarding Foreign Boycott Legislation in *Hearings: Arab Boycott*, pp. 476–80.

180. *Ibid.*, p. 478.

181. *Ibid.*

182. *Ibid.*, p. 479.

183. *Ibid.*

184. *U.S. News & World Report*, June 20, 1977, p. 64.

185. Mr. Alfred Moses, Chairman, Domestic Affairs Commission, American Jewish Committee, before U.S. House of Representatives, Committee on International Relations, *Hearings*, "Extension of the Export Administration Act of 1969," 95th Cong., 1st Sess., March 8, 1977, p. 79 at p. 81.

186. *Ibid.*, p. 90.

187. *Ibid.*, p. 91.

188. Letter from Mr. Irving S. Shapiro to Hon. Adlai E. Stevenson III, March 10, 1977, in *Hearings: Arab Boycott*, pp. 464–65.

189. *Ibid.*, pp. 481–82.

190. *Ibid.*, p. 482.

191. *Ibid.*, p. 489; see also *New York Times*, August 21, 1977, Sec. III, p. 1.

192. H.R. 5840, 95th Cong., 1st Sess., March 31, 1977.

193. *Id.*, §4A(a)(1).

194. *Id.*, §4A(a)(2)(D).

195. *Ibid.*, §4A(a)(1)(H).

196. *Id.*, §4A(a)(3).

197. *Washington Post*, March 31, 1977, p. A13.

198. *Ibid.*, March 30, 1977, p. D8.

199. The House version, however, prohibited unilateral selection where the U.S. contractor has "actual knowledge" that its intent was solely to implement boycott whereas the Senate version, having no "actual knowledge" test, provided that unilateral selection could not apply if a U.S. person participated in the selecting. The exception for compliance with the laws of the host country was somewhat more narrowly drawn in the Senate version but both bills gave the President discretion to grant limited exceptions for U.S. persons caught between our laws and those of a boycotting country. S. 69, §4A(a)(1)(A), (B), and (C); §4A(a)(2)(C); §4A(a)(2)(F).

200. Moses, *op. cit.* n. 185, p. 10.

201. *New York Times*, August 21, 1977, Sec. III, p. 5.

202. Moses, *op. cit.* n. 185, p. 11.

203. *Ibid.*, pp. 12–13.

204. *New York Times*, April 22, 1977, p. 26.

205. U.S. Senate, *Congressional Record*, May 5, 1977, S. 7148.

206. U.S. House of Representatives, *Conference Report To Accompany H.R.*

5840, "Export Administration Amendments of 1977," *Rept. No. 95–354,* 95th Cong., 1st Sess., May 18, 1977; henceforth *Conference Report HR 5840.*

207. Moses, *op. cit.* n. 185, p. 14.

208. *New York Times,* August 21, 1977, Sec. III, p. 5.

209. *Conference Report HR 5840,* p. 26.

210. U.S. Senate, *Congressional Record,* May 5, 1977, S. 7151.

211. *Ibid.,* S. 7152.

212. *Ibid.*

213. Interview with Mr. William A. Reinsch, legislative assistant to Sen. Heinz, Washington, D.C., June 15, 1978.

214. U.S. Senate, *Congressional Record,* May 5, 1977, S. 7190.

CHAPTER 9

1. *Washington Post,* August 4, 1978, p. A12.

2. *Ibid.*

3. *New York Times,* August 2, 1978, p. 21; article by Stanley Hoffmann entitled, "A Different World."

4. Foreign Relations Authorization Act, Fiscal Year 1978, of August 17, 1977, PL 95–105, 91 Stat. 844, Sec. 512.

5. U.S. Senate, *Congressional Record,* June 16, 1977, S. 9961.

6. *Ibid.,* S. 9960.

7. *Ibid.*

8. *Ibid.*

9. International Security Assistance Act of 1978, Sept. 26, 1978, PL 95–384, 92 Stat. 730, Sec. 21, 22 U.S.C. 2151 and 22 U.S.C. 2311.

10. James P. Richards, "The House of Representatives in Foreign Affairs," 289 *Annals of the American Academy of Political and Social Science* (September 1953), p. 69.

11. Mr. Charles Weissman, a Harpur College student majoring in political science, kindly and effectively assisted in the research and analysis of these statistics.

12. Randall B. Ripley, "Congressional Party Leadership and the Impact of Congress on Foreign Policy," in Commission on the Organization of the Government for the Conduct of Foreign Policy, *Congress and Executive-Legislative Relations,* Vol. 5, Appendix L (June 1975), p. 48.

13. *Ibid.,* p. 53.

14. *Ibid.,* p. 54.

15. U.S. Senate, Temporary Select Committee To Study the Senate Committee System, "Operation of the Senate Committee System . . . ," *Appendix to the Second Report,* John G. Stewart, "Committee System Management: Getting the Act Together—The Senate Leadership's Role in the Policy Process," 1977, p. 7 at p. 9; henceforth "Committee System Management."

16. *Ibid.,* pp. 9–10.

17. *Ibid.,* pp. 10–11.

18. *Ibid.,* pp. 12–13.

19. *Ibid.,* p. 11.

20. *Ibid.,* p. 13.

21. *See* Nelson W. Polsby, "Goodbye to the Senate's Inner Club," in Norman J. Ornstein, ed., *Congress in Change: Evolution and Reform,* New York: Praeger Publishers, 1975, p. 208 at pp. 212–13.

22. Committee System Management," pp. 16–17.

23. *Ibid.*, p. 17.

24. Interviews with Hon. Jonathan B. Bingham (D–N.Y.), Washington, D.C., June 16, 1978, and Mr. Hoyt Purvis, Staff Consultant on Foreign Relations, Senate Democratic Policy Committee, Washington, D.C., June 20, 1978; Rep. Bingham is a member of the Steering and Policy Committee of the House Democrat Majority caucus.

25. George B. Galloway, "Development of the Committee System in the House of Representatives," LXV *The American Historical Review*, No. 1 (October 1959), p. 17; *see also* p. 17, n. 1.

26. Joseph Cooper, "Jeffersonian Attitudes Toward Executive Leadership and Committee Development in the House of Representatives, 1789–1829," XVIII *The Western Political Quarterly*, No. 1 (March 1965), p. 45.

27. George Goodwin, Jr., *The Little Legislatures: Committees of Congress*, Amherst: University of Massachusetts Press, 1970, p. 4.

28. U.S. House of Representatives, Select Committee on Committees, *Report 93–916, Part II*, "Committee Reform Amendments of 1974 to accompany H.Res. 988," 93d Cong., 2d Sess., March 21, 1974, p. 9. Henceforth referred to as the *Bolling Committee Report, Part II*.

29. Goodwin, *op. cit.*, p. 10.

30. *Bolling Committee Report, Part II*, pp. 10–11.

31. *Ibid.*

32. *Ibid.*

33. Rule X, The Committees and Their Jurisdiction, in U.S. *Rules of the House of Representatives*, 94th Cong., 2d Sess., House Document No. 416, §669–691. *See also* H.Res. 988, 93d Cong., January 3, 1975. The House Permanent Select Committee on Aging does not have legislative jurisdiction but does have oversight jurisdiction, *ibid.*, §702(g).

34. Charles B. Brownson, *1977 Congressional Staff Directory*, Mount Vernon, Va.: Congressional Staff Directory, 1977.

35. Goodwin, *op. cit.*, p. 11.

36. U.S. Senate, Temporary Select Committee To Study the Senate Committee System, *First Staff Report*, "The Senate Committee System, Jurisdictions, Referrals, Numbers and Sizes, and Limitations on Membership," 94th Cong., 2d Sess., July 1976, p. 5; henceforth *The Stevenson Committee Staff Report*.

37. Goodwin, *op. cit.*, pp. 11–12.

38. *The Stevenson Committee Staff Report*, p. 5.

39. *Ibid.*, p. 6.

40. *Ibid.*

41. S.Res. 4, "Committee System Reorganization Amendments of 1977," 95th Cong., 1st Sess., February 4, 1977.

42. Nelson Polsby, "The Institutionalization of the U.S. House of Representatives," *American Political Science Review* (March 1968), p. 144 at pp. 153–56; *see also* William L. Morrow, *Congressional Committees*, New York: Charles Scribner's Sons, 1969, pp. 14–15.

43. *Ibid.*

44. John W. Baker, ed., *Clem Miller: Member of The House—Letters of a Congressman*, New York: Charles Scribner's Sons, 1962, p. 110.

45. Woodrow Wilson, *Congressional Government: A Study in American Government*, New York: Meridian Books, 1956, p. 66.

46. For example, on February 9, 1943, the House authorized the Committee on Appropriations "to examine into any and all allegations or charges that certain persons in the employ of the several executive departments and other executive

agencies are unfit to continue in such employment by reason of their present association or membership or past association or membership in or with organizations whose aims or purposes are or have been subversive to the Government of the United States." (Arthur W. Macmahon, "Congressional Oversight of Administration: The Power of the Purse I," LVIII *Political Science Quarterly*, No. 2 [June 1943], p. 166; *see also* U.S. House of Representatives, *Congressional Record*, 78th Cong., 1st Sess., H.Res. 105, H. 780.)

47. The Appropriations Committees had already tried to use their bills to prevent the employment of specified individuals. (*Ibid.*)

48. *Ibid.*, p. 167.

49. Dennison, *op. cit.*, p. 4.

50. *Ibid.*

51. *Ibid.*, p. 6.

52. Gary Orfield, *Congressional Power: Congress and Social Change*, New York: Harcourt Brace Jovanovich, 1975, p. 263.

53. Nicholas A. Masters, "Committee Assignments in the House of Representatives," 55 *American Political Science Review*, No. 2 (June 1961), p. 346.

54. *Ibid.*

55. David W. Rohde and Kenneth A. Shepsle, "Democratic Committee Assignments in the House of Representatives: Strategic Aspects of a Social Choice Process," 67 *American Political Science Review*, No. 3 (September 1973), p. 890.

56. Masters, *op. cit.*, p. 348.

57. *Ibid.*

58. Barbara Hinckley, *The Seniority System in Congress*, Bloomington: Indiana University Press, 1971, p. 86.

59. *Ibid.*, p. 89.

60. Randall B. Ripley, "Congressional Party Leadership and the Impact of Congress on Foreign Policy," in Commission on the Organization of the Government for the Conduct of Foreign Policy, *Congress and Executive-Legislative Relations*, Vol. 5, Appendix L (June 1975), pp. 48–49.

61. S.Res. 9 of 1975.

62. "Committee System Management," p. 16.

63. S.Res. 4, *op. cit.* n. 41.

64. Interview with Sen. Robert C. Byrd (D–W.Va.), Senate Majority Leader, Washington, D.C., June 23, 1978.

CHAPTER 10

1. Louis Henkin, " 'A More Effective System' for Foreign Relations: The Constitutional Framework," in Commission on the Organization of the Government for the Conduct of Foreign Policy, *Congress and Executive-Legislative Relations*, Vol. 5, Appendix L (June 1975), p. 9 at p. 11.

2. Rudolph Robert Rousseau, "Factors Affecting Decisions of the United States Senate on Bilateral and Multilateral Foreign Assistance Legislation, 1965 to 1974," Ph.D. dissertation, Fletcher School of Law and Diplomacy, January 1976, p. 361.

3. R. Roger Majak, "Report of a Staff Survey of Congressional Views on the Organization of Government Conduct of Foreign Policy," in Commission on the Organization of the Government for the Conduct of Foreign Policy, *Congress and Executive-Legislative Relations*, Vol. 5, Appendix L (June 1975), p. 121 at p. 123.

4. Richard Bolling, "The Management of Congress," 35 *Public Administration Review* (Sept./Oct. 1975), pp. 490–94, at p. 492.

5. U.S. Senate, Commission on the Operation of the Senate, *Final Report*, "Toward a Modern Senate," S.Doc. No. 94–278, 94th Cong., 2d Sess., December, 1976.

6. J. Leiper Freeman, *The Political Process: Executive Bureau–Legislative Committee Relations*, rev. ed., New York: Random House, 1965, p. 111.

7. Although these figures include clerical help, they primarily reflect an increase in professional specialists on members' staffs and on the staffs of committees. For an analysis of the staff explosion *see* Graham Allison and Peter Szanton, *Remaking Foreign Policy: The Organizational Connection*, New York: Basic Books, 1976, p. 101. Allison and Szanton's statistical data should be compared with Harrison W. Fox, Jr., and Susan Webb Hammond, *Congressional Staffs: The Invisible Force in American Lawmaking*, New York: The Free Press, 1977, p. 3. Fox and Hammond indicate that "The Legislative branch in 1976 employed over 38,000 persons, including 3,000 on committees, about 10,000 on personal staffs of Senators and Representatives, and 17,900 in supporting agencies. . . ." For fuller discussion, *see* David E. Price, "Professionals and 'Entrepreneurs': Staff Orientations and Policy Making on Three Senate Committees," 33 *Journal of Politics* (May 1971), pp. 316–33; Michael J. Malkin, "Congressional Committee Staffs: Who's in Charge Here?," *The Public Interest*, No. 47 (Spring 1977), pp. 16–40; Michael Andrew Scully, "Reflections of a Senate Aide," *The Public Interest*, No. 47 (Spring 1977), pp. 41–48; Warren H. Butler, "Administering Congress: The Role of the Staff," 26 *Public Administration Review* (March 1966), pp. 3–12; "Capitol Hill Staffs: Hidden 'Government' in Washington," *U.S. News & World Report* (April 4, 1977), pp. 37–40. *See also* Commission on the Organization of the Government for the Conduct of Foreign Policy, *Report* (June 1975), pp. 212–13. The first comprehensive study of Congressional staffs is Kenneth Kofmehl's *Professional Staffs of Congress*, Lafayette, Ind.: Purdue University Studies, 1962.

8. See Table 3, "Personal and Committee Staff," Fox, Jr., and Hammond, *op. cit.*, p. 171.

9. 1965 figures derive from Warren H. Butler, "Administering Congress: The Role of the Staff," 26 *Public Administration Review* (March 1966), p. 4, n. 4; 1977 figures were derived through computing entries in the 1977 issue of *Congressional Staff Directory*.

10. U.S. Senate, Committee on Rules and Administration, *Senate Manual Containing Standing Rules, Orders, Laws, and Resolutions*, S. Doc. No. 94–1, 94th Cong., 1st Sess., 1975, Rule 25.8; S.Res. 60 was passed, June 12, 1975.

11. *Ibid.*; also, S.Res. 4, "Committee System Reorganization Amendments of 1977," February 4, 1977, 95th Cong., 1st Sess.

12. Interview with Mr. Carl Marcy, former Chief of Staff, Senate Foreign Relations Committee, Washington, D.C., July 21, 1976.

13. *Ibid.*

14. Fox, Jr., and Hammond, *op. cit.*, p. 25.

15. Legislative Reorganization Act of 1946, PL 79–601, 60 Stat. 812, Chap. 753, §202(a).

16. *Ibid.*

17. *Ibid.*, §202(b).

18. *Ibid.*, §202(e).

19. *Ibid.*, §202(g).

20. Legislative Reorganization Act Amendment Act of 1970, PL 91–510, 84 Stat. 1141.

21. *Ibid.*, §301(a)(c), §302(b).

22. U.S. House of Representatives, Select Committee on Committees (the Bolling Committee), *Report To Accompany H.Res. 988*, "Committee Reform Amendments

of 1974," Rept. 93–916, Part II, 93d Cong., 2d Sess., March 21, 1974, pp. 73–74; for a full discussion *see also* Roger H. Davidson and Walter J. Oleszek, *Congress Against Itself*, Bloomington: Indiana University Press, 1977.

23. U.S. House of Representatives, *Congressional Record*, October 8, 1974, H. 34469.

24. U.S. Senate, *Manual, op. cit.* n. 10, Section 275.1 2 U.S.C. §72a.

25. Senate Resolution Authorizing Additional Expenditures by the Committee on Foreign Relations for a study of matters pertaining to the foreign policy of the United States, S.Res. 241, 93d Cong., 2d Sess., as amended by S.Res. 345, 93d Cong., 2d Sess.

26. U.S. Senate, Committee on Foreign Relations, Committee Print, "Background Information on the Committee on Foreign Relations," 3d rev. ed., 94th Cong., 1st Sess., May 1975, p. 48. This number includes professional and clerical staff.

27. U.S. Senate, Temporary Select Committee To Study the Senate Committee System, *Second Report*, "Operation of the Senate Committee System," Committee Print, Washington, D.C., 1977, p. 5; henceforth *Second Report: Operation of the Senate Committee System*.

28. U.S. House of Representatives, *Report of the Clerk of the House*, July 1, 1976, to December 31, 1976, Doc. No. 95–88, 95th Cong., 1st Sess., February 24, 1977, p. 212; updated by U.S. House of Representatives, Committee on International Relations, Print, March 1, 1978, unpub.

29. Interview with Mr. John J. Brady, Chief of Staff, House International Relations Committee, Washington, D.C., June 2, 1978.

30. *Second Report: Operation of the Senate Committee System*, p. 5.

31. U.S. House of Representatives, Committee on International Relations, *Rules*, 95th Cong., 1st Sess., February 3, 1977, p. 5.

32. *Ibid.*

33. U.S. House of Representatives, Commission on Administrative Review (the Obey Commission), *Final Report*, Vol. I, H.Doc. No. 95–272, 95th Cong., 1st Sess., December 31, 1977, p. 699; henceforth, *The Obey Commission Report*.

34. Based on Staff Biographies in *1978 Congressional Staff Directory*.

35. Fox, Jr., and Hammond, *op. cit.*, "Table 8: Education of Staff Professionals," p. 175.

36. *Ibid.*

37. *Ibid.*, p. 47, n. 2.

38. *The Obey Commission Report*, p. 707.

39. *Ibid.*, p. 706.

40. Interview with Mr. David Aaron, then legislative assistant to Sen. Walter Mondale and currently Deputy National Security Adviser, National Security Council, in Washington, D.C., August 3, 1976; also interview with Mr. William Buell, legislative assistant to Sen. Adlai Stevenson III, Washington, D.C., August 6, 1976.

41. For a brief discussion of Foreign Service Officers who have left the Service for work on the Hill, *see* Frederick Poole, "Congress v. Kissinger: The New Equalizers," *Washington Monthly* (May 1975), pp. 23–32.

42. *New York Times*, September 25, 1977, p. F5.

43. Interview with Mr. Les Janka, Senior Staff Member for Congressional Relations and Public Affairs, National Security Council, Washington, D.C., June 25, 1976.

44. Fox, Jr., and Hammond, *op. cit.*, p. 1.

45. Lloyd Hackler, a former Senate Aide and Washington lobbyist for the Ameri-

can Retail Federation, quoted in "Capitol Hill Staffs: Hidden 'Government' in Washington," *U.S. News & World Report* (April 4, 1977), p. 38.

46. Reported in Joseph Albright, "The Pact of Two Henrys," *The New York Times Magazine*, January 5, 1975, pp. 17, 22.

47. Interview with Hon. Thomas Harkin (D–Iowa), Washington, D.C., June 24, 1976.

48. The Senate Staff in 1978 appears to have had only one professional who was an avowed Republican, and, after years of Democratic control, even the staffer serving the minority was believed to be a liberal Democrat. The prevalence of liberals among staffers did not necessarily contradict the claim that staff serves all members, particularly since the senior Republicans then on the Committee—Case, Javits, Percy, Baker—had themselves been relatively liberal on most foreign policy issues.

49. Interview with Mr. William Anderson, Professional Staff Member, Foreign Operations Subcommittee of the House Appropriations Committee, Washington, D.C., June 8, 1978.

50. Interview with Hon. Richard Moose, formerly Staff Director, Senate Foreign Assistance Subcommittee of Foreign Relations Committee, Washington, D.C., July 9, 1976.

51. Michael Andrew Scully, "Reflections of a Senate Aide," *The Public Interest*, No. 47 (Spring 1977), p. 45.

52. Interview with Mr. Janos Michel, Deputy Legal Adviser, the Department of State, Washington, D.C., June 20, 1978.

53. Interview with Hon. Clement J. Zablocki (D–Wis.), Chairman, House International Relations Committee, Washington, D.C., June 15, 1978.

54. David E. Price, "Professionals and 'Entrepreneurs': Staff Orientations and Policy Making on Three Senate Committees," 33 *Journal of Politics* (May 1971), pp. 316–33.

55. Interview with Mr. Pat Holt, formerly Chief of Staff, Senate Foreign Relations Committee, Washington, D.C., June 9, 1976.

56. Price, *op. cit.*, p. 325.

57. For discussion *see* Arthur Schlesinger, "The Role of the President in Foreign Policy," in Commission on the Organization of the Government for the Conduct of Foreign Policy, *Congress and Executive-Legislative Relations*, Vol. 5, Appendix L (June 1975), p. 41.

58. U.S. General Accounting Office, *1977 Annual Report of the Comptroller General of the United States*, Washington, D.C., 1977, p. 8.

59. U.S. General Accounting Office, *The General Accounting Office*, Washington, D.C.: September 1976, p. 8; *see* the *New York Times*, June 25, 1978, Part V, p. 3.

60. Interview with Mr. J. Kenneth Fasick, Director, International Division, General Accounting Office, Washington, D.C., June 22, 1978.

61. *1977 Annual Report of the Comptroller General of the United States, op. cit.* n. 58, pp. 167–76.

62. Interview with Mr. J. Kenneth Fasick, Director, International Division, General Accounting Office, Washington, D.C., June 22, 1978.

63. Fox, Jr., and Hammond, *op. cit.*, p. 131.

64. *Ibid.*

65. *Ibid.*, p. 132.

66. Interviews with Mr. William Whitson, Director, and Dr. Stanley Heginbotham, Deputy Director, Congressional Research Service, Library of Congress, Washington, D.C., June 26, 1978, and June 20, 1978, respectively.

67. *Ibid.*

68. U.S. Senate, Committee on Foreign Relations, and U.S. House of Representatives, Committee on International Relations, Joint Committee Print, *An Analysis of Arms Control Impact Statements Submitted in Connection with the Fiscal Year 1978 Budget Request*, Prepared by the Foreign Affairs and National Defense Division, Congressional Research Service, Library of Congress, 95th Cong., 1st Sess., April 1977.

69. U.S. Senate, Committee on Foreign Relations, the Subcommittee on Foreign Assistance, *Report, Implications of President Carter's Conventional Arms Transfer Policy*, Prepared by Foreign Affairs and National Defense Division, Congressional Research Service, Library of Congress, 95th Cong., 1st Sess., December 1977.

70. U.S. House of Representatives, Subcommittee on Europe and the Middle East, Committee Print, *United States Arms Transfer and Security Assistance Programs*, Prepared by Foreign Affairs and National Defense Division, Congressional Research Service, Library of Congress, 95th Cong., 2d Sess., March 21, 1978.

71. Interview with Mr. Patrick Renehan, Professional Staff Member, Congressional Budget Office, Washington, D.C., June 23, 1978.

72. *Ibid.*

73. U.S. Congressional Budget Office, *Background Paper:* "Force Planning and Budgetary Implications of U.S. Withdrawal from Korea," Washington, D.C. (May 1978), p. 29.

74. U.S. Congressional Budget Office, *Staff Working Paper:* "The Effect of Foreign Military Sales on the U.S. Economy," Washington, D.C., July 23, 1976.

75. Interview with Mr. John J. Brady, Chief of Staff, House International Relations Committee, Washington, D.C., June 21, 1978.

76. U.S. Senate, Committee on Foreign Relations, "160th Anniversary 1816–1976," S. Doc. No. 94–265, 94th Cong., 2d Sess., August 30, 1976, p. 2.

77. James W. Gould, "The Origins of the Senate Committee on Foreign Relations," XII *The Western Political Quarterly*, No. 3 (September 1959), p. 678.

78. Commission on the Organization of the Government for the Conduct of Foreign Policy, *Report*, Washington, D.C., U.S.G.P.O. (June 1975), pp. 205–6; henceforth The Murphy Commission.

79. The Murphy Commission, to some extent, undermined its recommendation by stressing the domestic nature of most foreign policy issues of the future; e.g., *ibid.*, p. 196.

80. Legislative Reorganization Act of 1946, PL 79–601, 60 Stat. 812 (1946).

81. Legislative Reorganization Act of 1970, PL 91–510, 84 Stat. 1140 (1970).

82. U.S. House of Representatives, Select Committee on Committees, "Committee Reform Amendments of 1974, Report To Accompany H.Res. 988," *Rept. 93–916, Part II*, 93d Cong., 2d Sess., March 21, 1974, p. 3.

83. *Ibid.*, p. 38.

84. *Ibid.*

85. *Ibid.*, p. 32.

86. Roger H. Davidson and Walter J. Oleszek, *Congress Against Itself*, Bloomington: Indiana University Press, 1977, p. 180.

87. U.S. House of Representatives, *Rules*, H. Doc. 416, 93d Cong., 2d Sess., 1975, Rule X (K), pp. 368–70. The exception is sugar.

88. U.S. House of Representatives, Select Committee on Committees, "Committee Reform Amendments of 1974, Report To Accompany H. Res. 988," *Rept. 93–916, Part II*, 93d Cong., 2d Sess., March 21, 1974, p. 38.

89. Davidson and Oleszek, *op. cit.*, pp. 183–84.

90. U.S. House of Representatives, *Rules*, H. Doc. 416, 93d Cong., 2d Sess., 1975, Rule X (K), pp. 368–70.

91. Charles B. Brownson, ed., *Congressional Staff Directory, 1976*, Mt. Vernon, Va.: *Congressional Staff Directory*, 1976.

92. U.S. Senate, Temporary Select Committee To Study the Senate Committee System, *First Staff Report*, "Jurisdictions, Referrals, Numbers and Sizes, and Limitations on Membership," 94th Cong., 2d Sess., July 1976, p. 54.

93. U.S. Senate, Temporary Select Committee To Study the Senate Committee System, *First Report*, "Structure of the Senate Committee System: Jurisdictions, Numbers and Sizes, and Limitations on Memberships and Chairmanships, Referral Procedures, and Scheduling," *S. Rept. No. 94–1395*, 94th Cong., 2d Sess., November 15, 1976, p. 200.

94. *Ibid.*, p. 23.

95. *Ibid.*, p. 24.

96. U.S. Senate, Committee on Rules and Administration, *Report*, Committee Systems Reorganization Amendments of 1977, *S. Rept. No. 95–2* (Accompanying S. Res. 4), 95th Cong., 1st Sess., January 25, 1977, pp. 9–10.

97. *Ibid.*

98. Stephen K. Bailey, *Congress in the Seventies*, New York: St. Martin's Press, 1970, p. 59.

99. *Op. cit.* n. 92, pp. 130–34.

100. Richard Spohn and Charles McCollum, *The Revenue Committees: A Study of the House Ways and Means and Senate Finance Committees and the House and Senate Appropriations Committees*, New York: Grossman Publishers/Viking Press, 1975, p. 222.

101. Richard E. Fenno, Jr., *The Power of the Purse: Appropriations Politics in Congress*, Boston: Little, Brown, 1966, p. 271.

102. Holbert N. Carroll, *The House of Representatives and Foreign Affairs*, Pittsburgh: University of Pittsburgh Press, 1958, pp. 141–42.

103. Harris, *op. cit.*, p. 87.

104. U.S. House of Representatives, Committee on Appropriations, *Report*, "Foreign Assistance and Related Programs Appropriation Bill, 1975," *H. Rept. No. 94–53*, 94th Cong., 1st Sess., March 10, 1975, pp. 51–58, "Separate Views of Hon. Clarence D. Long: India: The Strange Case of Wasted Millions"; also, Statement of Hon. Clarence D. Long, Chairman, Subcommittee on Foreign Operations, House Appropriations Committee, before Subcommittee on International Development, Institutions and Finance, before Committee on Banking, Finance and Urban Affairs, March 14, 1978, unpub.

105. *Ibid.*

106. H.R. 12931, 95th Cong., 2d Sess., June 1, 1978.

107. *New York Times*, September 16, 1976, p. 26.

108. Foreign Assistance and Related Programs Appropriations Act, 1977, October 18, 1978, PL 95–481, 92 Stat. 1591, Secs. 610, 611, 22 U.S.C. 2169 and 22 U.S.C. 262d.

109. *Ibid.*

110. Interview with Mr. Keith Mainland, Clerk and Staff Director, House Appropriations Committee, Washington, D.C., June 27, 1978.

111. Letter to Hon. James J. Delaney, Chairman, Committee on Rules from Hon. Clement J. Zablocki, Chairman, Committee on International Relations, U.S. House of Representatives, Washington, D.C., June 16, 1978, unpub.

112. Interview with Hon. Clement J. Zablocki (D–Wis.), Chairman, House International Relations Committee, Washington, D.C., June 15, 1978.

113. Interview with Hon. George H. Mahon (D–Texas), Chairman, House Appropriations Committee, Washington, D.C., June 27, 1978.

114. PL 94–344, the Congressional Budget Act of 1974.

115. The jurisdictional problem described in text is also illustrated by the fact that several committees submitted estimates to the House Budget Committee relating to different aspects of foreign relations; e.g., House Agriculture Committee regarding P.L. 480 funds, House Banking and Currency Committee regarding international financial institutions and the Ex-Im Bank, and the House Appropriations Committee regarding foreign assistance. This, of course, in addition to the House International Relations Committee authorization recommendations. See U.S. House of Representatives Committee on International Relations, *Congress and Foreign Policy, 1976* (1977), pp. 50–53.

116. Memorandum to Members, Subcommittee on Foreign Assistance, Senate Committee on Foreign Relations, from Michael J. Glennon, Legal Counsel, Subject: "Appropriations Provisos Contained in H.R. 4842," dated March 29, 1977, unpub.

117. U.S. Senate, *Congressional Record*, June 14, 1977, S. 9694.

CHAPTER 11

1. George H. Haynes, *The Senate of the United States*, New York: Russell and Russell, 1960, Vol. I, p. 62; also, James A. Robinson, *Congress and Foreign Policy-Making: A Study in Legislative Influence and Initiative*, rev. ed., Homewood, Ill.: The Dorsey Press, 1967, p. 96.

2. E. S. Maclay, ed., *The Journal of William Maclay*, New York: D. Appleton, 1890, pp. 125–30. *See* Abraham D. Sofaer, *War, Foreign Affairs and Constitutional Power: The Origins*, Cambridge, Mass.: Ballinger Publishing Co., 1976, pp. 95–96.

3. Eleanor E. Dennison, *The Senate Foreign Relations Committee*, Stanford, Cal.: Stanford University Press, 1942, p. 23; also, Haynes, *op. cit.*, II, p. 716.

4. *Ibid.*

5. T. Franck and E. Weisband, "Lapdogs No More," *New York Times*, Nov. 29, 1976, p. L27.

6. Robert Ellsworth Elder, *The Policy Machine: The Department of State and American Foreign Policy*, Syracuse, N.Y.: Syracuse University Press, 1960, p. 93.

7. Graham H. Stuart, *The Department of State*, New York: Macmillan, 1949, p. 275.

8. *U.S. Commission on Organization of the Executive Branch of the Government* (The Hoover Commission), New York: McGraw-Hill Book Company, 1955, p. 131; henceforth *The Hoover Commission*.

9. *Ibid.* Hull was a Senator when President Roosevelt appointed him Secretary of State in 1933.

10. "The Department of State, 1930–1955: Expanding Functions and Responsibilities," 32 *U.S. Department of State Bulletin* (March 28, 1955), p. 531.

11. Joseph C. Rigert, "The Office of the Assistant Secretary of State for Congressional Relations: A Study of an Aspect of Executive Legislative Relations in the Formulation of Foreign Policy," June 1959, Masters Thesis, Georgetown University, p. 14.

12. The Commission on Organization of the Executive Branch of the Government, Task Force Report on Foreign Affairs, Washington, D.C.: U.S.G.P.O., 1949.

13. Estes Kefauver and Jack Levin, *A Twentieth-Century Congress*, New York: Duell, Sloan & Pierce, 1947, p. 150.

14. U.S. House of Representatives, Committee on Foreign Affairs, *Hearings*, "H.R. 3559 To Strengthen and Improve the Organization and Administration of the Department of State," 81st Cong., 1st Sess., 1949, pp. 2–3.

15. *Op. cit.* n. 12, p. 125.

16. Abraham Holtzman, *Legislative Liaison: Executive Leadership in Congress,* Chicago: Rand McNally, 1970, p. 13.

17. *The Hoover Commission,* p. 134.

18. Sanford Watzman, quoting Robert A. Flaten, "Congressional Relations," in Department of State *Newsletter* (April 1978), No. 200, pp. 7–8.

19. U.S. Department of State Criteria for Congressional Consultation on Executive Agreements, Submitted for the Record by Secretary of State William Rogers, U.S. Senate Foreign Relations Committee, *Hearings,* "Fiscal Year 1973 Department of State Appropriations Authorization," March 8, 1972, p. 33.

20. Elder, *op. cit.,* p. 106.

21. *Ibid.,* p. 107. In 1971, the bureau handled approximately 220 telephone inquiries from Congress per day and received almost 19,000 Congressional letters. Statement by David M. Abshire, 67 *U.S. Department of State Bulletin* (July–December 1972), p. 28 at 31.

22. Elder, *op. cit.,* p. 115.

23. Holtzman, *op. cit.,* p. 141.

24. *Ibid.,* p. 142.

25. *Ibid.*

26. U.S. House of Representatives, Committee on Appropriations, Subcommittee on the Departments of State, Justice and Commerce, The Judiciary and Related Agencies, *Hearings,* "Appropriations for 1973," Part 2, 92d Cong., 2d Sess., February 16, 1972, pp. 60–61.

27. U.S. House of Representatives, Committee on Appropriations, Subcommittee on the Departments of State, Justice and Commerce, The Judiciary and Related Agencies, *Hearings,* "Appropriations for 1972," Part 2, 92d Cong., 1st Sess., March 4, 1971, p. 49.

28. Holtzman, *op. cit.,* p. 170.

29. U.S. Senate, Committee on Foreign Relations, *Hearings,* "Panama Canal Treaties," 95th Cong., 1st Sess., Part I, September 26, 1977, p. 88.

30. 77 *U.S. Department of State Bulletin* (September 19, 1977), pp. 376–77.

31. *Op. cit.* n. 29, Part I, pp. 32–33.

32. *Ibid.,* p. 31.

33. *Wall Street Journal,* July 26, 1962, p. 1.

34. *Ibid. See also* Statement by David M. Abshire, 67 *U.S. Department of State Bulletin* (July–December 1972), p. 28 at pp. 31–32.

35. Holtzman, *op. cit.,* p. 187; also Robinson *op. cit.,* pp. 162–63.

36. Among the most effective favors is the ability of a Department to point up "a congressman's ability to induce executive leaders to reverse unfavorable administrative decisions affecting his constituency." Holtzman, *op. cit.,* p. 187.

37. Interview with Hon. Richard Moose, Staff Director, Senate Foreign Relations Subcommittee on Foreign Assistance, and subsequently Assistant Secretary of State for African Affairs, Washington, D.C., July 9, 1976.

38. Commission on the Organization of the Government for the Conduct of Foreign Policy, *Report,* June 27, 1975, Washington, D.C.: U.S.G.P.O., p. 201.

39. Roger Hilsman, "Congressional-Executive Relations and Foreign Policy Consensus," 52 *The American Political Science Review* (1958), p. 725 at p. 737.

40. Interview with Mr. Mark Moran, legislative assistant to Sen. John Tunney, Washington, D.C., June 22, 1976.

41. *Ibid.*

42. *Ibid. See also* Nathaniel Davis, "The Angola Decision of 1975: A Personal Memoir," in 57 *Foreign Affairs,* No. 1 (Fall 1978), pp. 109–24. That the Moran-

Davis meeting took place was confirmed by Davis. Meeting at Princeton, N.J., November 4, 1978.

43. U.S. Senate, Committee on Foreign Affairs, Subcommittee on African Affairs, *Hearings*, "U.S. Involvement in Civil War in Angola," February 3, 1976, Statement of Hon. Robert Ellsworth, pp. 59–87.

44. *Ibid.*, p. 50, Statement of Hon. Henry A. Kissinger.

45. Interview with Mr. Les Janka, Senior Staff Member for Congressional Relations and Public Affairs, National Security Council, Washington, D.C., June 23, 1976.

46. *Ibid.*

47. Interview with Hon. Robert J. McCloskey, Washington, D.C., June 24, 1976.

48. Interview with Mr. Les Janka, Senior Staff Member for Congressional Relations and Public Affairs, National Security Council, Washington, D.C., June 10, 1976.

49. *Washington Post*, June 5, 1978, p. A18.

50. Holtzman, *op. cit.*, p. 15.

51. Rudolph Robert Rousseau, "Factors Affecting Decisions of the United States Senate on Bilateral and Multilateral Foreign Assistance Legislation, 1965–1974," Ph.D. dissertation, Fletcher School of Law and Diplomacy, 1976, p. 363.

52. *Congressional Quarterly*, July 23, 1965, p. 1435.

53. *Ibid.*, April 24, 1976, p. 950.

54. Rousseau, *op. cit.*, p. 366.

55. *Congressional Quarterly*, April 24, 1976, p. 949.

56. For a listing of the roll call votes in which the conservative coalition had a significant part, and especially for a survey of conservative coalition victories, see *Congressional Quarterly Almanac*, Vol. 25, 1969, p. 1052; Vol. 26, 1970, p. 1144; Vol. 27, 1971, p. 84; Vol. 28, 1972, p. 65; Vol. 29, 1973, p. 946; Vol. 30, 1974, p. 991.

57. *Congressional Quarterly*, March 4, 1978, p. 581.

58. *Ibid.*, February 26, 1977, p. 363.

59. Rousseau, *op. cit.*, p. 367.

60. 77 U.S. *Department of State Bulletin* (October 17, 1977), pp. 484–85.

61. Letter of Transmittal in Senate Document S. Ex. N. dated September 16, 1977; also *op. cit.* n. 60, p. 486.

62. *New York Times*, February 3, 1978, p. 8.

63. *Los Angeles Times*, January 19, 1978, p. 18; *Washington Post*, January 10, 1918, p. A14.

64. U.S. Senate, Committee on Foreign Relations, *Report*, "Panama Canal Treaties," *Exec. Rept. No. 95–12*, 95th Cong., 2d Sess., February 3, 1978, Appendix B, Carter-Torrijos Understanding, October 14, 1977, p. 110.

65. *Ibid.*, pp. 110–11.

66. *Op. cit.* n. 63.

67. *New York Times*, January 9, 1978, p. 12.

68. The termination is provided for in Article V of the Treaty Concerning the Permanent Neutrality and Operation of the Canal, *op. cit.* n. 64, p. 218, and the Agreement in Implementation of Article IV of the Panama Canal Treaty, Article XXII, *ibid.*, p. 267.

69. Memorandum to All Members, Norvill Jones, Staff Director, U.S. Senate Foreign Relations Committee, Subject: "Treaty Procedure; Legal Effect of Changes," dated January 12, 1978, unpublished.

70. Interview with Dr. Romano Romani, Staff Director, Subcommittee on Im-

provement in Judicial Machinery, Senate Judiciary Committee, Washington, D.C., June 13, 1978.

71. *Ibid.* The idea was not entirely new. Senator DeConcini had actually introduced a much more innocuous version several months earlier.

72. *See* General Treaty of Friendship and Cooperation Between the United States of America and Panama, signed at Washington, D.C., March 2, 1936, Art. III, para. 6, 53 Stat. 1807, T.S. No. 945.

73. Interview with Hon. Warren Christopher, Deputy Secretary of State, Washington, D.C., June 27, 1978.

74. U.S. Senate, *Congressional Record*, February 9, 1978, S. 1688.

75. Interview with Dr. Romano Romani, Staff Director, Subcommittee on Improvement in Judicial Machinery, Senate Judiciary Committee, Washington, D.C., June 13, 1978.

76. Interview with Mr. Robert Beckel, legislative liaison, The White House, Washington, D.C., June 26, 1978.

77. *New York Times*, March 14, 1978, pp. 1, 7.

78. *Ibid.*, March 19, 1978, p. 17.

79. Interview with Mr. Samuel Goldberg, administrative assistant to Sen. Heinz, Washington, D.C., June 12, 1978.

80. Interview with Dr. Romano Romani, Staff Director, Subcommittee on Improvement in Judicial Machinery, Senate Judiciary Committee, Washington, D.C., June 13, 1978.

81. Interview with Hon. Warren Christopher, Deputy Secretary of State, Washington, D.C., June 27, 1978.

82. Interview with Dr. Romano Romani, Staff Director, Subcommittee on Improvement in Judicial Machinery, Senate Judiciary Committee, Washington, D.C., June 13, 1978.

83. Interview with Sen. Robert C. Byrd (D–W.Va.), Senate Majority Leader, Washington, D.C., June 23, 1978.

84. Interview with Mr. Robert Beckel, legislative liaison, The White House, Washington, D.C., June 26, 1978.

85. *Ibid.*

86. *New York Times*, March 16, 1978, pp. 1, 3.

87. *Congressional Record*, March 16, 1978, S. 3817.

88. Interview with Sen. Robert C. Byrd (D–W.Va.), Senate Majority Leader, Washington, D.C., June 23, 1978.

89. *Ibid.*

90. Interview with Mr. Robert Beckel, legislative liaison, The White House, Washington, D.C., June 26, 1978.

91. Interview with Sen. Robert C. Byrd (D–W.Va.), Senate Majority Leader, Washington, D.C., June 23, 1978.

92. Interview with Hon. Warren Christopher, Deputy Secretary of State, Washington, D.C., June 27, 1978.

93. *New York Times*, April 10, 1978, p. D9.

94. *Ibid.*, April 11, 1978, pp. 1, 9.

95. *Ibid.*, April 12, 1978, p. 1.

96. *Ibid.*

97. *Ibid.*, April 13, 1978, p. 22.

98. Interview with Dr. Romano Romani, Staff Director, Subcommittee on Improvement in Judicial Machinery, Senate Judiciary Committee, June 13, 1978, Washington, D.C.

99. *New York Times,* April 14, 1978, p. 1.

100. Interview with Sen. Robert C. Byrd (D–W.Va.), Senate Majority Leader, Washington, D.C., June 23, 1978.

101. Interview with Mr. Hoyt Purvis, Staff Consultant on Foreign Relations, Senate Democratic Policy Committee, Washington, D.C., June 20, 1978; also the *New York Times,* April 18, 1978, pp. 1, 7.

102. Interview with Sen. Robert C. Byrd (D–W.Va.), Senate Majority Leader, Washington, D.C., June 23, 1978.

103. *New York Times,* April 18, 1978, pp. 1, 7.

104. The other DeConcini resolution denying U.S. liability for any accrued arrears in the year 2000 was passed by a vote of 90 to 2 on April 17. Also passed the same day was the reservation, earlier negotiated by Senator Baker with General Torrijos, which repeals the treaty's mutually exclusive rights and obligations applicable to construction of any new sea-level canal. *Ibid.*

105. *New York Times,* April 19, 1978, p. 16.

106. U.S. Senate, *Congressional Record,* June 5, 1978, S. 8517.

107. Interview with Mr. Robert Beckel, legislative liaison, The White House, Washington, D.C., June 26, 1978.

108. *Washington Post,* October 17, 1978, p. A2.

109. Roland Young, *This Is Congress,* 2d ed., New York: Alfred A. Knopf, 1946, pp. 247–54; Charles S. Hyneman, *Bureaucracy in a Democracy,* New York: Harper & Bros., 1950, pp. 557–79; *see also* Robinson, *op. cit.,* p. 117. A recent discussion of "an advising and consenting" council of state, which again rejects the idea, is found in *Congress, Information and Foreign Affairs,* prepared by the Committee on Foreign Relations by Foreign Affairs and National Defense Division, Congressional Research Service, Library of Congress, September 1978, pp. 102–3, Washington, D.C.

110. Robinson, *op. cit.,* p. 117.

111. *Congress, Information and Foreign Affairs, op. cit.,* p. 97.

112. *New York Times,* December 18, 1978, p. 1; 79 *U.S. Department of State Bulletin* (January 1979), p. 25.

113. U.S. Senate, *Congressional Record,* June 6, 1979, S. 7030–39.

114. *Ibid.,* S. 7058.

115. *New York Times,* April 9, 1979, p. A19.

116. *New York Times,* October 17, 1977, p. A1; November 3, 1977, p. A3; November 14, 1977, p. 16; November 18, 1977, p. A1.

117. Press Conference of June 9, 1978. Transcript: U.S. Senate Office Memorandum, June 12, 1978. Sen. Alan Cranston. Unpub.

118. *New York Times,* April 14, 1979, p. 2.

119. *Ibid.*

120. *SALT II, A Basic Guide,* U.S. Department of State, in SALT II, Reference Guide, Office of the President of the United States, May 1979, p. 6 (limited distribution).

121. Interview with Ms. Madeleine Albright, National Security Council staff, Washington, D.C., June 7, 1979.

122. Richard Burt, "Search for an Invulnerable Missile," *New York Times Magazine,* May 27, 1979, p. 34.

123. *SALT II, A Basic Guide, op. cit.,* p. 4.

INDEX

Aaron, David, 234
Abourezk, James, 31, 85, 87, 88, 117
Abzug, Bella, 23, 27, 69
Action Committee on American-Arab
  Relations, 190–91
Adams, John, 63, 144
Adams, John Q., 139
Addabbo, Joseph, 17, 19, 170
Adee, A. A., 264
Afghanistan, 92
AFL/CIO, 188, 189, 197, 198
Agency for International Development,
  78–79, 86, 94, 239, 252, 263
Agnew, Spiro, 182
Agriculture Department, 93–95, 263
Aid Authorization for Greece and Turkey
  (1947), 78
Airborne Warning and Control System
  (AWACS), 105–6
Airforce Association, 193
Albert, Carl, 21, 26, 31, 44, 166–68
Albertson, Marian, 53
Albright, Madeleine, 241, 291
Allen, James, 153, 212
Allende, Salvadore, 47, 119
Allison, William B., 139
American Arab Association, 108
American Civil Liberties Union, 176
American Conservative Union, 198
Americans for Democratic Action, 188,
  199
American Hellenic Educational Pro-
  gressive Association (AHEPA), 191
American Hellenic Institute, 192

American Iron and Steel Institute, 195
American Israel Public Affairs Committee
  (AIPAC), 187–90, 193, 197, 206, 207
American Jewish Committee, 187, 203
American Jewish Congress, 201, 203
American Legion, 193, 198
American Near East Refugee Aid, 191
American Palestine Committee, 195, 196
Amin, Idi, 91
Amitay, Morris, 187, 188, 189, 193
Angermueller, Hans, 206
Angola and Angolan war, 34, 35, 46, 49,
  51, 71, 91, 93, 110, 118, 130, 157,
  236, 271
Anti-Defamation League (ADL), 187,
  201, 202, 203
Appropriations Committees, 16, 17, 79,
  220, 231, 249–51, 253–56; see also
  House Appropriations Committee;
  Senate Appropriations Committee
Arab boycott, 200–209
Arab League, 200
Argentina, 90, 91, 92, 93, 94, 97, 182
Arms Control and Disarmament Agency,
  112
Arms Export Control Act, 108, 239, 288
Arms Export Control Board, 95
arms sales and exports, 62, 80, 82, 85,
  88, 96, 98–111, 160, 181–85, 196,
  211, 240, 241, 243, 245, 285, 288; see
  also Hawk missile sales; military as-
  sistance
Arthur, Chester, 6
Ash, Roy, 17, 18

347

Aspin, Les, 29, 120, 127, 196
Atomic Energy Act of 1954, 78
Atomic Energy Act Amendments of
  1974, 79
Atwood, Brian, 37, 184, 241, 267
Australia, 142

Babcock and Wilcox Co., 111
Bader, William, 251
Badillo, Herman, 92
Bafalis, L. A., 38
Baker, Howard, Jr., 109, 124, 198, 267,
  282, 283, 289, 292
Bandar, Bin Sultan, 184, 185
Barbour Resolution (1816), 246
Bas v. Tigny, 63, 65
Bay of Pigs invasion, 116, 117
Bayard, James A., 139
Bayh, Birch, 130, 133
Beckel, Robert, 277, 278, 279, 281, 285,
  291
Bechtel Corporation, 182, 203
Begin, Menachem, 185
Bell, Griffin, 77, 81
Bennet, Douglas, Jr., 151, 241, 267
Berger, Paul, 206
Bermuda, 145
Beveridge, Albert, 221
Biaggi, Mario, 37
Biden, Joseph, 26
Bingham, Jonathan, 61, 99, 102, 103,
  107, 111, 113, 184, 201
Black, Hugo, 174, 175
Blumenthal, W. Michael, 207, 277
Boland, Edward P., 127, 133
Bolling, Richard, 227
Bolling Committee and Commission,
  231, 246–47, 250
Bonker, Don L., 51, 105, 168
Borah, William, 138, 213
Boyatt, Thomas B., 120
Boyatt memorandum, 120
Brademas, John, 37, 38, 41–44, 170
Brady, Jack, 232, 246, 251
Brazier, Don R., 17
Brazil, 86, 88, 90, 91, 92, 145
Broomfield, William S., 167
Brown, George, 188, 198
Brown, Harold, 109, 277
Brownell, Herbert, 78
Bryen, Stephen D., 102, 108
Brzezinski, Zbigniew, 277
Buchanan, James, 6
Budget Act (1974), 256
Budget and Accounting Act (1921), 242

Budget Committees, 253–56; *see also*
  House Budget Committee; Senate
  Budget Committee
Budget Office (Congress), 6
Bumpers, Dale, 290
Burt, Richard, 289
Burton, Theodore E., 141
Business Roundtable, 194, 202, 203,
  204, 206, 207
Butler, Pierce, 135
Byrd, Harry, 123
Byrd, Robert C., 74, 107–9, 153, 211,
  212, 216, 225, 275, 278–83, 289, 290,
  292
Byrnes, Jimmy, 264

Caglayangil, Ihsan, 44
Calhoun, John C., 221
Callaghan, James, 36
Cambodia, 13, 14, 23–30, 33, 34, 71,
  73, 74; *see also* Paris peace accord
Cambodian bombing, 14–19, 21, 22, 24,
  29, 158–59
campaign contributions, 171, 172, 177–
  79
Canada, 111, 182
Cannon, Howard, 123, 281
Cannon, Joe, 220
Caramanlis, Konstantin, 36, 37, 182
Carter, Jimmy, 5, 9, 72, 76, 81, 92, 96,
  105, 107, 110, 113–14, 128, 130, 132,
  134, 144, 146, 153–54, 157–58, 184,
  191, 201–3, 277–80, 287–88, 291
Carter, Rosalynn, 277
Carter Administration, 74–75, 81, 85,
  91, 93, 133, 152, 157, 185, 211–12,
  240, 241, 268, 273–76, 278, 281, 282,
  289
Case, Clifford P., 14, 51, 71, 101, 102,
  106, 149, 152
Case Act, executive agreements, 150
Case-Church Amendment, 18
Case-Zablocki law, 150
Castro, Fidel, 55, 122, 185, 273
caucus system, 216–21, 223, 224; *see
  also* committee system
Central Intelligence Agency, 46–52, 55,
  62, 82, 115–18, 120–21, 123, 129–34,
  181, 236, 248, 271, 291
Central Intelligence Agency Act, 116
Chamber of Commerce, 181, 194, 198,
  202, 206
Chayes, Abram, 65
Chile, 47, 85, 86, 88, 91–94, 97, 119,
  122

Christopher, Warren, 93, 109, 153, 276–83, 285
Christopher Committee, 93–96
Church, Frank, 14, 71, 107, 109, 118, 121–22, 153, 154, 195, 276, 278, 283, 293
Church Committee, 50, 117–23, 125, 128, 234
Clark, Dick, 30, 50, 51, 53, 56, 57, 61, 150, 157, 224, 271
Clark v. Valeo, 80
Clay, Henry, 139, 218, 220
Clerides, Glafkos, 36, 43
Cleveland, Grover, 6
Clifford, Clark, 180.
Colby, William, 50, 52, 121
Commerce Department, 94, 112, 202, 205, 208, 261, 263
committee system, 132–34, 213, 217–28, 230–32, 243, 245–49; *see also* caucus system; *entries under names of House and Senate committees*
Common Cause, 199
Conference of Presidents of American Jewish Organizations, 187
Congressional Budget and Impoundment Control Act (1974), 242
Congressional Budget Office, 228, 242, 244–45
Congressional leadership, 27, 34, 39, 41, 44, 43, 73, 85, 86, 213–21, 224, 292
Congressional rank and file, 24, 25, 29, 34, 35, 37–40, 85, 88, 210–13, 220, 227, 245, 263, 284
Congressional Research Service, 79, 228, 242–44
Congressional staff, 148–49, 228, 229, 231–45, 254–55, 263; *see also* Senate Resolution 4
Congressional vetoes, 62, 69, 76–82, 89, 99, 102, 105, 108, 109, 112–13, 124, 150, 190; *see also* Executive veto
Connally, John, 182
Constantinides, Evagorus, 192
Conway, Jack T., 199
Cook, Crawford, 181
Coolidge, Calvin, 6
cooption, 132–34, 240–41, 250
Cotton, Norris, 15
Coughlin, Bill, 52
covert operations, 125–28, 133, 248, 257
Cranston, Alan, 30, 52, 53, 61, 87, 88, 152, 153, 276, 278, 289
Cuba, 35, 46–51, 53–55, 66, 90, 93, 110, 122, 130, 131, 157, 185, 271, 273
Cuban Missile Crisis, 64

Culver, John, 69, 70, 105, 106, 190, 290
Curtiss-Wright case, 156
Cyprus, 34–36, 38, 39, 41, 43, 44, 71–72, 74, 110, 120, 191
Czarnecki, Marian, 241

Davis, Cushman K., 140
Davis, Nathaniel, 47, 57, 271
Dayan, Moshe, 185
Dean, John, 21
Declaration of Geneva, 36
DeConcini, Dennis, 275–76, 278–81, 283–84, 290
Defense Department, 16, 17, 18, 25, 28, 51, 52, 53, 66, 78, 93, 94, 100–102, 104, 106, 112, 115, 118, 196, 212, 241, 245, 261, 263, 269, 272–73, 289, 291, 293
Defense Intelligence Agency, 116, 123, 129
Defense Security Assistance Agency, 100
Democratic caucus, 223, 224, 247
Democratic Committee on Organization, Study and Review, 247
Democratic party, 31, 215, 238
Democratic Policy Committee, 112, 216
Denktash, Rauf, 43, 182
Denton, Donald L., 251
Derian, Patricia, 95
Derwinski, Edward J., 61, 107, 167
Desai, Morarji, 113, 184
Diem, Ngo Dinh, 122
Dies, Martin, 220
Director of Central Intelligence, 128, 130
District of Columbia Committee, 178
Dole, Robert, 92, 211, 278
Dominican Republic, 66, 67, 97, 122
Douglas, William, lobbying, 175
Downey, Thomas, 147, 148, 196–97
Dutton, Frederick G., 180, 267

Eagleton, Thomas, 18, 21, 37, 39–44, 69, 70, 75, 241
Eagleton Amendment (Foreign Assistance Act), 19, 20, 21, 29, 32, 41
Earle, Ralph, 290
Ecevit, Bulent, 37, 182
Egypt, 104, 106, 107, 133, 142, 143, 182, 185, 243
Eisenhower, Dwight David, 4, 67, 78, 273
Eizenstat, Stuart, 205, 206

El Salvador, 90, 91, 97
Ellsworth, Oliver, 139, 183
Ellsworth, Robert, 271
Emergency Committee for American Trade, 194–95, 206
Energy Department, 112
Environmental Policy Center, 198
Environment Defense Fund, 198
Epstein, Benjamin R., 202
Ervin, Sam, 145
Ervin Committee, 15, 21
Ethiopia, 57, 88, 90, 94
European Community, 114
executive agreements, 62, 141–45, 149–54
Executive Order 12036, 128, 133
Executive veto, 20, 69, 70, 88, 103, 272
expertise, 227, 228, 232–34, 245
Export-Import Bank, 92, 93, 94, 245

Faisal, Turki, 184
Fascell, Dante, 107–9
Fasick, Kenneth, 243
FBI, 115, 118, 123, 132, 170
Federal Election Campaign Act, 178
Federal Regulation of Lobbying Act, 174
Fenno, Richard E., 250–51
Fillmore, Millard, 6
Findlay, Paul, 75
First Amendment, 173, 174–75, 178, 179–80
Fish, Hamilton, 200
Flaten, Robert A., 110
Flynt, John J., 25, 27, 28, 166, 182
Foley, Tom, 170
Food for Peace program, 79, 263
Ford, Gerald R., 21, 25, 26, 28, 31, 33, 39, 41, 45, 46, 53, 55, 56, 71–73, 81, 82, 88, 101, 120, 161, 272–73, 285
Ford Administration, 26, 42–44, 74–75, 93, 102–4, 201
Foreign Agents Registration Act, 174, 176, 177, 180
Foreign Aid Appropriations law, 252
foreign assistance, 62, 86, 89, 91, 167–68, 240, 249, 252, 272–74; see also military assistance
Foreign Assistance Acts, 29, 49, 79, 85, 86, 89, 98, 117, 273–74; see also Eagleton Amendment
Foreign Assistance and Arms Export legislation, 5
Foreign Debt Commission, 141
Foreign Military Sales Act, 79
Foreign Military Sales Program, 245
Foreign Operations Subcommittee, 40

Foreign Service, 234, 264, 269–70
Formosa, Mutual Defense Treaty, 158
40 Committee (CIA), 48, 50
Fosdick, Dorothy, 189
Fox, Harrison W., 233
France, 72, 143, 183
Fraser, Donald, 27, 31–32, 61, 85, 86, 89, 96, 169
Friedersdorff, Max, 100, 101
Friends' Committee on National Legislation, 86
FRLA (1946), 178
Frye, William P., 140
Fulbright, William, 4, 5, 27, 67, 176, 181, 239, 248, 262–63

Gallagher, Cornelius, 171
Gallatin, Albert, 16, 139
Gardner, John, 199
Garfield, James A., 6
Garment, Leonard, 189
Garn, Jake, 289
Gasch, Oliver, 287
General Accounting Office, 6, 105, 106, 150, 176, 177, 228, 242–43
General Services Administration, 128
Geneva trade negotiations, 148
Gerry, Elbridge, 64
Giaimo, Robert N., 20, 55
Giap, General, 23
Glenn, John, 111, 249, 290
Goldberg, Sam, 241
Goldwater, Barry, 30, 121, 130, 158, 186, 248, 275, 287
Granum, Rex, 280
Gravel, Mike, 190
Gray, George, 140
Greece, 35, 36, 37, 38, 42, 43, 86
Guatemala, 90, 91
Guinea, 94

Habib, Philip, 26
Haiti, 66, 97, 180
Hamilton, Alexander, 63, 64, 219
Hamilton, Lee, 44, 108, 205
Hamilton-Whalen bill, 205
Hammond, Susan Webb, 233
Hanna, Richard, 170
Hannah, John, 171, 252
Hanoi, 13, 22–23, 25
Hansell, Herbert J., 277
Hansen Committee, 247
Harding, Warren, 6, 140, 141
Harkin, Tom, 85, 86, 87, 92, 93, 236

Harkin Amendment, 87, 88, 89
Harrington, Michael, 119
Harrison, Benjamin, 6, 139
Harrison, William Henry, 6
Harrowby, Lord, 136
Hart, Gary, 121, 132, 289, 290
Hartman, Arthur A., 38
Hatfield, Mark, 235
Hatfield, Paul, 278, 279
Hawaiian Island annexation, 139
Hawk missile sales, 100–104, 183, 187, 188
Hay, John, 136, 137, 140
Hay-Pauncefote Treaty, 136, 138
Hayakawa, S., 185
Hayden, Tom, 52
Hayes, Rutherford B., 6, 25
Hébert, F. Edward, 24, 223, 247
Heinz, H. John, 207, 208, 241
Helms, Jesse, 185, 289
Henkin, Louis, 65
Hersh, Seymour, 132
Herter, Christian, 146
Hesburgh, Theodore, 199
Hilsman, Roger, 270
Hoar, George F., 140
Hodges, Kaneaster, 278
Hoffman, Paul, 146
Hoffmann, Stanley, 211
Holt, Pat, 239
Holtzman, Abraham, 267
Holtzman, Elizabeth, 69
Hoover, Herbert, 6, 77, 141
Hoover Commission, 264, 265
House of Representatives:
—Agriculture Committee, 170
—Appropriations Committee, 17, 20, 21, 25, 116, 169, 252, 253, 267
—Armed Services Committee, 24, 170, 196, 247
—Banking and Currency Committee, 246, 247
—Budget Committee, 249, 250
—Democratic Committee on Committees, 222
—Democratic Steering Committee, 17
—Education and Labor Committee, 247
—Ethics Committee, 127, 171, 172, 176
—Foreign Affairs Committee, 24, 28, 149–50, 213, 247
—Foreign Operations Subcommittee, 252
—Government Operations Committee, 248
—Interior and Insular Affairs Committee, 248
—International Organizations Subcommittee, human rights, 85

—International Relations Committee, 54, 72, 85, 89, 95, 101, 107–8, 111, 113, 118, 131, 154, 165, 167, 182, 184, 204, 205, 231–33, 240–41, 246, 249, 254–55
—Interstate and Foreign Commerce Committee, 248
—Judiciary Committee, 129, 175
—Merchant Marine and Fisheries Committee, 248
—Permanent Select Committee on Intelligence, 126–31, 134, 248
—Public Works and Transportation Committee, 248
—Rules Committee, 192, 253
—Science and Technology Committee, 248
—Standards of Official Conduct Committee, 126, 127, 166
—Un-American Activities Committee, 220
—Ways and Means Committee, 147, 222, 224, 247, 250
House of Representatives-Senate Conference Committee(s), 19–20, 21, 40–41, 69, 70, 93, 99
Hruska, Roman, 19
Hughes, Harold E., 49
Hughes-Ryan Amendment, 117–18, 129–31
Hull, Cordell, 145, 264, 286
human rights, 8, 80, 82, 84–97, 160, 166, 169, 199, 211, 236
Human Rights Bureau, 95, 96
Human Rights Convention, 96
Humphrey, Hubert, 25–26, 28, 41, 61, 88, 106, 122, 187, 206, 232, 237, 240, 241, 272
Hussein, King of Jordan, 100–103, 183, 184

India, 111, 113, 114, 184, 252
Indonesia, 86, 88, 90–93, 95, 96
Ingram, George, 240
Inonu, Ismet, 191
Inouye, Daniel, 125, 126, 132
Inter-Agency Group on Human Rights and Foreign Assistance, NSC, 93
Inter-American Development Bank, 92, 93–94
Inter-American Human Rights Commission, 97
Interior Department, 261
Internal Revenue Service, 115, 166
International Atomic Energy Agency, 112
International Commission of Jurists, 97
International Development Agency, 237

International Development Association, 256–57
International Financial Institutions, 92, 94
International Labor Organization, 197
International Monetary Conference, 139
International Sugar Agreement, 195
International Water Boundary Commission, 140
Iran, 91, 97, 104–6, 130, 134, 157
Israel, 101, 106–7, 109, 110, 142, 161, 182–84, 187, 200–209
Israeli-U.S. secret Agreement E, 142
Ivory Coast, 49

Jackson, Andrew, 5, 137
Jackson, Bill, 53
Jackson, Henry, 152, 153, 186, 189, 289, 292
Jackson, Robert H., 78
Jackson-Vanik Amendment, 189, 197, 236; see also Jewish emigration
Japan, trade councils, 181
Javits, Jacob, 19, 30, 61, 68–71, 81, 109, 154, 158, 189–90, 208
Jaworski, Leon, 25, 171, 172
Jay, John, 135, 139
Jay Treaty, 136
Jefferson, Thomas, 63, 84, 136
Jewish emigration, 103, 160, 189, 197, 236
Johnson, Andrew, 82
Johnson, Hiram, 140
Johnson, Lyndon B., 67, 191, 214–15, 273
Joint Chiefs of Staff, 100, 109, 187, 188, 290
Joint Committee on Atomic Energy, 111–12
Joint Committee on the Organization of Congress, 174
Joint Committees, committee system, 218
Jordan, 100, 101, 103, 104, 181, 183, 184, 187
Jordan, Hamilton, 277, 290
Jordan, William, 251, 255
Joseph, Burton M., 202, 204–5, 206
Justice Department, 79, 108, 166, 171, 172, 175–78, 180, 202, 236, 262

Kampelman, Max, 206
Karl-i-Bond, 97
Kendall, William T., 73
Kennedy, Edward, 24, 53, 95, 122, 186, 192, 195, 196, 230, 236, 248

Kennedy, John F., 4, 64, 78–79, 215, 273
Khmer Rouge, 13, 14, 15, 22, 27–28, 33
Kim Dong Jo, 171, 172
Kim, Hancho, 172
King-Hawkesbury Convention, 136
Kirkland, Lane, 198
Kissinger, Henry, 15, 24–26, 37–43, 50, 54, 56, 57, 88, 101–2, 105–6, 109, 120–21, 142–43, 187, 189–90, 237, 241, 271–72, 277
Kleindienst, Richard, 180
Korea, 85, 88, 90–94, 97, 142, 150, 211–13, 243, 245
Koreagate scandal, 166–72
Korean Central Intelligence Agency, 166, 167, 171
Korean War, 66–67, 166–67, 169
Korologos, Tom C., 196
Kreps, Allyn, 153
Kyprianou, Spyros, 182

Labor Department, 94, 261
Lacovara, Philip A., 177
La Follette-Monroney Committee, 174
Lance, Bert, 182
Laos, 13, 21, 23, 25, 117
Law of the Seas Conference, 147, 197
League of Nations, 78
Lebanon, 67, 71–74, 110, 211
Leggett, Robert L., 170
legislative management officers, 261, 287
Legislative Reorganization Act, 218, 219, 231, 242, 244, 246, 248
Lend-Lease Act (1941), 78
Leventhal, Harold, 80
Lewis, Gabriel Galindo, 280–83
liaison, limits of, 286–88
liaison staff, LMO, 261–270
Lincoln, Abraham, 64
Linowitz, Sol, 267–68, 277
Lippmann, Walter, 287
Lipshutz, Robert J., 96
Lissakers, Karen, 240
lobbies and lobbyists, 165, 172–94, 196, 199–200, 208–9
Lodge, Henry Cabot, 137, 138, 140, 213, 262
London Naval Conference, 141
London-Zurich accord, 35
Long, Clarence, 18, 92, 113, 251, 252
Long, Russell, 18, 19, 20, 195, 278, 279
Long Amendment, 18
Lon Nol government, 14, 158
Lowenstein, James G., 239
Luanda, 236
Lumumba, Patrice, 122

McCarran, Patrick, 220
McCarthy, Joseph, 220
McClelland, John L., 19
McCloskey, Paul, 27, 57, 75
McCloskey, Robert, 52, 101, 272
McClure, James A., 153
McClure Amendment, 154
McCormack, John W., 78
McCormack Act, 176
McCreary, James B., 139
McCrory, Ray, 290
McFall, John J., 167, 168, 170, 171
McGovern, George, 21, 88
McHenry, James, 63
McIntyre, Thomas, 290
McKinley, William, 66, 139, 140
McNamara, Robert S., 92, 199
Madden, Ray J., 192
Madison, James, 63, 64, 139, 145, 173, 262
Mahon, George, 19, 20, 26, 40, 55, 253
Mainland, Keith, 253
Makarios, Archbishop, 35, 36
Mansfield, Mike, 15, 21, 26, 37, 39, 44, 73, 123–24, 190–91, 215–16
Mantel, Robert, 240
Marcuss, Stanley, 208
Marcy, Carl, 230
Marshall, George C., 146, 275
Marshall Plan, 146, 191
Mathias, Charles, 176, 290
Maw, Carlyle, 37, 88, 193
Mayaguez incident, 33, 71, 73, 74
Mead, Margaret, 199
Meany, George, 188, 189, 198
Mehdi, T. M., 191
Merchant Marine Act, 174
Mexican War, 65
Micronesian independence movement, 132
Middle East policy, 8
Middle East war (1973), 45, 99
military assistance, 88, 89, 90, 95, 167, 171; *see also* arms sales and exports; foreign assistance
Military Construction Authorization, 79
military intervention, 142, 150
Mill, John Stuart, 172–73
Miller, William, 118
Mills, Wilbur D., 224
Mineta, Norman, 127
Mink, Patsy, 69, 70
missile sales, 100, 104, 106; *see also* Hawk missile sales; military assistance
Mitchell, William D., 77
Molander, Roger, 291–92
Mondale, Walter "Fritz," 91, 120–21, 234, 241, 277, 278, 280, 291

Monroe, James, 144
Moore, Frank, 277
Moore, R. Walton, 264
Moose, Richard M., 239, 240, 269
Moran, Mark, 52, 53, 55, 236, 271
Morgan, John T., 138, 139
Morgan, Robert, 235
Morgan, Thomas, 87
Morgan-Zablocki bill, 68, 69
Morocco, 95, 96
Morris, Gouverneur, 144
Morris, Robert, 83
Moses, Alfred, 203–4, 206
Moss, Ambler, 280
Moynihan, Daniel Patrick, 181, 278
Moynihan, Michael, 181
Mozambique, 91, 92, 211
Mulcahy, Edward, 51
Murphy, John M., 169, 170
Murphy Commission, 9, 214, 223, 227, 246, 269
Muskie, Edmund, 176, 241, 255, 256, 292
Mutual Defense Treaty (1954), 158
Muzorewa, Abel, 185

NASA, 248
National Association of Arab Americans, 190
National Association of Manufacturers, 173, 202, 206
National Conference on Soviet Jewry, 189
National Front for the Liberation of Angola (FNLA), 46, 47, 48, 50, 54, 56
National Jewish Community Relations Advisory Council (NJCRAC), 206
national security, 3, 4, 90, 105, 124–25, 130, 247, 249
National Security Act (1947), 115
National Security Agency, 116, 122, 128, 129
National Security Council, 6, 56, 93, 94, 118, 234, 235, 241, 261, 271, 272, 285, 291
National Security Industrial Association, 196
National Union for the Total Liberation of Angola (UNITA), 46–50, 54, 56
Nedzi, Lucien N., 118, 119
Nelson, Gaylord, 61, 99, 104, 239
Nelson-Bingham law, 98–102, 106, 107, 110, 240
Neto, Augustinho, 50
Neustadt, Richard, 146
Neutrality Act, 98

Neutrality Proclamation (1793), 63
Neutrality Treaty, 281
New Directions, 199
Newfoundland, 145
New Zealand, 142
Nicaragua, 66, 90, 92, 93, 96
Nidecker, John E., 170
Nixon, Richard M., 3, 13, 20–23, 25, 29,
    47, 67, 70, 82, 158, 170, 189, 215,
    274, 285, 291
Nixon Administration, 15–18, 23–24, 93
North Atlantic Treaty Organization, 35,
    36, 43, 45, 146–47
North Yemen, 288
nuclear exports, 8, 82, 111–14, 184
Nuclear Regulatory Commission, 112,
    113
Nunn, Sam, 186, 212, 276, 278, 290,
    292
Nyerere, Julius, 51

Obey Commission Report, 233, 234
O'Brien, Larry, 273
O'Connell, John, 181
Office of Management and Budget, 6,
    17, 116, 240
Office of Technology Assessment, 228,
    242
Olney, Richard, 137
O'Neill, Thomas P., 167, 168, 196, 216
Oregon Territory treaties, 137
Organization for Economic Cooperation
    and Development, 252
Organization of American States, 147
Ottinger, Richard, 113
Overseas Development Council, 239–40

Panama, 66
Panama Canal treaties, 8, 136, 142, 198,
    211, 216, 225, 248, 267, 274–86,
    288, 291
Paolillo, Charles, 239, 240
Paraguay, 97
Parallel Unilateral Policy Declarations
    (P.U.P.D.), 152–53, 154
Paris peace accord, 13–16, 23, 161
Park, Tongsun, 166, 167, 170, 172, 177
Park, Chung Hee, 167, 170
Passman, Otto, 40, 169, 171, 252
Pathet Lao, 13
Patman, Wright, 223
patronage, 269, 273, 274, 278
Pearl Harbor, 64
Peking, 66, 97
Pell, Claiborne, 192, 195

People's Republic of China, 46, 47, 49,
    97, 186
Percy, Charles, 111
Perle, Richard, 189
Pershing, John Joseph, 66
Peru, 97
Philippines, 86, 88, 90–94, 97, 140, 142,
    211, 243
Phnom Penh, 14, 26, 33, 34, 71, 74
Pierce, Franklin, 6
Pike, Otis G., 51, 119, 121
Pike Committee, 50, 119–20, 126–28
Poage, W. R., 223
Political Action Committees, 179, 197
Polk, James K., 65, 137
Polsby, Nelson, 219
Ponomarev, Boris, 186
Popular Movement for the Liberation of
    Angola (MPLA), 46, 48, 49, 50, 54,
    271
Portugal, 46, 86
Pot, Pol, 159
Powell, Jody, 108, 291
Price, David E., 238
Price, Melvin, 170
Proxmire, William, 104, 201
Public Utilities Holding Company Act,
    174

Rafshoon, Gerald, 285, 291
Reorganization Acts, vetoes of, 77
Republican party, 31, 238
Reston, James, 165
Reynolds, James, 198
Rhee, Jhoon, 167
Rhodes, John, 39
Rhodesia, 92, 185, 243
Ribicoff, Abraham, 108, 111, 176, 187,
    189, 249
Richards, James P., 212–13
Richardson, Elliot, 18, 24
Richbourg, Donald E., 251
Rio Pact (1947), 64
Roberto, Holden, 47, 54
Robinson, Joseph, 140, 141
Rockefeller, Nelson, 28
Rockefeller Commission, 118
Rogers, William, 15, 180, 282, 283
Rogul, June Silver, 189
Romani, Romano, 276, 279
Rooney, John, 267
Roosevelt, Franklin D., 4, 64, 78, 98, 145,
    264, 273, 276
Roosevelt, Theodore, 66, 137
Rosenthal, Benjamin S., 31, 39, 40–43,
    100, 101, 107, 185, 193, 201, 204
Rosenthal Amendment, 39

Rousseau, Rudolph, 273
Rousselot, John H., 75
Rossides, Eugene, 192
Row, Chin Hwan, 170
Ruckelshaus, William, 180
Rush-Bagot executive agreement, 144
Rusk, Dean, 267, 268
Ryan, Leo, 49, 169

Saba, Michael, 108
Sadat, Anwar, 106, 133, 185
Saigon, 26, 28, 29, 33, 34, 46, 49, 71, 73, 74
St. Clair, Arthur, 83
Sampson, Nikos, 35, 36
Sancar, Ilhami, 43
Sarbanes, Paul, 38, 41–44, 276, 283
Saudi Arabia, 99, 104, 106–9, 160, 180–82, 184–85, 190, 211
Savimbi, Jonas, 49, 51
Schlesinger, Arthur, Jr., 66, 288
Schlesinger, James, 24, 36, 44
Schneider, Mark, 53, 95
Schneider, Rene, 122
Schorr, Daniel, 126
Schwarz, F. A. O., Jr., 118
Scott, Hugh, 40
Security Assistance Act, 212
Seko, Mobutu Sese, 97
Senate:
—African Subcommittee, 50
—Appropriations Committee, 18, 39, 116, 123, 238
—Armed Services Committee, 24, 29, 123, 129, 212, 248, 249, 288–90, 292
—Banking and Currency Committee, 205, 248
—Budget Committee, foreign assistance, 249, 250
—Democratic Policy Committee, 216–17
—Finance Committee, 141
—Foreign Assistance Subcommittee, 28
—Foreign Relations Committee, 27, 157, 181, 216, 239, 248, 249
  AIPAC and, 187, 188
  arms sales, 99, 101, 102, 106, 108, 109, 239
  bombing cut-off, 20
  budget process, 254–57
  Cambodian assistance, 28
  Clark Amendment, 51
  Cypriot civil war, 38
  Executive relations, 284
  foreign influence in, 185
  human rights, 78–88
  Intelligence Committee and, 130–31
  intelligence oversight role, 118, 123

Israeli-U.S. secret Agreement E, 143
  security in, 130, 131
  staff of, 231, 232, 235, 245
  war powers, 66
—Government Affairs Committee, 176, 249
—Judiciary Committee, 129, 140, 141, 248
—Select Committee on Intelligence, 125–34, 225, 292 (see also Church Committee)
—Select Committee on Presidential Campaign Activities, 15, 21
—Select Committee on the Committee System, 214
Senate Resolution 4, 219, 225, 228, 230–32, 240, 249
Senate Resolution 109, 248
Senate Resolution 239, 146
Senate Resolution 400, 122–26, 129–30
Senate staff, 120–21, 124–25, 227, 230
Senegal, 49
Shaba evacuation, 72, 74, 75
Shapiro, Irving S., 202, 204, 207
Sikes, Robert L., 17
Silver, Tina, 189
Sinai agreement, 142, 161
Sirica, John, 25
Sisco, Joseph, 36, 38
Slack, John M., 251
Smith, Ian, 185
Smoot, Reed, 141
Sofaer, Abraham, 65
Solarz, Stephen, 107
Somalia, 185–86
Somoza, Anastasio, 96
South Africa, 47, 49, 50, 54, 55, 182
South East Asia Defense Treaty, 64
Soviet Union, 8, 35, 46–51, 53, 54, 56, 86, 90, 91, 103, 105, 110, 145, 147–48, 160, 183, 186, 189, 197, 289–92
Spain, 86, 140
Sparkman, John, 44, 67, 101, 105, 109, 130, 151, 153, 205, 268, 275, 289, 293
Speer, Edgar B., 195
Spiegel, Dan, 241
Springer v. Government of the Philippine Islands, 78
State Department, 6-8, 20, 21, 36–39, 41, 46, 47, 51, 52, 56, 65, 74, 86, 88–90, 93, 94, 96, 97, 99, 101–2, 104, 107, 112, 118, 120, 132, 138, 143, 148–50, 152, 154, 155–56, 184, 188, 195, 202, 205, 212, 234, 236, 241–42, 251, 261, 263–70, 272, 273, 276–77, 280–81, 285, 291

Stavrou, Leon, 192
Stennis, John, 44, 123, 290, 292
Stern, Paula, 99
Stevens, Ted, 170
Stevenson, Adlai, 42, 53, 110, 201,
    204–7, 232, 248, 261
Stimson, Henry O., 265
Stitt, Nelson, 181
Stockwell, John, 48, 50, 51
Stone, Richard, 109
Strategic Arms Limitation Talks and
    Treaties, 7, 131, 144, 146–48, 152,
    186, 249, 288–93
Stratton, Samuel, 119
subcommittee system, 218, 228–29, 232
Sullivan, Jack, 241
Supreme Court, 63, 81, 145, 156, 174–
    75, 178
Sutherland, George, 156
Switzer, Rebecca, 236
Switzerland, 271
Syria, 92, 211

Taft, William Howard, 66, 137
Taiwan defense pact, 287–88
Talisman, Mark, 189, 236
Talmadge, Herman E., 278
Tanzania, 51
Taboulareas, William P., 207
Taylor, Zachary, 6
Teng Hsiao-ping, 186
Thailand, 21, 92
Thieu, 22
Thomson, Sue Park, 167
Tonkin Gulf Resolution, 14, 67, 79
Torrijos, Omar, 198, 268, 275, 277, 280,
    282, 283
Tower, John, 123, 201
trade, 189, 194–95, 197, 200–201, 247,
    257
Trade Act of 1974, 79, 103, 147
Trade Reform Act, 195
Treasury Department, 93, 94, 160, 202,
    261
Treaty of Versailles, 77, 140
treaty powers, 64, 135–41, 146–51
Trujillo, Rafael, 122
Truman, Harry S., 66, 146
Truman Doctrine, 191
Tunney, John, 37, 51, 53, 57, 236, 271
Tunney Amendment, 53, 54, 56
Turkey, 35–45, 91, 110, 182, 192, 193,
    211, 285
Turner, Stansfield, 127, 130, 131, 133,
    157, 289, 291
Tyler, John, 6

Udall, Morris, 111, 238
Uganda, 243
Ulman, Haluk, 37
Underwood, Oscar, 140
United Arab Emirates, 181
United Kingdom, 35, 36, 84, 144, 182
United Nations, 36, 257
United Nations Conference on Trade
    and Development, 147
United Nations Security Council, 67
U.S. Criminal Code, 169
U.S.-Japan Trade Council, 181
U.S. v. Rumely, 174
U.S. v. Harriss, 174, 175
Uruguay, 90, 91, 93, 252
U-2 incident, 116

Van Buren, Martin, 5
Vance, Cyrus, 5, 81, 90, 96, 107, 109,
    152, 199, 207, 241, 277
Vandenberg, Arthur, 146, 147, 248
Vanik, Charles, 189
Vera Cruz, 66
Versailles Conference, 138
Veterans of Foreign Wars, 193, 198
Vietnam, 13, 14, 15, 21, 23, 25, 27–29,
    30–31, 34, 86, 91, 93, 101, 122, 161,
    186
Vietnam Contingency Act, 30
Vietnam War, 8, 13, 64, 98, 117, 157,
    210, 239
Viguerie, Richard, 198
Villa, Pancho, 66

Warner, Rawleigh, Jr., 203
Warnke, Paul, 147, 153, 290
War of 1812, 139
war powers, 15, 29, 63–71, 135
War Powers Act, 5, 62, 71–82, 84, 117,
    135, 157, 161
Warren, Earl, 174
Warren, Gerald L., 21
Washington, George, 63, 136
Washington Naval Conference, 140
Watergate affair, 15, 70, 119, 120, 146,
    175, 210
Waxman, Henry A., 26
West, John, 181
Westmoreland, William, 277
Wexler, Anne, 285, 291
Whalen, Charles, 44, 199, 205
Wiley, Alexander, 286
Williams, Harrison, 201
Wilson, James, 144